The Next Step

Integrating
the Software Life Cycle
with SAS® Programming

making pgms portable. 34

Paul Gill

Comments or Questions?

The author assumes complete responsibility for the technical accuracy of the content of this book. If you have any questions about the material in this book, please write to the author at this address:

SAS Institute Inc.
Books by Users
Attn: Paul Gill
SAS Campus Drive
Cary, NC 27513

If you prefer, you can send e-mail to sasbbu@sas.com with "comments for Paul Gill" as the subject line, or you can fax the Books by Users program at (919) 677-4444.

Table of Contents

Acknowledgments vii

Preface ix

Chapter 1:   **Introduction** 1
Purpose..1
Research..2
Interpretation 2
Audience 2
Using This Book 3
Quick Tour..3

Chapter 2:   **Overview of the Software LIfe Cycle**............................5
Why Use the Systems Approach to Programming? 6
Unique Characteristics of Large Software Systems 7
Quick Reference 8
An Example: Applying the Key Components of the Software Life Cycle   10
Summary 14
Exercises 14
References..14

Chapter 3:   **Managing the Project**..15
Introduction 15
Library Management 15
Project Considerations 23
Database Management..26
Getting the Programming Team Started 31
External Documentation..32
Making Programs Portable 34
Summary 34
Exercises 35
References..35

Chapter 4:   **Analyzing the Problem**..37
Introduction 37
The Problem 38
Risk/Reward..38
Analysis Tools 39
Structured Analysis 43
Data Modeling 45
Evaluating a Language 46
Summary 47
Exercises 48
References..48

Chapter 5: **Laying the Foundation with Good Design** **49**
    Introduction **50**
    Concepts of Modular Design **50**
    The Definition of a Module **55**
    Module Qualities **58**
    Module Cohesion **59**
    Module Coupling **65**
    Converting Modules to SAS Code **73**
    Documentation of Modules/Arguments **79**
    Prototyping Methods **81**
    Principles of Good Design **82**
    Writing a Utility Module from Scratch **84**
    Summary **87**
    Exercises **87**
    References **88**

Chapter 6: **Improving Readability and Providing**
                      Internal Documentation **89**
    Introduction **89**
    Readability **90**
    Commenting Code **103**
    Summary **114**
    Exercises **114**
    Reference **114**

Chapter 7: **Structured Programming Techniques** **115**
    Introduction **116**
    History **116**
    Background Theory **117**
    Proper Organization of Data Step Statements **120**
    Considerations for Variables **131**
    Measuring Software Quality **134**
    Putting It All Together: Converting from Design to Structured Code **139**
    Summary **148**
    Exercises **148**
    References **148**

Chapter 8: **System Coding Principles** **151**
    Introduction **152**
    System Coding Principles **152**
    Table-Driven Code **163**
    Error Handling **165**
    Dynamic Code **166**
    Seamless Coding **169**
    System Coding Concerns **174**
    Initialization Options for Customized Software **178**
    A Reporting System **180**
    Code Generators: Reporting at the Next Level **184**
    Summary **186**

Exercises **187**
References **187**

Chapter 9:   Program Verification and Testing Methodology **189**
Introduction **190**
Black Box Testing **191**
White Box Testing **198**
Black Box versus White Box Testing **211**
Gray Box Testing **212**
Structured Testing Methodology **216**
Bugging a Program **223**
Comparison Testing Techniques **223**
Summary **225**
Exercises **225**
References **228**

Chapter 10:   Digging Out with Debugging Techniques **229**
Introduction **230**
The Anatomy of Bugs **230**
General Debugging Strategies **231**
Debugging Tactics **234**
Preventive Maintenance **242**
Regressive Bugs **244**
Debugging Dynamic Code **245**
Macro Debugging Tips **246**
The SAS DATA Step Debugger **249**
Summary **255**
Exercises **256**
References **256**

**Chapter 11:   Putting It All Together with a Demonstration:
The Site Map System** **257**
Introduction **258**
Background **258**
Important Terms **258**
Problem Definition **259**
Analysis **260**
Design **261**
Coding **266**
Testing **267**
User Acceptance **270**
Maintenance **271**

Chapter 12:   Answers to Exercises **273**

Appendix 1:   Coding Samples **283**

Appendix 2:   Definitions for the Site Map System **339**

Appendix 3: A Links Primer..**341**

Definition of a Link **341**

Invalid Link Relationships..**343**

Appendix 4: Tutorial of Navigation Rules **345**

Introduction..**345**

Pointer Approach..**345**

Sample Site **346**

Logic for Navigation **346**

Appendix 5: Summary of Navigation Rules **357**

Introduction..**357**

Navigation Strategy...**357**

Error Checks...**361**

Index...**363**

Acknowledgments

Since this is my first book, I have become a little wiser. I now realize the enormity of such a project. This publication would not have been possible without the tremendous effort from the following individuals:

The technical review team. Reading a book of this size and analyzing the code is a painstaking commitment. Thanks to: **Martha Johnson**, **Kathy Wisniewski**, **Ian Whitlock**, **Tom Dawson**, and **Sue McGrath**. Also, special thanks to **Mike Kalt** for his expertise in transforming SAS/GRAPH output to hardcopy.

Tim Latendress. Tim deserves a standing ovation for his commitment on this project. Besides serving as a technical reviewer, Tim read and critiqued the manuscript a number of times. His eye for detail and his excellent suggestions elevated this book to another level.

Terry Williams. Terry reviewed my grammar, syntax, and style. His overall critique was also invaluable in shaping this publication. His encouragement and sense of humor were greatly appreciated over the course of this project.

Judy Whatley. As Acquisitions Editor, Judy had an enormous task. Her many duties included editing, working with the publishing department, and coordinating the whole project. I would also like to thank her for letting me try a book a little out of the norm. It has been a great joy to work with her.

Eric Schuman. I am very fortunate to have a world class illustrator on this project. Eric's creativity, imagination, and humorous slant have been a terrific addition to this book.

All the editors and production staff at SAS Institute. I appreciate all the hard work in making such a project possible. Submitting a manuscript is just one very small piece in the production process. It is an incredible thrill to see the finished product!

Irma. My wife has been incredibly tolerant during this long journey. As promised, we can now take our honeymoon!

Preface

Whether you are a novice or advanced SAS user, you have probably stumbled upon the following pearls of truth:

- All data processing managers have coded software at some point in their career.

- Customers really know what they want. In fact, they wouldn't dare change the specifications.

- Computer software development has accelerated light years ahead of hardware development.

- Software development is financially and emotionally rewarding.

- Computer programming is still one of the few stress-free jobs available to honest-to-goodness career seekers.

Even if you haven't made these discoveries, you may have had an experience like the following:

"Sandra!" exclaims the boss, "Those programs that we need for the XYZ company on Monday... well... We need to make some changes. You see, there is a change in the record layout of the master file, and we need to modify those 75 programs to take advantage of this new format. Could you change these programs by, say .... Friday?"

Sandra attacks the assignment with vigor. She enthusiastically toils at her task, working late into the night for the better part of the week. After analyzing the required changes for each program, she brings each source module into the program editor and makes the appropriate modifications. Friday morning rolls around, and she proudly presents her revised programs to her manager. "Gee... ah, Sandra," says her boss, "I just found out—there was a slight mis-communication with our client. We are going to use the old format with just a few modifica-tions. Do you think we can make those changes by, say .... Monday?"

Like Sandra, you have probably learned the hard way that developing complex programs or complete software systems is dramatically different from developing simple, nonreusable, ad hoc programs. This book is dedicated to all those software professionals who want to dis-cover this journey of painless systems development.

x

Chapter 1   # Introduction

Purpose **1**

Research **2**

Interpretation **2**

Audience...**2**

Using This Book **3**

Quick Tour **3**

Becoming proficient in building software systems is not a function of perspiration, inspiration, or even experience for that matter. Building a complete system is like building a house from the ground up. It requires planning—a LOT of planning.

This publication is a culmination of the author's experiences as they relate to developing complete systems using SAS software. While the SAS programming language has a long history, many SAS programmers have not been exposed to systems development. Perhaps there is a historical perspective behind this phenomenon. SAS was originally developed as a powerful statistical language. However, the DATA step functionality has greatly expanded, including the addition of the macro language. Furthermore, multiple new SAS products were developed for virtually every type of business or scientific application. Becoming comfortable with all the new language elements was certainly enough of a challenge, but learning to write SAS code in an organized, modular way was not a high priority.

Purpose

The purpose of this publication is to demonstrate structured, modular programming techniques for creating complete systems using SAS software. However, readers who simply want to learn how to develop more complex programs will also find this publication to be invaluable. The focus of this publication is the development of software as it relates to the full software life cycle. Specifically, this publication walks through all phases of program development, from analysis to user acceptance.

The base SAS language was chosen to demonstrate these principles because it is the core of the SAS System. The base product is a rich language which contains all the constructs that you need to create complete, structured, modular programs.

Choosing material to be included in the text was a difficult task. However, as a general rule, the book tends to focus on "classical" techniques. These methods date as far back as the 1960's, when programmers were looking for guidance in developing software systems. All of these methods are still valid today for teaching programmers the fundamentals of software development.

The literature is exhaustive on topics such as modular and structured systems development, as well as the software life cycle. However, very little has been written relating these concepts directly to the SAS programming language. Hence, a significant portion of this publication weaves these elements together. Most chapters begin with a theoretical treatment of structured programming theory or key concepts that relate to a particular component of the software life cycle. After digesting the underlying principles, the reader is taught how to relate these principles to specific constructs in the SAS programming language.

Research

A number of different sources provided material for this publication. First and foremost is the author's experience relating to systems development. Another good source of material was a perusal of other software systems, written both in SAS and in other programming languages. Finally, a number of books and articles were reviewed that relate to all aspects of the software life cycle. This was invaluable for modeling the chapters in this book.

Interpretation

Much of the material presented here is the author's interpretation of modular programming theory as it applies to the SAS programming language. You may not agree with every idea, construct, or philosophy presented here. What is really important is to urge you, the reader, to *think* about what you are doing when you are coding with the SAS language.

It is easy to become involved in rote coding practices. Take a chance, and try something different. Play with the SAS language as much as you can. Undoubtedly, you will discover that experimentation is the programmer's best teacher.

Audience

Much of the material in this book focuses on philosophy rather than specific programming technique. Hence, this book can be beneficial to a wide range of programming experiences. Furthermore, the platform that you work on is irrelevant. So, if you can confidently write simple SAS programs, then you can learn from the instruction in this book. In fact, this publication is useful for anyone who has six months experience up to advanced programming ability.

Although the information in this book focuses on the base product, users who work with other SAS products can certainly benefit from the principles of systems development. It should benefit anyone who wants to move to the next level of systems development using SAS software.

Finally, this publication does not teach elementary SAS programming constructs, nor does it attempt to teach syntax. It assumes that the reader understands the basic syntax for the SAS language.

Using This Book

All source code was tested on the SAS System, Release 6.12, for the Windows environment (TS020). While there may be an occasional reference to code specific to Windows, most of the code is portable to a wide variety of operating environments. This feature is intended to allow readers from different environments to benefit from the material in this publication.

You may find that you read the book sequentially as a project develops, or that you may skip around and read only chapters of interest. In either case, the material in each chapter is highly independent, so you won't lose the flow if you decide not to read the book in sequential order.

Much of the code in this book is presented as small code fragments. This should allow you to grasp the salient concepts and then apply them to their own situations. You may see ellipses (...) embedded within the code snippets. This means "other SAS code here." This omitted code is immaterial for the discussion at hand.

Also, for brevity, certain constructs are omitted from code fragments. For example, using KEEP and RETURN statements is highly recommended in other parts of the text. However, they are often omitted from the code fragments only because they tend to obscure the salient points of the demonstration code. Similarly, defensive coding practices and comprehensive error checking are encouraged throughout the book. However, due to space limitations, these constructs may be omitted in code segments and in Appendix 1, "Coding Samples."

Quick Tour

Here is a brief overview of each chapter:

Chapter 2, "Overview of the Software Life Cycle," provides a preliminary, tongue-in-cheek look at the entire software development process. This chapter should be useful for preparing you for the long (though relatively painless) journey ahead. The content presented here should be particularly useful for those who may not be familiar with the range of terminology relating to systems development and the software life cycle.

Chapter 3, "Managing the Project," introduces you to the general concerns required to handle large projects, from assigning programming tasks, to providing external documentation.

Chapter 4, "Analyzing the Problem," describes the beginning of the software life cycle. This chapter discusses several key concepts regarding problem definition, heuristics, and analysis.

Chapter 5, "Laying the Foundation with Good Design," allows for the transition between analysis and coding. The key elements presented include modularity and the means of communicating data between modules. Also included is a formal discussion of building SAS modules with an emphasis on both intramodule and intermodule strength.

Chapter 6, "Improving Readability and Providing Internal Documentation," explores two areas that are often ignored in program development. The first section discusses principles for improving the readability of a program. The second section suggests ways to improve source code documentation.

Chapter 7, "Structured Programming Techniques," examines the principles of building program structure. Little details in coding can have profound effects in systems development. This chapter explains details about structured methods and the theoretical framework behind them.

Chapter 8, "System Coding Principles," addresses coding concerns involved in building a complete software system. In addition, this chapter explores the development of a modular reporting system using the DATA _NULL_ step.

Chapter 9, "Program Verification and Testing Methodology," describes testing, an often overlooked part of the life cycle equation. You will learn about testing techniques that go beyond the random nature of typical systems testing.

Chapter 10, "Digging Out with Debugging Techniques," provides useful techniques for finding and repairing program bugs. In addition, this chapter contains an introduction to the SAS DATA step debugger.

Chapter 11, "Putting It All Together with a Demonstration: The Site Map System," is a concise description of a project developed for the Environmental Protection Agency. This chapter briefly walks through all phases of the software life cycle so you can appreciate the process of systems development.

Chapter 12, "Answers to Exercises," provides answers to all of the problems presented at the end of each chapter.

Appendices: Appendix 1, "Coding Samples," is a collection of SAS code that is referenced within the chapters. These are usually small programs that are too large to be embedded within the text. The remaining appendices (2 through 5) are useful for those who want to explore the details of the project discussed in Chapter 11. These appendices provide definitions and details about algorithms used to generate the code.

References are provided at the end of each chapter, including both the bibliography and cited references.

Chapter 2   # Overview of the Software Life Cycle

Why Use the Systems Approach to Programming? **6**

Unique Characteristics of Large Software Systems **7**

Quick Reference **8**
  Problem Definition 8
  Analysis 8
  Design 8
  Coding 8
  Testing 9
  Debugging 9
  Internal Documentation 9
  External Documentation 9
  User Acceptance 9

**An Example: Applying the Key Components
of the Software Life Cycle** **10**
  Background/Problem Definition 10
  Requirements Analysis 11
  Prototyping 11
  System Level Design 11
  Module Level Design 12
  Coding 12
  Unit Testing 12
  Integration Testing 12
  System Testing 12
  Debugging 13
  Internal Documentation 13
  Regression Testing 13
  External Documentation 13
  Installation 13
  User Acceptance 13
  Maintenance 14
  And the Aftermath 14

Summary **14**

Exercises **14**

References **14**

Why Use the Systems Approach to Programming?

Have you become comfortable programming a certain way? After being given an assignment, do you dash straight to your desk and start pounding out keystrokes on your terminal? This method works fine for small or simple programs. But, can it stand up to the pressure of a full-blown development process? Probably not.

Think back to some of your first assignments. Your first program as a novice SAS programmer may have been nothing more than a little data manipulation, sorting, and printing:

```
data final ;
    set solar ;

length planet $10 ;

if loc = 1 then
    planet = "Earth" ;
else
if loc = 2 then
    planet = "Venus" ;
else
if loc = 3 then
    planet = "Mercury" ;

run ;

proc sort data = final nodupkey ;
    by planet ;
run ;

proc print data = final ;
    title "Best planets for a hot summer vacation" ;
run ;
```

There is not too much that can go wrong here. Oh sure, you could forget to set up a LENGTH statement for the variable PLANET and you could get some unexpected truncation as a result. But a look at the output would alert you to this obvious mistake.

What if, on the other hand, you developed a payroll system with 5000 lines of code? Let's say that the system was completed in March and has worked well for the past 10 months. Suddenly, it's January, and everybody's paycheck is off by $500! You need to fix the problem . . . and fast!!! What could be wrong? Running through your mind (in a state of semi-panic) are the following possibilities:

- There were changes to the federal, state, and local tax tables.
- The system has several new macro functions.
- In December, several programs were hastily patched to fix other problems.
- It's a new year; perhaps something was hardcoded in the system relating to the date.
- For the first time, there are more than 100 employees in the company.
- Recently, the payroll system was hooked up to the employee data system.
- Or . . . it could be anything!

Here is where using proper system programming techniques can help you isolate and correct the problem in a systematic and controlled manner. By writing code modularly and with clean interfaces, you can often isolate the problem by employing methodical debugging techniques. On the other hand, if this system was written as a bundle of 5000 lines of source code, you can look forward to a long night! In this predicament, debugging often takes the form of randomly displaying dozens of variables and thousands of records. The basic strategy of many a weary SAS programmer is: "If I put enough PUT statements and PROC PRINTS in my code, I should eventually be able to find the problem!"

What exactly is the "systems approach to programming"? Here is a working definition: "the utilization of modular and structured techniques to build an operational software system."

A short definition of terms is in order here. A *modular program* is a system broken into functional units. *Structured programming* is the application of coding techniques that help translate abstract thoughts into well-constructed code segments. Future chapters expand on these definitions.

What are the advantages of using the systems approach?

- Debugging programs is easier because a bug can be isolated to a particular module.
- Total development time is less. Note: There are project managers who believe that all the extra analysis and design time common to systems development actually lengthens the time needed to complete the project. While it is true that more time is spent in up-front planning, time savings in coding, testing, and debugging is almost always realized over the remainder of the project. In fact, many times, these savings are dramatic.
- Programmers can be assigned a specific task in the project without interfering with the tasks of others on the team.
- Enhancements are usually implemented much more quickly than with traditional systems.
- Management is more in control of the system since they are not supervising a big bowl of spaghetti.
- It is possible to create a logical ordered plan for testing.

Unique Characteristics of Large Software Systems

Developing a software system that is ten times larger than another software system does not necessarily result in a proportionate increase in effort. As a system increases in size, so does its complexity. Many problems that are unique to large software systems are not encountered when writing smaller systems, or for that matter, individual programs.

As an analogy, think about joggers who run an easy two miles every morning before work. What kinds of aches and pains do typical runners experience? Perhaps they develop some early morning stiffness, hunger pangs, and general lethargy as a result of a low morning sugar level. On the other hand, what happens to marathoners who run 26 miles? Long distance runners will gladly spew forth their list of war wounds: blisters, cramps, nausea, heat exhaustion, vomiting, disorientation, severe muscle soreness, dehydration, and stress fractures.

Although a large system development process can lead to an analogous set of ailments, it isn't necessarily inevitable if proper systems methodology is implemented.

Here is a list of unique requirements for a large project:

- There is a need for more formal communication. This may involve more meetings and memos.
- Coding becomes a significantly smaller percentage of the total project effort.
- Analysis, design, testing, and debugging effort increase.
- Teamwork becomes more important than individual talent.
- Project management becomes critical.
- Documentation requirements increase substantially. System architecture, functional requirements, integration issues, data dictionaries, user manuals, test plans, quality assurance plans, and online help are just a few of the additional documents required.

Quick Reference

The systems approach to programming involves applying the software life cycle. Figure 2.1 provides a view of the major components of this process.

In this reference section, two sets of definitions describe the key components of the software life cycle: (1) the textbook definition (Sommerville 1982, pp. 3–5, Weinberg 1980 pp. 13–17) and (2) the typical programmer's definition.

Problem Definition

Textbook: The concrete definition of the task to be solved. This expression should be quite specific and void of ambiguity. For example: "A program is needed that calculates the distance from the lowest point in Death Valley to the highest point of Mt. Rainier at midnight, July 3, 2012. The distance is defined as the linear distance and is irrespective of any obstacles."

Programmer: So, like, what's the problem?

Analysis

Textbook: Clarifying the nature of the programming task. Included in analysis is determining exactly (1) What is needed? (2) When is it needed? (3) Why is it needed? (4) Who is the end user? (5) What is the operating environment? (6) What are the inputs and outputs? (7) What files are required? (8) What constraints are imposed? (9) What are the computing performance requirements?

Programmer: 20/20 hindsight.

Design

Textbook: Converting abstract thought into a well defined set of processes that describe the overall sequence of events in a system.

Programmer: Flowcharts that you whip together long after the project is over.

Coding

Textbook: Implementing the program design using a programming language.

Programmer: The semantic constructs that create my "masterpiece."

Testing

Textbook: Verifying that the implementation (coding) meets the software requirements. It is the set of procedures that demonstrates the correct operation of the software in its intended environment. An additional definition of testing is to demonstrate the existence of software defects.

Programmer: Proof that the program works.

Debugging

Textbook: The set of procedures that begins with the discovery of a software defect and ends when the defect has been removed.

Programmer: Not needed. The program works.

Internal Documentation

Textbook: The narrative, accompanying the source code, that elaborates on the purpose of the program, describes the function of specific routines, clarifies the use of instructions, and provides a discussion of algorithms.

Programmer: Vastly overrated script that describes the system.

External Documentation

Textbook: Any narrative that is external to the source code but is related to the current system. This may include user instructions, problem definition, historical perspective, design documents, data dictionaries, source code listings, sample output, test plans, test results, and description of algorithms.

Programmer: Vastly overrated script that describes the system.

User Acceptance

Textbook: The user agrees that the current system conforms to the specifications as originally specified, or in the face of changing requirements, the current system meets with their approval. There may be an accompanying "sign-off" if there is a contract involved.

Programmer: The day the project is over or the day the large bonus rolls in!

There appears to be a slight difference between a programmer's definition of the key components and the textbook definition. Perhaps the following observations can explain this discrepancy:

- Many programmers are inherently lazy. They do the minimal amount of work to complete the requirements of the job. (No! That couldn't possibly be right.)
- Programmers may not have been taught the correct implementation of the software life cycle.
- Budgetary constraints force management and programmers to take shortcuts.

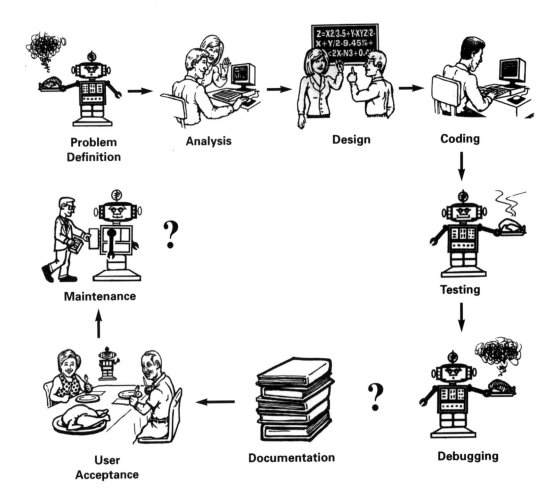

Figure 2.1 *The Programmer's Dream. In the ideal system, the components of the software life cycle flow from one phase to the next. In reality, many elements are revisited for a number of iterations. Note that Maintenance and Debugging can proceed in virtually any direction.*

An Example: Applying the Key Components of the Software Life Cycle

This example uses a scenario to illustrate the key concepts of the software life cycle; these concepts were defined previously.

Background/Problem Definition

Mr. Farmer: I asked for a wake-up call at 4:30, and it's 5:30 already. Can't you people handle a simple request?!

Mr. Boxer: Hello, hello, operator, I got your call. You rang me four times. You can try waking up someone else now.

Mr. Rock N. Roll: Hello, this is Room 1228. I was supposed to get a wake-up call at 2:00 in the afternoon and you woke me up an hour early.

Mrs. Sales: Yes, this is Mrs. Sales in Room 942. I missed my marketing meeting at "Dinosaurs for Us" at 9:30. I want to speak to the manager, or better yet the owner, and fast!

Sounds like a problem here. The hotel's manual system of waking up guests could no longer handle the volume load. After expanding the hotel capacity by 60% in the last year, it was time for an automated system.

Beth: Hello, Mr. Clark. Triumphant Software sent me over to handle your problem. We specialize in converting manual systems to automated systems using the SAS programming language. But first, we have to identify your problem in greater detail.

Requirements Analysis

Beth: Mr. Clark, we are going to have a number of meetings over the next few months to help us understand the problem completely. I will put together a document that describes, in detail, exactly how the system will work. After we get your approval, we can start the development phase.

Prototyping

Mr. Clark: I have a lot of confidence in your company. After all, your organization is highly recommended. But, I do have some concerns. Your team will be off on its own for many months. What if I'm not happy with the system when I see the end product?

Beth: You should hear some of the horror stories! That is why we want you involved in the design. We want your expertise and input in the development. In fact, we are going to develop a small version of the system — a prototype. We will continually refine the prototype until you and your management team are completely satisfied.

System Level Design

Beth laid out the plans for the automated system from a general perspective using flowcharts and diagrams. As the blueprints sharpened in her mind, she used the process of *stepwise refinement* to bring greater detail to the design documents she was preparing. Stepwise refinement is the process of dividing a task into successively smaller functions. This process of division is repeated until the task is at its most elemental level and, therefore, lends itself to solution. Stepwise refinement has been shown to be particularly effective with software design.

At this point, she didn't concern herself with the details, but rather with the flow of the system. She set up a database using PROC SQL views and indexing features of the SAS base language. The component data sets and variable names were compiled into a database dictionary. The programming team received a sample of the layout, which was generated using PROC PRINT and PROC CONTENTS.

Module Level Design

Beth identified the following key elements of the new system:

- **data collection module:** gathers the data into a transaction buffer (a transaction data set) using a simple user interface created with the %WINDOW statement.
- **data validation module:** verifies that all user requests are valid, such as the wake-up time and the room number.
- **user request module:** massages the data in preparation for the communication protocol.
- **communication module:** automates the wake-up call system by using a command sequence.
- **feedback module:** verifies that requesters receive their phone calls as planned.

Coding

Beth distributed detailed functional *specifications* (that is, descriptions about how the system was to work) among the team of programmers. Each programmer was assigned one module, except for the user request and communication modules. Because of their inherent complexity, these two modules required a team of three programmers each. The code was to be completed in six months.

Unit Testing

After coding, each of the five component parts underwent thorough testing. The project leader created mock data for the team. Everyone was happy that their routine was working perfectly.

Integration Testing

Roberto: Hey, Craig! When I ran my communication module stand-alone, everything was working just dandy, but now we have some serious problems. I keep getting a message that the macro variables COM_PORT, PROTOCOL, and TASKLIST are undefined. What gives?

Suzie: Roberto, I'm not sure the problem is in Craig's module. I not only received those warning messages, but every fifth call or so, I got a message that the external file COMMPATH could not be located.

Debbie: Well, this won't solve all the problems, but we just updated the global symbol table for macro variables, and COM_PORT was changed from %LOCAL to %GLOBAL.

Beth: Well, I think it's time for another meeting. I thought we had these problems ironed out. Let's walk through the system flow. I also want to do a dynamic data flow analysis to track the status of variables throughout the system.

System Testing

Beth: Is everyone ready for the big test? I gave everyone on the team a list of their duties. Let's start slowly. Larry, Miguel, and Eddie will be calling in at two minute intervals. Their wake-up call requests will start at 10:00 and will be spaced one minute apart. We'll stop after 12 calls.

Roberto: That's no problem. Why don't we really stress the system to the max, like 100 calls in a 30 second period?

Rachel: Yeah, and 50 of these requests would be for exactly 10:00!!

Beth: Patience, patience, patience. We will create stress and volume load tests, but only after we prove the system can handle the simple requests first. By slowly increasing the stress, we can more closely monitor the program. This should make debugging a lot easier.

Debugging

Roberto: Well, I feel pretty stupid. For some reason, people were getting their wake-up calls 10 minutes apart instead of one minute apart. Hmmm. I have a few theories. Perhaps, I have a bug in my SUBSTR command and I'm pulling in two bytes instead of one. Also, I need to examine how I am using the INTCK function. Let me check it out, and I'll make the fix as soon as I can.

Beth: Fine, but don't rush. Properly debugging a system means sitting down and doing an organized analysis. We don't want to fix one bug and create another.

Internal Documentation

Roberto: No problem. My source code is heavily commented including a detailed description of my algorithms. I learned a long time ago that undocumented code is useless code.

Regression Testing

Miguel: Roberto, I'm happy that the programming changes you made are not affecting any other components of the system. Fortunately, I created a battery of reusable tests, and the output is now comparable to earlier test runs.

External Documentation

Beth: Mr. Clark, I have prepared two manuals for your hotel chain. The first is a training manual that includes an instructional video for the new user. The second is a user manual that is also a comprehensive reference. This can be digested after you play with the system for a while. Also, if you are having problems entering requests on the system, just press F1 for a complete description of commands.

Installation

Beth: Mr. Clark, we have finished the system testing, and you seem to be pleased. We are now ready to install the finished product live. Of course, we still have to re-test the system thoroughly. We certainly don't want to wake anyone in the middle of the night.

User Acceptance

Mr. Clark: The system is working great. I think your company did a terrific job. We have tested it thoroughly here at the hotel, and we are confident and ready to go live.

Maintenance

Ring! Beth answers the phone.

Mr. Clark: Hello, Beth. How are you doing? You know Beth, instead of a wake-up call using the computer voice, I have a better idea. How about allowing the guest to dial in and request waking up to music? They could select jazz, rock and roll, elevator music, or whatever. And they could request snooze calls, say one to ten minutes apart... yeah... and..., they could order breakfast... and .....

And the Aftermath...

Beth: (to team) I just had a nice discussion with Mr. Clark and his staff. They were incredibly impressed with the system and our professional approach. I hope everyone is ready for more business. They would like our company to automate their reservation system. Is it too early to pass out the Christmas bonuses?!

Summary

Developing large or complex software systems includes a number of requirements that are not evident in small or simple programs. Specifically, the coordination of people and coding takes on a new meaning. Utilizing structured and modular methods is effective in guiding the team along this difficult journey. Working through the software life cycle with proper planning and focus enables project teams to realize their goals.

Exercises

1. From your experience, describe the typical software life cycle for the development of ad hoc (non-reusable) programs.

2. In your opinion, how has the implementation of the modern software life cycle changed since the earlier days of systems development?

3. List several reasons why many organizations resist using the full software life cycle when developing comprehensive systems?

4. Bugs can occur anywhere in the software life cycle. In what phase are bugs likely to be disastrous to a project?

5. Here is a true scenario. A manager once reasoned the following: Two programmers developed a complete software system in one year. The system required a complete rewrite in two months. The manager pulled out his calculator and said "Well, we need the equivalent of two man-years. All we have to do is hire ten more people, for a total of twelve bodies. Then we can make the deadline!" Critique this reasoning.

References

Ince, D. and Andrews, D. (1990), *The Software Life Cycle*, London: Butterworths.

Sommerville, I. (1982), *Software Engineering*, London: Addison-Wesley.

Weinberg, V. (1980), *Structured Analysis*, Englewood Cliffs, NJ: Prentice-Hall.

Chapter 3   # Managing the Project

Introduction **15**

Library Management **15**
   Library Organization 16
   Backing Up Files 20
   Source Code Organization 21
   Creating a %INCLUDE Library 23

Project Considerations **23**
   Project Standards 23
   Establishing a "To-Do" List 24
   Assigning Programming Tasks 25
   Test Plans 26

Database Management **26**
   Format Considerations 26
   Beware of the Efficiency Trap 28
   Quality Assurance 29
   Transforming the Data 29

Getting the Programming Team Started **31**
   Print the Raw Data 31
   Creating a Job Stream 32

External Documentation **32**

Making Programs Portable **34**

Summary **34**

Exercises **35**

References **35**

Introduction

Before laying down a single line of code, it is imperative to set up standards and procedures for the project. Organization is critical for developing successful large scale systems. As the number of individuals increases on a project, the number of lines of communication also expands. Ensuring software quality on a large project requires as much planning as development. This chapter addresses a number of those organizational considerations.

Library Management

After starting a project, you may realize that everything is in a state of disarray. Most likely, you have created libraries for source code and macro functions and formats and raw data and external files . . . and the list goes on and on. Let's look at some ideas for getting organized.

Library Organization

A project's source code and related documentation can be organized using vendor-supplied packages, or a company can develop its own organization from scratch. As for vendor-supplied packages, suffice it to say that they are well worth their money. The main drawback is that if you are not satisfied with a particular feature, customization is rarely available. In that case, the alternative is to create an in-house library management system.

Here is a suggested way of creating your own work environment. For demonstration purposes, consider a directory structured system. This would be directly applicable to an environment such as VMS, UNIX, or DOS. However, the principles of organization are certainly transferable to other operating systems.

First, create an empty directory structure. It is important to keep each subdirectory "clean" because each subdirectory has a unique function. That is, there should be no sharing of files or functions between subdirectories. This is an absolute requirement because a number of utility functions need a directory list for automated processing. For instance, you may want to create a tool that "runs a report for every file in this directory." This is only possible with the complete segregation of files.

A typical directory structure would have the following format (a backslash indicates subdirectories):

```
ROOT
        \ADHOC
        \BACKUP
                \OCT1296
                \NOV1496
                \NOV2996
                . . . and so on.
        \DATA
        \DATADUMP
        \DOCUMENT
        \EXTFILES
        \INCLUDES
                \GENERAL
                \PROG_INC
                \FORMATS
        \LOG
        \MENU
        \ORIGDATA
                \SASDATA
                \LOOKUPS
        \REPORTS
        \SCRATCH
        \SOURCE
        \UTILITY
        \VIEWS
```

ROOT is the anchor directory. Each complete software system (or subsystem) has an identical (or almost identical) directory structure. For example, imagine developing a fuel reporting system for a number of different states. The root directory names may look like the following:

> D:\FUEL\OHIO
> D:\FUEL\PENNA
> D:\FUEL\KANSAS
> *... and so on.*

Nothing should reside in this root directory except the directories themselves. Figure 3.1 describes how all the major modules work in unison to create a list of final reports.

Here is a closer look at the directory structure. The entries are listed alphabetically:

ADHOC

contains ad hoc (or "quick and dirty") requests by users. These programs never generate "production" level programs. Ad hoc program entries are often requests from various departments, managers, or users who simply want a program that is outside the realm of the production environment. While mnemonic names are usually preferable for creating files, the number of ad hoc requests can become massive and preclude the possibility of meaningful file names. In that case, name the files consecutively: PROG_001.SAS, PROG_002.SAS, PROG_003.SAS, and so on. The final step involves creating a directory or contents file — DIRECT.SAS. Here is a sample of the first two entries in the directory file:

```
Program   Author     Created    Requester
PROG_001  Bill Steb  10-17-91   Athletic Dept./Mrs. Wiggins

Description
Runs a statistical analysis to ascertain whether the maximum
levels of oxygen consumption are statistically different among
three groups of soccer players who underwent different aerobic
training programs.

Program   Author     Created    Requester
PROG_002  Ted Bear   10-18-91   Athletic Dept./Mr. Kendall

Description
Creates a report that lists the members of the men's soccer
and women's volleyball teams.
```

BACKUP

contains backed up source files and, optionally, data files. The creation date identifies the subdirectory. Optionally, you can create a batch file that automates the backup process.

DATA

contains permanent SAS data sets used directly by the programming team. These data sets are created after massaging the data in the ORIGDATA subdirectory (see ORIGDATA later in this section).

DATADUMP

holds the results of procedure output. By rerouting output using PROC PRINTTO, you can route all PROCEDURAL output to this directory. Then you can redirect the output back to the REPORTS directory right before the final step in your program. This rerouting occurs automatically when you submit SAS programs as part of a job stream. This method avoids cluttering the output file or terminal with nonreport debugging output. In addition, storing output here gives you the option to browse online and/or print at will.

DOCUMENT

contains study documentation. Unless the documentation is required company wide, storing all project data in its own subdirectory is usually simplest. If the list of documents becomes large, you can create subdirectories that reflect function. Organizing by date is usually confusing and does not allow you to easily locate a file.

EXTFILES

holds any external files. For example, this directory may contain flat files for program input or graphic files for export.

INCLUDES

contains all modules that are to be %INCLUDEd into your production level programs. Utilizing %INCLUDE modules greatly enhances structured/modular programming and simplifies maintenance. Depending on the size of the project, it is possible to break up the INCLUDES directories into several subdirectories such as GENERAL, PROG_INC, and FORMATS.

GENERAL contains nonspecific common modules such as abort routines and initialization, cleanup, or routing of output. PROG_INC (for "program %INCLUDEs") contains source code common to specific programs. For example, you may want to develop three different reports that utilize common code to create a tabulated type of report output. This common code should reside in this subdirectory. FORMAT contains user-created formats developed with PROC FORMAT. This is not to be confused with a permanent library for storing SAS formats.

LOG

contains SAS log files routed to this subdirectory for later perusal. This technique of routing log files is useful when programs are submitted as a job stream. Then, utility programs can scan through the group of log files searching for warnings and errors.

MENU

holds code to produce production menus.

ORIGDATA

contains SAS data originally created by the resident database. This is the data originally created after the transfer of data into the SAS data sets. The two subdirectories are SASDATA, which holds actual SAS data, and LOOKUPS, which are lookup tables created by the database administrator.

REPORTS

holds final reports. This is the location of final report output created by PROC or DATA _NULL_ output. The PRINTTO procedure can route reports to this directory.

SCRATCH

can be used as a temporary storage area. Most often, this directory functions as a storehouse for temporary source files or work files. The project team understands that this is a temporary area, and that the directory could be erased at any time if disk space becomes critical. Backup source code does not belong here.

SOURCE

contains all source code required to generate production reports. This directory does not contain %INCLUDE modules — rather, they belong in the INCLUDES subdirectory.

UTILITY

contains SAS code that is not required for generating system reports, but which may be useful for programming tasks. These include programs that list directory members, create frequency distributions of raw data, or batch the submission of reports.

VIEWS

stores SAS views, which may be useful in order to simplify data retrieval.

Note: The organization of files must be tailored to the philosophy of your project team. For example, some teams prefer to use specific libraries for source and compiled macro functions.

Figure 3.1 illustrates the directory structure contributing to final reports.

STEP 1: Beginning of project. Create SAS formats and scrub the original SAS data sets into another directory (DATA).

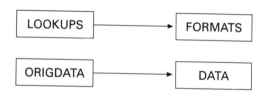

STEP 2: Each directory works on DATA and contributes to REPORTS.

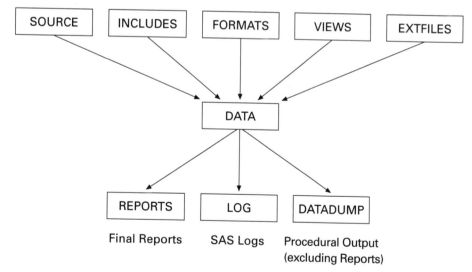

Figure 3.1   *Segregating files by function allows for easier maintenance, especially when running an entire group of source modules as a batch run. Final reports reside in their own directory for easy viewing and/or printing. The SAS logs are also segregated so that utilities can scan the files and report errors while running jobs in batch. Finally, all output, up to but not including the final step is routed to its own directory. This allows programmers to continue debugging output (using PROC PRINT) in the source without destroying the REPORTS subdirectory.*

Backing Up Files

Backing up files is like taking out an insurance policy on the software system. For a very small investment (a few minutes time and a little bit of disk space), you get the assurance that a lost or damaged source file does not spell disaster. Fortunately, almost all organizations have a backup plan in the event of a catastrophe. But, be cautious when relying on the company's backup system as a safety net. Many places perform a bulk backup, from which restoration can be a very time consuming process. In addition, backups may not be done as frequently as needed to make them useful (for example, every other Friday).

Larger organizations usually have two or perhaps three main libraries for storing source code. For example, a company may store its code in directories like the following:

PRODUCTION
production level source code

TEST
code that must be tested thoroughly before it is moved to production

DEVELOP
a complete development environment for the programming team

Typically, each of these libraries is backed up frequently due to the critical nature of this software. Doing nightly backups is considered standard practice.

Smaller organizations are less likely to have such rigorous library-control and backup procedures in place. If you are unsure of the reliability of your backups, then you should take matters into your own hands and perform your own. You can backup your personal software at a routine interval, say every day or every week.

One effective method is to create a backup directory whose subdirectory names reflect the backup date. For example, the subdirectory names might be JUL0695 or 070695. Obviously, this can take up a lot of disk space, so files have to be purged routinely. What is the best way to do this? Consider the following list of backup directories ordered by date:

```
                    070295
     purge ==>      092795
                    101295
     purge ==>      111495
                    111895
     purge ==>      012796
                    022196
                    031796
                    042296
```

As noted in the above diagram, simply deleting the oldest generations is not recommended. There are two reasons for purging files at intervals. For one, you may want to revert to an algorithm used in a previous version. Secondly, you may accidentally overwrite a "good" file with a completely different file. As a result, you could be backing up the "bad" file for many generations. Instead, purge files at a routine interval.

An alternate (or complementary) method for protecting disk space involves using a file compare program. If the file has not been modified since the last backup, then you don't back it up again. This practice can save valuable disk space.

For system-wide data, back up data on more than one medium. It is interesting that more than one MIS director has lost their job because they relied solely on using the network. Tape (dirt cheap!), local disk, disk cartridges, and floppies are also available for extra insurance. Some organizations have gone to the extreme of creating parallel systems that are backed up nightly. In case of network failure, the parallel system is immediately available for use. For critical applications, well managed companies routinely store one whole copy of the system off site (for example, in a bank vault).

Not to be overlooked is the technique of routinely producing hardcopy of the source code. Even in the absence of scanning technology, you can avoid a catastrophe. Most programs can be retyped in an hour or two, if need be.

Source Code Organization

When you are developing a complete software system, libraries of utility programs are essential for the project team. This section focuses on the organization of macro and %INCLUDEd code. You have several options available to you, and each has its advantages and disadvantages.

Using the SAS Macro Autocall Facility

Using the SAS autocall facility ensures that macros are stored in one common area. You specify the following combination:

```
options mautosource ;
options sasautos = (libref1, libref2,...librefn) ;
```

When a library member is found with the same name that is invoked, the macro processor does the following:

1. compiles and stores the source and macro definitions in the session catalog
2. executes any open code in that member
3. executes the macro within it using the same name that was invoked.

The advantages of using the autocall facility are as follows:

- The macro name and external file have the same name so you don't have to worry where "so-and-so" macro resides.
- Macros are stored in a common area that allows easy access by everyone on the project team.

Here are two warnings if you want to use the autocall facility properly:

1. Don't place more than one macro function into the external file. If you place multiple macros into one file, the additional macros are also included when the file is called. However, this destroys the whole concept of autocall! Programmers should not worry about a macro's location.

2. Don't include nonmacro code in this file. This included code only executes the first time the macro is called. Keeping open code in an external file can contaminate the programming environment and invite unexpected bugs. Remember, this is a macro library.

Using the Compile Stored Macro Facility

Another option that you have for organizing your source code is to use the compiled stored macro facility. To utilize this facility, set the following library specification and options:

```
libname mylib 'SAS-data-library' ;
options mstored ;
options sasmstore = mylib ;
```

The primary advantages of this method include:

- As with the autocall facility, all the macros reside in the same location, which is helpful for organizing the macro libraries. The difference is that compiled macros are stored.

- Because compiled macros, not source code, reside here, you can save some CPU time by not having to recompile the macros on each call. The macros only have to be compiled once before they are placed into the library.

Now the potentially bad news. The source code that created the macro could be *anywhere*. To circumvent this problem, designate a certain library to be the location of all macro source code. The name of the source module should be the same name as the compiled macro module. Version control with macros is *always* a problem at many organizations. Can you be sure that the source and compiled code match?

Consider the situation where a macro bug surfaces while you are running a production program. Imagine the horror when you discover that the source and compiled macro do not match. What do you do now?! Nothing but test the source and recompile. SAS Institute has utilized the compiled stored macro facility very successfully. Two reasons for the Institute's success are:

1. They have instituted very strict controls and standards. The entire process conforms to very exacting specifications. Most companies do not have the discipline (or know-how) to institute such controls.

2. They are primarily a software development organization. Many companies are performing in a real-time environment. If a programming bug appears, it must be fixed quickly. If there is a version control problem, then it could spell catastrophe!

Creating a %INCLUDE Library

Another option for organizing your source code is to create an %INCLUDE library. You set up filename definitions that point to these external files:

```
filename parser "fileref" ;
filename putpage "fileref" ;
filename abortit "fileref" ;
```

Then you can %INCLUDE these files into your program as needed:

```
%include parser ;
```

While losing some of the advantages of using the autocall facility and compiled macro libraries, this method has its own advantages:

- By assigning the same name to the fileref and the physical file name, organization is simplified:

```
filename parser   "c:\includes\parser.sas" ;
filename putpage  "c:\includes\putpage.sas" ;
filename abortit  "c:\includes\abortit.sas" ;
```

- It is possible to mix open code with macros in the component library members. This technique is useful because libraries can be grouped by function. Furthermore, it is immaterial whether the code is in the form of a macro. It is interesting to note that many programmers insist on building modules solely out of macro code. This is unfortunate because this philosophy limits the power of the SAS programming language. %INCLUDE libraries may contain any of the following:

  1. pure macro code.

  2. all nonmacro code.

  3. a combination of macro and nonmacro code.

  4. a group of %LET statements used to build global symbol tables. (These are useful when you are initializing the project environment or creating a core set of constants for table driven code.)

  5. an external file that builds SAS code or provides control information.

Project Considerations

Here is a look at a few of the elements that are required to ensure quality programming.

Project Standards

Prior to the onset of a project, an organization should have a set of standard operating procedures (SOP). Some programmers claim that project standards take away from their creativity. Nothing could be further from the truth! Sure, telling programmers to use a DO WHILE instead of DO UNTIL is unnecessarily restrictive. On the other hand, setting up standards to increase the lines of communication is indispensable and does not in any way inhibit creativity. One type of standard is for report layouts. For instance, you can set up the following standards for reports:

Left margin	1.5"
Right margin	1.0"
Top margin	1.0"
Bottom margin	1.0"
Footnotes	left justified
Project titles	left justified
Report specific titles	center justified
Headings	centered
Numeric fields	right justified, decimal aligned
Text fields	left justified
Printer font	LINEPRINTER size 8
Underline below headings	
Underline separating last line on page and footnotes	

Similarly, you can set up standards for online development:

Left margin	0.25"
Right margin	0.25"
Top margin	0.25"
Bottom margin	0.25"
Footnotes	left justified, yellow
Project titles	left justified, yellow
Report specific titles	center justified, red
Headings	centered, yellow
Numeric fields	right justified, decimal aligned, black
Text fields	left justified, black
All input fields	blue
Background color	white
Error fields	red, blinking
Font	SASFONT size 8
Underline below headings	
Underline separating last line on page and footnotes	

Programs also require documentation standards. These standards may include the format for the program header, macros, %INCLUDE modules, and level of comment detail expected. For more information on program documentation, refer to Chapter 6, "Improving Readability and Providing Internal Documentation."

Additionally, you should install a standardized change request log if your team operates in a heavy maintenance environment.

Establishing a "To-Do" List

To ensure order on a project, it's useful to establish a checklist (preferably online). Each individual on the project should have update/read access to the checklist. Figure 3.2 provides a short sample list for a project from the coding phase to the end of the project.

☑   <u>Move</u> source from production to test

☑   Coding complete

☑   Internal documentation

☐   External documentation

☐   Unit testing

☐   Integration testing

☐   System testing

☐   Compare source file with previous version

☐   Compare last data set with previous (Reports only)

☐   <u>Move</u> source from test to production

☐   Customer sign off

Figure 3.2   *An online checklist prevents tasks from "falling through the cracks."*

Assigning Programming Tasks

Systems building typically involves teams of programmers. What is the best way to divide up the task of coding once the analysis and design phases are complete? There are a number of ways to break out the coding tasks. However, there is only one steadfast rule: do not let two or more programmers work on the same module at the same time. No matter how good you think your version control is, it is still likely that programmers will write over each other's work. If the program is large and requires segmentation, create temporary %INCLUDE modules and let each programmer work on his or her own %INCLUDE module. Then, when the program is over, these modules can be copied back inline to the master program.

Here is a sample shell in which six programmers (one of which is you) are working on the same program:

```
MASTER.SAS program
%include dan ;
%include sheila ;
%include bill ;
.... your source code goes here
%include terry ;
%include steven ;
end of MASTER.SAS program
```

Assigning Tasks by Skill Level

Assuming that you can assign separate modules to each programmer, logical breakouts might involve assignment by skill level. The following table provides a rough guideline of assigning tasks by skill set.

Senior Level Programmers	Junior Level Programmers
utility programs	PROC FORMAT
module interfaces	title/footnote files
high level modules	low level modules
drivers and stubs	%INCLUDE modules
macro functions	report programs
advanced DATA _NULL_	PROC PRINT/PROC REPORT

Test Plans

The time to develop test plans is early on during the project, well before the coding is complete. Waiting until the last minute ensures that testing cannot be as comprehensive as it should be. In addition, the test plan can be biased after the coding step is complete because the tester may already be too familiar with the data. Details for developing test data can be found in Chapter 9, "Program Verification and Testing Methodology."

Database Management

Developing a clean, user-friendly database is paramount before the programming team lays down the first line of code. Here are a few recommendations to achieve this goal.

Format Considerations

Raw data can be stored in a variety of formats. It is not unusual for the original data to be stored in a database that is ultimately transferred to SAS data sets. One critical decision is how you want the data to be formatted for your data sets. Do you want data transferred as codes or preformatted values? For example, consider a rural area that has a number of dangerous roads because of sharply banked curves. As a software engineer, do you want "severity of curve" coded as 1, 2, or 3? Or, do you prefer a preformatted character variable such as "Mild," "Moderate," or "Severe"?

The major advantages of having preformatted values include:

- The data set is already self-documenting.

- The database administrator has probably already developed formats, which could save you from having to write your own with PROC FORMAT.

- You don't have to worry about making critical errors created by a mistake in your PROC FORMAT statement. For example, suppose that you accidentally code the formats incorrectly. Later on, when analyzing the output of your work, you could unknowingly make incorrect conclusions based on your faulty conversion.

The major advantages of using numeric codes include:

- Even with prior formatting, you may prefer to create your own lookup tables. You may also want the option of formatting the data differently according to the situation.

- You may want to shift the burden of quality assurance to your own programs. In this way, you can verify the formats yourself.

- Many PROCs require numeric variables for analysis.

- If the codes are contiguous (that is, codes = 1 to 5 all inclusive), you can process data as loops.

- Automating the creation of formats is fairly straightforward. For a coding example, refer to Coding Sample 1 in Appendix 1, "Coding Samples."

A final warning is in order here. Sometimes it is tempting to create user formats by running a frequency distribution on the data and setting up the corresponding lookup tables. This is especially true when the data appear to be contiguous. However, doing so can result in unexpected surprises when the database gets updated. Consider a variable, SEVERITY, which has values of "Mild," "Moderate," and "Severe" for preformatted values, or 1,2,3 for numeric codes: It appears that all values are accounted for. You then develop a report, set up the headings, calculate spaces, do your analysis, and so on. Now, assume the database gets updated. To your surprise, there are actually two more values of SEVERITY — "Dangerous" and "Extremely Dangerous." Now there are two possible conditions. If you fail to code defensively (more on this in later chapters), these two values cannot be accounted for in the reports.

```
if severity = "Mild" then
    ... SAS statement
else
if severity = "Moderate" then
    ... SAS statement
else
if severity = "Severe" then
    ... SAS statement
```

On the other hand, if you did code defensively, you now realize that the formats are incorrect. Hence, you have to rebuild the format tables. In addition, you have to recode the report to account for these new unexpected values. This means recoding headings and recalculating locations of the variables. This is a good time to do some finger pointing!

Beware of the Efficiency Trap

Writing efficient code is beneficial for many reasons, but you can become so obsessed with efficiency that design decisions become based on saving a little bit of disk space or memory at the expense of common sense. Consider the case of using a numeric field for laboratory values. Perhaps you need to differentiate between "types" of missing values. In order to conserve space, the database utilizes numeric codes to handle problem data. Here is a possible scenario:

```
2222 = "Not recorded"
3333 = "Not done"
4444 = "Lost data"
5555 = "Waiting on validation"
6666 = "Ongoing"
```

This is a very dangerous practice. It is quite possible that laboratory tests could take on these values to represent valid results. How would you know whether a white blood cell count is really 2222 or "not recorded"? A lesson here (that is transferable to any system) is that one variable should serve one and only one purpose! What are your alternatives in the above example? You can do one of the following:

- use special SAS System missing values:

    ```
    missing R D L W O ;
    ```

    However, be sure to explicitly document these values:

    ```
    ***************************************************************** ;
    *** The following conventions are used to designate special  *** ;
    *** values:                                                  *** ;
    ***                                                          *** ;
    ***      R = "Not recorded"                                  *** ;
    ***      D = "Not done"                                      *** ;
    ***      L = "Lost data"                                     *** ;
    ***      W = "Waiting on validation"                         *** ;
    ***      O = "Ongoing"                                       *** ;
    ***                                                          *** ;
    ***************************************************************** ;
    ```

- create a separate variable that contains a variable's status (beware, this method can use a lot of space!)

- consider creating a character variable and using standard names for each of these missing conditions, such as LOST DATA or ONGOING. Then you can recode these to missing values before performing calculations or displaying their values.

- create an auxiliary file that contains information about anomalous records. Do not record normal missing values.

Quality Assurance

One major quality assurance concern is to ensure that the data transferred from the in-house database are equivalent to the data stored in the SAS data sets. How do you know that the transfer was successful and without error? One approach is the following:

1. Request that the database administrator write out the data to a text (ASCII) file in the following format. The first line of the file is a header that contains the variable names separated by commas. All succeeding lines contain the value of the variable. For example:

```
ord_id,bookname,distrib,customer,ord_date
12,Whistling in the Wind,Cameron,Sedgewick,07-12-95
135,Painless Moving,Kellerman Dist,Long,08-04-95
347,Computers are Like Partners,Smith,Perrimon,08-15-96
1012,Odyssey of the Longshoreman,Bell Dist,Bellows,12-04-95
3490,Mellow and Marvelous,Pack Wholesale,Von Helling,11-30-96
```

2. Ensure that the names of the text files correspond to the names of the SAS data sets. There should be one text file for each corresponding SAS data set. For example,

SAS Data set	Text file
ORDER	ORDER.TXT
BOOK_INV	BOOK_INV.TXT
RETAIL	RETAIL.TXT

3. Create a SAS program that loops through the text files one at a time. Each iteration creates a data set from the input text file.

4. Run PROC COMPARE to compare the two data sets: the data set created from the text file and the original SAS data set. If everything goes well, the results of the compare should report no differences! For a coding example, refer to Coding Sample 2 in Appendix 1.

Transforming the Data

With the exception of very small organizations, the programmer and the database administrator rarely share the same role. As a result, the programming team may experience a few surprises after data transfer. Because the SAS team may have little or no say about the data format, they must make a few adjustments. Their primary task is to create two separate subdirectories off the root: ORIGDATA contains the original SAS data, and DATA contains the scrubbed version of the data. For the rest of the project, the team works off of the DATA subdirectory. To massage the data, set up a master program and call it NEWDATA.SAS. This module is extremely useful for a number of reasons:

- Renaming variables can bring clarity to their meaning. You could, for example, rename K-9 to DOG_NAME.

- Renaming variables can improve consistency. For instance, all "key" variables should have the same name across data sets for easy merging.

- Altering a variable's TYPE or LENGTH can also provide consistency. For example, a variable may be coded as numeric in one data set and character in another. Or, the LENGTH of a character variable may be different in two data sets.

- This is a good opportunity to attach labels to variables.

- Global variables can be established for the project. These variables can then be placed in a master lookup data set. Here, for example, you can create a customer information data set that contains a customer's first order. Additionally a number of general customer parameters can also be collected in this data set. Then, any program can merge back against this data set to collect vital information. The biggest advantage may be the avoidance of data redundancy. For example:

```
*************************************************************** ;
*** Collect important variables for each customer. This   *** ;
*** will save programming team from constantly merging     *** ;
*************************************************************** ;

data custinfo ;
    merge customer
          orders
          credit
          address
          ;
    by cust_id ;

if first.cust_id then
do ;
    firstord = ord_date ;
    output ;
end ;
...
...   other code to output variables to custinfo data set
...
run ;
```

- Bad or missing data can be recoded to ".".

- Variables can be globally changed to select only a portion of the variable that is relevant to your project. For instance, you may not want to use the entire nine character zip code, so you may wish to substring the field to select only the first five characters.

- Formats can be associated with variables.

- Special data sets can be created for this project.

- Only those variables required for the project are kept.

- You can reorganize the contents of the data sets. This has two major benefits:

  1. The data sets might not be logically organized. Experience can guide you to the most efficient way to build an application. Typically, each application requires a core set of data sets. For instance, in programming for a hotel chain, a good kernel of programs would include:

     Reservations
     Wake-up calls
     Room Service
     Catering
     Personnel
     Maid Service
     ... *and so on*.

     An investment in time spent, up front, reworking the organization of the data sets typically saves a tremendous amount of time in the long run. Whenever a particular field is required for a report, it is a simple matter to locate it. The programming team should not be spending a lot of time fumbling around, wondering where to find information.

  2. The data set might have too few or too many variables. If there are too few variables in the data set, then you have to spend extra effort in the programs to merge and concatenate data sets. If there are too many variables in the data set, then you spend too much time searching for the appropriate variables. This may cause the user to select the wrong variable because of the number of similar variable names in the data set.

Getting the Programming Team Started

The programming team will be eager to start their tasks. Here are a few tasks to get them well on their way.

Print the Raw Data

One of the first chores when you start a new system is to become familiar with the data. At the start of the project, print the following:

1. the SAS data set layouts (using PROC CONTENTS)

2. the actual data (using PROC PRINT)

3. a frequency distribution of all the data. Not only does browsing the distribution provide familiarity with the data, but it also gives you a preview of possible outlier data. For a coding example, refer to Coding Sample 3 in Appendix 1.

Creating a Job Stream

The next task is to set up a program that runs all your programs in a continuous job stream. You could, for example, write code like the following:

```
%include arizona ;
%include kansas ;
%include nevada ;
%include ohio ;
```

and so on, for all the source modules. However, this file needs continuous maintenance to handle any additions, deletions, or name changes to the source code. For an automated approach, refer to the coding example in Coding Sample 4 in Appendix 1.

External Documentation

External documentation can take on many forms. Selecting the appropriate documentation is, to a great extent, based on the size and complexity of the project. Some types of external documentation that may be useful for systems include: user instructions, problem definition, historical perspective, requirements analysis, system definitions, design documents, data dictionaries, source code listings, sample output, test plans, test results, problem descriptions and resolution log, and description of algorithms.

Here, for the sake of brevity, only two critical forms of documentation are examined: system definitions and a data element dictionary.

System definitions are the project definitions that are agreed upon as a team. They can have a great impact on how you eventually write the SAS code. One of the greatest sources of system-related bugs is not in the code itself, but in misinterpretations of the functional specifications.

For example, assume that a new pain reliever for arthritis is being tested for efficacy. Patients enrolled in this study are expected to take this oral medication three times a day, and each dose is to be taken at least four hours apart. In addition, the patient is expected to take the medication no sooner than one hour after a meal. Now, if you need to calculate the patient's study compliance, you must be armed with the proper definition of compliance. Even though the clinical study protocol specifies a specific dosing regimen, the investigator may decide that this definition is too stringent. Hence, you may want to set up a list of definitions. It is important to set up these terms without abstraction and as close to mathematical terms as possible:

> **Compliance:** is calculated for daily compliance only. The day cycle begins at 6 a.m. Patients are compliant if they receive 2 doses at least 6 hours apart, or if they receive 3 doses at least 3 hours apart. Administration in regards to meals is ignored.

PROC FORMAT statements, %INCLUDE modules, or macro definitions are most likely to be set up to handle the appropriate definition of compliance. It is critical that these definitions be reviewed periodically (and, of course, before software is released) because the programming team depends on the correct translation of the specifications. An error in the creation of SAS code to create these definitions can have a rippling effect throughout the system.

Another important piece of documentation is the data element dictionary. SAS provides PROC CONTENTS and the dictionary tables, which are extremely useful for visualizing the ordering of data. However, one important missing element is the range of valid values for a field. It is preferable not to use the LABEL field for listing value ranges. The principal role of the LABEL field is to provide a general description of the field itself. Thus, it would be useful to add a field that describes valid ranges such as 1-9, 10-15, 16-24. At times, the valid range may be complex and based on multiple factors such as the following:

Primary Part	Manufacturer	Value
chassis	Hentgen	1-12
chassis	Brittle MTX	16-44, 47-65
chassis	Fallaway	10-25, 34-92, 101-104
brakes	Stop-All	3-33, 44-57
brakes	Blue Val	2-26, 28, 30, 32, 34
and so on.		

For the sake of completeness, the rules for validating the field should also be included if they are different from simple range checking. Also, you may want to specify when the field is validated in the system procedure guide.

Another requirement for reports and for online programming is to define the report and screen layouts with the appropriate SAS variables. If the variables do not come directly from the data, then describe how the variable is derived or calculated. In addition, list the report formats below the variables.

One final important note: Whenever possible, external documentation should be online. Nothing is more frustrating than working with outdated specifications.

Here is a sample layout of a report that lists a patient's concomitant medications:

Wonder Drug Phase III
Patient Data Listing #17

Patient's Concomitant Medications
(All Patients Randomized)

Patient ID	Days on Study	Medication	Medication Class	Indication	Start Date	Stop Date
pat_num	(1)	concom	medclass	indicate	initdate	end_date
$	4.-r	$	class.	$	mm/dd/yy	mm/dd/yy

Note: Only medications post-baseline are listed.

(1) = Medication Date minus First Treatment Date. If patient received no treatment dose, then use Medication Date minus Randomization Date.

Making Programs Portable

Early on in a project, you must think about portability issues. Are you going to develop for one configuration or for multiple configurations? That is, are you going to develop for more than one platform? This can be a critical decision because you may have to write additional code (perhaps substantially more) to accommodate portability. However, if you don't think the program needs to be portable, then it may be wiser not to build-in this protection because of the substantial savings in cost development. Here is a list of suggestions to make programs portable:

- Whenever possible, avoid embedding operating system commands in the source code.

- Be wary of using constructs that are available only in the latest release of SAS. At times these newer elements are specific to a particular operating system. Be sure to consult with the SAS technical reports as well as the operating system companions to determine the portability of a construct.

- If you must embed code related to the operating system, always place it in a different module. That way, you can play "plug-and-play" by changing only the modules related to the operating system.

- Utilize the automatic macro variable &SYSSCP to determine the operating system, and &SYSVER to determine the version. In that way, you can conditionally execute code based on the environment. For example:

```
%macro file_def ;
    %if &sysscp = VMS %then
    %do ;
        ... filename and libname defs for VMS
    %end ;
    %else %if &sysscp = WIN %then
    %do ;
        ... filename and libname defs for Windows
    %end ;
    %else %if &sysscp = OS %then
    %do ;
        ... filename and libname defs for MVS
    %end ;
%mend file_def ;
```

Summary

As the size of a project grows in complexity, so does the need for clear communication among the members of the programming team. For instance, properly managing libraries of code is critical in minimizing programmer frustration. Also, failing to install appropriate standards invariably results in finger pointing as soon as an important file disappears.

Reorganizing data, providing adequate documentation, and developing utility modules can be invaluable in saving development time and improves quality assurance.

Finally, you must assess portability requirements because the cost factor may be dramatically reduced if only one system has to be coded.

Exercises

1. List at least one advantage and one disadvantage of organizing libraries using:

   a. SAS macro autocall facility

   b. compiled macro facility

   c. a general %INCLUDE library

2. Creating variables that have preformatted values without using a concomitant lookup table has an inherent danger. Explain.

3. From 8 to 5, you work in the MVS environment. However, you take your work home to a Windows environment. What automatic system variable can assist you in porting the code between these environments?

4. Collecting system definitions into a common library is critical for the success of a project. Revise the following definition to achieve the precision required for proper documentation:

   Drug PAIN-AWAY is effective if it reduces fever.

5. Assume that you are working in a large organization. You have the option of creating two types of macro libraries either one large, centralized library, or a number of decentralized libraries. Cite advantages and disadvantages of each.

References

Borenstein, N. (1991), *Programming as if People Mattered,* Princeton: Princeton University Press.

Cady, D. (1996), *Bulletproof Documentation*, New York: McGraw-Hill.

Enger, N.L. (1976), *Documentation Standards for Computer Systems*, Fairfax Station, VA: The Technology Press.

Hohmann, L. (1997), *Journey of the Software Professional*, Upper Saddle River, NJ: Prentice-Hall.

Purba, S., Sawh, D., and Bharat, S. (1995), *How to Manage a Successful Software Project*, New York: John Wiley & Sons.

Putnam, L.H. (1992), *Measures for Excellence: Reliable Software on Time, within Budget*, Englewood Cliffs, NJ: Yourdon Press.

Whitten, N. (1990), *Managing Software Development Projects*, New York: John Wiley & Sons.

Chapter 4   # Analyzing the Problem

Introduction **37**

The Problem **38**
    Problem Definition. 38
    Expanded Problem Definition 38

Risk/Reward **38**

Analysis Tools **39**
    Decision Tables 39
    Tree Searching: Brute Force 40
    Tree Searching: Backtracking and Pruning 41
    Digraph-Directed Graphs 42

Structured Analysis **43**
    Preliminary Assessment. 43
    Functional Requirements. 43
    Feasibility Studies. 44
    The Core Components of Structural Analysis 44

Data Modeling **45**

Evaluating a Language **46**

Summary **47**

Exercises **48**

References **48**

Introduction

What really separates the human being from the conglomerate box of parts that is called a computer? It is the power of the human mind to analyze. In the first phase of analysis (and even design), you have to forget about computers and languages, and conjure up a solution that is understandable in human terms.

There is no magic tool that can simplify analysis to its atomic elements. Don't be lured into thinking that, by utilizing certain tools and techniques (such as Action Diagrams), that systems analysis is easy. It isn't. Programmers will stand around the break room and debate which technique is the best, but in reality, the argument is moot. These are tools — nothing more, nothing less. If you want to be good at analysis, stir up your creative juices. Look at the problem from different perspectives. Don't be caught up in the mechanics of analysis. If a tool helps you organize your thoughts, use it. Otherwise, forget it.

The Problem

Before embarking on the journey of analysis, it is imperative that you carefully define the problem. This allows you to develop a solution through heuristic methods or structured analytical techniques.

Problem Definition

The first step in the software life cycle is to state the problem in the form of a problem statement. This should be one or two concise statements of the problem. Then you can amplify the discussion in subsequent paragraphs. Here is a sample problem statement:

> Arbor Airport is losing an unacceptable number of passenger bags on both domestic and international flights.

Expanded Problem Definition

The expanded problem definition starts with the problem statement and expands it in greater detail. The expanded definition may be a paragraph or it could fill a chapter, depending on the application area. Using the above example, the expanded definition might read:

- At Arbor Airport, 7.3% of all passengers report missing luggage on domestic flights.
- 3.9% of all passengers report missing luggage for international flights.
- On average, 1.7 bags are unclaimed every day.
- Overall, 99.3% of passengers recover their luggage within 7 days, 99.8% within 14 days.
- . . . and so on.

Risk/Reward

Many problems require you to weigh the risks and benefits of each possible solution. Consider a company that is a developing a toy targeted for an October 1st distribution. Because this toy is likely to be a big hit for the Christmas season, the company is anxious to make the deadline. However, in April, the toy is exhibiting mechanical difficulties. The company has the following options:

- Continue everything "as is" with the expectation that everything will be fine by the deadline.
- Abandon the project completely.
- Hire a number of design and testing specialists to debug the problem.
- Abandon development on the current toy and start designing a new one.
- Modify the design to reduce the chance of mechanical problems at the risk of decreasing its marketability.
- Develop a second toy concurrently with the chance that one of them will be ready for the Christmas season.

This kind of analysis involves looking at the complete risk/reward spectrum. Just a few of the factors that may shape the analysis in this example include: the company's financial situation, its market share, its projected sales of the product, its marketing ability, its confidence in its technical staff, and its experience with "problem" toys in the past.

Perhaps you won't have the opportunity to work on a project as exciting as toy design. However, as a software engineer, you will be confronted with the following kinds of risk/reward decisions on an almost daily basis:

- promising to make a deadline that might be tough to make
- shortening the testing phase on a project to fulfill an earlier delivery date
- subcontracting a portion of the programming effort
- not writing a program to be portable
- spending a lot of time on an efficiency rewrite
- not documenting a program.

Analysis Tools

Attaining proficiency at analysis means being a good problem solver. Here are just a few tools to get you started. The most fundamental tool is drawing. It is invaluable in shaping the thought process. Don't be shy about the using the chalkboard to work through a thorny problem. Often, you may have to try several different representations until you discover a means of correctly visualizing the problem.

Decision Tables

When the number of conditions is not too great, you can use decision tables to assist you in resolving a problem. By creating tables, you can be sure that you have accounted for all conditions and outcomes. For example, flipping a coin 6 times creates a set of 6 binary conditions (heads or tails). Thus, there are 2^6 or 64 possible combinations. Without tables, how do you account for each of these combinations?

Imagine that you sneak home from work a little early. How should you spend the afternoon? You would likely think (probably on a subconscious level) about all the relevant conditions (such as, the weather or your motivation) and consider possible actions (such as take a nap or go jogging). Let's try to organize these thoughts into a table like Table 4.1.

First, list all of the possible conditions that could influence your decision. For brevity, you can abbreviate "Yes" to "Y" and "No" to "N". If the condition is immaterial in your decision, then designate it with a "—". Below this, list all the possible outcomes. To the right of these outcomes, place an "x" next to the item that describes the outcome based on the conditions listed above. For example, look at rule #4 in Table 4.1 and read down. You can interpret the column as follows: I do not have sore muscles, I am not tired, I am motivated, and the weather is good. Hence, I will (continuing to move down the column) go jogging and then go to the jacuzzi.

RULE # =>	1	2	3	4	5	6	7	8	9	10	11	12	13	14	15	16
Sore muscles	N	N	N	N	N	N	N	N	Y	Y	Y	Y	Y	Y	Y	Y
Tired	N	N	N	N	Y	Y	Y	Y	N	N	N	N	Y	Y	Y	Y
Motivated	N	N	Y	Y	N	N	Y	Y	N	N	Y	Y	N	N	Y	Y
Good weather	N	Y	N	Y	N	Y	N	Y	N	Y	N	Y	N	Y	N	Y
Take a nap					x	x							x			
Go jogging	x		x	x		x	x				x	x			x	x
Go to jacuzzi		x		x					x		x		x		x		x
Get massage									x	x	x	x				

Table 4.1   *A decision table helps to organize conditions and outcomes. The top half of the table describes all possible conditions. The bottom portion of the table describes all possible outcomes.*

There are two rules that can help you to simplify decision tables by eliminating columns. Look for action sequences that are identical for two columns. For instance, in Table 4.2, the first two columns yield the same action sequence on the bottom of the diagram, so you can collapse these two columns into the column shown at the right:

Y	Y	======>	Y
N	N	======>	N
Y	N	======>	–
Y	N	======>	–

Table 4.2   *Collapsing conditions into a single column*

You can also collapse "don't care" entries (that is, the condition is immaterial), as shown in Table 4.3:

N	N	======>	N
–	Y	======>	–
–	Y	======>	–
–	Y	======>	–

Table 4.3   *Collapsing of "don't care" entries*

Decision tables have many practical applications in software engineering, especially when the number of conditions is not too great. For example, you can use decision tables to determine traffic light sequencing at a street intersection.

Tree Searching: Brute Force

While decision tables are effective when the conditions are relatively few, they are cumbersome when dealing with a large number of conditions or decisions. Here is where tree searching strategies can be helpful. Starting with a simplistic example, consider a problem in which there are only two possible outcomes at each decision point. For example, a leading cereal producer has the option of advertising on nationwide TV over a three-month period. For each month, they can choose whether or not to advertise, and can then measure the effects of advertising on gross revenues for the period. For such a small number of decisions, you can certainly draw a diagram. Figure 4.1 depicts this situation.

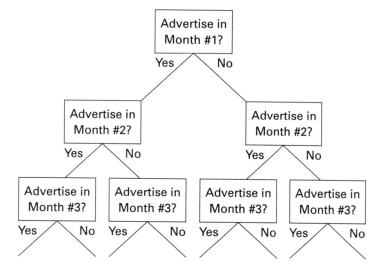

Figure 4.1 *This diagram shows there are eight possible permutations, based on this company's decision to advertise.*

For a more advanced example, consider the game of chess. On the first move, the player with the white pieces has 20 choices, and his opponent also has 20 choices. Hence, there are 400 possible combinations for the first move alone. It does not take long before the number of combinations mushrooms into the millions. To make "intelligent" decisions, the computer evaluates each position. It scores the position based on important gaming tactics such as "mobility of pieces," "control of the center," and "safety of the king." Then the computer plays the "what-if" game. If I move here, what is the new evaluation score? And if my opponent does that, then what is the new score? In fact, the computer evaluates every single move and countermove, searching through thousands (or millions) of these "what-if" move combinations. Each position receives a rating, and, within the time limit, the computer selects the position that yields the highest score. Since the computer evaluates every possible move, no matter how ridiculous looking, the strategy is called "brute force."

Even if you aren't a game aficionado, brute force has a number of exciting applications. A strange complex of symptoms may bewilder even the most brilliant physician. However, with a brute force algorithm, you can enter the list of symptoms, and the program can search its massive index and suggest a list of possible diseases.

Tree Searching: Backtracking and Pruning

Often, decisions are based on uncertainty. There may be a number of alternatives, and each of them seems to have a certain attractiveness. Hence, you revisit each of these alternatives, probing and exploring each concept deeper and deeper, then backtracking to another "tunnel" and exploring these areas. At some point, you may discover that a given strategy is no longer tenable, so you abandon further exploration. Abandoning such a search path is called *pruning*.

Examine Figure 4.2. A brave (or foolish) soul has wandered into a network of caves with nothing more than a flashlight. He tries different tunnels, but "backtracks" when a path does not seem promising (that is, he has been walking for a long period of time with no rescue in sight). At other times, he abandons a path completely ("pruning") because of the inherent dangers. Most likely, the obstacles in Figure 4.2 cause the wanderer to "prune" these search paths.

Figure 4.2   *High speed search algorithms are dependent on effective "pruning" and "backtracking" techniques. For example, it is necessary to "prune" paths that show little promise. Then you can "backtrack" to continue on a more fruitful path. As shown, the arrows would be a typical "pruned" path.*

Tree searching, backtracking, and pruning are exceptionally useful in artificial intelligence applications. Because the number of search paths can mushroom to astronomical proportions, the computer proves invaluable in searching many paths in a relatively short time frame. Tree searching strategies have been highly successful in medicine, automotive diagnostics, computer diagnostics, and game programming.

Digraph-Directed Graphs

A verbal or even written description of a problem may not shed light on a solution, but drawing it out on paper is usually very useful. Consider Wacky Airlines, a zany airline company that prides itself in providing the customer with the "scenic" tour. Consider the situation in which you want to find the best way to get from Los Angeles to Charlotte. Using the following verbal descriptions is not overly helpful: "Flight 197 departs Los Angeles and stops at San Francisco, Amarillo, and Miami. Flight 202 departs San Francisco and stops at Baltimore and Kansas City." And so on for all the flight connections. Figure 4.3 illustrates how a digraph is useful.

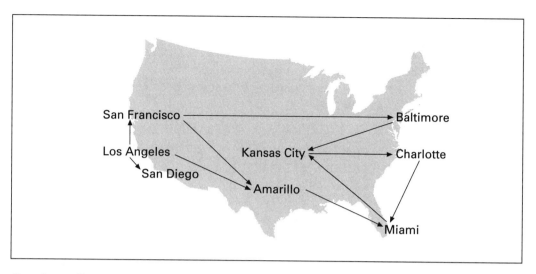

Figure 4.3 *Drawing a digraph can simplify even the most complex paths.*

As a journeyman SAS programmer, you will eventually have the honor of maintaining another programmer's bowl of spaghetti (source code). In such a situation, you might find that a digraph can be valuable in tracing program flow.

Structured Analysis

More formal methods of analysis are also available if you like to organize your thoughts. Structured analysis provides you with a means of bridging the gap between problem solving and design. Here is a quick overview.

Preliminary Assessment

The first step is to gather information from any and all sources in order to learn as much as possible about the problem. You may have to interview people, perform surveys, have group meetings, read any available current system documentation, and analyze the current system (if there is one).

Functional Requirements

Using the "lost luggage" example, this list of user requirements specifies, in concrete terms, the functional requirements of the system that you want to design:

- A monitor displays the status of all luggage within one hour of flight arrival.
- All customer complaints are handled through a centralized station rather than through the individual airlines.
- Customers are able to obtain more detailed information about their particular luggage with a status tracking viewer.
- . . . and so on.

Feasibility Studies

The next phase, if needed, is to perform a feasibility study. Feasibility studies are not always required because an organization may have already made their decision. However, there may be a transition from a manual to an automated system requiring further analysis. Several of the factors may include:

- Cost is usually the most important factor. Can the organization afford to develop the system? Is it cost effective in the long term? Are there any budgetary constraints? How will investors react at this time to an expensive project?

- Is the project do-able? Is the technology too experimental? Does the organization have the expertise to develop the system? What types of utilities, compilers, applications, communications software, and hardware need to be purchased?

- What external factors could affect the success of the project?

- What are the timeline constraints? What is the projected start date? When is a reasonable implementation date? Could implementation occur early enough to solve the user's problems?

As the next step, the organization receives the results of the feasibility study in the form of an initial study report. At some institutions, a steering committee reviews the feasibility assessment. This is particularly true in business application industries, where there is competition for available resources.

The Core Components of Structured Analysis

The traditional means of structured analysis involves four major components. The current system and the proposed system are viewed from both physical and logical components. The physical component describes how the system is assembled; the logical component specifies the function of the system. Figure 4.4 illustrates this sequence of analysis.

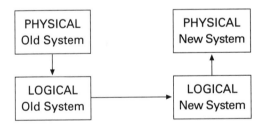

Figure 4.4   *The traditional view of systems analysis.*

This traditional method of analysis has its share of critics because there is a substantial time investment in evaluating the old system before analyzing the new proposed system. Why invest so much time and effort in analyzing an operation that is obsolete? Although the traditional method still has its share of proponents, many modern day theorists have emphasized data modeling for new systems.

Data Modeling

Data modeling is a means of providing a documentation framework for a system's data. Data modeling is an important concept for SAS programmers because it provides the theoretical framework for correctly setting up the SAS database. Creating a SAS data set is not just a matter of collecting a number of elements and storing them in a common area. There are a number of subtleties that you, as the analyst, must be aware of so that members of the programming team can easily abstract the data. One of the more popular methods of depicting data is through a diagramming tool known as an Entity Relationship Diagram (ERD).

The principal component of the ERD model is an *entity,* which is any kind of element that can store data. For instance, an entity can be a customer, a job opening, or a personal computer. These data elements contain *attributes,* which are the facts about a particular entity. Consider a potential customer on a company's mailing list. The customer's attributes may include full name, home address, date of birth, occupation and home phone number. For a personal computer, its attributes might include its RAM, BIOS, monitor, hard disk, processor type, and casing.

The database relationship of entities can be described by two major rules: ordinality and cardinality. *Ordinality* specifies the minimum number of occurrences between two entities. For instance, one entity might be a magazine, and another entity a homeowner whose personal information is generated from a mailing list. The two elements are related because the homeowner can order a magazine. The homeowner can exist in the database without ordering a magazine. On the other hand, a magazine entry must have been ordered by an owner in order for the magazine to exist in the database. Thus, the ordinality for the relationship is 0 and 1 respectively. *Cardinality* is the maximum number of elements that can exist between the elements. Using this example, one homeowner can order many magazines, and a given magazine can be ordered by many homeowners. Hence, this is a 1-to-many relationship for both directions of the entity relationship. Figure 4.5 depicts a primitive ERD of this scenario. In this figure, rectangles are entities, and the diamond is an action that associates entities. The ordinality is on the left side of the colon, and the cardinality is on the right side of the colon.

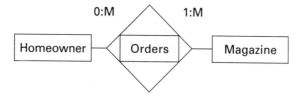

Figure 4.5   *The entity relationship between homeowners and magazines.*

After completing the task of data modeling, you are ready to answer the following questions:

- Should you store the data in SAS data sets or in another vendor package?
- How do you avoid data redundancy?
- What kind of indexing scheme is appropriate? Should the keys be simple or compound?
- Should the database have the look and feel of a hierarchical database or a relational database?
- How do you organize the data sets?
- Do you define variables as character or numeric? What would be appropriate lengths for these variables? How can you effectively use the LABEL field? Should default formats and informats be assigned to the variable?
- How should you handle variables greater than 200 bytes?
- How should the database be documented?
- What efficiency considerations are of concern?
- Should a "Black Box" querying system be developed with, say, SQL or macros?
- What are the appropriate procedures to handle changes to the database schema? How will you notify the project team?

Evaluating a Language

With a plethora of languages available on virtually all types of platforms, how do you choose a language appropriate for a project? There a number of parameters that you can use to judge the utility of a language. You must not be so shortsighted as to think there is one magical language that handles all requirements. There are numerous tradeoffs, and the project should determine the proper choice of target language. For example, the languages that execute very rapidly are also the most time consuming to develop. Likewise, the ones learned very quickly usually lack the rich set of constructs that permit the development of serious systems.

Some theorists suggest that the choice of language be postponed until the end of the design phase because design should be language independent. However, can a company afford to spend a tremendous amount of money on planning, analyzing, and designing, and then suddenly realize that they do not have the personnel or expertise for the long journey ahead?

The end of the analysis phase is the perfect time to evaluate possible implementations. Some of the factors that may influence the choice of language are the following:

memory utilization disk space requirements execution speed	Machine Efficiency
ease of enhancements difficulty in debugging readability	Maintainability
ability to prototype ease of development structured constructs lends itself to modularity object oriented constructs	System Building
mathematical calculations string manipulation quick and dirty programs application diversity GUI development real-time applications	Programming Power
portability interface to other languages interface to databases	External Factors
availability of programmers price and support cost	Miscellaneous

Summary

This has been a very quick tour through problem definition and analysis. These two phases of the software life cycle should be implementation independent. However, when you are in the transition between analysis and design, it may be prudent for you to start thinking about implementation. This may include choice of language, operating system, database construction, and so on.

Exercises

1. What are some of the reasons that organizations consider feasibility studies?

2. Current trends in analysis tend to focus on the proposed system while not belaboring on the current system. What would be an exception?

3. Many organizations use SAS software for their applications development, but store their core data in a different kind of database. Why do you think this is so? Will this trend continue, or do you envision SAS becoming the centralized data repository?

4. Why is data modeling important for the SAS programmer?

5. How would you define analysis? The definition of analysis should give you a hint on how to proceed with the analysis of a project. Explain.

References

Barker, R. (1989), *Case*Method Entity Relationship Modeling*, Wokingham, England: Addison-Wesley.

Brown, S.I. and Walter, M.I. (1993), *Problem Posing Reflections and Applications*, Hillsdale, NJ: Lawrence Erlbaum Associates.

Goodman, S.E. and Hedetniemi, S.T. (1977), *Introduction to the Design and Analysis of Algorithms*, New York: McGraw-Hill.

Rubenstein, M.F. (1986), *Tools for Thinking and Problem Solving*, Englewood Cliffs, NJ: Prentice-Hall.

Silver, E.A. (1985), *Teaching and Learning Mathematical Problem Solving: Multiple Research Perspectives*, Hillsdale, NJ: Lawrence Erlbaum Associates.

Weinberg, V. (1980), *Structured Analysis*, Englewood Cliffs, NJ: Prentice-Hall.

Chapter 5   # Laying the Foundation with Good Design

Introduction **50**

Concepts of Modular Design **50**
Top-Down Design 50
Bottom-Up Design 52
Combination Approach 53
Stepwise Refinement 54

The Definition of a Module **55**
Module Size 55
Definition of a SAS Module 56

Module Qualities **58**

Module Cohesion **59**
Coincidental Cohesion 59
Logical Cohesion 60
Temporal (Classical) Cohesion 61
Procedural Cohesion 62
Communicational Cohesion 63
Informational Cohesion 63
Functional Cohesion 64

Module Coupling **65**
Content Coupling 66
Tramp Coupling 67
Control Coupling 67
Common Coupling 68
Stamp Coupling 69
Data Coupling 71

Converting Modules to SAS Code **73**
Creating the Module Interface - Passing Parameters 75
Number of Arguments 79

Documentation of Modules/Arguments **79**

Prototyping Methods **81**

Principles of Good Design **82**

Writing a Utility Module from Scratch **84**
General Tips for Designing Modules 84
The Design Process for Writing a Utility Module 85

Summary **87**

Exercises **87**

References **88**

Introduction

Good software design is the foundation of software engineering. A well designed system can result in straightforward implementation. On the other hand, a poorly designed system can result in project failures, no matter how proficient the coding team. Although good design skills require a certain degree of creativity, a number of principles can guide designers of all skill levels. The most important principle of design is the concept of modularity.

Concepts of Modular Design

Modular design is the cornerstone of systems building. Hence, we need a concise definition of a module. A *module,* in the broadest sense, is a block of code delineated by a starting and ending boundary. A well designed program (or system) is a collection of these modules or blocks of code. By breaking programs into smaller pieces, the task of system building becomes more manageable. Subsequent sections in this chapter examine various SAS structures which may be considered a module.

Properly developing a modular system forces the programmer to think about the problem in great detail. In fact, one of the benefits of good design is that the process helps to clarify the analysis and problem definition phases of the software life cycle. Frequently, more questions arise during design development. This is important because a good designer wants to ensure that program development conforms to the specifications of the system. It is not unusual for the designer to interact with the end user or system analyst to ensure that they are using sound judgment in the design process.

Modular design is especially impressive in its effects on the latter stages of the software life cycle. With proper design, structured programming becomes a natural extension for converting modular constructs into easily maintainable code. However, this is only true when the interfaces between modules are described cleanly and carefully. Good design results in systematic testing and debugging, in contrast to the random nature of testing and debugging that is encountered in typical software systems.

There are several ways to achieve modular design. The three most widely recommended approaches are Top-Down design, Bottom-Up design, and a combination of the two.

Top-Down Design

Top-Down design is based on the principle of "abstraction." *Abstraction* is a way of focusing on the similarities of objects and categorizing the objects into groups based on these properties. For example, the game of baseball is an abstraction that describes our national pastime. In order to refer to the game of baseball, you don't have to describe the details of the game, such as pitching, or running the bases, or laying down a sacrifice bunt. You can simply converse with someone using the term "baseball." From this highest level of abstraction, you can then formulate more detailed levels of abstraction. For instance, you can use the word "pitching." You don't have to describe the process of one person throwing the ball towards the catcher. Going a step further, you can say that that the pitcher has a good "curveball." You don't have to get involved in the actual mechanics of how the pitcher rotates his wrist and adjusts his grip on the ball. Obviously, the levels of abstraction can be defined to atomic detail.

This same principle of abstraction applies to the creation of good systems design. You think about a process at a very generalized level. Then you can refine your thoughts and think about applications at a more detailed level. Though this process of refinement may require a number of iterations, it is a vital component of systems building.

When developing systems from the top down, you can create a hierarchy of modules that are (usually) coded and tested from the top down. For instance, assume that you are developing a very simple system that determines whether an individual is addicted to television. In this system, you design a hierarchy of three modules:

1. MAINLINE contains initialization routines and is the main driver for the system.

2. GETSTATS inputs all the demographic data as well as the number of hours of TV watched per week.

3. ADDICTED classifies an individual as "sane" or as a "TV-aholic and beyond help."

Figure 5.1 depicts this structure.

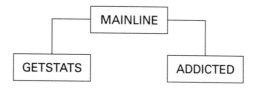

Figure 5.1   *MAINLINE calls the modules GETSTATS and ADDICTED.*

Stubs

Assume that the coding is complete for MAINLINE and ADDICTED. You cannot test the program fully because GETSTATS has not been completed. The solution to this problem is to create a dummy module, or *stub*. In this case, you can create a dummy for GETSTATS. Here is a simple way to code the GETSTATS stub:

```
data _null_ ;

link getstats ;
link addicted ;

return ;

getstats:
age = 52 ;
sex = "male" ;
jobtitle = "longshoreman" ;
tv_hours = 34 ;
return ;


addicted:
(The code for this subroutine is completed)
return ;

run ;
```

Notice that you do not need to actually write the input routines. You can simply hardwire some sample values back to the calling routine because these are the direct outputs from GETSTATS.

Often stubs are nothing more than simple routines that let the calling module know that the stub is alive and kicking. For instance, many stubs can be coded as simple routines that write to the log:

```
im_alive:

file log ;
put "Yes you entered the im_alive subroutine!" ;

return ;
```

Stubs are examined more closely in Chapter 9, "Program Verification and Testing Methodology."

Bottom-Up Design

At the other end of the spectrum is Bottom-Up design. This design philosophy is built on the concept of *concatenation*. You develop a small piece of the program and continually add to it other small pieces or modules. The most striking difference between Top-Down and Bottom-Up design philosophies is based on sequence. In Top-Down design, you start at the highest level of abstraction and gradually move down to the detail modules. With Bottom-Up design, you start with the detail levels and eventually move upward to design the higher level constructs. An example where concatenation may be successful is the creation of a word processing system. You can design small chunks of functional units and build them into a complete system. For instance, you can design a module that performs spell checking, another that is a thesaurus, and finally one that counts the words in a document. Then, you can combine these modules into a "tools" function. This approach works particularly well when intermodule communication is minimal. If one lower level module does not have to know the inner workings of another low level module, then all you have to do is ensure that the calling function to these low level modules is handled smoothly. One advantage of this type of design is that output is produced very quickly if coding proceeds after developing each module. This may be advantageous when the financial commitment to a project is uncertain. If a project is terminated, then all the bottom level modules can become functional with little or no modification.

When the developer codes and tests from the bottom up, testing becomes problematic because low level modules must communicate through a higher level module. The solution is to create driver modules. Assume that you wish to develop a computerized fitness program that can improve an individuals strength, flexibility, and endurance. You decide to name these modules STRENGTH, FLEX, and ENDURE. Driving the whole system is a module called ASSESS. Figure 5.2 shows this structure:

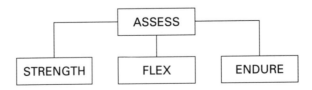

Figure 5.2   *ASSESS calls the three lower level modules.*

Writing a recommended exercise prescription depends on a preliminary fitness assessment. However, because you are developing the system from the bottom up, the assessment data are not ready. Thus, you must create a driver module that can supply data to the lower level fitness modules. Here is an example:

```
data fitness ;
...
link assess ;
...
return ;

assess:
flex_scr = 7.5 ;
str_scr = 6.8 ;
end_scr = 8.8 ;
age = 23 ;
weight = 137 ;
bodycomp = "Ectomorph" ;

%flex
%endure
%strength

return ;

run ;
```

The concept of drivers is covered in greater detail in Chapter 9.

Combination Approach

At times it may be most effective to employ a combination of Top-Down and Bottom-Up design. This approach may be recommended for any of the following reasons:

• A powerful set of utility modules has been developed. As a designer, you want to ensure that these modules are utilized in the final product.

• The financial commitment to a long-term project may be uncertain. How long can you expect investors to contribute without even a glimpse of the final product? Developing just a piece of the system from the ground up can keep their appetites whetted.

• You may realize early on in the project that certain low level modules are required. For instance, table-lookups, database retrievals, and error handling routines are not expected to change to any great degree. These can be developed while concurrently designing high level functions.

• The customer has created specifications early in the project for low level modules. This usually takes the form of report layouts. Part of the team can be designing and coding the DATA _NULL_ steps while others are simultaneously designing higher level functions such as the user interface.

However, as the designer, you should realize that the combination approach requires considerable foresight. Developing a system that requires a lot of intermodule communication can become unwieldy. What may happen halfway through a project is that designers "bend" their modules to conform to the system requirements.

Stepwise Refinement

Regardless of the type of design, the ultimate goal of the designer is to establish a hierarchy of relationships. This is usually expressed graphically in the form of a structure chart. For a simple example, assume a group of friends decides to make pizza instead of ordering out. Since they've never made pizza before, they envision the steps depicted in Figure 5.3.

1. Put sauce on crust.

2. Put cheese on crust.

3. Put in oven.

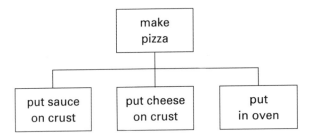

Figure 5.3   *The first "cut" at making a great pizza.*

Presto! Out comes the pizza. OK, maybe not that tasty yet, but experience is starting to pay off. Here is the recipe for a great pizza:

1. Start with a bakery crust.

2. Put tomato sauce and a bag of cheese on the crust.

3. Spread the veggies on top.

4. Bake at 425 degrees for 15 minutes.

5. Lower temperature to 375 degrees and bake for five minutes.

6. Sprinkle oregano on top.

7. Serve piping hot!

Well, maybe not a world class pizza, but not bad for a second try. After a little contemplation, we're ready for the real masterpiece:

1. Stone grind the wheat to make the crust.

2. Crush four homegrown tomatoes to a fine puree and spread on the crust.

3. From your own backyard garden, pick some fresh herbs and sprinkle them on the sauce.

4. Milk the cow and let the milk stand for a good while.

5. When the milk has coagulated, apply to the top of sauce.

6. Finely chop garden-fresh mushrooms, onions, and parsley. Spread on top of the cheese.

7. Preheat the oven to 450 degrees.

8. Bake for ten minutes.

9. Lower heat to 350 degrees.

10. Bake for five minutes.

11. Serve piping hot!

This "recipe" of stepwise refinement is exactly what is required to develop Top-Down programs. Start at a very high level of abstraction and continue through a number of iterations to complete the design.

The Definition of a Module

As described at the beginning of this chapter, a module is defined as a series of program statements that has a definite starting and ending point. Think of a module as a "block" of code. As discussed shortly, an ideal module is the smallest unit of source code that describes a program function. Here are several examples of modules:

- A routine that causes a line to word wrap properly.

- A routine that calculates employee pay.

- A routine that performs an indexed table search.

Module Size

How big should a module be? The literature varies greatly with opinions about optimal module size. However, most designers recommend modules that span anywhere from 10 to 200 lines of source code. The most frequently quoted figure seems to be around 50 lines of code. This is arbitrary, but the point is that a properly defined module should perform only one function. Very often a function can be coded within this 50 line limit. Another important reason for keeping modules small is related to attention span. When all the source code is listed on one page, you can grasp the concept without too much difficulty. However, when the code spans two or more pages, it is easy to lose focus. In addition, as a module increases in size, so does its complexity.

Fortunately, many SAS modules can be developed with less than 50 lines of code. Most likely, you will create modules that range from 5 to 500 lines of code. However, the typical range will probably be 10 to 30 lines of code. This can be attributed to the fact that SAS is a high-powered, fourth generation language. With 30 lines of SAS code, you can accomplish quite a lot of work compared to other programming languages. This is especially true if the code contains SAS functions and PROCS. Many of the suggestions in the literature are related to lower level languages such as assembler, mid-level languages like C, or third generation languages like COBOL. For example, one SAS instruction may accomplish what would require many lines in assembler or C. For COBOL, the difference is certainly smaller, but nonetheless there is a tangible difference.

The number of lines of code only serves as a general guideline. The actual size of the module should be dictated by the logical structure of the code.

Definition of a SAS Module

The SAS programming language behaves a little differently from many traditional programming languages. Let's examine a typical SAS program and a typical traditional program as illustrated in Figure 5.4.

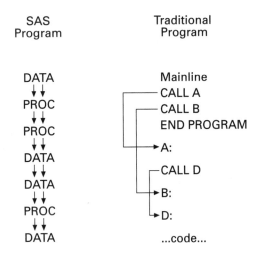

Figure 5.4   *A SAS program has a structure that is markedly different from other programming languages.*

Note how SAS is basically a sequentially ordered language. The program proceeds from top to bottom, compiling and executing each section of code in sequence. Many other programming languages compile and then execute a complete program. A typical, well-structured program executes a mainline routine which, in turn, calls other functions. In addition, other modules may be compiled separately and then linked to each other, thus forming an executable module. These differences are significant because the traditional definition of a "module" is based on this type of program structure.

In the following sections, each SAS construct is examined individually to determine which of these can be classified as modules. Here is the list of candidates:

- complete SAS program

- DATA step

- PROC

- SAS function

- SAS-defined macro

- block of code called by a LINK statement

- user-defined macro

- group of SAS statements within a DO loop

- other SAS statements within the DATA step

- code %INCLUDEd into your program.

Complete SAS Program

While it may seem that a complete program is a module, it usually is not. You might reason that if each of your programs performs one function, then each program could be considered a module. In reality, this is almost never the case. Ask yourself—what does this program do? You might say, "It prints a report. Therefore, it performs one function and is thus a functional module." However, your program really accomplishes a lot more than that. In fact, your program may actually perform all of these functions:

1. reads an external file or SAS data set

2. rearranges data for report output

3. initializes fields or sets counters

4. prints titles and headers

5. prints the requisite detail information

6. accumulates totals

7. prints totals

8. prints footnotes.

Using this example, there are eight (or more) functions. To determine whether you have a functional module, ask yourself—do you need to use the word "and" to describe it? If you do, then you do not have a functional module.

There are those who might call a complete program a "program module," particularly when it is part of a system. However, sticking with the classic definition, a complete program is rarely a module, but is rather a collection of modules.

DATA Step

The DATA step can be either a module, or more likely a collection of modules. To determine if the DATA step is a module, ask yourself the following questions:

1. How large is the DATA step? If it contains hundreds (or even thousands!) of lines of code, then it fails the size test. It is most likely that this DATA step is performing numerous functions.

2. What is the function of the DATA step? If it appears to accomplish one task or several related tasks, then you may consider the DATA step a module. There is some latitude taken here that deviates from the strict definition of a module. Note the exact wording "one or several related tasks." Because SAS has a slightly different structure from other programming languages, it would be too restrictive if a DATA step could only perform one task.

SAS Procedure

A procedure is a powerful collection of compiled code. As such, it can be argued that it performs multiple functions. Examine PROC UNIVARIATE. It can calculate a large number of descriptive statistics, create an output data set, perform analysis on a BY group, and identify the lowest and highest five observations in a printed data set. However, this is accomplished with a few lines of code. Is it a module? Perhaps this could be called a super module.

SAS Function/SAS Library Macro

SAS functions (such as SUBSTR) or SAS macro functions (such as %SCAN) meet the requirement of being one single independent function. However, these functions are only one line of code. You wouldn't place a single line of code into its own module. So for all practical purposes, neither a SAS function nor a SAS macro function is a callable routine. Therefore, you wouldn't consider either of them to be a module.

A Block of Code Called by a LINK Statement

The LINK statement calls a block of code for execution. This called routine is a good candidate for a functional module.

User-Defined Macro

Now you're becoming a student of modular programming theory! This is an excellent construct in part because of its ability to hide data. More on this later in this chapter.

Group of SAS Statements within a DO Loop

Although a DO loop may at times act like a function, it fails the modularity test because it does not have distinct physical boundaries to set it apart from the rest of the code. As such, it is not callable.

Other SAS Statements within the DATA step

Same reason as above for the DO loop.

%INCLUDE

This is probably the most underutilized construct for building systems. It is callable, has one function if written properly, and is easy to maintain.

Module Qualities

So far, this chapter has presented a broad definition of a module. This section describes the qualities of a good module.

Independence

A module is *independent* when its operation is completely isolated from the effects of other modules. The only interaction between independent modules should be the passing of parameters from one module to the next.

Simplicity

A good module performs only one function. Small modules are easier to develop and maintain.

Minimizes Parameter Passing

Minimize the number of parameters passed between modules. If you are passing too many parameters, you may need to redesign the module. A large number of arguments usually indicates that you are passing a lot of data to control the inner workings of another module.

Minimizes Side Effects

Information returned to the calling module should only be a parameter list because it is crucial that a module minimize its side effects. A SAS macro can help ensure this by defining macro variables to be local. This causes them to disappear after the module has finished executing. This is the primary advantage of using only macro variables in a macro function.

Module Cohesion

A module's *cohesion* describes its inner strength. It is, in essence, the glue that makes a solid construction. This topic is discussed at great length here because it is one of the key elements the reader must understand to create a good module. Cohesion is usually rated on an ordinal scale. The seven types of cohesion that describe a module's strength are listed in Table 5.1.

Module Type	Effectiveness
Functional	Excellent
Informational	Above Average
Communicational	Average
Procedural	Average
Temporal	Very Weak
Logical	Very Weak
Coincidental	Totally Unacceptable

Table 5.1 *The types of module cohesion.*

These types of cohesion are examined here from worst to best. In that way, you can better appreciate the incremental improvements in each type of cohesion. In addition, you learn how module design translates into code implementation.

Coincidental Cohesion

Coincidental cohesion occurs when the program statements within a block of code are related only coincidentally. In other words, they may not be related at all.

Here is a sample of code that demonstrates coincidental cohesion:

```
a = left ( b ) ;
link acc_rec ;
%payroll
d = reverse ( c ) ;
e = substr ( f, 3, 1 ) ;
link emp_name ;
```

These six statements apparently have no relation to one another:

Statement 1 removes leading spaces from a variable.
Statement 2 calls a routine relating to an accounts receivable function.
Statement 3 calls a routine relating to a payroll function.
Statement 4 reverses the characters in a string.
Statement 5 selects the third character from a string.
Statement 6 calls a routine relating to employee name.

You could call this type of structure "random coding." Why would someone actually write such code? There are many reasons. One is that someone may have written modules that they thought were too small and so combined them into a larger module. The two component parts may not have been as related as the programmer thought they were.

A second reason relates to the nature of the SAS programming language. Many SAS programmers have developed a mind set of a two-way design. In other words, they think of all design in terms of the DATA step and procedures. If you can't do it with a PROC, then you can do it with the DATA step. Unfortunately, what may often happen is that programmers try to squeeze every possible operation into one DATA step, even if it runs hundreds of lines of code.

The third reason is efficiency. Many books on SAS software efficiency teach that it is better to do as much as possible in one step because the program executes more quickly.

Coincidental cohesion relates to lack of organization. Thus, it is the most difficult type of module to maintain. The two major difficulties with these modules are:

1. Tracing logic flow can be next to impossible.

2. They are not reusable. The statements in a coincidental module have a very specific role, such that the code cannot be generalized for use in another program. It is interesting to note that you can rarely use the code of a DATA step, "as is," in another program.

Logical Cohesion

A module has logical cohesion if all of the components in the module perform common, logically related functions. While better than coincidental cohesion, it ranks very low on the scale of effectiveness. General kinds of logical cohesion include:

1. a module that handles all input and output functions

2. all mathematical formulas required for certain calculations

3. code required to maintain a linked list of elements, such as adding, deleting, and inserting records.

Here is sample code that performs logical cohesion.

```
file_io:

if rec_type = getsas then
   set new_data ;
else
if rec_type = new_recs then
do ;
   infile newfile ;
   input @001 part_one ;
end ;
```

```
      else
      if rec_type = out_rec then
         output out_data ;

      return ;
```

This type of construct is very undesirable because you need to set a flag to determine the actions of the statements in the module called FILE_IO. Another problem with this construct is that the calling routine must know the inner workings of the called module.

Temporal (Classical) Cohesion

A module is temporal or classical when its actions relate to events in time. It exhibits properties similar to logical cohesion, but logical cohesion results in the conditional execution of a module. Types of temporal modules include:

1. Initializing a module if this is the first record read.

2. Calculating totals if this is the end of the file.

3. Printing a report if all header records have been read.

A temporal module may look like this:

```
      data _null_ ;

      array grades {*} $1 grade_01-grade_10 ;

      set children end = last_one ;
         by rec_type child ;

      length testlist $100 ;
      retain ;

      ************************************************************;
      **** Initializing module if this is first record read.***;
      ************************************************************;

      if first.child then
         link init ;

      if last.child then
         link totals ;

      return ;

      ***********************************************************  ;
      **** Initialization routine.                      ***  ;
      ***********************************************************  ;

      init:
      test_cnt = 1 ;
      testlist = " "   ;
      return ;
```

```
**************************************************** ;
**** Calculate totals.                         *** ;
**************************************************** ;

totals:

do until ( grades { test_cnt } = " " ) ;
    test_cnt + 1 ;
    testlist = trim ( left ( testlist )) || grades { test_cnt } ;
end ;

return ;
run ;
```

This example looks innocent enough. However, examine the module INIT. The variable TEST_CNT is initialized to 1. A bug surfaces because, within the module TOTALS, TEST_CNT is incremented before the test list is built. The test list is built beginning with the second observation instead of the first one. This bug could be avoided if the initialization of TEST_CNT occurred in TOTALS. Temporal modules teach programmers a valuable tip: whenever possible, initialize variables within the same module that manipulates that data.

The main disadvantage of temporal cohesion is that, although the components are weakly related to one another, they may be more strongly related to functions in other modules. Temporal cohesion means that if a change is made to the basic structure of the core data, multiple modules must be changed to maintain the system.

1→2→3 Procedural Cohesion

The next strongest element on the scale is procedural cohesion. Such elements are related by sequence. Examples of procedural cohesion are:

1. Finding a part in a database and determining its unit cost, and then determining a subtotal and a total cost.

2. Finding a defect, repairing it, and reporting the defect on an audit log.

Here is an example of procedural cohesion:

```
%macro rec_club ( cust_ssn = ,
                  custname = ) ;
    %order      /* Read the customer order file */
    %trw_chk    /* Check the credit file */
    %inventry   /* Look at the inventory data set, in stock? */
    %ship_it    /* create letter file and update ship file */
%mend rec_club ;

%rec_club ( cust_ssn = 209-55-8936 ,
            custname = Will Karlson )
```

Procedural cohesion is stronger than temporal cohesion because the elements relate more closely to each other, yet is still not reusable code.

Communicational Cohesion

This form of cohesion is similar to procedural cohesion, except that operations work on the same data, as in the following:

```
%macro do_all ;
    %intrans    /* Read transaction data into SAS data set */
    %sortit     /* Sort the transaction and master data sets */
    %upd_mast   /* Update the master data set */
%mend do_all ;
```

But, as before, this code is not reusable. This example is an ineffective way to create modules. The common thread is that a number of functions work on the same piece of data. This factor alone does not justify creating macro functions.

Informational Cohesion

This type of cohesion has more than one function, but each function has a separate entry and exit point. Each section of code must be independent of each other, and they must all work on the same data.

One construct that almost fits the definition of informational cohesion is the SELECT statement:

```
select (action) ;
    when (1)    new_text = left (text) ;
    when (2)    new_text = substr (text,1,1) ;
    when (3)    new_text = substr (text,1,3) ;
    when (4)    new_text = reverse (text) ;
    when (5)    new_text = upcase (text) ;
    otherwise   new_text = "ERROR ON INPUT" ;
end ;
```

This construct satisfies several important conditions:

1. Each function operates on the same data string, called TEXT.

2. Each function has one entry point that is decided by the value of action.

3. Each function has one exit point, which is the closing END statement.

4. Each function works independently of every other function. The action of one function does not in any way change or affect the outcome of other functions.

SELECT, by itself, is not really callable. However, you can simulate informational cohesion by placing the SELECT statement into its own routine:

```
destiny:

select (vacation) ;
    when (1)    link bahamas ;
    when (2)    link china ;
    when (3)    link florida ;
    when (4)    link india ;
    when (5)    link tibet ;
    otherwise   link badplace ;
end ;

return ;
```

Functional Cohesion

Functional cohesion is the strongest cohesive structure. By definition, this type of module performs only one function. Here is a macro function, RENAME, which serves one purpose. Clearly, its function is to rename a series of variables. It is tight and self contained, and it should not interfere with the execution of other modules:

```
%macro rename ( old_name = ,
                new_name = ,
                name_cnt = ) ;
   %local count ;
   rename
   %do count = 1 %to &name_cnt ;
       &old_name&count = &new_name&count
   %end ;
   ;
%mend rename ;
```

If appropriate, you could certainly add error checking to this routine. For example, you could verify that the length of OLD_NAME (or NEW_NAME) + the length of NAME_CNT is not greater than eight characters. Or you could determine if the OLD_NAME prefix actually exists. These are certainly acceptable enhancements because they support the function of this routine. On the other hand, mixing calculations into this routine is not acceptable because the module now has taken on multiple roles.

As another example, consider a %INCLUDE module that contains a PROC FORMAT for laboratory values:

```
proc format ;

*************************************************************** ;
*** Grades for White blood cells.                        *** ;
*************************************************************** ;

value wbc_gr
 4.00 <-high = 0
 3.00 <-4.00 = 1
 2.00 <-3.00 = 2
 1.00 <-2.00 = 3
 low-1.00    = 4
 other       = 0
 ;

*************************************************************** ;
*** Grades for Platelets.                                *** ;
*************************************************************** ;

value plat_gr
 130.00 <-high    = 0
 75.00  <-130.00 = 1
 50.00  <-75.00  = 2
 25.00  <-50.00  = 3
 low-25.00       = 4
 other           = 0
 ;

... and so on, to create laboratory grades for all laboratory tests.

run ;
```

This module has one purpose, and that is to create toxicity ratings for all laboratory values in a clinical protocol. Because this is contained in a %INCLUDE module, all changes occur in one place. This greatly simplifies maintenance because only one file has to be modified if the toxicity scale needs to be adjusted.

The advantage of functional modules is that they can be ported to other applications and they are reusable. In fact, a good test to determine if a module is functional is to try to port it to another system. If the module is workable with little or no change in the code (and fits the definition of one role), then you have achieved functionality. If, on the other hand, the module requires a significant amount of change to work in another system environment, then you probably have a module of lower cohesive strength.

Writing modules functionally has a number of advantages over all the other programming constructs:

- The module can be coded independently. You can, as many organizations do, assign one programmer the task of coding a specific module. That programmer does not have to know the internals of other modules in the system, with the exception of the interface (more on the module interface later).

- Module testing and debugging occur independently. You can create your own inputs to the module, process the routine, and examine the output.

- When modules are functionally coded, defects in the code can be isolated to the appropriate module.

- This type of component is easier to understand than others. Because it performs only one function, it is easier to follow. Also, because of its limited scope, the module is often more manageable in size.

- Maintenance is often easiest with functional modules. If the component becomes obsolete, it can simply be removed, and a new piece can be coded and plugged into its place.

Module Coupling

Module coupling refers to the interdependence of modules. If two modules can function totally independently of each other, then the two modules are said to be "loosely coupled." If, on the other hand, the modules are highly dependent on each other, they are said to be "tightly coupled." The goal of any structured system is to attain complete module independence. Table 5.2 is a schematic of the types of coupling (arranged from best to worst) and their utility in building systems.

Type of Coupling	Usefulness
Data	Excellent
Stamp	Usually Acceptable
Common	Problematic
Control	Problematic
Tramp	Variable
Content	Dangerous

Table 5.2 *Types of module coupling.*

This section describes all types of coupling, from worst to best. In this way, you can more fully appreciate the differences in each type of coupling.

Content Coupling

In content coupling, the calling module must know about the inner workings of the called module. There are several ways that modules can be content coupled, but the most dangerous is when one module modifies the code in another module. In this example, the macro variable &COND attempts to change the code in another module:

```
%let cond = ;

data module_a ;

infile records ;
input @001 require $1 ;

if require = "Y" then
    call symput ( 'cond', 'and degree = "Y" ' )   ;
...
run ;

data module_b ;

degree = "N" ;
has_sat = "Y" ;

if has_sat = "Y" &cond then
    put 'CONGRATULATIONS, YOU ARE HIRED AT $100,000 PER YEAR!!' ;
else
    put 'WE WILL KEEP YOUR RESUME ON FILE.' ;
...
run ;
```

Here everything went as expected. Because the applicant did not have a college degree, he or she was not eligible for this executive position. Now, suppose you make an innocent change to the second DATA step (marked in bold):

```
data module_b ;

degree = "N" ;
has_sat = "Y" ;
has_gre = "Y" ;

if has_sat = "Y" or has_gre = "Y" &cond then
    put 'CONGRATULATIONS, YOU ARE HIRED AT $100,000 PER YEAR!!' ;
else
    put 'WE WILL KEEP YOUR RESUME ON FILE.' ;

run ;
```

The modified line now resolves to:

```
if has_sat = "Y" or has_gre = "Y" and degree = "Y" then
```

Without parentheses, the AND/OR combination creates an unexpected bug. (The applicant gets the executive position without the college degree!) This happens because the first module must know the contents of the second module.

Tramp Coupling

With tramp coupling, data flow through many intermediate modules. Data created in one part of the program may be far removed from the place where it is actually used. While in some languages tramp coupling can be very hazardous, it is probably less of a problem in SAS. SAS carries many variables throughout the program, and the programmer usually anticipates this by coding accordingly. In this example, the variable LASTNAME should have been calculated in the DATA _NULL_ (or close to it) and not carried, unused, throughout the program:

```
data report ;
...
lastname = substr ( fullname, 1, 15 ) ;
...
run ;



.

.

numerous DATA steps and/or PROCEDURES
.

.
```

Now, the programmer has lost track of the field length and does not allocate the proper space for LASTNAME:

```
data _null_ ;
    set report ;

put @001 lastname
    @011 ","
    @012 firstnam ;

run ;
```

Control Coupling

Control coupling occurs when one module passes one or more parameters to a subordinate module in order to control its behavior. Keeping the level of control at a higher level prevents control decisions from being buried in low level modules.

For example:

```
data control ;

office = "Vice President" ;
link office ;

return ;


office :
```

```
            if office = "President" then
                 link pres_rtn ;
            else
            if office = "Vice President" then
                 link  vice_rtn ;
            else
            if office = "Manager" then
                 link  man_rtn ;

            return ;
            ...
            ...
            run ;
```

A safer way to write this code is:

```
            data control ;

            office = "Vice President" ;

            if office = "President" then
                 link pres_rtn ;
            else
            if office = "Vice President" then
                 link  vice_rtn ;
            else
            if office = "Manager" then
                 link  man_rtn ;

            return ;
            ...
            ...
            run ;
```

Common Coupling

Common coupling results when two modules reference the same global data. In general, the use of global macro variables can be extremely useful in systems development. However, here are a few precautions:

- Do not modify a macro variable intended to be a "constant." In this case, a safer method is to move it to a DATA step variable. Here is an example of how common coupled modules can cause a bug.

  In your initialization file, you set up a macro that lists your favorite sports:

  ```
  %let favsport = Hockey, Tennis, Golf ;
  ```

  In program one, to improve the appearance of the report, you uppercase the list of favorite sports:

  ```
  %let favsport = %upcase ( &favsport ) ;
  ```

In program two, you only want to send a subscription of "Golf" magazine to those people who list GOLF as one of their favorite sports:

```
check = index ( "&favsport", "Golf" ) ;
```

Unfortunately, the golf nut does not get his free subscription because "Golf" is now "GOLF." Yes, it is best to uppercase both sides of the index function as part of defensive programming practice. Nevertheless, the point is that the variable's value was unexpectedly changed.

- A good rule of thumb is to define all your global macro "constants" in one place. One method is to list all system-wide globals at the beginning of an initialization file with an underscore prefix. Then list all your program-specific global macro "constants" at the beginning of the source program (without the underscore prefix). In this way, it is almost impossible to overwrite globals.

- Another good practice is to set up variables as global only if they are truly wide reaching in scope. Sometimes after redesign, you may discover certain variables were defined as global but in reality were only utilized by a single program. In this case, move the macro variable back into the source program.

Stamp Coupling

Two modules are stamp coupled if two modules require different parts of the same data structure. In the following example, someone wants to be prequalified for a home loan. The current record layout for the customer financial profile is:

Full Name
Age
Length of Time at Current Residence
Savings Account
Total Value in Stocks
Checking Account
Life Insurance
Other Assets

A sample record can be laid out as:

```
Bill Finnerty, 53, 2.4, 8000, 1224, 23112, 0, 8400
```

Because the formulas for calculating the worth of each of these involves numerous calculations, you create a separate module to calculate the potential cash value for each item. For brevity, the contents of only the stocks and checking modules are listed:

```
%macro stocks ;
    stockval = scan ( cashline, 5, "," ) ;
    ... SAS statements to calculate cash value
%mend stocks;

%macro checking ;
    checkval = scan ( cashline, 6, "," ) ;
    ... SAS statements to calculate cash value
%mend checking ;
```

```
data _null_ ;

infile cash truncover ;
input cashline $200. ;

%checking
%savings
%stocks
%life
%other

run ;
```

Suppose that the standard savings account is split into a regular savings account and a money market account. The file format changes to:

Full Name
Age
Length of Time at Current Residence
Savings Account
Money Market Account
Total Value in Stocks
Checking Account
Life Insurance
Other Assets

Now you must change the SCAN statements in each module to point to the correct field. Because you have to change all of the modules that reference this change in file structure, you have decreased the maintainability of the system. The macros CHECKING, SAVINGS, STOCKS, LIFE, and OTHER are said to be stamp coupled to each other. A good rule to eliminate the effects of stamp coupling is to handle file i/o in one place. As in the previous example, the code for only the macros STOCKS and CHECKING is listed:

```
%macro stocks ;
    SCAN function removed from this routine.
    ... SAS statements to calculate cash value
%mend stocks;

%macro checking ;
    SCAN function removed from this routine.
    ... SAS statements to calculate cash value
%mend checking ;

data _null_ ;

infile cash truncover ;
input cashline $200. ;

saveval = scan ( cashline, 4, "," ) ;
%savings

markval = scan ( cashline, 5, "," ) ;
%markval
```

```
stockval = scan ( cashline, 6, "," ) ;
%stocks

checkval = scan ( cashline, 7, "," ) ;
%checking

lifeval = scan ( cashline, 8, "," ) ;
%life

otherval = scan ( cashline, 9, "," ) ;
%other

run ;
```

Data Coupling

The ultimate goal in systems design is to create modules that are data coupled. Two modules are data coupled if they communicate by parameters, so that the argument list contains only one parameter or a homogeneous group of data items with no control flags. Parameter passing, or data coupling, is covered in great detail in a later section.

Here are a couple of examples that demonstrate data coupling. In the first example, one module needs to have a second module sort an array. The routine requires two parameters: the name of the array and the sort order requested by the user, whether ascending or descending. The called module determines the algorithm for sorting the array.

Here is the <u>called</u> module:

```
%macro sort_ary ( name = ,
                  order = A ) ;

    %local ary_size ; * Practical array size,ignores blank fields ;
    ...
    ...
    %if &ary_size gt 1000 %then
    %do ;
        ... SAS code to sort large arrays
    %end ;
    %else
    %do ;
        ... SAS code to sort small arrays
    %end ;
    ...
%mend sort_ary ;
```

and this is the <u>calling</u> module:

```
data new_data ;
...
%sort_ary ( name = the_list ,
            order = D )
...
run ;
```

Note that the called routine does not need to pass any flags to the control module. Because parameters are passed downward only, this is an example of data coupling.

In the next example, a program prints a report about steel breakout systems. The calling module (DATA _NULL_) links to a subroutine called RPT_HEAD. The calling routine passes three parameters that are user-defined titles in the variables _TITLE1, _TITLE2, and _TITLE3. The parameter list contains variables organized by common function. In addition, no flags need to be transferred back to the calling module. Hence, this is also a good example of data coupling.

Here is the <u>calling</u> routine:

```
data _null_ ;
...
SAS code in preparation to print report
...
_title1 = "Wellington Steel Breakout Report" ;
_title2 = "# of Interrupts" ;
_title3 = "(Full breakouts only)" ;
...
link rpt_head ;
...
return ;
```

and here is the <u>called</u> routine:

```
rpt_head:

retain _pagecnt 0 ;   * page counter ;

******************************************************************** ;
*** Calculate time, date and page number.                     *** ;
******************************************************************** ;

_time = time ( ) ;
attrib _time format = time. ;
_date = today ( ) ;
_pagecnt = sum ( _pagecnt , 1 ) ;

******************************************************************** ;
*** Calculate positions for report titles.                    *** ;
******************************************************************** ;

_loctit1 = int (( 132 - length ( trim ( _title1 ))) / 2 ) ;
_loctit2 = int (( 132 - length ( trim ( _title2 ))) / 2 ) ;
_loctit3 = int (( 132 - length ( trim ( _title3 ))) / 2 ) ;
```

```
*****************************************************************  ;
*** print standard report header.                         ***  ;
*****************************************************************  ;

put // @ 001 'Run Date:'
       @ 011  _date mmddyy8.
       @ 020  _time
       @ 119 'Page No.'
       @ 128 _pagecnt 3. ;

put    @ _loctit1 _title1 ;
put    @ _loctit2 _title2  ;
put    @ _loctit3 _title3  ;

return ;
```

Further enhancements of this routine would involve passing in the linesize and then calculating the field positions based on this parameter.

Converting Modules to SAS Code

This chapter has, so far, been a lengthy discussion about the principles of modularity. This information was intended to prepare you for the following discussion about how to create a module using SAS software. There are five major candidates for module development:

1. PROCS

2. DATA steps

3. Internal subroutines

4. MACRO functions

5. %INCLUDEd code

Obviously, these choices are not mutually exclusive. You could, for example, %INCLUDE a macro, or create a DATA step enveloped within a macro. However, to simplify this discussion, assume that options 3 through 5 are embedded within the DATA step or are called from a library. Therefore, the first decision is whether to create a procedure or a DATA step. Usually the choice is pretty straightforward. If a PROC can adequately fulfill the needs of the job, then you certainly want to use a PROC. PROCs are very powerful, and they simplify the coding substantially. In addition, because the PROCS have been thoroughly tested, your chance of creating buggy code is dramatically reduced.

However, as your data manipulation skills improve, you may find that the reporting procedures, such as PROC PRINT, PROC TABULATE, and PROC REPORT, can easily be replaced by your own, more powerful, DATA _NULL_ routines. This is not to say that these reporting procedures are removed from your arsenal, but over time, they may be relegated to quick and dirty reporting tools.

In addition, it is easy to reroute other PROC output to an external file. This external file can then be parsed to create virtually any type of report format. This is highly advantageous when you are developing programs for customers who are very exacting in their format requirements. Nothing is more frustrating than writing a PROC TABULATE and then having a customer complain that heading number "four" should be right justified instead of centered. A word of caution about parsing external files: The procedure is often not portable, and it can be influenced by different versions of SAS. Hence, it is especially important to use good programming technique when you are parsing. The most important technique is to avoid using hardcoded columnar values. Instead, use the character functions, such as SCAN or INDEX. By doing so, maintenance should be easier if the output format changes.

Assume that you have chosen the DATA step for the task. You then have to decide whether to use (1) inline code (2) a macro (3) an internal subroutine, or (4) %INCLUDEd code.

(1) Inline code (writing code simply as a DATA step) is often a good choice if the code is not reusable and not overly complex.

(2) Macros are probably the most controversial of the SAS constructs. It seems that there are two factions of macro users. The first (and unfortunately larger segment of SAS users) shuns macros almost completely because they are difficult to code, more difficult to read, and almost impossible to debug. The other group seems to take macros to the other extreme. This camp believes that virtually all code should be written as macros. They also believe that all "libraries" of routines should be written as macros. The reality of the situation is that programmers should be somewhere between these two extremes. At times macros, are extremely powerful—the perfect tool for the job. At other times, they are overkill. They should not be created for the sake of creating a macro, or because everyone on the project team does so. For example, have you ever seen this kind of code?

```
%macro total ;
    data _null_ ;
    ... entire SAS program
    run ;
%mend total ;

%total
```

Here are situations where macros might be the best tool for the task:

- when you need to do repetitive tasks that cross DATA step or procedure boundaries.

```
%macro repeatit ;
    data &new_set ;
        set &old_set ;
    ...
    ...
    run ;
    proc print data = &new_set ;
    run ;
%mend repeatit ;
```

- if you need to create a variable list, such as &SCORE_01—&SCORE_10.

- if you need to process variables as a list:

```
%do i = 1 %to &max_vars ;
    var&i
%end ;
```

- when you want to create a series of programs that have only minor differences.

- to create Black Box systems; that is, when you develop systems that hide the details from the programmer. This is particularly useful for developing programming tools.

As mentioned previously, macros are ideal for repetitive tasks. However, using %INCLUDE and LINK statements may be more straightforward. Both these constructs are easier to code and debug. Creating macros introduces an extra layer of translation. An additional concern is that quoted values, while straightforward in open code, can be quite complex in the context of macros.

(3) Internal subroutines take two forms: (a) SAS has implicit calls to subroutines with the HEADER= option in the FILE statement. This is useful for repetitively printing header information at the top of every page. (b) The LINK statement is most advantageous when you have to repetitively execute code that is not reusable in other programs. If the DATA step is small and the routine is executed only one time, then there is nothing to be gained by placing the code into an internal subroutine. However, DATA steps often become lengthy (which seems to be a common practice among SAS programmers). In these cases, creating a small driver section and linking to subroutines can considerably simplify the clutter and enhance readability.

(4) %INCLUDE code takes on two forms. One is the type that permanently resides on disk and is called into the program at the appropriate location. Usually, for organizational purposes, you may decide to place all these include modules into a library. This practice is not a requirement, but it facilitates organization and systems development as discussed in Chapter 3, "Managing the Project." The second type of %INCLUDE module is code that is written out to a file (usually a temporary file) and then %INCLUDEd into the program at a later point in the program. This is a very valuable technique when developing data driven systems. This technique is discussed further in the section "Writing Dynamic Code" in Chapter 8, "System Coding Principles."

Creating the Module interface - Passing Parameters

Passing Parameters Using the Macro Functions

When you pass parameters to a macro, you have two choices: you can use keyword parameters or positional parameters. As the name implies, *positional parameters* are determined by their relative position in the parameter list. *Keyword parameters* designate a specific word as the argument, and they are preferred for the following reasons:

- The keyword parameter is more likely to be self documenting. Most programmers are considerate enough to use a word that describes the function of the parameter. Whereas, with positional parameters, programmers often designate a variable by its relative position such as PARM1, PARM2, PARM3, and so on.

- New parameters are much easier to add because you don't have to worry about the relative position of the variable.

- You can initialize a keyword parameter with a default value. This creates a more user-friendly macro, especially if many arguments are passed into the macro function.

- The chance of incorrectly passing a value to the wrong parameter in the argument list is much greater if you use the positional list. This is largely because positional parameters tend not to be as self documenting.

- The use of commas as place holders with positional parameters tends to be confusing. For example, with a macro invocation such as %macro list (M,,,N,,,O,,,P), it is easy to mis-count the number of commas required between each selected argument.

Despite all of the arguments against positional parameters, there are situations where you might prefer to use a positional parameter list. If you have code that automatically generates a list of macro variables (such as &VAR01–&VAR10) that differ not by function but are truly relative, then a positional list might be useful. An example of this would be a list of test scores, such as &SCORE_01–&SCORE_10. In this example, code from within the macro can treat these scores as a macro variable list. On the other hand, a list of unrelated parameters is not a good candidate for positional parameters (for example, &PARM1 is a start date, &PARM2 is a score, and &PARM3 is a subtotal).

One of the most important factors to remember when you use macros is to avoid contaminating the programming environment. Remember that macro variables can have effects throughout your program. If you don't control the scope of your macros, bugs can surface far removed from their creation. When designing interfaces, you should keep the environment as clean as possible. Specifically, this means that when variables are passed into a module, a function performs its action and returns only the requisite information back to its parent module. Following are some points to keep in mind that can help to ensure this clean passing of parameters.

Within a macro function, declare macro variables as local:

```
%local income ;     * Individual personal income ;
%local depend ;     * Number of dependents ;
%local localtax ;   * Calculated local income tax ;
```

By using this convention, these variables die when the routine has terminated its action. This is considered such an important aspect of modular design that several languages create this type of variable by default (for example, the C programming language). It is difficult to keep track of all variables in a large system, and you certainly don't want to corrupt other people's hard work!

To help you understand how SAS creates macro variables in their appropriate referencing environment, here is a concise explanation of local macro variable behavior:

1. During macro execution, the macro processor attempts to change the value of an existing macro variable, regardless of environment. This action has a higher priority than does creating a new variable.

2. If there is no existence of that variable in any environment, then that variable is created in the current environment. You can save yourself a lot of heartache by declaring your variables using %LOCAL.

Two global macro variables can also contaminate each other. Thus, it is a good idea to have a convention for naming these variables. One approach is to name all system-wide globals with a leading underscore, such as _ABORTIT or _ERRFLAG. All global macro data could use this common area. Then, if needed, an individual program or module could create its own global variables as needed (without the underscore) without interacting with one of the system global macro variables. Remember, however, that only variables with a leading underscore should then be passed as control information.

With this tip in mind, you should nevertheless still avoid declaring your variables as global in the local environment unless there is a pressing reason for doing so. A preferred method for using global variables is to set them in a global table during the initialization phase at the top of the programming hierarchy. The primary reason is that, by defining all the globals in a common area, there isn't much chance that one part of the program can create a global that is modified by a different part of the program. For instance, the initialization of a program could contain a segment of code that sets up the global environment:

```
%let _rpttype = Summary Table ;
```

Then, you can modify the global variable in the local environment, if needed:

```
%let _rpttype = Detail Listing ;
```

Note that this does not violate a previous rule regarding the modification of macro variables. Each program contains an initialization routine, and _RPTTYPE is reset to Summary Table at each invocation of the program. By sticking to this convention, you are less likely to create a gigantic stack of global variables that are being used by other parts of the program.

Another recommendation is to not create new DATA step variables within the macro function. These can overwrite data values set up in another part of the DATA step. Obviously, this is a judgment call. At times your program may require heavy data manipulation or mathematical calculations that require the utilization of DATA step variables. Just be aware that this option is always available.

Passing Parameters Using a SAS Data Set

This is a useful way to communicate control information to other parts of the system. One of the advantages of this method over using the global macro environment is that keeping data within a SAS data set is, to a certain extent, "information hiding." In other words, if a module doesn't need to know about a particular block of data, then don't let it know about it. This means that you should not open multiple data sets in one DATA step unless you really need to.

The same caution applied to system global variables applies here. You might need to read in a secondary data set after reading your primary SAS data set. To avoid contaminating the environment (for example, overwriting the PDV), determine a convention for naming system-wide control variables. As you might have done with macro functions in the previous section, you might decide to use a leading underscore, such as _CONTROL or _TRANS.

Passing Parameters Using an External File

Another option is to pass data in an external file. This is most useful in a system in which other programming languages may require reading that same file. For simplicity, a simple ASCII file (text file) is readable by virtually every software product. If at all possible, let only one language update the file and preferably at the same place in the system. If you don't adhere to this standard, the potential problems that you could encounter are many and they vary greatly depending on the operating system and supplemental software used to control concurrent access. Lockout, deadlock, and update corruption are all possible.

Passing Parameters Using Open Code

If a program needs to communicate with other parts of the program internally, you can use the LINK statement to connect to a subroutine. Communication through LINK implies that you wish to pass data that are required only for the current routine and not outside of the module. One of the disadvantages of LINK is that it is difficult to "hide" information from the called subroutine. All functions in the called routine have access to the PDV as well as to all global variables. However, LINK is a powerful way to organize code, and it encourages modularity.

To pass data to a subroutine, set up code to pass input through input parameters and output through output parameters:

```
data _null_ ;
...
status  = "Single" ;
calc    = "State Tax" ;
state   = "California" ;

link calc_tax ;
...
return ;


calc_tax:
...
... calculations
...
tot_tax = tax_01 + tax_02 + tax_03 ;
return ;
```

You can also establish a convention for passing parameters based on the type of argument, such as:

    i_ = prefix for an input variable
    o_ = prefix for an output variable
    io_ = prefix for an input/output variable

Hence, in the above example, you can substitute arguments using this convention (parameters marked in bold):

```
data _null_ ;
...
i_status  = "Single" ;
i_calc    = "State Tax" ;
i_state   = "California" ;

link calc_tax ;

return ;


calc_tax:
...
... calculations
...
o_tax    = tax_01 + tax_02 + tax_03 ;
return ;
```

Passing Parameters Using Global Macro Variables

The %LET statement (in open code) and the CALL SYMPUT statement allow you to create variables whose scope can span the SAS session. CALL SYMPUT provides good flexibility for creating data values at execution time. %LET, when used in open code, sets the value of a variable at compile time. %LET is a also a great way to increment pointers within a macro function:

```
%let new_cnt = %eval ( &new_cnt + 1 ) ;
```

Number of Arguments

Ideally, it is advisable to minimize the number of arguments that are passed to a subroutine. More than a few arguments passed is usually a sign of a pathological design interface. When the number of arguments is large, it is often related to the usage of data to control the execution of the called module. To circumvent this problem, move the control information into the calling module.

Documentation of Modules/Arguments

In order for a module to be effective, it must contain comprehensive internal documentation. Refer to Chapter 6, "Improving Readability and Providing Internal Documentation," for more details about documentation techniques.

Here is a program that was developed for a T-shirt designer in preparation for the lucrative Halloween season. Match the numbers to the descriptions below.

```
************************************************************** ;
***                                                      *** ;
*** Module:    Draw_it.sas  ❶                            *** ;
***                                                      *** ;
*** Type:      Include module  ❷                         *** ;
***                                                      *** ;
*** Function: Determines the best type of monster that can be*** ;
***           created with the given input specifications.❸ *** ;
***                                                      *** ;
*** Input:     &height = height of the monster in inches. *** ;
***            This value can not exceed 100. ❹          *** ;
***                                                      *** ;
***            &pounds= weight of the monster in pounds.This *** ;
***            value cannot exceed 500  ❹                *** ;
***                                                      *** ;
*** Output:    Output is returned via macro parameters.  *** ;
***                                                      *** ;
***            &mon_type (monster type) is returned to the *** ;
***            calling routine.  ❺                       *** ;
***            possible monster types include:           *** ;
***                                                      *** ;
***            Frankenstein   ❻                          *** ;
***            Bride of Frankenstein                     *** ;
***            The Mummy                                 *** ;
***            The Creature from the Black Lagoon        *** ;
***            The Thing                                 *** ;
```

```
***                                                               *** ;
***                   &err_flag is indication if error detected ❼ *** ;
***                                                               *** ;
***                   "YES" if error detected         ❽          *** ;
***                   "NO" if no error detected                  *** ;
***                                                               *** ;
***                   &err_msg is the error message returned ❼    *** ;
***                                                               *** ;
***                   "No height specified"  ❽                   *** ;
***                   "No weight specified"                      *** ;
***                   "Height must be between "X" and "X"        *** ;
***                   "Weight must be between "X" and "X"        *** ;
***                   "No monster could be calculated with these *** ;
***                   input specifications, perhaps try other    *** ;
***                   values"                                    *** ;
*** Usage:     This is a macro call of the form:                 *** ;
***                                                               *** ;
***                   %monster ( height = 67 , pounds = 456 )  ❾  *** ;
***                                                               *** ;
*** Limits:    Because of the algorithm, certain monster types *** ;
***            cannot be calculated at this time.  ❿             *** ;
***                                                               *** ;
*** Author:    Ted Stanford/Designs Unlimited ⓫                  *** ;
***                                                               *** ;
*** History:   Program written 07-12-1994 ⓬                      *** ;
***                                                               *** ;
*****************************************************************;
```

Here is a description of each of the elements marked above:

❶ Identify the name of the module. The name should be descriptive of the function. Sometimes the name may not be intuitively obvious. In that case, place parentheses around the description of the term, for example, supertrk.sas (Superfund Tracking System).

❷ Describe the type of module. Options might include: (a) Program, which is a complete SAS program; (b) %INCLUDE, which is code to be copied into your program; (c) Macro function, which is a user-created macro; and (d) Flat file, which may contain text such as control information. You may wish to break down any of these categories further if it helps to organize the system. For example, some programmers like to specify macros by function such as utility macro, report macro, mathematical macro, string manipulation macro, and so on.

❸ Describe the function of the module in simple terms. You can provide additional documentation here or you can embed it within the code. Typically, if the information is useful to the user, you can include additional documentation at the top of the program. If these details are inconsequential to the user, place the additional documentation within the code. Ideally, the function should be like a "black box" to the user, who should not have to worry about programming details.

❹ Specify the input parameters. Let the user know of the valid input values. If there are default input parameters, let the user know.

❺ Specify the output parameters. Also, specify the mode of output. Is the data to be passed back via macro parameters or perhaps a flat file?

❻ Show the kind of output returned to the user.

❼ Almost all routines require a method of handling errors. Pick a convention and stick with it. Notice the generic error message:

```
Height must be between "X" and "X"
```

Try to keep the constants out of the comments to allow for easier maintenance.

❽ Show the possible return codes.

❾ Provide at least one example of how to use the routine.

❿ Discuss any limitations.

⓫ Put your name on the routine. That way, you can get a phone call at 2 a.m. if there is a production problem.

⓬ Some companies don't like to use this section because it seems that this documentation is never updated. Nevertheless, it is listed here because some project teams insist on using it.

Prototyping Methods

Every few years, a hot new topic in software engineering springs forth and promises to cure all the ills of computer software. Third generation languages, fourth generation languages, CASE tools, Expert Systems, Object Oriented Programming, and Relational Databases were just a few of these evolutionary concepts.

In the early 1980's, a new concept stepped up to the podium. It was called prototyping. The idea took on many different forms and names, including Rapid prototyping and Rapid Application Prototyping. Regardless of the name, the principal idea was to change the way designers built systems. For many years, programmers went through a preliminary analysis, may have consulted the end-user, but then went off on their own to build a project. Of course, this process resulted in numerous system failures. The programming team would develop this finely tuned system (or so they thought). When the project was complete, they would unveil the curtain, eagerly waiting for the customer's approval. That's when the coding team would hear the morose music. The client had a completely different idea in mind!

As a result of many disappointing software systems, designers practiced a little introspection. Perhaps... yes... perhaps they were ignoring the customer. Yes, that's it. The customer should be involved throughout the entire design and implementation process! Hence the birth of rapid application prototyping. The end-user would become intimately involved in the software life cycle, but especially in the design phase of the project. In this way, the programming team could develop a model, evaluate it, and proceed along the appropriate path based on this evaluation. This process could theoretically involve many iterations of design, but, in the end, customer satisfaction should be quite high.

The term rapid prototyping implies that the development process moves along much more swiftly than traditional systems, but this is not really the case. Prototyping is a kind of insurance that minimizes the risk on the project. It certainly could be argued that the utilization of prototyping techniques moves a project more quickly to the final product.

The two major classifications of prototyping are (1) throwaway and (2) evolutionary. *Throwaway prototyping* is a way of modeling a system with the advanced knowledge that any code developed for the system would be trashed at the end of the preliminary design. This is most likely to occur when someone prototypes in one language (usually a very high level language) and then develops in another (often a lower level language to dramatically improve execution speed). *Evolutionary prototypes* are systems in which much of the code used to develop the model is also used to develop the final product.

In general, prototyping methods refer to online user interfaces because this is an area of systems development that users can understand and contribute. In SAS, the SAS/AF or SAS/FSP products are the most beneficial tools. However, with the base SAS product, you can create interfaces with a combination of WINDOW, %WINDOW, and PROC PMENU.

Principles of Good Design

This section provides a summary of the principles of good systems design.

Be Sure You Understand the Problem Completely

If needed, interview people involved in the project, read any available documentation, and brainstorm with others.

Use the Right Tool for the Job

When selecting software for a project, there are four possibilities:

1. The right tool is selected for the wrong reasons. This can be attributed to good fortune. This usually happens because the programming team has habitually used a certain programming language.

2. The right tool is selected for the right reasons. Good job! You have done your homework.

3. The wrong tool is selected for the wrong reasons. This may happen for any of the following reasons:

    - The company always uses "so-and-so" language. "It is what we know best."

    - There may not be in-house technical expertise with the appropriate language. In addition, the cost of re-training the programming staff may be prohibitive.

    - The analysis was inadequate. This may be, in part, related to time pressure.

4. The wrong tool is selected for the right reasons. This is usually from lack of experience. The analysis was correct, but the decision maker did not realize the strengths and weaknesses of various programming languages.

Do Not Write a Single Line of Code Before Adequate Analysis and Design

This may be the most fundamental and important aspect when developing a complete software system. You must resist coding at all costs until you are completely ready for the coding phase. While inadequate planning may be harmless when developing simple ad hoc programs, it is disastrous when building complete systems. You need to think carefully about your game plan. Any system that you develop must be robust and inviting to change.

Develop Three Lists: The "Must Have" List, the "Would Be Nice" List, and the "Future Enhancements" List

In an ideal world, a company's budget is limitless, as is the time frame for completing a project. However, on planet Earth, short-term profit is the ruling class. Hence, it is imperative to classify milestones on a priority basis.

The "Must have list" is what you promise for the customer. This is a set of minimum requirements that must be met. Do not try to finish every enhancement in the first pass. Software development almost always takes longer to code and test than planned. This "must have" list helps you to focus on the task at hand.

The "Would be nice list" is an extension of the first list. These are NOT promised to the customer. If you can complete some or all of them, then great! If not, you can leave them for future enhancements. The reason that you develop this list is that it helps you think about the full range of design considerations. The design has to be flexible so it can handle any enhancements.

Creating the "Future enhancements list" also helps to focus on the design. Unlike the second list, do not attempt to finish any of these now. Also, by looking forward and keeping a design flexible, there is a chance to build more business for the future.

Divide and Conquer: The Process of Stepwise Refinement

Manned space missions don't just happen—they take a lot of planning. Each component of the project is broken down into very small manageable modules. The best way to do this is to divide the project into a series of processes. Each of these processes can be subdivided into tasks. These tasks, in turn, can be broken down further into atomic elements. Anything done in small increments makes a project manageable. Writing this book all at once seemed a formidable task, but by breaking the task into chapters, sections and subsections, the project became do-able.

The process of creating a design chart really requires a number of iterations (see Figure 5.5). Don't worry about how much progress you make on each pass. Just like conquering writer's block, start putting anything on the paper. In addition, don't worry about error checking or coding details at this time. That can be left for detailed design. You can use any kind of diagramming scheme that you feel comfortable with.

While you are in the midst of design, many times something might pop up in your mind relating to the project. The best thing to do is to write these comments on a memo pad so you don't forget some important detail.

After looking over Figure 5.5, you might be wondering how many boxes should be subordinate to a parent box? In other words, how many boxes should branch from the box above it? Most authors recommend the range of two to seven boxes. At the lower range, if one box branches from the one above it, it is possible (though not required) that the two modules should be combined into one unit. At the upper end of the range, seven is considered maximal, not based on empirical evidence but rather from psychological experiments about memory retention. Miller, a noted psychologist, suggested that the human capacity for storage is at its maximum with seven chunks of information at a time (Miller 1957 pp.81–97). In the same light, it has been theorized that if the unit is broken down into too many subunits, then you lose the feeling of continuity among those disassembled units.

Often elements are reorganized during design. This type of module "shuffling" is typical during the design process. Sometimes, modules that appear to be too small can be combined with another module. On the other hand, you may break up large modules at any step because of the realization that the module is too complex.

You may discover that just the mechanical act of putting ideas on paper spurs new ideas. How do you know when to stop? The general idea is that each of these boxes should be a module. If you are at the point where breaking the module further causes you to think about coding details, then you have gone too far.

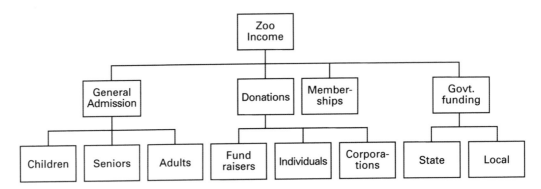

Figure 5.5   *Consider the task of writing a program that tracks all income for the city zoo. Before writing any code, sit down and map out the structure with a design chart.*

Writing a Utility Module from Scratch

Successful systems development requires the creation of workable library tools that can be utilized by different programs. If these routines are developed with sufficient flexibility, the programming team can create software systems with a substantial reduction of effort. In addition, the output is more reliable and more likely to adhere to the original user specifications.

General Tips for Designing Modules

- When designing the module, remember that it must be flexible. It should be able to handle virtually any type of data.

- Do not try to skimp on space by not allocating sizes large enough. This can come back to haunt you. When working with strings, and there is any doubt about their size, declare their length as $200.

- Design your module for the worst case scenario.

- Stress test your module. As in the design phase, test your module using data extremes. Details about stress testing can be found in Chapter 9, "Program Verification and Testing Methodology."

- If appropriate, set up default parameters for the routine and let the user know you are doing so. For example, you can set the input data set default to &SYSLAST, which is the last data set created. You can also set the output data set default to be the same as the input data set.

- The documentation should be thorough. It is especially important that the input and output parameters be specified. Also, if data sets are being modified, note any changes to the contents of the data set.

- Make it easy to use. For example, just because your module contains complicated macro code does not mean the user should be a macro master.

- Do not contaminate the user environment. If you are adding variables to a data set, let the user know. Before the project begins, select a convention for designating global variables, and stick with it.

- If the programmer does not use the routine properly, do not pass back vague information, such as "Invalid Parameter". Be specific. A much better error message is "Invalid data set name 'mydata.people' passed to routine 'f:\cement\myhelp.sas.'"

- If the program contains a serious error, do not continue to let the job run. Stop the program and send an error message to both the log and output queue. You may also consider writing to an error log and sending a return code if your operating system permits this.

- Whenever possible, avoid including operating system commands embedded within the SAS code. Utilizing operating system instructions dramatically decreases the portability of the product.

- When exiting your routine, delete any scratch data sets you created.

- Get others involved in the design. Tell them what you are trying to do. They might have some good ideas. Everybody loves to give their opinion even if they don't want to write the code.

- Your code must be especially meticulous. If a utility module is buggy, a lot of programs may be affected!

The Design Process for Writing a Utility Module

The first step of the design process for writing a utility module is to define the problem carefully.

Problem definition:
Several fields are being truncated in a report. The current report specifications allow only 10 characters for the name, 28 characters for an individual's favorite candy bars, and 24 characters that lists their favorite parks.

Example:

Name	Favorite Candy Bars	Favorite Parks
Bill	Gooey and Sweet, Syrupy Flav	Grand Canyon, Yosemite,
Steve	Carmel Mountain, Chocolate T	Kings Canyon, Bryce Nati
Mary	Rich and Delicious, Loads of	Torrey Pines, Glacier Na

Solution:

Write a wordwrap parsing routine. When getting close to the end of an output field, determine if there is enough room to write the word on this line. If not, go to the next line.

Considerations:

When analyzing the problem, it sometimes helps to sketch it out. Use the blackboard for more complicated problems. It's a great way to brainstorm with a team.

Here are some things that come to mind when developing this routine:

- The user could be passing in character variables of any length.

- The user may want to have multiple variables wordwrapped.

- Allow for the option of indenting the second and subsequent lines of the parsed variable.

- Allow the input data set to be parameterized.

- Do not change the order of the observations. This ensures that you are simply inserting records where needed.

- Change the data set as little as possible while still giving the user the flexibility to use a couple of variables to assist with formatting.

- Provide a clear description of problems that the user may encounter while using the parser. For instance, they may specify 12 characters for a field when the parser may need a minimum of 14 positions.

- Consider a dictionary to determine the proper hyphenation of words. That could save space. This enhancement is a little bit more involved than is needed at this time, so add it to the "Would Be Nice List."

Other "Would be Nice" enhancements could be:

- Let the user pass in macro variables to be parsed out. The routine could then pass back data in the form of &_WORD_01, &_WORD_02, &_WORD_03, and so on.

- For even more flexibility, allow parsing on other boundaries besides words. Let the user pass in delimiters, such as hyphen or slash, to serve as acceptable delimiters for wordwrap.

- When rebuilding the parsed string, eliminate any extra spaces. For instance, if the variable has three spaces between a word, compress it to one because its looks better on the report. A variable such as &_COMPRES = "Yes" or "No" would let the user decide.

The complete source code for the parsing routine can be found in Coding Sample 5 in Appendix 1, "Coding Samples." Enhancements to this routine are presented in Coding Sample 6, in Appendix 1.

Summary

In conclusion, strong system design sets the tone for the remainder of the project. Coding modules that exhibit a high degree of independence are imperative for developing a strong foundation. In addition, building modules by function also improves the likelihood that well structured code ensues. All phases of design, from very high level to very low level, lend themselves to the principle of stepwise refinement. This allows you to assemble a project into manageable pieces. Finally, creating clean interfaces between modules helps to minimize the side effects of module interaction.

Exercises

1. What is the underlying principle of Top-Down design?

2. What is the underlying principle of Bottom-Up design?

3. What is the danger of declaring a DATA step variable in DATA step #1 but not using the variable until DATA step #25 (tramp coupling)?

4. For each of the following, decide if the construct is (1) Probably a module, (2) Possibly a module, or (3) Probably not a module:

    a. a PROC
    b. block of code called by a LINK statement
    c. user-defined macro
    d. statements within the DATA step, such as a DO loop
    e. complete SAS program
    f. code %INCLUDEd into your program
    g. DATA step
    h. SAS function (for example, RANUNI)
    i. SAS defined macro

5. How do you know that you have created a good, functional module?

6. What would be an acceptable reason for using positional parameters with a macro function?

7. Why would you use an external file to control processes in a system?

8. Why is software prototyping becoming more popular? What are the two main types of prototyping methodologies?

9. What is the safest way to manipulate a GLOBAL macro variable?

10. Why would you develop "Would Be Nice" and "Future Enhancements" lists early in the project? Wouldn't it be better to just concentrate on the current task?

References

Aron, J.D. (1974), *The Program Development Process: Part 1, The Individual Programmer*, Reading, MA: Addison-Wesley.

Bruce, P. and Pederson, S.M. (1982), *The Software Development Project*, New York: John Wiley & Sons.

Connell, J.L. and Shafer, L.B. (1989), *Structured Rapid Prototyping*, Englewood Cliffs, NJ: Yourdon Press.

Ghezzi, C., Jazayeri, M. and Mandrioli D. (1991), *Fundamentals of Software Engineering*, Upper Saddle River, NJ: Prentice-Hall.

Higgins, D.A. (1986), *Data Structured Software Maintenance*, New York: Dorset House Publishing.

King, D. (1984), *Current Practices in Software Development*, New York: Yourdon Press.

Miller, G.A. (1957), "The Magical Number 7 Plus or Minus Two: Some Limits on our Capacity for Processing Information," *Psychological Review*, 63, 81–97.

Myers, G.J. (1975), *Reliable Software Through Composite Design*, New York: Mason/Charter.

Sommerville I. (1982), *Software Engineering*, London: Addison-Wesley.

Yourdon, E. (1977), *Techniques of Program Structure and Design*, Englewood Cliffs, NJ: Prentice-Hall.

Ziegler, C. (1983), *Programming System Methodologies*, Englewood Cliffs, NJ: Prentice-Hall.

Chapter 6   # Improving Readability and Providing Internal Documentation

Introduction **89**

Readability **90**
    Create a Good Layout 90
    Please..., Only One Source Code Statement Per Line! 91
    Separate Blocks of Code 91
    Alignment. 92
    Use Parentheses 94
    Wide Monitors 95
    White Space 95
    Continuation Lines 96
    Remove Literals 96
    Mixed Case 97
    Tips for Creating Meaningful Names 98

Commenting Code **103**
    Flowerbox Style Comments 104
    End-Line Style Comments. 105
    Top-Line Style Comments 106
    Mixing Case 106
    Variable Length Boxes 107
    Statement Style versus Delimited Style Comments. 107
    Macro Style Comments. 108
    Levels of Documentation 108
    Commenting Data Declarations 112
    Logging Changes in Source Code 113

Summary **114**

Exercises **114**

Reference **114**

Introduction

Writing documentation is probably the programmer's least favorite task. Maybe that's because the fruits of documentation are rarely visible. Have you ever heard a manager say, "It's a shame the program doesn't work, because that's the sweetest documentation I have ever seen!" A programmer who documents religiously is like a scrappy baseball player. The player sacrifices himself by hitting to the right side of the infield and advances his teammates to the next base. It doesn't show up in the box scores though, so who really cares?

If you think about it, how often does a company have a comprehensive manual of Standard Operating Procedures (SOP)? Or better yet, how often have you seen an SOP for Programming Documentation? Not very often.

There are two major ways to document programs. One is to write a narrative that accompanies the system. This narrative can either be *internal* (that is, commentary contained within the source code) or *external* (commentary not contained within the source code). Internal documentation is the main subject of this chapter. External documentation is discussed in Chapter 3, "Managing the Project." The other means of improving documentation is the enhancement of readability. This involves techniques both to improve the clarity of code and to use good naming conventions.

Readability

Ideally, you should be able to read source code as if you were reading a good novel (maybe not quite as exciting). Well written source code should flow and have a smooth quality. Unfortunately, computer languages tend to be a bit cryptic and, despite claims made by many egotistical programmers, code is not self documenting. Here is a list of guidelines to help you write clearer code.

Create a Good Layout

One important fundamental for improving code readability is to create a clean layout. For example, here is a section of code that works perfectly well:

```
proc sort data= patient out=new_pat (keep=pat_id age
sex_id tum_type treat_id) nodupkey;by pat_id;run;
data _null_;set new_pat nobs=pat_cnt;call symput
('pat_cnt',pat_cnt);stop;run;
```

It works, but it is painfully unreadable. With a little bit of reorganization, the code is much more intelligible:

```
proc sort data = patient out = new_pat ( keep = pat_id age
    sex_id tum_type treat_id ) nodupkey ;
    by pat_id ;
run ;

data _null_ ;
    set new_pat nobs = pat_cnt ;

call symput ( 'pat_cnt', pat_cnt ) ;
stop ;

run ;
```

Please…, Only One Source Code Statement Per Line!

The origin of stacking multiple programming statements on one line is uncertain. It might have its roots in the pre-recycling days when programmers hid under the alias of conservation freaks. Sure, it saves space, but at what cost? Coding only one statement per line allows you to concentrate on one entity at a time. Furthermore, if you are using a line-based debugger, you can effortlessly trace through the source code.

Separate Blocks of Code

You can improve the readability of your source code by organizing source code in "blocks." You should be able to tell at a moment's glance the logical units in a program. These logical units include:

- DATA steps

- PROCS

- subroutines (called by the LINK statement)

- %INCLUDE modules

- macro definitions

- "clumps" of code that logically relate to each other. These may encompass any of the following:

  - variable declarations
  - DO loops
  - SELECT statements
  - TITLE statements
  - FOOTNOTE statements
  - LIBNAME statements
  - FILENAME statements
  - groups of related assignment statements
  - INPUT statements
  - PUT statements

Strive for good separation. For example, Figure 6.1 illustrates using at least one blank line between each of the logical units. Some programmers have used underscores, dashes, asterisks or equal signs to separate DATA step and PROC boundaries. This is also quite useful in achieving visual separation. Just don't get carried away with too many different types of separators because this can lead to confusion.

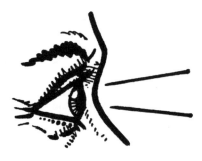

```
proc print ;
run ;

proc tabulate data = reside ;
    class state county ;
    var years ;
    table state, county ;
run;

data _null_ ;
    put "I'm bored" ;
run ;
```

Figure 6.1 *Providing white space between blocks of code allows the separation necessary for effective reading of source code. Separating blocks alerts you to changes in coding constructs.*

When printing source code, it is also beneficial to use the compiler PAGE option at the beginning of each new routine:

```
page ;

*** new routine ***
```

This will force a page eject for each new module. This is quite useful for rapid debugging because, when you compile your listings in a documentation binder, you can quickly find the routine that you are looking for.

Alignment

Consistent alignment is important. Not everyone on the programming team is going to abide by the same rules of layout, but if nothing else, you should strive for consistency. For example, don't lay out a macro parameter list in one place as in the following:

```
%macro military ( rank = , serial = , name = ) ;
```

and in another as:

```
%macro money
        (
            savings = ,
            checking = ,
            cash =
        ) ;
```

Align related elements. In this example, you can align the locations, the variable names, and the formats for the PUT statement:

```
put @ 001   coffee   cafe.
    @ 005   tea      steep.
    @ 007   soda     pop.
    @ 024   juice    oj.
    @ 038   milk     leche.
    @ 125   water    agua.
    ;
```

For the SELECT statement, line up cases and actions:

```
select (color) ;
    when ("blue")
          do ;
              put "sad songs" ;
              put "more sad songs" ;
          end ;
    when ("white")
          do ;
              put "pure white snow" ;
              put "winter on my mind" ;
          end ;
    otherwise
          do ;
              put "neither white nor blue" ;
              put "can rid me of sadness" ;
          end ;
end ;
```

Align equal signs for elements processed as a group:

```
war        =    army ;
soldiers   =    many ;
tanks      =    3000 ;
pilots     =    3298 ;
```

The use of indention is crucial for IF-THEN-ELSE constructs as well as any type of DO loop construct. Here are examples of sloppy indention, which can result in serious debugging problems:

```
do i = 1 to dim ( graphics ) ;
    do j = 1 to dim ( plot ) ;
do m = 1 to 17 ;
    r + 1 ;
end ;
    end ;
       rec_cnt + 1 ;
end ;
```

Rearrange the DO-END constructs so that each DO statement aligns with its corresponding END statement:

```
do i = 1 to dim ( graphics ) ;
    do j = 1 to dim ( plot ) ;
        do m = 1 to 17 ;
            r + 1 ;
        end ;
    end ;
    rec_cnt + 1 ;
end ;
```

When appropriate, use a SELECT statement to improve clarity instead of using multiple IF-THEN-ELSE statements. Usually this is advisable when the list of cases grows to more than about three or four. Compare the readability of the following two sections of code:

Example 1:

```
if yardage le 100 then
    caddysez = "wedge" ;
else
if yardage le 120 then
    caddysez = "9-iron" ;
else
if yardage le 140 then
    caddysez = "7-iron" ;
else
if yardage le 160 then
    caddysez = "5-iron" ;
else
if yardage le 180 then
    caddysez = "3-iron" ;
else
if yardage gt 180 then
    caddysez = "I recommend a three-wood and a prayer" ;
```

Example 2:

```
select ;
    when ( yardage <= 100 ) caddysez = "wedge" ;
    when ( yardage <= 120 ) caddysez = "9-iron" ;
    when ( yardage <= 140 ) caddysez = "7-iron" ;
    when ( yardage <= 160 ) caddysez = "5-iron" ;
    when ( yardage <= 180 ) caddysez = "3-iron" ;
    when ( yardage >  180 ) caddysez =  "I recommend " ||
        "a three-wood and a prayer" ;
end ;
```

Use Parentheses

Use parentheses to clarify expressions. No matter how well you can remember compiler evaluation rules, the reader after you may not have this unusual gift. Also, for optimization purposes, subsequent releases of a compiler may change the order of evaluation. The following equation is more coherent with parentheses:

```
earnings = bonus + years * 12 ;
earnings = bonus + ( years * 12 ) ;
```

Wide Monitors

Perhaps you have one of the newer wide screen monitors. If you do, resist the temptation to use the width of the entire display area for entering source code. There are three fundamental reasons. First, the number of characters displayed on your screen is a function of your monitor size and (if appropriate) terminal emulation. Therefore, other team members may not have the same advantage of viewing extra wide source code. If they pull your code into their work environment and find that they have to continuously scroll left and right, they may pull you aside for some choice comments.

Secondly, if a single line of code has upwards of 100 characters, then you are probably developing expressions that are too complex. Try to keep it simple.

Finally, utilizing the width of a large screen encourages deep nesting of DO loops and IF-THEN-ELSE constructs. That's not a good practice!

White Space

For mathematical equations, there is certainly no harm in using extra spacing between expressions:

```
slug_avg =  (( single  * 1 ) +
             ( double  * 2 ) +
             ( triple  * 3 ) +
             ( homerun * 4 )) * 1000 / at_bats ;
```

Consider separating operators and operands with a little more white space. Compare the following three expressions, each one with more white space than the other:

```
a=reverse(trim(left(substr(belt,3,2)))));

a = reverse ( trim ( left ( substr (belt,3,2 ))));

a = reverse ( trim ( left ( substr ( belt, 3 , 2 )))) ;
```

This practice is particularly advantageous when passing a number of positional arguments to a macro routine. Check out the following vision test. Quick, what argument number is "4"?

```
%wordwrap ( 3,,,,,,,,4,5)

%wordwrap ( 3 , , , , , , , 4 , 5 )
```

Here is an oddball convention that is actually quite useful. Place a space between the closing semicolon and the previous character or operator. It's effective because one syntax error that seems to plague the SAS programmer is the all too common missing semicolon. Try it—you might just eliminate one of your nasty syntax errors!

```
%let amnesia = semicolon;
%let amnesia = semicolon ;
```

Continuation Lines

Since you are not using the full 120 characters available on the screen (because you are listening to the aforementioned advice), you must eventually deal with continuation lines. How should you handle them? One method is to break at a sensible point so that each part is as self contained as possible, such as after the following:

a complete word
an arithmetic operator

It is poor practice to break within (1) parentheses or (2) an arithmetic expression, as shown in the following:

```
put @001 "this is an example of a bad break " (
   grades1-grades5 ) ( 5 * 3.2 ) ;

savings = ( quarter + penny + dime + nickel  ) * ( 7 *
   numweeks ) ;
```

Here is the same code, reformatted with better breaks:

```
put @001 "this is an example of a better break "
   ( grades1-grades5 ) ( 5 * 3.2 ) ;

savings = ( quarter + penny + dime + nickel  ) *
   ( 7 * numweeks ) ;
```

Note also the indention for the continuation lines. Two spaces is typically recommended.

Remove Literals

Whenever possible, remove literals from the code even if they are constants. For instance, have you ever tried to recall the hexadecimal equivalents for various superscripts and subscripts? To preserve your sanity, create an external file with the following variable definitions and %INCLUDE it where needed.

```
retain    super_0 'b0'x  ; * Superscript of 0 ;
retain    super_1 'b9'x  ; * Superscript of 1 ;
retain    super_2 'b2'x  ; * Superscript of 2 ;
retain    super_3 'b3'x  ; * Superscript of 3 ;
```

For instance, this statement:

```
put "E = mc" super_2 ;
```

displays the following statement:

$$E = mc^2$$

You can also have fun with graphics by predefining variables to represent their graphic equivalent:

```
%let paramark = 'b6'x ;        * Paragraph mark ;
%let smallbox = '81'x ;        * Small box ;
%let vert_bar = '82'x ;        * Vertical bar ;
%let doubvert = '93'x ;        * Double vertical bar ;
%let u_r_corn = '86'x ;        * Upper right corner ;
%let u_l_corn = '84'x ;        * Upper left corner ;
```

To make the code more readable, use the PUT conversion instead of testing variables against literals. In the following code, replace the first example with either of the following code fragments. In addition to enhancing readability, this practice minimizes logic errors:

```
If medicine = 3 then ...

if upcase ( put ( medicine, med. )) = "MORPHINE" then ..
if upcase ( put ( medicine, med. )) = upcase ( morphine ) then ..
```

Mixed Case

Another way to improve readability is to write most of the code in lowercase but to put selected elements in uppercase. Any of these constructs are candidates for uppercase:

all variables
"constant" variables
statement labels
comments
references to labels
variables passed to routines (such as macro variables)
data set names
macro keywords

Here is how sample code might appear using some of these conventions. Caution! If you use this technique, someone might label you a C programmer:

```
data _null_ ;
    set books ;

retain    BOOKMARK 1 ;
retain    PAGE_CNT 0 ;
retain    CURRPAGE 0 ;
length    BOOKNAME $12 ;

%story ( book = MY_BOOK ,
        the_loc = CURR_LOC )

if PAGE_CNT gt 0 then
    link MOREPAGE ;

return ;

MOREPAGE:
if CURRPAGE gt BOOKMARK then
    put "No peeking to end of story" ;
return ;

run ;
```

Tips for Creating Meaningful Names

These code formatting rules can get you well on your way to creating readable programs. However, no matter how neat your code is, if you use variable names that have no meaning, then your program can be difficult to follow. Because of the variable name limitation of eight positions, you have to choose your names carefully. The most important factor in choosing a name is to minimize translation. Otherwise, every time that readers have to pause to decipher your code, they may lose the logic. This diminishes the chance that they will fully comprehend your code. Ideally, the variable name should conjure up the appropriate image immediately. For example, PAYROLL is straightforward, but PR, PROLL, PYROLL, and PAYR all require the reader to stop and translate.

As an analogy, imagine learning a foreign language such as Spanish. It is relatively easy to learn that "parte" means "part." However, learning that "triste" means "sad" requires considerable effort. In short, just because a variable's meaning is obvious to you does not mean that it is intuitively obvious to someone else. Moreover, the bias that is inherently based on your own programming and background can easily spill over into the design of your variable names. You can improve your naming skills by periodically reviewing your code.

Standardized Naming Conventions

Should variable names be standardized for a project? This question brings up mixed feelings. Certainly it is a good idea to use the same name for a variable across all data sets in a project. However, some people are much better than others at naming variables. How would you like it if someone created variable names that were all only two characters long? Certainly, you can create variable names by committee. Unfortunately, this usually results in a "lose-lose" situation because everyone feels that their contributions are minimized.

Module Names

Creating meaningful module names is critical in developing large software systems. Programmers should not have to scan source code to verify that a module is the appropriate one. For many modules, the use of a verb and object can adequately describe the contents of the module. If space allows, an underscore between the verb and object is useful. Examples of good module names include:

```
CALC_TAX    GET_REC
SORTLIST    DEL_REC
ADD_PART
```

You can create another good class of names by using the return argument as the module name. For instance, many functions use this method: STD, SKEWNESS, MAX, SUM, and so on. You can use this same technique with such names as:

```
NEXT_EMP    P_VALUE
PAT_ID      LABGRADE
END_TIME    NEW_VAR
```

Variable Names

Maintain consistency when naming variables. It is almost always desirable to use the same name for a variable across data sets. This is important because the MERGE, UPDATE, and MODIFY statements depend on the consistency of names. For example, if a customer identification number is CUST_ID in one data set, don't call it CUST or CUST_NUM or NUM_CUST in other data sets.

Similarly, be consistent with the attributes of a variable. If the customer identification number is defined as character length 10 in one data set, don't change it to character length 8 in another data set. Or, worse yet, don't define it as numeric in subsequent data sets. If there is even a possibility that a variable contains character data, then define it as a character variable. This can save you from maintenance headaches when someone suddenly realizes that all the references to a variable need to be changed.

Also, be consistent with prefix and suffix names. If you use CNT as a reference to "count," don't use CNT both as a prefix and a suffix. Settle on a convention. For example, if you use REC_CNT in one part of the system, then don't use CNT_REC in another. Furthermore, strive to be consistent with naming conventions for prefixes and suffixes. If you like NO for "number," then don't mix all the variations such as PART_NO, PART_NUM, PARTNUMB, PARTNMBR, and PART_NM. Reserve your creativity for design and program logic.

Choose your variable names carefully. This is probably the most important factor that determines whether or not someone else can understand your program. Except for indexes, try to use as many letters as possible that can adequately describe the meaning of the variable. No need to be stingy here. Because SAS allows only eight characters for a variable, you don't have to worry about developing carpal tunnel syndrome. Here is a simple way to decide if a variable has a good name: Give your list of variables to someone else on the programming team. Ask them to tell you the meaning of each one without looking at the accompanying documentation.

If you're having trouble coming up with a good name, then it's a good time to pull out the thesaurus and get some ideas. It's great for programmer's block!

If you've been using a variable and you suddenly realize that the name is ambiguous, then change it. This may happen as a system becomes larger and you realize that more and more variables are starting to look alike. Fortunately, most program editors provide a simple way to perform a global "find and replace." But, be careful. The variable you are changing might be part of another variable. Include leading and trailing spaces in the "change" command as needed. Additionally, if the variable name is also an English word, you may inadvertently change the documentation. That's why, in this case, it is best to do a "global search and change with confirmation."

Use the log to your advantage. Clean up variables that you don't need. You can easily notice them in the log message:

```
NOTE: Variable USELESS is uninitialized.
```

If you need to use pairs of variables that represent an opposite condition, use unambiguous combinations such as:

START/FINISH	BEGIN/END
ADD/DELETE	LOCK/UNLOCK
UP/DOWN	ON/OFF
HIGH/LOW	

When you must distinguish the various forms of a variable such as its mean, median, standard deviation and so on, use suffixes to create the new variable names. The advantage of this practice is that readers see the core part of the variable first, which helps them to differentiate one set of variables from another. For example, you might want to create several new variables from your statistical PROCs:

```
proc univariate data = stats ;
    var baseline ;
    output out = newstats mean = basemean
    median = base_med std = base_std
    min = base_min max = base_max ;
run   ;
```

Try to use names that you can remember and that are also easy to pronounce. QZETIRMA isn't a bad variable name—if you're from Venus!

Avoid variable names that look almost identical. For instance, the following pairs of names are confusing:

R2D2/R_TWO_D2	DARTHVDR/DRTHVADR
BACK_PAY/PAY_BACK	HIGH_VAL/HI_VAL
STD_DEV/STAN_DEV	MASTPLAN/MSTPLAN
LITIGATE/LITGATE	

Return the status of a condition by using meaningful values such as "done," "found," "ok," "finished," "end-of-file," and so on.

Filerefs and librefs should also be descriptive. Names such as LIB5, LIBNAME1, FILE01, FILEREF3, and THEFILE, are not effective. On the other hand, MASTLAB, WORDWRAP, and PUTPAGE are much more illuminating.

Avoid using names that demonstrate your particular orientation to other programming languages or operating systems:

```
filename   file_ptr 'fileref' ;
filename   handle01 'fileref' ;
filename   makefile 'fileref' ;
libname    partit01 'libref' ;
libname    winexe   'libref' ;
```

Avoid using one letter to signify a part of the word. Here are a few misleading variable names :

```
retain parttime ;   * prime art time ;
retain tend_bar ;   * time to end of bar exam ;
retain stickem  ;   * standard tick emollient ;
```

Beware of using "clone" variable names such as LIB1, LIB2, LIB3. Reserve these names for variable lists where processing is simplified. Also, stir up those creative juices. The names in the list SCORE_01–SCORE_20 are much better than VAR_01–VAR_20.

Steer clear from letter combinations that look alike. The most lethal combinations include (O,0), (1,l) and (1,I). Using lowercase lettering causes fewer problems than does using uppercase lettering.

Because SAS limits variable declarations to eight characters, sometimes a little ingenuity is required to create names that are meaningful and unambiguous. Some suggestions to overcome this eight-character limitation include:

- Use standard computer abbreviations such as EOF or IO.

- Use the first few letters of each word and, optionally, provide an underscore to separate parts of a word: INC_TAX instead of INCTAX, PAY_STUB instead of PAYSTUB.

- Use standard industry abbreviations. For example, if you are developing medical applications, you can use:

SYS_BP	for systolic blood pressure
DIA_BP	for diastolic blood pressure
BASE_HR	for baseline heart rate
CANDA_01	for version #1 of computer-aided New Drug Application
DOSE_Q6H	medicine for a dosage of once every six hours
DOSE_TID	medicine for a dosage of three times a day

- Avoid suffixes that don't add meaning to the word, such as "ing" or "ed."

Working Variable Names

At times you may need to use external modules that modify an input data set. As with the use of global variables, it is a good idea to devise a convention for naming these variables. One way is to use a leading underscore in these routines to prevent overlaying a value in the Program Data Vector. Another advantage of using such "marked" variables is that you can write a routine that can DROP all variables that have a leading underscore. This can be useful when you write a utility routine that uses a large number of working variables.

Questionable Variable Names

Several dangerous naming conventions have been adopted by the data processing industry. One is the use of FLAG or SWITCH or any of the numerous variations such as FLAG1, SWITCH2, FLG, or SW_01. Sure, FLAG alerts the reader that the variable is a flag, but what is it flagging? At the risk of developing typing tendonitis, why not create names such as:

IS_FOUND	FOUND
READ_OK	ERR_STAT
FILE_OK	HAS_LINK
HAS_KID	HAS_LOCK
IS_CHILD	MATCH
ALL_DONE	LAST_ONE

Another popular but ambiguous variable that has become commonplace is TEMP:

```
temp = index ( pages, book ) ;
if temp gt 0 then ...
```

Instead, you can use a more meaningful name:

```
found = index ( pages, book ) ;
if found then ...
```

Avoid using negative conditions such as NOTFOUND, NOT_DONE, NO_REC, NO_BUILD, or NO_INIT, and so on. Using these kinds of variable names can complicate IF-THEN-ELSE logic:

```
if not (notfound or last_rec ) then ...
```

This code is easier to comprehend if you use FOUND instead of NOTFOUND:

```
if found and not last_rec then ...
```

Of course, you can avoid using literals in your code with just enough laziness to make you a true programmer:

```
%let fourteen = 14 ;
```

Instead, use a name to describe the condition:

```
%let max_days = 14 ;
```

Avoiding literals is extremely important when you are creating table-driven systems. This is discussed at length in Chapter 8, "System Coding Principles."

Switch Variable Names

For two-way switches (ON-OFF), it is a bad idea to use numerics. There is no uniform agreement about the meaning of 0, -1, 1 or any other positive number. Frequently, programmers write code similar to the following:

```
If ret_code = 1 then
    put "Good job" ;
else
if ret_code = 0 then
    put "Major problem here" ;
else
    put "No valid return code set." ;
```

Each operating system has its own rules for error codes. For instance, in the EDX operating system, "-1" signifies success, and positive numbers indicate an error. Similarly, the MVS operating system returns "0" for successful job completion, but returns positive codes for warning or error codes. And to really complicate matters, SAS has built in Boolean logic in which "missing" or "0" signifies false and positive values as true. Obviously, your own orientation can sway the way in which you utilize flags. Regardless of your programming exposure, a sensible option for keeping some sanity on the project is to use the following pairs of values for your switches: True/False, Yes/NO, T/F, or Y/N. Then the construct becomes readable:

```
If upcase ( got_val ) = "TRUE" then
    put "Good job" ;
else
if upcase ( got_val ) = "FALSE" then
    put "Major problem here" ;
else
    put "No valid return code set." ;
```

It may be preferable to standardize return codes by placing them into a table that allows access by the entire programming team. These can be set up as %LET statements as part of start-up processing. Then you would never again have to reference numbers within the code:

```
%let true  = 1 ;  * Placed in initialization file ;
%let false = 0 ;  * Placed in initialization file ;

If  got_val = &true then
    put "Good job" ;
else
if got_val = &false then
    put "Major problem here" ;
else
    put "No valid return code set." ;
```

Remember that, when using this technique, you want to make sure that you use the globals throughout the system, or else you defeat the purpose of the mnemonic names. Write your code like this:

```
if last_one then
    ret_code = &true ;
```

but, not like this!

```
if last_one then
    ret_code = 1 ;
```

You may find that using macro variables makes the code less readable because of the leading ampersand. In that case, you can set up a list of globals with RETAIN statements in your initialization module. Just be sure that your organization has a convention so that these globals do not clash with data variable names.

Commenting Code

Commenting your source code is about as enticing as a ham and liverwurst sandwich. However, the judicious use of comments is essential for building large software systems. Why is this so? Usually, maintenance changes involve creating enhancements or fixing program bugs, and often doing so under time pressure. Hence, you don't want to spend an inordinate amount of time wading through modules. Put simply, if you are reading code to find where to make the fix, you are in serious trouble. Combined with the stress of deadlines, debugging becomes an unenviable task.

Comments in your code should function like an index or a road map. By reading the comments, you can quickly find the part of the program or module that needs correcting. Once you find the appropriate section, then it is usually a matter of reading a relatively small section of source code. Now the big test. The next time a bug creeps up in a program, determine how long it takes to find the code that is likely to have caused the error. If, on average, it takes longer than ten minutes, then you are probably reading the code and not the comments.

For comments to be an effective road map, they need good visual separation from the code so that they stand out clearly. If you have comments embedded all over the place in a random fashion, then you might as well be reading the code.

Is there any disadvantage to commenting code in general? Yes, there is. The comments had better match the code. If you don't update the comments when you update the source, then the road map is out of date—useless and misleading. Surely, if that happens more than occasionally, you might not trust the comments at all! This is where good project management plays an important role. Management should require that source code be commented before accepting the code into production. Although this might sound dictatorial, running successful large projects requires a different mind set than does running ad hoc programs.

Flowerbox Style Comments

Perhaps the most effective commenting method is the flowerbox style, with at least one space separating it from the source code. This provides the visual clues necessary for easy maintenance. Here is an example:

```
*********************************************************** ;
*** Format for site category                         *** ;
*********************************************************** ;

value $categ
      'A' = 'ABANDONED'
      'B' = 'CHEMICAL PLANT'
      'C' = 'CITY CONTAMINATION'
      'D' = 'DIOXIN'
      ;


*********************************************************** ;
*** Create abbreviation name formats.              *** ;
*** Activity formats are listed alphabetically before events.*** ;
*********************************************************** ;

value $name
      'AC' = 'ADM-ORDR'
      'AN' = 'RDRA-NEG'
      'AV' = 'ADMIN-CR'
      'CA' = 'CON AGMT'
      ;
```

With this kind of comment block scattered through your code, you can visually pick them out very quickly, read them, and move on. Are these comments an effective use of time? Well, try this. Get a stopwatch and scan a thousand line undocumented program. How long did it take to decipher the code? Now compare this experience with scanning a well commented program. Enough said.

End-Line Style Comments

At the detail level, you may see this type of end-line commentary:

```
if _n_ = 1 then      /* if this is the first record */
do until ( last_rec ) ;  /* do until last record read */
    input in_line $varying133. in_len ;  /* varying length */
    check = index ( in_line, "&stopsign" ) ;  /* find stop flag */
    if check gt 0 then  /* if stop flag found then */
        fetch_it = 'no' ;  /* do not grab this record */
    if fetch_it = 'yes' and _type = 'TITLES' then /* title rec? */
    do ; /* do the following */
        titlecnt + 1 ;  /* Add 1 to the number of titles */
        tit_ary ( titlecnt ) = in_line ; /* Move to title array */
    end ; /* end of do loop */
    if fetch_it = 'yes' and _type = 'FOOTNOTES' then /* fnote? */
    do ; /* do the following */
        foot_cnt + 1 ;  /* Add 1 to footnote count */
        foot_ary ( foot_cnt ) = put ( in_line, $char133. ) ;
    end ; /* end of do loop */
end ; /* end of do loop */
```

That code is pretty messy. It can be cleaned up a little by simply aligning the comments and removing the superfluous remarks for the start and end of DO Loops:

```
if _n_ = 1 then                          /* if first record */
do until ( last_rec ) ;                  /* do until last */
    input in_line $varying133. in_len ;  /* input line   */
    check = index ( in_line, "&stopsign" ); /* find stop flag */
    if check gt 0 then                   /* stop flag found? */
        fetch_it = 'no' ;                /* do not fetch */
    if fetch_it = 'yes' and              /* if title record */
       _type = 'TITLES' then
    do ;
        titlecnt + 1 ;                   /* bump title count*/
        tit_ary ( titlecnt ) = in_line ; /* move tit. to ary */
    end ;
    if fetch_it = 'yes' and              /* if footnote rec. */
       _type = 'FOOTNOTES' then
    do ;
        foot_cnt + 1 ;                   /* Bump footnote cnt*/
        foot_ary ( foot_cnt ) =          /* put in foot.array*/
          put ( in_line, $char133. ) ;
    end ;
end ;
```

Note that several problems have emerged with end-line commenting:

1. Alignment. Every time you add a line of code, you may have to wrap the source code to the next line just so that you can squeeze in the comment. In the above example, for instance, you had to wrap two lines just to be able to comment the line. This continuation is a mechanical break and may not be as effective as lining up the code for more intuitive reading.

2. The comments, by nature, must be extremely short. Do they add much if your code is well written?

3. It is difficult to get an overall feel of the function of the block of code. Even by reading the comments instead of the code, you are at such a detailed level that you may not be sure how the code fits into the scheme of things.

Instead, reserve the end-line style for commenting data declarations because the LENGTH and RETAIN statements occupy very little space on the line.

Top-Line Style Comments

Another popular style of commenting is the top-line style:

```
/* point to the first element */
rank1 = int ( new - 1 ) / ( len ) + 1 ;
calc1 = mod ( scode, r_code ) ;
new_val = calc1 * tot_cnt ;

/* point to the second element */
rank2 = int ( new - 2 ) / ( len ) + 1 ;
calc2 = mod ( scode2, r_code ) ;
new_val = calc2 * tot_cnt ;
```

These comments tend to get lost within the code and it is difficult to scan the source and pick them up quickly. But, as they say, it's hard to break old habits.

Mixing Case

Another method of improving visual separation between the comments and source code is to use uppercase for one and lowercase for the other:

```
/*   CREATE A VIEW THAT CONTAINS INFORMATION ABOUT OVERDUE
     LIBRARY BOOKS AT THE MAIN CAMPUS LIBRARY. */

proc sql ;
    create view in.books as
        select p.idcode, my_name, ove_due, due_date
        from in.main as m, in.lookup as l
        where p.idcode = l.idcode ;
```

Here is the reverse version:

```
/*   create a view that contains information about overdue
     library books at the main campus library. */

PROC SQL ;
    CREATE VIEW IN.BOOKS AS
        SELECT P.IDCODE, MY_NAME, OVE_DUE, DUE_DATE
        FROM IN.MAIN AS M, IN.LOOKUP AS L
        WHERE P.IDCODE = L.IDCODE ;
```

This method provides pretty good visual separation. The biggest difficulty is that, with many people working on the project, some like to code in uppercase and others in lowercase. Perhaps a referee could settle this case.

Variable Length Boxes

Another commenting style is to use a variable length box size that matches the comments:

```
************************************ ;
*** Calculate students per class  *** ;
************************************ ;

proc freq data = students noprint ;
    tables class_id /out = classcnt   ;
run ;

*********************************************************** ;
*** Calculate all classes each student is registered for.*** ;
*********************************************************** ;

proc freq data = students noprint ;
    tables grad_id*class_id / out = students ;
run ;
```

While this may look a little better cosmetically, it suffers from the same maintenance problems discussed earlier. Namely, when the code changes, you not only have to change the comment, but you have to re-adjust the pretty print around it. This discourages documentation changes even if you think of a better descriptive comment. The advantage of constant size boxes is that you simply create a keyboard macro and, with one key stroke, you have a template for the comment. In addition, changing comments is not a problem. You simply type in overstrike mode if the original comment is longer than the original.

Statement Style versus Delimited Style Comments

The statement style comment is simply a leading asterisk and a trailing semicolon:

```
* Hey, you are putting too many comments in the code! ;
```

The delimited style uses the slash asterisk combination:

```
/* Hey, you are putting too many comments in my code! */
```

You can certainly mix the two styles, but not without consequence. If you consistently use statement style comments, you can comment out blocks of code with delimited style comments. For example, you can code this:

```
/*
.... SAS code
* Hey, you are putting too many comments in the code! ;
* You do not believe my code is self documenting? ;
... SAS code
*/
```

but certainly not this:

```
/*
... SAS code
/* Hey, you are putting too many comments in the code!
   You do not believe my code is self documenting? */
... SAS code
*/
```

Macro Style Comments

In addition to the statement and delimited style comments, SAS allows you to use a macro comment within a macro function. A sample comment may look like:

```
%macro new_data ;
    %*                                 ;
    %* This macro creates a new DATA step   ;
    %*                                 ;
    proc append base = old_one new = new_one ;
    run ;
%mend new_data ;
```

Macro style comments (unlike statement style comments) do not appear in the log if you set the system option MPRINT.

Levels of Documentation

There are three levels of documentation: program level, module level, and detail level.

Program Level Documentation

Program level is the overall header documentation that appears at the beginning of a program. For an example, match the numbers in the following program to the descriptions that follow the program.

```
****************************************************************** ;
***                                                          *** ;
*** Module:    Makelink.sas (Make a link string for site) ❶ *** ;
***                                                          *** ;
*** Type:      SAS Program ❷                                 *** ;
***                                                          *** ;
*** Function:  This program creates link strings that mirror *** ;
***            the sequence of events and activities that    *** ;
***            are associated with a Superfund site.  Each   *** ;
***            string contains fields that point to the next *** ;
***            activity or event in sequence.  An example    *** ;
***            sequence is:                                  *** ;
***            01RA2 01RA1 01RD2 01RD1 01CO1 NS01            *** ;
***                                                          *** ;
***            Note that the strings are listed in reverse   *** ;
***            order with the bottom of the pipeline listed  *** ;
***            first and the top of the pipeline listed last.*** ;
***                                                          *** ;
***            The basic logic of the program is as follows: *** ;
***            * Create every possible combination of link   *** ;
***              strings.                                     *** ;
***            * Remove duplicate strings.                    *** ;
***            * Remove substrings totally contained in       *** ;
***              other strings.                               *** ;
***            * Remove parallel strings.  These strings run  *** ;
***              parallel to other strings but represent a    *** ;
***              shorter more direct path of events.          *** ;
***            * Insert project support events within its     *** ;
***              associated operable unit. ❸                  *** ;
***                                                          *** ;
*** Input:     The link data are stored in a national data-  *** ;
***            base sasdata.site11 ❹                          *** ;
***                                                          *** ;
*** Output:    Output is written to a file that which con-   *** ;
***            tains the region, EPA identification number,  *** ;
***            site name, and linked list of events and      *** ;
***            activities ❺                                   *** ;
***                                                          *** ;
*** Limits:    An output link string cannot contain more     *** ;
***            than 200 characters because of the SAS        *** ;
***            limitation of 200 characters per variable.❻    *** ;
***                                                          *** ;
*** Author:    Eduardo Permatowitz ❼                          *** ;
***                                                          *** ;
*** History:   Program written 12-17-96 ❽                     *** ;
***                                                          *** ;
****************************************************************** ;
```

❶ Identify the name of the module. The name should be descriptive of the program. Because eight characters may be limiting, place parentheses around the description that describes the derivation of the term, for example, FLUSHBUF (Flush the Input Buffer).

❷ Describe the type of module. Is it a program, macro function, or an %INCLUDE statement construct?

❸ Describe the function of the program in simple terms. You might want to summarize major logic flow, as in the above example.

❹ Specify the input data. Does it come from an external file, a database, a SAS data set, or a cards image?

❺ Specify the output. Is it a SAS data set, an external file, or a database?

❻ Discuss any limitations of the routine.

❼ Put your name on the routine. This allows you to receive proper credit or discredit, as warranted.

❽ Some programmers don't believe in using the history section because this documentation is updated on a hit-or-miss basis. Nevertheless, it is listed here because some project teams require it.

Module Level Documentation

Module level documentation describes routines that are smaller than a program, namely modules %INCLUDEd in the program, macro definitions, and code called by a LINK statement. For a complete description of this documentation, refer to the section "Documentation of Modules/Arguments" in Chapter 5, "Laying the Foundation with Good Design."

Detail Level Documentation

Detail level documentation involves commenting a single line of code or a small code fragment. These comments are critical for the roadmap. What information should the detail level commentary include? It should describe, in summary fashion, both "what" the code does and "why" the programmer is doing it. While most programmers are pretty good at describing "what" the code does, they fail to let readers get into their mind. The "why" helps readers understand the routine, especially when the logic is complex. For example, you may have taken the more complex programming route to provide an extra "bell" or "whistle." However, if you don't let readers know why, they may assume that you wrote inefficient code.

When discussing "what" the code does, don't simply repeat the code:

```
*************************************************************** ;
*** Add 1 to emp_cnt.                                      *** ;
*************************************************************** ;

emp_cnt + 1 ;
```

If you have to comment this line, then describe its purpose in clear terms:

```
*************************************************************** ;
*** Point to the next employee in the payroll list.       *** ;
*************************************************************** ;

emp_cnt + 1 ;
```

Comment Density

How many comments are appropriate? It's doubtful that many programs are over-commented. However, almost all programs suffer from a lack of commentary. Perhaps the programmer felt that he or she would be the only one maintaining the code to the end of civilization. The funny thing is that many programmers who say that often pick up their code after a few months and find that they have no idea what they were trying to do originally. The comments are there to refresh your memory as well as to help readers.

"Documentation density" is a software metric that describes the amount of documentation in a program. The formula is quite simple:

Documentation Density = number of comment lines /
(total lines of program – blank lines)

When counting comment lines, count only actual text, not the borders or hyphens or asterisks that you have included to make the comments stand out. For example, if a program contains 20 lines of comments within a program that is 110 lines long and has 10 blank lines, then the formula equates to:

$$\text{documentation density} = 20 / (110 - 10)$$
$$= 20/100$$
$$= 20\%$$

The appropriate documentation density depends on the programming language. Low-level languages are, by nature, more difficult to understand, so they require more documentation. Here is a general guideline for commenting code according to the programming language:

Assembler	90–100%
C	50%
COBOL	10–20%
SAS	10–20% ??

A well documented Assembler program requires comments on almost every line of code. Moving up the scale, C requires a substantial degree of documentation. Although C is far removed from Assembler-level programming, it is inherently cryptic. In addition, C programmers seem to take pleasure in developing "tricky" code that uses an endless series of pointers. COBOL, on the other hand, is a large step away from the first two languages. It is intuitive and straightforward, and it allows many characters to describe variables, which assists in documenting the program. This allows you to follow the program without a large number of comments.

The next step up on the evolutionary scale includes SAS. SAS is arguably a 4th generation language and a step up from COBOL. However, SAS is much richer with its powerful set of operations and functions. This greater programming flexibility can tempt programmers to develop complex programs. In particular, DATA step manipulation can become quite involved. As a result, the documentation density suggested for COBOL is also appropriate for SAS.

Commenting Data Declarations

Previous sections examined good variable naming conventions. But good naming conventions are not enough. You should also use comments to describe the variables. When building a system, you will likely need a set of system global variables. You should describe the meaning and use of these variables with care:

```
*************************************************************** ;
***                                                       *** ;
***               G L O B A L   V A R I A B L E S         *** ;
***                                                       *** ;
*************************************************************** ;
%let builder  = hemsley, daughton ;    * Available builders   ;
%let material = brick, wood, glass ;   * Primary materials     ;
%let zip_loc  = 92129, 92145, 94233 ;  * Where can build?      ;
```

Complex programs need their own declaration portion. In this section, alphabetize the entries. This does not require much effort and can simplify the life of the maintenance programmer, particularly when the list of variables is quite large:

```
*************************************************************** ;
***                                                       *** ;
***                   V A R I A B L E S                   *** ;
***                                                       *** ;
*************************************************************** ;

retain apple     "A" ;  * The ultimate food for health        ;
retain bacon     "B" ;  * Best food for artery cleansing       ;
retain candy     "C" ;  * One a day keeps the dentist busy     ;
retain doughnut  "D" ;  * The policemans idea of fine dining   ;
retain granola   "G" ;  * Health foods are overrated           ;
retain popcorn   "P" ;  * Easy on the butter please            ;
```

Instead of one long alphabetic list, you may prefer to organize variables alphabetically within logical groupings. However, don't try to create too many categories or the reader may spend too much time sifting through the stacks of variables:

```
*************************************************************** ;
***                                                       *** ;
***                   V A R I A B L E S                   *** ;
***               Used to Build LINK strings              *** ;
***                                                       *** ;
*************************************************************** ;
retain addspace    0 ;  * Spaces to add to end of string       ;
retain cnt         0 ;  * Index used to build arrays            ;
retain copy_cnt    0 ;  * Current # of elements in copy array   ;
retain from_pos    7 ;  * Points to linked activity or event    ;
retain limit     169 ;  * Maximum string length allowed         ;
retain max_cnt     0 ;  * Maximum # records in count array      ;
```

```
******************************************************************** ;
***                                                            *** ;
***                       V A R I A B L E S                    *** ;
***                    Used to route printer output            *** ;
***                                                            *** ;
******************************************************************** ;
%let landcode = '1B266C314F'x  * Printer landscape esc sequence;
%let orient = portrait ;       * Default print - portrait mode ;
%let print = print ;           * Print file specifications     ;
%let redirect = TERMINAL ;     * Where redirect report output  ;
%let reset    = '1B45'x ;      * Resets printer to normal mode ;
%let studyrun = NO ;           * Is this a batch study run ?   ;
%let sysfoot = 0 ;             * Assume 0 system footnotes     ;
```

Variable declarations should be on their own page because the maintenance programmers may want the list of variables easily at their disposal. Most programmers complain that improper naming of variables or lack of their understanding may be the biggest obstacle to program maintenance.

At what point of coding development should you put comments into the code? One strategy is to write a block of commentary and then write the associated code, then write another block of commentary and then its associated code, and so on. This practice actually serves several useful purposes:

- You are assured that the code is commented. You'll have no excuses later on when you are under tight deadlines to quickly slap together some documentation.

- It allows you to focus more carefully on the code about to be written.

- Sometimes you will discover logic flaws while writing the comments. If needed, you can then go back to the design board.

When the code is ready to be put into production, walk through the comments and code one more time. This time, embellish the remarks to clarify the more salient points.

Logging Changes in Source Code

Some programmers mark their changes with their name and date, as in the following example:

```
proc freq data = fruits noprint ;
    tables type / out = types ;   /* smr 12/17/79 */
run ;
```

In the above case, someone made a change, but what was modified? Perhaps if you rummage through the trash can, you can find the original code.

```
proc freq data = fruits ;
    tables type /* lowsugar */ ; /* smr 12/17/79 */
run ;
```

In the second case, the original code is flagged by being commented out. Do you really care what the original code intended to do? The commented out code is extremely irritating and confusing. Usually people mark their changes because they aren't confident that the modification was correct. If you are unsure of your changes, then use version control. In other words, make sure you have a backup copy of the code that can be restored if needed.

Summary

By now, you are totally convinced that proper documentation is essential for building a complete software system. You are nodding your head. Are you doing that just to appease the author? Perhaps you are not convinced. Just don't wake me at midnight when you're in a real jam!

Exercises

1. For your Christmas bonus, your boss buys you a slick, workstation-sized monitor. Why should you be cautious about using the full width of the screen to enter your source code?

2. Why are numeric flags dangerous?

3. What are a couple of good ways to name modules?

4. Assume that "24" represents the number of work categories. What is a safer way to code the following:

    ```
    do k = 1 to 24 ;
     .....
    end ;
    ```

5. Noting that SAS Institute intended to increase the number of characters available for variable names, some experienced SAS users said that this would not change their programming habits. In fact, they believed that the shorter the variable name, the better. Why do you think people take this attitude?

6. What are useful tricks to handle the eight-character limit for SAS variables?

7. What is probably the biggest advantage of highly visual comments?

8. What is the biggest disadvantage of comments?

9. What are the principal weaknesses of "end-line" comments?

10. What is the biggest advantage and disadvantage of using upper case for the source and lower case for the comments or vice-versa?

11. Describe "documentation density." How is it affected by the programming language?

Reference

Kelly, D.A. (1983), *Documenting Computer Application Systems*, New York: Petrocelli Books.

Chapter 7   # Structured Programming Techniques

Introduction **116**

History **116**

Background Theory **117**

Proper Organization of Data Step Statements **120**
  Construct Breakout Mechanisms 120
  DATA Step Breakout Mechanisms 121
  Straight-Line Code 121
  IF-THEN-ELSE Constructs 122
  Loops: The Basics 126
  General Control Issues with DO Loop Constructs 127
  Using LEAVE and CONTINUE 128
  GOTO Is a Four Letter Word 130

Considerations for Variables **131**
  Referencing Variables 131
  Persistence of Variables 131
  Initializing Variables 133

Measuring Software Quality **134**
  McCabe's Cyclomatic Complexity 134
  McCabe's Essential Complexity 136
  Knot Count 137
  Halstead Software Science Metrics 137
  Scoring SAS Complexity 138

**Putting It All Together: Converting from Design to
Structured Code** **139**
  First Cut 139
  Second Cut 139
  Third Cut 139
  Final Cut 140
  Write the Pseudocode 141
  Translate from Pseudocode to ... Pseudocode?? 141
  Translate from Pseudocode to SAS Code 142
  Clean It Up 144

Summary **148**

Exercises **148**

References **148**

Introduction

This chapter examines the structural aspects of SAS code. Topics include the formation of various programming elements and their relationship to each other. By adhering to the principles of structured coding, you can develop code that is more likely to be free of careless programming bugs and easier to maintain.

As with many programming terms, the phrase "Structured Coding" has different meanings to different authors. The definition presented here refers to the formation of programming elements. Specifically, this chapter examines the aspects of writing code within a module. Related concepts, such as modularity, are discussed in Chapter 5, "Laying the Foundation with Good Design." System coding concerns are discussed in Chapter 8, "System Coding Principles."

History

The 1960's was an era of creativity, revolution, and excitement. This was certainly true in the computer industry, where new programming languages sprouted as quickly as designers could envision them. In the mid-1960's, E.W. Dijkstra raised the eyebrows of many theorists with his radical papers on structured programming. Most notable was a paper that discounted the use of the GOTO construct as a valid software construct (Dijkstra 1979). In short, his work demonstrated that not all high-level languages require the use of the GOTO construct. It is important to realize that Dijkstra did not favor complete abolition of the GOTO construct but rather replacing it in most instances with other structured programming constructs. Furthermore, he believed that the indiscriminate use of the GOTO led to the creation of unstructured programs that were difficult to maintain.

Numerous papers ensued, arguing both for and against the use of GOTO (Hopkins 1979, Wolf 1979, Ashcroft 1979). As a result of this controversy, programmers began to examine programming languages from a broader viewpoint. Computer scientists started to explore many other aspects of program structure. While starting as a GOTO controversy, the discussion moved across the entire spectrum of coding constructs. Some interesting questions arose:

- Are there other coding constructs to avoid when developing structured programs?

- How deeply can you nest a DO-END construct?

- How deeply can you nest an IF-THEN-ELSE construct?

- What is the best way to sequence instructions?

This is just a subset of the questions investigated in this chapter. While previous chapters focused on general programming strategies, this chapter focuses on programming at the microscopic level. In large software productions, coding detail becomes more important than it does in ad hoc programs. Weaknesses in one module, or even in a section of one module, can have a rippling effect throughout the system. It is imperative that programmers pay attention to the fine points of structured coding.

Background Theory

Bohm and Jacopini demonstrated that, in theory, all structured programs could be developed with merely three programming constructs (Hughes 1977, p.61). The three fundamental constructs are:

- sequence
- selection
- iteration

Sequence implies that code executes one instruction after the next in consecutive order.

instruction ==>   instruction ==>   instruction ==>   instruction ==>

Here is an example of sequence:

```
first  = 'one' ;
second = 'two' ;
third  = 'three' ;
fourth = 'four' ;
```

Selection (as depicted in Figure 7.1) implies that different instructions execute based on the evaluation of an expression.

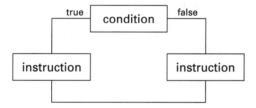

Figure 7.1   *"Selection" allows the program to branch to more than one path.*

Here is an example of selection:

```
if true then
    put "this is true" ;
else
    put "this is false" ;
```

Iteration refers to the execution of a set of instructions "X" number of times. Figure 7.2 illustrates the DO-WHILE version that evaluates the test condition at the top of the loop:

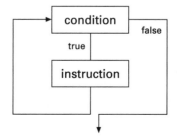

Figure 7.2   *Iteration allows for program repetition.*

Here is an example of iteration:

```
i = 1 ;
do while ( i <= 10 ) ;
    put "I will do this ten times" ;
    i = i + 1 ;
end ;
```

As previously mentioned, all code can theoretically be written using only these three constructs. However, using only these building blocks is somewhat restrictive for developing complete programs. Three other constructs are acceptable because they are essentially derivations of the original three basic building blocks:

- the nested IF statement

- case-type statement

- a breakout mechanism

The *nested IF* allows for more complicated expressions than does the simple IF construct:

```
if make = "chevy" then
    if model = "camaro" then
        if submodel = "Z-28" then
            put "Nice wheels!" ;
        else
            put "Get a real car!" ;
```

Perhaps the biggest advantage of using nested IF constructs is the ability to simplify what would otherwise be complex AND/OR expressions:

```
if make = "oldsmobile" and ( cost lt 1000 or make = "cutlass")
    and ( age gt '1jan1989'd or color = "lime" ) and
    (seller = "motivated" ) then
        option = "Make an offer!" ;
```

This code can be rewritten more simply as:

```
if make = "oldsmobile" then
    if cost lt 1000 or make = "cutlass" then
        if age gt '1jan1989'd or color = "lime"  then
            if seller = "motivated"  then
                option = "Make an offer!" ;
```

Case is a convenient way of dealing with multiple IF statements. In SAS, the SELECT statement fits this role:

```
select ( typefood ) ;
    when ( carbo )    calories = 4.1 ;
    when ( protein )  calories = 4.1 ;
    when ( fat )      calories = 9.0 ;
end ;
```

When case-type statements were originally implemented in programming languages, programmers used them like traffic cops, redirecting code in many different directions. Usually the GOTO was the culprit and was therefore considered unacceptable in structured programs. Here is an abusive example of SELECT:

```
select ( money ) ;
    when (1) goto pauper ;
    when (2) goto lowclass ;
    when (3) goto midclass ;
    when (4) goto snobbery ;
end ;
```

However, the judicious use of the SELECT statement can be an extremely valuable construct:

```
select (rank) ;
    when (1) put "Private First Class" ;
    when (2) put "Corporal" ;
    when (3) put "Sergeant" ;
    when (4) put "Lieutenant" ;
    when (5) put "Major" ;
    when (6) put "Colonel" ;
    when (7) put "General" ;
    otherwise put "Invalid military rank" ;
end ;
```

Remember, using fall-through logic to collect default cases is just as dangerous as using fall-through logic with IF-THEN-ELSE constructs. For example, in the above example, it would have been dangerous to let the OTHERWISE case default to "General." OTHERWISE is most useful to catch invalid cases so that you can act appropriately with invalid data.

There are four reasonable ways to order the elements in the SELECT clause. Normally, the order is a moot point but, occasionally, SELECT may have a multitude of test cases. Then you may want to order the test cases by:

- Alphabetic order: this allows for quick visual location of test cases.

- Numerical order: this also allows for quick visual location of test cases.

- Logical order: cases can be organized by categories such as chronology (such as, Monday to Sunday) or ranking (Private to General).

- Descending frequency: this can be useful for debugging because the most frequently occurring cases are near the top of the SELECT expression.

If each element in a SELECT structure requires a significant amount of code, then you are better off writing a subroutine for each element.

Here is a questionable use of the SELECT statement. A dangerous practice is stripping off letters and using part of a field as an index:

```
command = substr ( command, 1, 1 ) ;

select ( command ) ;
    when ( "I" ) link indent ;
    when ( "T" ) link trans ;
    when ( "D" ) link delete ;
    when ( "P" ) link printrtn ;
    otherwise put "ERROR: We have a new code not tabled." ;
end ;
```

While this code may look harmless, difficulties arise when you add new commands far removed from this section of code. For example, you might add a new command, elsewhere in the program, named INSERT. Because both INSERT and INDENT start with an "I," the error trapping in the OTHERWISE statement becomes useless.

Proper Organization of DATA Step Statements

This section discusses details about organizing DATA step statements.

Construct Breakout Mechanisms

When your code is deeply nested within a DO loop or IF-THEN-ELSE construct, it may be necessary to avoid executing it. For example, assume that you are doing a table lookup using a very sophisticated and lengthy algorithm. You may very well want to get out of the DO loop, as in the following example:

```
do until ( found or end_file) ;
    ...
    numerous SAS statements
    ...
    if found then (GET ME OUT OF THIS LOOP!!)
    ...
    numerous SAS statements not to be executed if found
...
end ;
```

Sometimes it is quite messy to avoid executing a section of code. Usually, this may involve setting one or more flags and, so, structured coding theorists permit a breakout. Breakout mechanisms in SAS are LEAVE, CONTINUE, and GOTO statements. Later on in this chapter, these elements are examined in greater detail.

DATA Step Breakout Mechanisms

Because of the sequential nature of SAS processing, a number of DATA step breakout mechanisms are available to prevent the processing of more observations.

To break out of a DATA step entirely, ABORT and STOP statements are both useful escape mechanisms. From a systems standpoint, their execution prevents the execution of code that could otherwise cause programming bugs. This is most likely to occur in systems that rely heavily on counters and flags to control processing (which is, incidentally, not a good practice in general). For example:

```
data master ;
    set trans end = last_one ;
...
...
if bad_rec = &yes then
    abort ;

if last_one then
    call symput ('tot_recs', _n_ ) ;

run ;
```

Likewise, the DELETE statement, WHERE clause, and subsetting IF statements can select only those observations required for the present DATA step:

```
data master ;
    set trans end = last_one ;

where polparty =: "Radical" ;

a_cnt + 1 ;

run ;
```

Straight-Line Code

One popular method of coding is to perform a related action on different variables in the same code fragment. This can lead to unnecessary transformations or improper handling of a given variable, as in the following example:

```
var_one  = substr ( big_var, 2, 2 ) ;
var_two  = substr ( big_var, 4, 2 ) ;
varthree = substr ( big_var, 6, 2 ) ;

var_one  = translate ( var_one, ",", " " ) ;
var_two  = translate ( var_two, ",", " " ) ;
varthree = translate ( varthree, ",", " " ) ;

var_one  = upcase ( var_one ) ;
var_two  = upcase ( var_two ) ;
varthree = upcase ( varthree ) ;
```

At first glance, you might consider this to be well-structured code. After all, the code appears to be well organized and it is logically grouped by function. However, as is demonstrated shortly, the span of a variable is spread longer than is necessary. Instead of concentrating on one variable at a time, you must commit three to memory. Here is the code fragment, reorganized to minimize the span of variables:

```
var_one = substr ( big_var, 2, 2 ) ;
var_one = translate ( var_one, ",", " " ) ;
var_one = upcase ( var_one ) ;

var_two = substr ( big_var, 4, 2 ) ;
var_two = translate ( var_two, ",", " " ) ;
var_two = upcase ( var_two ) ;

varthree = substr ( big_var, 6, 2 ) ;
varthree = translate ( varthree, ",", " " ) ;
varthree = upcase ( varthree ) ;
```

As you can see, this structure presents a straightforward approach to processing each variable.

In order to execute a sequence of modules, avoid consolidating initialization code into one module. Similarly, do not add the termination information into the last module. For instance, embedding an initialization routine in the first module (%ROAD_MAP) and final calculations in the last module (%BEST_WAY) prevents the possibility of rearranging the module order later:

```
%road_map (contains the initialization routine)
%getroute
%best_way (contains the termination routine)
```

A safer structure is to place initialization and termination code into their own routines, as indicated by the arrows :

```
==>    %init_rtn
       %road_map
       %getroute
       %best_way
==>    %decision
```

IF-THEN-ELSE Constructs

There are many ways to write IF-THEN-ELSE constructs. While the differences may be subtle, they can be important for organizing code in order to minimize logic errors. One recommended technique is to list the most commonly occurring case first:

```
if choice = "Horror" then
    ticket = 6.75 ;
else
if choice = "Drama" then
    ticket = 6.25 ;
else
if choice = "Old Time Classic" then
    ticket = 4.25 ;
```

This practice can be useful when debugging because the maintenance programmer has to scan through fewer cases. This can be particularly important if the number of IF-THEN-ELSE constructs becomes large. Now, the previous example is not quite complete. It is always a good idea to have a default case if other branches have not been met:

```
if choice = "Horror" then
    ticket = "6.75"  ;
else
if choice = "Drama" then
    ticket = "6.25" ;
else
if choice = "Old Time Classic" then
    ticket = "4.25" ;
else
    ticket = "You forged this ticket!!" ;
```

Another typical problem is failing to match up the tests of equality:

```
if work_hrs le 40 then
    paygrade = "Regular" ;
else
if work_hrs gt 40 and work_hrs lt 70 then
    paygrade = "Overtime" ;
else
if work_hrs gt 70 then
    paygrade = "Workaholic" ;
else
    do ;
        file log ;
        put work_hrs= ;
        put "*** We have a SERIOUS problem here ***" ;
    end ;
```

According to this example, if you work exactly 70 hours, you won't get paid. The last ELSE is always useful for catching values that "fall through the seams."

Another handy solution, when working with a large set of cases, is to use formats. The biggest advantage is that it is easier to visually align the test cases and note if there is a break in the ranges:

```
proc format ;
value work_val
0-40     = "Regular"
41-69    = "Overtime"
70-high  = "Workaholic"
other = "*** We have a SERIOUS problem here ***"
;
run ;
```

Within your DATA step, you can substitute the previous IF-THEN-ELSE construct with:

```
paygrade = put ( work_hrs, work_val. ) ;
```

Many constructs can be easier to read with a little bit of maneuvering. Take for example this code, which does nothing when the case is true:

```
if true then ;
else
     put @col_01 out_var ;
```

Rewriting this code results in:

```
if not true then
     put @col_01 out_var ;
```

or it can be simplified with:

```
if false then
     put @col_01 out_var ;
```

Some programmers, in their exactitude, like to demonstrate that all test cases have been covered. While some may debate its practicality, some ivory tower theorists suggest that this technique ensures complete logic coverage. You can recode the above example to handle the "do nothing" case as follows:

```
%let nothing = ;        * Defined in initialization module ;

if true then
do ;
     &nothing ;
end ;
else
     put @col_01 out_var ;
```

Or, if you prefer to avoid the DO-END construct because you are only dealing with one line of code:

```
%let ignore = ;        * Defined in initialization module ;

if true then
     &ignore ;
else
     put @col_01 out_var ;
```

Many IF-THEN-ELSE expressions are more readable after a little reordering. For example, the following two statements are equivalent:

```
if ( not wealthy or not handsome ) then
     link get_lost ;
if not ( wealthy and handsome ) then
     link get_lost ;
```

Although programmers may debate which is the better construct, the first expression is probably easier because you can evaluate one condition at a time. In the second example, you have to evaluate the whole expression and then negate the condition. This can be rather confusing, especially when the condition to be evaluated is complex.

In general, it is easiest to cancel out the double negatives into a positive expression. In fact, it is possible to make a lot of code more readable by avoiding negative tests of expressions. The following first example is certainly more readable than the second:

```
if goodread or gooddisk ;

if not bad_read or not bad_disk ;
```

Nesting

To enhance readability, consider reordering nested IF-THEN-ELSE constructs. In the following example, you have to do some mental gymnastics to locate the value of penalty:

```
if speed gt 55 then
    if speed gt 65 then
        if speed gt 75 then
            if speed gt 85 then
                penalty = '100 bucks' ;
            else
                penalty = '80 bucks' ;
        else
            penalty = '60 bucks' ;
    else
        penalty = '50 bucks' ;
else
    penalty = '0 - you lucked out' ;
```

Reworking the structure can restore your sanity:

```
if speed gt 85 then
        penalty = '100 bucks ' ;
    else
    if speed gt 75 then
        penalty = '80 bucks' ;
    else
    if speed gt 65 then
        penalty = '60 bucks' ;
    else
    if speed gt 55 then
        penalty = '50 bucks' ;
    else
        penalty = '0 - You lucked out!' ;
```

Macro Variables

IF-THEN-ELSE constructs can easily become too complex, as in this case:

```
if char in ( " ", "?", ".", "M", "m" ) then
    chartype = "missing" ;
```

To simplify, use macro variables defined in an initialization file. The previous code fragment can be rewritten as:

```
%let misschar = ' ', '?', '.', 'M', 'm' ; /*Define in init file*/
if char in ( &misschar ) then
    chartype = "missing" ;
```

Loops: The Basics

The SAS System provides a number of constructs that are useful for iteration. Here are three major methods of loop control:

1. Do a loop a fixed number of times:

```
do loop_cnt = 1 to dim ( my_array ) ;
...  sas code
end ;
```

2. Do a loop until a condition is true:

```
do until ( cond = &finish ) ;
...  sas code
end ;
```

3. Do a loop while a condition is true:

```
do while ( morerecs = &true ) ;
...  sas code
end ;
```

Important safeguards for using loops correctly include:

- Initialize a variable close to where it is used.

- Pay close attention to counters and accumulators. The "off-by-one" problem is very common when executing DO loops.

- Be sure you reinitialize a variable at the appropriate location.

Stating the evaluation simply in the DO loop helps to avoid logic errors. The following first example is easier to understand than the second:

```
do while ( not done ) ;
```

```
do while ( done = false ) ;
```

If a DO loop construct spans more than about 25 lines, you should consider making the contents of the loop a callable routine. When a DO loop flows across more than one page, it becomes extremely difficult to follow the logic. Similarly, if a DO loop contains more than about three levels of indention, the logic also becomes difficult to follow. This is a good time to call a subroutine via the LINK statement or a macro function. Here is a common example where a DO loop can extend over a page in length:

```
if ticket = notavail then
do ;
... 75 lines of SAS code
end ;
else if ticket = avail then
do ;
...    75 lines of SAS code
end ;
```

You can simplify with:

```
if ticket = notavail then
    link findmore ;
else if ticket = avail then
    link calcfare ;
```

This moves the details out of the mainline code and promotes both readability and maintainability.

General Control Issues with DO Loop Constructs

Coding errors are often due to the improper indexing of a DO loop. In general, you want to use mnemonic names for DATA step variables. However, it is certainly acceptable to use one-letter variables for array subscripts —programmers use them by convention. The letters I, J, and K are particularly favorable. In fact, most letters towards the middle of the alphabet are pretty safe to use. However, be cautious about using the letters at the beginning and end of the alphabet. You certainly want to avoid choosing letters that might be used as variables in other parts of the program. The letters X, Y, and Z may very well be used in a graphics coordinate system to designate the various axes. Likewise, A, B, and C are letters that quickly come to mind when a programmer needs a "quick and dirty" variable.

However, when you are nesting DO loops (or using multidimensional array structures), it is imperative that you use good names for the subscripts because failing to do so can easily result in logic errors.

Here is the kind of mistake that can easily appear when using nondescriptive index names. Suppose you have set up a two dimensional array, 8 x 8, to represent the grid of the chessboard. In SAS software, you can represent this as follows:

```
array chess {8,8} $6 ;
```

Figure 7.3 displays the chessboard (and pieces) that correspond to this array.

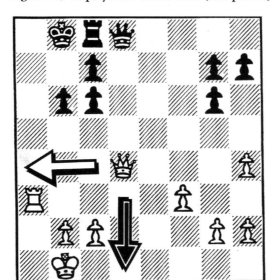

Figure 7.3   *This is certainly a winning position for "White."*

Whenever a player wants to make a move, he assigns a chess piece to the array coordinate where he wants to move.

The computer asks, "What is your play?" After considerable deliberation, the player thinks he has found the winning move! The player responds (as indicated by the black arrow in the figure):

```
chess { i, j } = "Queen" ;
```

"You should consider resigning!" declares the computer, as it swiftly captures your queen.

The player faints in disbelief because he meant to play the following (as indicated by the white arrow in the figure):

```
chess { j, i } = "Queen" ;
```

This could have been avoided by using more descriptive variables names:

```
chess { column, row } = "Queen" ;
```

or, for the seasoned competitor:

```
chess { file, rank } = "Queen" ;
```

Using LEAVE and CONTINUE

Sometimes it is necessary to break out of a DO loop prematurely. In the following code fragment, you have a dilemma. You don't want to use a DO-UNTIL construct because that would force you to execute the DO loop at least once. And to complicate matters, you don't want the patient to be placed on any diets unless the total number of calories is more than the calories burned.

Here is the first try:

```
tot_cals = 0 ;
%exercise ( walk_cnt = 3 , jog_cnt = 2 , swim_cnt = 5 )        <==
tot_cals = tot_cals + eat_cals - exercise ;                    <==

do while ( tot_cals ge cal_burn ) ;
    %new_diet
    %morediet
    %milkdiet
    %eggsdiet
    %exercise ( walk_cnt = 3 , jog_cnt = 2 , swim_cnt = 5 )   <==
    tot_cals = tot_cals + eat_cals - exercise ;               <==
end ;
```

The problem is that two lines have been repeated (marked here with arrows). This is a potentially difficult maintenance problem because someone may have the audacity to modify these two lines in the future. The programmer making the fix would have to be aware that the lines have to be changed in both places to avoid an error. Here, in this second try, is a way to circumvent this problem:

```
%let forever = 0 ;

do until ( &forever ) ;
    %exercise ( walk_cnt = 3 , jog_cnt = 2 , swim_cnt = 5 ) ;
    tot_cals = tot_cals + eat_cals - exercise ;
    if tot_cals lt cal_burn then
        leave ;
    %new_diet
    %morediet
    %milkdiet
    %eggsdiet
end ;
```

Some theorists argue that breakout mechanisms such as LEAVE and CONTINUE are nothing more than disguised GOTOs. Here is the same example with a "hidden GOTO":

```
%let forever = 0 ;

do until ( &forever ) ;
    %exercise ( walk_cnt = 3 , jog_cnt = 2 , swim_cnt = 5 )
    tot_cals = tot_cals + eat_cals - exercise ;
    if tot_cals lt cal_burn then
        goto loopexit ;
    %new_diet
    %morediet
    %milkdiet
    %eggsdiet
end ;

loopexit: ;
```

While LEAVE and CONTINUE statements are convenient, use them with caution. Several general guidelines include:

- Within a DO loop, use only one LEAVE or CONTINUE statement.

- Try to rearrange the code to avoid using these breakout mechanisms.

- If the test expression for LEAVE or CONTINUE is quite complex, it is likely that the code needs to restructured.

- If setting too many flags is required to avoid the use of a breakout, it is probably better to keep the LEAVE or CONTINUE statement in the code.

- LEAVE is especially useful when you need to abort a routine.

- CONTINUE is more likely to be affected by logic changes.

GOTO Is a Four Letter Word

Getting back to the old GOTO controversy—is the GOTO construct (or the %GOTO) ever justified? Some structured programming theorists argue that the presence of even a single GOTO in a program automatically makes it an unstructured program. The indiscriminate use of GOTO is the cause of maintenance nightmares, and it is certainly not needed with the SAS language. Using a GOTO statement within a DATA step is almost never needed. In almost all cases, you can restructure code to avoid the use of the GOTO.

Acceptable Use of the GOTO Construct

Here is an example where the %GOTO may be useful in a macro function. There are situations where you must exit the macro function. Most notably, you may want to leave the macro function when there is an error and you therefore do not want to do any further processing:

```
%macro sum_recs (in_data) ;
    %if &in_data = %then
    %do ;
        %put ERROR: Please supply a value for in_data ;
        %goto sum_exit ;
    %end ;
    ...
    ... 100 lines of code to process in_data
    ...
    %sum_exit:
%mend sum_recs ;
```

Unacceptable Use of the GOTO Construct

Here is an important warning for the reader. Do not use the computed %GOTO. It takes the form of:

```
%goto &guess ;
```

This is analogous to the computed GOTO of years gone by. As previously mentioned, conditionally branching to other parts of code is poor programming practice. The computed %GOTO has an additional diabolical feature. The programmer does not know the destination of the computed %GOTO while reading the source code!

Considerations for Variables

It is as important to be careful with organizing your DATA step variables as it is with organizing your code. Here are several salient points for organizing data.

Referencing Variables

Keep all references to a variable as close as possible to each other. Spreading references to a variable throughout a DATA step increases the chances of inadvertently modifying the variable. With the exception of macro code, which can create local macro variables, all variables are "alive" for the duration of the DATA step. A way to measure this effect is to evaluate the "span" of a variable. *Span* is the number of lines between the references to a variable. For example, if variable COUNTER is referenced at lines 7, 13, 14, and 16, then the variable has spans of 6, 1, and 2. In addition, you can calculate an average span as:

$$\text{average span} = (\text{sum of spans}) / (n - 1)$$
$$= (6 + 1 + 2) / (4 - 1) = 3$$

where n = the number of references to a variable. Ideally, you want to have a very small average span.

A related measurement is the lifetime of a variable. A variable's *lifetime* is the difference between the first and last time it is referenced within a module. Thus, if a variable is first referenced at line 12 and last referenced at line 112, its lifetime is 100 lines.

Persistence of Variables

Related to the concept of span and lifetime is the persistence of a variable. *Persistence* refers to a variable's longevity. In general, you want to strive for a short longevity because then there is less opportunity for a variable to cause data destruction. That is, as long as the variable is alive, it can corrupt another variable, or the variable itself can be corrupted. Ideally, you want a variable to do its job and then cease to exist. You can categorize the persistence of variables as the following lengths of their existence:

1. the entire SAS session. This includes global macro variables defined in your SAS AUTOEXEC file, as well as any automatic macro variables provided by SAS, such as &SYSTIME, &SYSDATE, &SYSLAST, and &SYSVER.

2. from creation time to the end of the SAS session. This includes global macro variables.

3. for as long as you want. This involves variables carried from the DATA step and PROC steps that produce an output data set.

4. for a block of code. This includes local macro variables and variables not carried forward in DATA steps and PROCS.

Here is a list of suggestions to help you minimize persistence (or the effect of persistence):

- Use the KEEP data set option or statement. While it can be debated as to whether KEEP or DROP is the better choice, KEEP is favored. One of the biggest problems leading to coding errors is that of carrying forward variables that no longer have a usefulness. All too often, programmers hurriedly change code by creating a working variable and then fail to clean up the environment. The odds are pretty good that they won't add it to the DROP list. A good habit is to run PROC CONTENTS after each DATA step when you think you are finished writing a program. If you are carrying excess baggage, this can help you find it and handle it accordingly.

- While KEEP is usually preferred over DROP, there are a couple of exceptions. For example, DROP may be useful when utility modules are written that require an input data set. Then (using the convention of leading underscores for utility variable names), you can simply DROP any variables that begin with a leading underscore. For a second example, you may use a procedure that collects extra variables, such as _TYPE_ or _FREQ_, which are not needed for further processing. In such a case, using DROP is quite acceptable.

- Don't modify a globally defined macro variable. Instead, move it to a working DATA step variable and modify the DATA step variable as needed:

```
namelist = "&namelist" ;
namelist = substr ( namelist, 1, 10 ) ;
```

or

```
namelist = substr ( "&namelist", 1, 10 ) ;
```

- In special cases, you might consider using a CALL SYMPUT routine instead of SET to do a secondary lookup. For instance, assume that you need one variable in one data set that resides in the first observation. The usual way of handling this involves two SET statements. The danger is that, if you don't use a KEEP statement on the lookup data set, you may carry unwanted variables into the Program Data Vector:

```
data _null_ ;
    set master ;

if _n_ = 1 then
    set lookup ;

if key_val = my_key then....
```

An alternate strategy is to carry forward a single macro variable:

```
data _null_ ;
    set lookup ;

call symput ( 'the_key', key_val ) ;
stop ;

run ;

data _null_ ;
    set master ;

if &the_key = my_key then.....
```

- Use local macro variables and explicitly define them as local in scope. If practical, write macro functions entirely with local variables (not DATA step variables). This can serve to minimize the side effects of a macro function.

- Don't define a macro variable as global unless it really is.

- Don't forget that you can use the KEEP option in both the SET statement and the DATA statement rather than on the DATA statement alone.

Initializing Variables

What causes improper variable initialization? Usually it is the result of one of the following scenarios:

Scenario 1: A variable was never assigned a value. You may have defined a variable with a LENGTH statement, but neglected to give it an initial value. For DATA step variables, you have several ways to initialize a variable:

- provide a value in an initialization routine

- use the RETAIN statement

- provide a value just before the variable is used.

Depending on the situation, any of these options might be the correct choice. But there are several considerations to keep in mind. When you use a RETAIN statement, a variable is set prior to any data being read, and so it is a safe way to ensure that all variables are initialized. RETAIN is most useful for initializing constants because there is no need to change their value. However, if these constants are global to the system, it is best to %INCLUDE them in the initialization segment of the DATA step.

The third option is preferable when initializing variables whose values may change. If the variable needs a default value, then you consider using an accompanying RETAIN statement. Structured programming theory suggests that the third choice (and a RETAIN statement, if appropriate) is often the best because it ensures that the variable is always initialized at the correct time.

Scenario 2: Another possibility is that a variable was initialized improperly. For example, a variable may be set according to another variable's value. In this example, a part code has three sections: part description (defined in a lookup table), location in file, and quantity in stock. To determine the location of the part, you search on the fifth through seventh character positions. For example, a sample part code may have a layout such as 1417-335-1917. Your code might read:

```
initpart = substr (  partcode, 6, 3 ) ;
```

Use this coding technique with caution because it is very sensitive to changes in data structure. A safer technique (though still sensitive to modifications in the data structure), used in conjunction with complete error checking, is either of the following:

```
initpart = scan ( partcode, 2 ) ;
```

or,

```
initpart = scan ( partcode, 2, "-" ) ;
```

Scenario 3: Assigning a value to a variable in an initialization routine without a concomitant RETAIN statement causes the variable to be reset to missing on the next execution of the DATA step.

Scenario 4: A duplication of variable names in the Program Data Vector could cause the initialized variable to be overwritten. Assume that, in this example, the data set OLDMONEY also contains the variable INIT_SUM. Apparently the programmer forgot about it. Hence, INIT_SUM has its value changed inadvertently:

```
data _null_ ;
    set newmoney ;

init_sum = 0 ;

if _n_ = 1 then
    set oldmoney ;

run ;
```

Measuring Software Quality

A good way to ascertain the overall structure and quality of a program is through a method called software metrics. This branch of computer science provides a tool for measuring structural quality and robustness of a system. Here are several major uses for software metrics:

- It can determine which modules are problematic and likely to be risky or difficult to modify.

- It can suggest when a module has become too complex and should be subdivided into one or more component modules.

- It can be used during the testing phase of the program to determine modules that are likely to be difficult to test.

- It can predict the number of errors likely to occur in a module.

This section describes several of the major software complexity metrics.

McCabe's Cyclomatic Complexity

McCabe's method measures logic complexity by counting the number of logic paths (Martin and McClure 1988, p.73):

```
if trial = "Phase 1" then
do ;
    if num_pats gt 100 then
        est_cost = "5 Million" ;
    else
    if num_pats gt 50 then
        est_cost = "3 Million" ;
    else
    if num_pats gt 20 then
        est_cost = "1 Million" ;
end ;
```

```
else
if trial = "Phase 2" then
do ;
     if num_pats gt 300 then
         est_cost = "25 Million" ;
     else
     if num_pats gt 150 then
         est_cost = "15 Million" ;
     else
     if num_pats gt 100 then
         est_cost = "10 Million" ;
end ;
else
if trial = "Phase 3" then
do ;
     if num_pats gt 1000 then
         est_cost = "75 Million" ;
     else
     if num_pats gt 500 then
         est_cost = "35 Million" ;
     else
     if num_pats gt 100 then
         est_cost = "20 Million" ;
end ;
```

To calculate the number of logic paths, count the number of IF statements and add 1. In the previous code fragment, there are 13 logic paths, so this piece of code has a cyclomatic complexity of 13. McCabe recommends a maximum cyclomatic complexity of 10 for one module. However, the logic in the previous example is pretty straightforward and intuitive. That code is probably not a violation of McCabe's theorem. Here is a more difficult construct:

```
if trial = "Phase 1" then
do ;
   if drug_cat = "Cardio" and ( site in ("South", "North" )) then
       est_cost = phaseval * site_fac ;
   else
   if drug_cat = "Cardio" and ( site in ("West", "East" )) then
       est_cost = max_val * site_fac ;
   else
   if drug_cat = "Renal" and center not in ("Sloan", "GT" ) then
       est_cost = max_val * site_fac ;
   else
   if drug_cat = "Renal" and  center in ("Sloan", "GT" ) then
       est_cost = ren_cost * num_pats * mark_up ;
end ;
else
```

```
          if trial = "Phase 2" then
              if drug_cat = "Cardio" or drug_cat = "Hormonal" then
                  if site = "West" and num_pats lt min_pats and num_pats gt
                    max_pats then
                          est_cost = ren_cost * num_pats * mark_up ;
                  else
                          est_cost = max_cost * num_pats * mark_up ;
          else
          if trial = "Phase 3" then
              if drug_cat = "Cardio" or drug_cat = "Hormonal" then
                  if site = "East" and num_pats lt min_pats and num_pats gt
                    max_pats then
                          est_cost = end_cost * num_pats * mark_up ;
                  else
                          est_cost = min_cost * num_drs * new_rate ;
```

In this example, the cyclomatic complexity is only 12, yet certainly it is much more difficult to manage than the previous example. Note also that this example has more AND/OR operators, which also adds to the complexity. In fact, McCabe has a modified version of this metric. Called Extended Cyclomatic Complexity, it also counts the number of AND/OR operators.

To reduce cyclomatic complexity, consider the following suggestions:

- Use formulas to calculate a value.

- Take advantage of PROC FORMAT to set up lookup tables.

- Consider using the SELECT statement, which is easier to read than nested IF-THEN-ELSE constructs.

- Break down complex IF-THEN-ELSE constructs by using the LINK statement to connect to internal subroutines.

McCabe's Essential Complexity

This metric measures how well a program is structured. It is a simple count of the number of GOTO statements that do not go directly to an exit statement (such as a label before a RETURN statement). The formula is:

Percent Structuredness = # returning branches / total branches

Obviously, you want 100% in any module.

Knot Count

This is an other measure of how well a program is structured. It measures the number of logic crossings created by GOTO statements. To determine the knot count, draw a line from the beginning to the end of each IF-THEN-ELSE construct. Then draw a line from each GOTO to its destination. Everywhere the lines intersect (indicated by an arrow) is considered a knot, as shown in Figure 7.4.

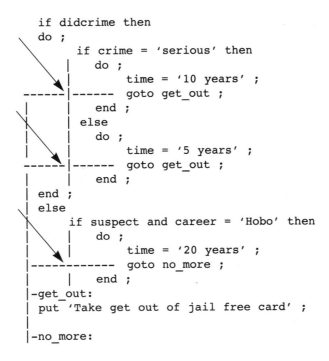

```
   if didcrime then
    do ;
        if crime = 'serious' then
    |      do ;
    |           time = '10 years' ;
------|------  goto get_out ;
 |    |      end ;
 |    |    else
 |    |      do ;
 |    |           time = '5 years' ;
------|------  goto get_out ;
 |    |      end ;
 | end ;
 | else
 |      if suspect and career = 'Hobo' then
 |    |      do ;
 |    |           time = '20 years' ;
|------------  goto no_more ;
 |    |      end ;
|-get_out:
| put 'Take get out of jail free card' ;
|
|-no_more:
```

Figure 7.4   *The GOTO statement creates a knot at the intersections.*

The above example has 3 knots. With few exceptions, as noted in the GOTO section, you can write most modules with a knot count of 0. If you must write a GOTO, minimize the knot count.

Halstead Software Science Metrics

Another measurement of software metrics is the Halstead Software Science Metrics (Martin and McClure 1988, p.71). This method is based on the calculation of program keywords and data variables. Here is a summary of the key statistics. Each of the counts is for a module or complete program:

<u>Length</u> = Total # of Operators + Total # of Operands

<u>Estimate Length</u> =
   (# Unique Operators * Log (# Unique Operators)) +
   (# Unique Operands * Log (# Unique Operands))

<u>Volume</u> = (Total # of Operators + Total # of Operands) *
      Log (# Unique Operators + # Unique Operands)

<u>Effort</u> = Volume / Language Level

where Language Level is a large number for a high-level language and is a small number for a low-level language. An exact value has not been quoted for the SAS language, although it should be relatively high.

In essence, the effort to develop a program is proportional to the code's Volume and is inversely proportional to the level of the language.

Scoring SAS Complexity

All of the previous metrics are useful tools for evaluating software complexity in general. In addition, all of these measurements are appropriate for the SAS programming language and are useful to measure the complexity of modules. However, it would be useful to tailor these metrics to SAS. The following evaluation is completely subjective, yet it can stir up some interesting discussion. Programmers' particular strengths and weaknesses will certainly affect their views of a module's complexity. For example, some programmers are uncomfortable with multidimensional arrays. But such arrays are not a problem for other programmer's, who happen to have strong visualization skills. Nevertheless, Figure 7.5 provides a rough guide.

More Complex

Hardcoded values without concomitant documentation

Array with three or more dimensions

Indirect macro variable reference with 3 or more ampersands

PROC TRANSPOSE

Multiple flags in a DATA step to control program flow

Two dimensional array

Multiple conditions that control DO-LOOP iterations

Indirect macro variable reference (i.e. two ampersands)

Macro functions

PROC SQL sub query

PROC SQL

MERGE

Macro quoting function

Less Complex

Figure 7.5 *SAS scoring complexity.*

Remember that many of the elements listed in Figure 7.5 can demonstrate extreme variability of complexity. For example, PROC SQL can be a simple request to select all variables, or it may involve complex joins and subqueries. Nonetheless, being aware that code can often be simplified goes a long way towards improving the readability of code.

Putting It All Together: Converting from Design to Structured Code

What is the procedure for converting from design to actual code? One popular way is to create an intermediate step that translates your design thoughts into English-like statements. After creating these English-like statements, you can then move directly into the coding step. Two methods (which are essentially identical) are called Pseudocode and Program Design Language (PDL). Here is the process described in greater detail:

Write a paragraph that describes the routine. Be specific about input, process, and output, and list them in that order. Now, rewrite the paragraph to include the details of error handling and module interface. Then, create a good name to describe the routine. Finally, write a header comment to describe the function of the routine. Don't hesitate to rewrite the paragraph as often as required to fine tune your thoughts.

First Cut

This routine calculates a professional baseball player's overall batting skill level and determines if the player is a good candidate for the Baseball Hall of Fame. Traditional evaluation systems underestimate the importance of power, hence this formula contains a heavier power weighting than normal. Data are input from an external file that contains virtually every batting statistic for each player. The player receives a total score and is evaluated as a possible candidate for the Hall of Fame.

Second Cut

This routine calculates a professional baseball player's overall batting skill level and determines if the player is a good candidate for the Baseball Hall of Fame. Data are input from an external file that contains fields for Career At-Bats, Batting Average, Slugging Average, On-Base Percentage, and Home Runs. The player's overall rating is based on these factors. In addition, adjustments are made for the epoch the player played in, as well as the ballpark and league. The module produces two outputs: an overall ranking score, and a "Yay" or "Nay" for a player's vote for his Hall of Fame candidacy.

Third Cut

This routine calculates a professional baseball player's overall batting skill level and determines if the player is a good candidate for the Baseball Hall of Fame. Data are input from an external file that resides on the C: drive and is named C:\STATS.DAT. The data are stored in character format:

Career At-Bats	column 1-6
Batting Average	column 7-9
Slugging Average	column 10-12
On-Base Percentage	column 13-15
Home Runs	column 16-19
League	column 20
Epoch	column 21
Ballpark	column 22-50

The player's overall rating is based on the following formula:

Rating =   (Career At-Bats /525 * 10) plus
             (Batting Average) plus
             (Slugging Average * 2) plus
             (On-Base Percentage * 1.5) plus
             (Home Runs * 3)

Rating is adjusted by:

Rating = Rating * 0.95 if American League
Rating = Rating * 1.10 if 1900–1960
Rating = Rating * 0.90 if 1961–1988
Rating = Rating * 0.88 if 1989 to present
Rating = Rating * Ballpark adjustment factor

In case there is any overlap, the rating is adjusted by At-Bats.

Output Parameters are (1) Rating factor (numeric) (2) Vote (1 byte) "Y" or "N" (3) Error Message (200 characters).

Final Cut

In addition to everything in the third cut, you add the following:

The module's name is HALLFAME. The input parameters to the routine are data variables for Career At-Bats, Batting Average, Slugging Average, On-Base Percentage, Home Runs, the League the player was in, the Epoch the player played in, and his home Ballpark. Data are passed to an internal subroutine because the program is not portable. The input parameters are not modified. If any of the input parameters is missing, then an error message returns; otherwise, the error message field is blank. Multiple error messages may be returned such that each message is separated by a slash. The vote field is set to "Y" if the player's overall rating exceeds 3000; otherwise, it is set to "N." If a player does not have a minimum of 5000 Career At-Bats, then the player is disqualified from consideration. Set his vote to missing and return an error message that the player does not have a sufficient number of at-bats to qualify. Note: For simplicity of calculations, assume that a ballplayer played for the same team, in one time period, and in the same ballpark his entire career.

Write the Pseudocode

Now translate the above ideas into pseudocode. It is important to use English-like statements. Avoid the use of computer lingo and especially any SAS expression or construct.

```
*************************************************************** ;
*** This routine calculates a baseball player's overall     *** ;
*** batting skill level and determines if a player is a      *** ;
*** a good candidate for the Baseball Hall of Fame.         *** ;
*************************************************************** ;

    set error message to empty
    set rating to empty
    set vote to empty
    input line containing variables for statistics
    if field for at bats, batting average, slugging average,
        on base percentage or home runs is missing then
        do
            set error message to indicate field is empty
            return from routine
        end
if at bats is lt 5000 then
        do
            set error message to indicate player not considered
            return from routine
        end

  rating =  ( at bats / avg plate appearances for season)
              X longevity factor +
              batting average +
              slugging average times 2 +
              on base percentage X 1.5 +
              home runs X 3

    rating = rating * league adjustment
    rating = rating * epoch adjustment
    rating = rating * park adjustment

    if rating greater than 3000 then
        vote = Yes
    else
        vote = No

    return from routine
```

Translate from Pseudocode to... Pseudocode??

Stop! Don't write the SAS code just yet. Now is the perfect time to walk through the logic carefully. Many errors can be discovered at this point. Refine the pseudocode until you are confident of the logic flow.

Translate from Pseudocode to SAS Code

The next step involves translating each line of pseudocode into one or more lines of SAS code directly below it:

```
************************************************************* ;
*** This routine calculates a baseball player's overall   *** ;
*** batting skill level and determines if a player is a    *** ;
*** a good candidate for the Baseball Hall of Fame.        *** ;
************************************************************* ;

set error message to empty
length err_msg $200 ;
err_msg = " " ;

set rating to empty
rating = . ;

set vote to empty
vote = " " ;

input line containing variables for statistics
filename stats "c:\stats.dat" ;

infile stats ;
input  @ 01 at_bats    $6.
       @ 07 bat_avg    $3.
       @ 10 slug_avg   $3.
       @ 13 on_base    $3.
       @ 16 homeruns   $4.
       @ 21 league     $1.
       @ 22 epoch      $1.
       @ 23 ballpark   $28.
       ;

if field for at bats, batting average, slugging average,
   on base percentage or home runs is missing then
   do
      set error message to indicate field is empty
      return from routine
   end

if at_bats = . then
     err_msg = trim ( left ( err_msg )) ||
       "At bats is missing/" ;
if bat_avg = . then
     err_msg = trim ( left ( err_msg )) ||
       "Bating average is missing/" ;
if slug_avg = . then
     err_msg = trim ( left ( err_msg )) ||
       "Slugging Average is missing/" ;
if on_base = . then
     err_msg = trim ( left ( err_msg )) ||
       "On Base Percentage is missing/" ;
if homeruns = . then
     err_msg = trim ( left ( err_msg )) ||
       "Home runs is missing/" ;
```

```
if at bats is lt 5000 then
do
    set error message to indicate player not considered
    return from routine
end
if at_bats lt 5000 then
    err_msg = trim ( left ( err_msg )) ||
        "Player ineligible, has less than 5000 at-bats" ;

if err_msg ne " " then
    return ;

rating =  ( at bats / avg plate appearances for season)
            X longevity factor +
            batting average +
            slugging average times 2 +
            on base percentage X 1.5 +
            home runs X 3

rating = (( at_bats / 550 ) * 10 ) +
        ( bat_avg )         +
        ( slug_avg * 2 )  +
        ( on_base * 1.5 ) +
        ( homeruns * 3 )
         ;

rating = rating * league adjustment
if league = american then
    rating = rating * .95 ;

rating = rating * epoch adjustment
if epoch = early then
    rating = rating * 1.10 ;
else
if epoch = middle then
    rating = rating * .90 ;
else
if epoch = late then
    rating = rating * .88 ;

rating = rating * park adjustment
rating =  rating * input ( put ( ballpark, parkadj. ), 6.2 )   ;

(Don't worry, we're going to move this later!)

proc format ;
value $parkadj
"Astrodome"     = 1.40
"Busch"         = 1.20
"Candlestick"   = 1.00
"Coors"         = 0.75
"Connie Mack"   = 1.10
"Forbes"        = 1.10
"Fenway"        = 0.85
"Fulton County" = 0.90
"Jack Murphy"   = 1.10
"Kingdome"      = 0.95
"Olympic"       = 1.00
```

```
"Polo Grounds"    = 1.20
"Skydome"         = 0.93
"Wrigley"         = 0.88
"Yankee Stadium"  = 1.20
;
run ;

if rating is greater than 3000 then
    vote = Yes
else
    vote = No

if rating gt 3000 then
    vote = "Y" ;
else
    vote = "N" ;

return from routine
return ;
```

Clean It Up

As a last step, do the following:

- Remove the pseudocode and replace it with comments.

- Replace literals in the code with variables.

- Rearrange any code to make it more readable.

```
************************************************************ ;
*** This routine calculates a baseball player's overall  *** ;
*** batting skill level and determines if a player is a   *** ;
*** a good candidate for the Baseball Hall of Fame.       *** ;
************************************************************ ;


************************************************************ ;
***   Create format to adjust the rating according to the  *** ;
***   park.  An "average" park has a rating of 1.00.  A     *** ;
***   park rated below 1.00 would be a hitter's ballpark and *** ;
***   a park rated higher than 1.00 would be a pitcher's    *** ;
***   ballpark                                              *** ;
************************************************************ ;

proc format ;
value $parkadj
"Astrodome"      = 1.40
"Busch"          = 1.20
"Candlestick"    = 1.00
"Coors"          = 0.75
"Connie Mack"    = 1.10
"Forbes"         = 1.10
"Fenway"         = 0.85
"Fulton County"  = 0.90
"Jack Murphy"    = 1.10
"Kingdome"       = 0.95
"Olympic"        = 1.00
"Polo Grounds"   = 1.20
```

```
"Skydome"         = 0.93
"Wrigley"         = 0.88
"Yankee Stadium"  = 1.20
;
run ;

filename stats "c:\stats.dat" ;

data _null_ ;

*********************************************************** ;
***                                                   *** ;
***                V A R I A B L E S                  *** ;
***                                                   *** ;
*********************************************************** ;

length err_msg $200 ;      * Collect errors in message field   ;

retain american   "A" ;    * American league                   ;
retain al_adj     .95 ;    * Adjustment for American league    ;
retain early      "E" ;    * Early baseball period             ;
retain earlyfac 1.10 ;     * Adjust for early epoch 1900-1960  ;
retain hr_fac       3 ;    * Home run factor                   ;
retain late       "L" ;    * Late baseball period              ;
retain late_fac   .88 ;    * Mod period adjust 1989 to present ;
retain mid_fac    .90 ;    * Middle time period adjust 1961-1988 ;
retain long_fac    10 ;    * Adjustment for player longevity   ;
retain middle     "M" ;    * Middle baseball period            ;
retain min_bats 5000 ;     * Minimum At bats to qualify for Hall ;
retain obp_fac    1.5 ;    * On Base Percentage factor         ;
retain seasbats   525 ;    * Average number of At bats in a season;
retain slug_fac     2 ;    * Slugging factor                   ;
retain vote_fac 3000 ;     * Score required for Yes vote for Hall ;
....
link rating ;
...
SAS code to print report
...
return ;

rating:

*********************************************************** ;
*** Initialize return variables.                      *** ;
*********************************************************** ;

err_msg = " " ;
rating  = . ;
vote    = " " ;

*********************************************************** ;
*** Input player statistics.                          *** ;
*********************************************************** ;

infile stats ;

input @ 01 at_bats    $6.
      @ 07 bat_avg    $3.
```

```
            @ 10 slug_avg    $3.
            @ 13 on_base     $3.
            @ 16 homeruns    $4.
            @ 21 league      $1.
            @ 22 epoch       $1.
            @ 23 ballpark    $28.
            ;

**************************************************************** ;
*** If any variable used to calculate the player rating is  *** ;
*** missing, then append the error message to the error     *** ;
*** message line.                                           *** ;
**************************************************************** ;

if at_bats = . then
    err_msg = trim ( left ( err_msg )) ||
      "At bats is missing/" ;
if bat_avg = . then
    err_msg = trim ( left ( err_msg )) ||
      "Batting Avg. is missing/" ;
if slug_avg= . then
    err_msg = trim ( left ( err_msg )) ||
      "Slugging Avg. is missing/" ;
if on_base = . then
    err_msg = trim ( left ( err_msg )) ||
      "On Base % is missing/" ;
if homeruns = . then
    err_msg = trim ( left ( err_msg )) ||
      "Home runs is missing/" ;

**************************************************************** ;
*** If the player does not have the minimum number of      *** ;
*** at-bats to qualify for a rating, then return to calling *** ;
*** routine by setting an error message.                   *** ;
**************************************************************** ;

if at_bats lt min_bats then
    err_msg = trim ( left ( err_msg )) || "Player ineligible," ||
      " not enough at-bats/" ;

**************************************************************** ;
*** If an error is detected, return to the calling routine. *** ;
**************************************************************** ;

if err_msg ne " " then
    return ;

**************************************************************** ;
*** Calculate the player's base rating irrespective of any  *** ;
*** adjustment factors.                                     *** ;
**************************************************************** ;

rating =    ( at_bats / seasbats) * long_fac    +
            ( bat_avg )                          +
            ( slug_avg * slug_fac )              +
            ( on_base  * obp_fac )               +
            ( homeruns * hr_fac )
            ;
```

```
**************************************************************** ;
*** Adjust for the league.  There is evidence that the   *** ;
*** leagues do not yield the equivalent amount of runs.   *** ;
**************************************************************** ;

if  league = american then
    rating = rating * al_adj ;

**************************************************************** ;
*** Adjust for the epoch that the player played in. Hitting *** ;
*** has waxed and waned over the years.              *** ;
**************************************************************** ;

if epoch = early then
    rating = rating * earlyfac ;
else
if epoch = middle then
    rating = rating * mid_fac ;
else
if epoch = late then
    rating = rating * late_fac ;

**************************************************************** ;
*** Adjust for the ballpark factor.                  *** ;
**************************************************************** ;

rating =  rating * input ( put ( ballpark, parkadj. ), 6.2 )  ;

**************************************************************** ;
*** Decide if the player gets into the hall of fame, by com- *** ;
*** paring his rating against the critical standard factor. *** ;
**************************************************************** ;

if rating gt vote_fac then
    vote = "Y" ;
else
    vote = "N" ;

return ;

run ;
```

Several important concepts come to light after using Pseudocode:

- Probably the greatest benefit of using PDL is that you can discover logic and design errors along the way. For instance, the error message field was designed a little differently than usual. Normally, when discovering an error, you might consider returning immediately to the calling routine. Here, the programmer tried to be more user friendly by collecting all the errors in the error message field and then returning after the completion of error checking. You may have realized, early on, that it is very easy to overflow the message field.

- Documentation is written while you are coding, not later (which may translate to never).

- You can check your logic at any stage along the way. You may want to give your pseudocode to a team member for a critique of the analysis and design. While you may feel defensive about your code, your ego could permit a scrutiny of your design.

Summary

Using the individual SAS constructs correctly results in more reliable code. Just like a team working together toward a common goal, the individual program statements are not simply stand-alone entries. They, too, must work as part of a functional unit. By using these concepts, you can decrease coding errors and your modifications can be more straightforward.

Exercises

1. Under what circumstances are the LEAVE and CONTINUE constructs recommended?

2. In general, you don't want to nest IF-THEN-ELSE constructs beyond three levels. How can you rework code to minimize nesting?

3. A variable's persistence refers to its longevity. How do you minimize a variable's persistence?

4. Why is Pseudocode an effective method of translating design thoughts into SAS code?

5. What are the principal causes of improper variable initialization?

6. Why is measuring software complexity a valuable tool for analyzing your code? In your opinion, is metric complexity more useful as a prospective tool (future programs) or as a retrospective tool (to analyze the current project)?

7. Why are formats generally preferred over nested IF-THEN-ELSE constructs?

8. Suggest one way to rework this code fragment so it is easier to read and maintain:

```
if ( prelim = &fever or prelim = &rash ) and
   ( nitetime = &chills or nitetime = &sweats ) and
   ( signs = &pale or signs = &flushed ) then
        call = urgent ;
```

9. Why is it important that the span of a variable be minimized?

10. When is GOTO an acceptable construct?

References

Ashcroft E. and Manna Z. (1979), "The Translation of 'Go To' Programs to 'While' Programs," *Classics in Software Engineering*, ed. E.N. Yourdon, New York: Yourdon Press.

Bycer, B.B. (1975), *Flowcharting: Programming, Software Designing, and Computer Problem Solving*, New York: John Wiley & Sons.

Ejiogu, L.O. (1983), *Structured Programming*, New York: Petrocelli.

Hopkins, M.E. (1979),"A Case for the Go To," *Classics in Software Engineering*, ed. E.N. Yourdon, New York: Yourdon Press.

Hughes, J.K. and Mithtom, J.I. (1977), *A Structured Approach to Programming*, Englwood Cliffs, NJ: Prentice-Hall.

Linger, R.C., Mills, H.D. and Witt, B.I. (1979), *Structured Programming: Theory and Practice*, Reading, MA: Addison-Wesley.

McGowan, C.L. and Kelly, J.R. (1975), *Top-Down Structured Programming Techniques*, New York: Van Nostrand Reinhold.

Martin, J. and McClure, C. (1988), *Structured Techniques: The Basis for CASE*, Englewood Cliffs, NJ: Prentice-Hall.

Orr, K.T. (1977), *Structured Systems Development*, New York: Yourdon Press.

Tausworthe, R.C. (1977), *Standardized Development of Computer Software*, Englewood Cliffs, NJ: Prentice-Hall.

Ullman, J.D. (1976), *Fundamental Concepts of Programming Systems*, Reading, MA: Addison-Wesley.

Weiland, R.J. (1983), *The Programmer's Craft*, Reston, VA: Reston Publishing.

Wolf, W.A. (1979), "A Case against the Go To," *Classics in Software Engineering*, ed. E.N. Yourdon, New York: Yourdon Press.

Yourdon, E. and Constantine, L.L. (1979), *Structured Design Fundamentals of a Discipline of Computer Program and Systems Design*, Englewood Cliffs, NJ: Prentice-Hall.

Zelkowitz, M.V., Shaw, A.C. and Gannon, J.D. (1979), *Principles of Software Engineering and Design*, Englewood Cliffs, NJ: Prentice-Hall.

Chapter 8   # System Coding Principles

Introduction **152**

System Coding Principles **152**
  Strive for Simplicity 152
  Code Defensively 153
  Handle Missing Values Consistently 154
  Centralize Coding Changes 155
  Allow for Field Expansion 156
  Think about Long Term Maintenance 156
  If You Are Going to Automate, Then Automate! 157
  Some Things Just Can't Be Coded 159
  Pretend You Are the Customer 159
  Hide the Details from the Code 160
  Define Standards for Status Variables 161
  Keep Modules Small and Simple 161
  Don't Hardcode, Don't Hardcode ... but if you must 162

Table-Driven Code **163**

Error Handling **165**
  Where to Route Error Messages 165
  Where to Perform Error Checking 165

Dynamic Code **166**

Seamless Coding **169**

System Coding Concerns **174**
  Black Box Systems: Good or Bad? 174
  Data Duplication 175
  System Control Flags 176
  Portrait and Landscape Printing 177

Initialization Options for Customized Software **178**
  Utilize the SAS AUTOEXEC and CONFIG Files 178
  Utilizing a %INCLUDE Startup File 179
  Create a Startup Shell that Runs an Initialization Program 180

A Reporting System **180**
  Segregate Titles and Footnotes 180
  Eliminate Coding Steps 181
  Allow for Flexibility in Routing Output 182

Code Generators: Reporting at the Next Level **184**

Summary **186**

Exercises **187**

References **187**

Introduction

For many of us, programming is coding. So far, this book has suggested that you postpone coding in order to ensure that you first lay the proper foundation with good design, project management, and documentation. This chapter is not a lesson on SAS coding techniques per se, but rather a philosophy of coding that is paramount for building a complete software system.

System Coding Principles

This section presents a number of principles that are vital for building a complete software system.

Strive for Simplicity

Don't confuse coding with diving, ballet, or figure skating. There are no points allotted for elegance. The code with the least amount of complexity, trickery, or fancy constructs is simply the easiest to maintain. Several suggestions for simplifying your code structure include:

1. Minimize the internal communication hooks on a project. Every time you introduce a new interface, the complexity increases. This does not contradict the earlier point that modularity simplifies a project. In general, modularity is advantageous, but this is true only to a point. If you overmodularize, such that you are breaking down each source module into a few lines of code, then you actually increase the complexity. When you overmodularize, data must pass through more channels, and each of these channels must be wide open and without ambiguity.

2. Minimize the external communication hooks on a project. Often, you have opportunities to introduce other languages or software packages into a project. It is best to avoid this practice whenever possible. At first, using other languages or software might look like a quick fix to a difficult problem. But that is often all these are—quick fixes. Use your creativity. Most likely, the SAS programming language by itself can solve your problem. The SAS Technical Support line, the World Wide Web, and online bulletin boards can all supply you with a number of useful ideas that you probably never thought of before.

3. Resist using a construct just because it is your favorite. There is a tendency to try to do a project with a limited subset of the SAS language because you may become convinced that it is the only proper tool. Some programmers try to do everything with PROC SQL, or with macros or PROC TABULATE or PROC REPORT or DATA _NULL_ or PROC FORMAT. It is pretty interesting to see some of the code that has been written using clever techniques. Unfortunately, programmers sometimes forget that there is often a much simpler way to accomplish a task. Being a well rounded SAS user improves your ability to select the right tool for the job.

Code Defensively

Moving from ad hoc programming to systems development requires a shift in mind set. There is a good chance that you or someone else on the team will modify the program in the future. This translates into *defensive coding*, which is code written to prevent problems that may result from any of the following:

- changes in data passed into the program

- changes in the program specifications

- changes in code that interface with the routine

- changes in the coding algorithm.

One of the most obvious examples of defensive programming is the use of the LENGTH statement to avoid truncation. Here is an example of a forgotten LENGTH statement:

```
fruit  = "Peach" ;
fruit  = "Watermelon" ;
veggie = "Onion" ;
veggie = "Green beans" ;
put "My favorite veggie/fruit combo is " veggie fruit ;
```

This program prints "Green Water" as your favorite combo. Hmmm.

Positioning of the LENGTH statement is critical. For example, suppose that you are developing a module that requires a LENGTH statement for a new variable. During unit testing, you can leave the variable definition in the module. However, when you are confident that the module is working properly, you can then move the LENGTH statement into the calling program, preferably at the top of the source code. Improper positioning of the LENGTH statement can result in unexpected truncation of these variables.

Failing to use the RETAIN statement is certainly one of the silliest bugs that plague the SAS community. In fact, they can be elusive bugs because the variable in question may be re-initialized on many, but not all, DATA step iterations. This may happen, for example, when a variable is reset for a new BY group without using a RETAIN statement. Most variables need to be retained anyway, so you may want to declare it at the beginning of the program. This also provides an opportunity for you to provide subsequent readers with a helpful comment:

```
RETAIN arti_cnt 0 ;   * Geological artifact count in Egypt ;
```

Never assume proper data alignment. For example, data might be justified left, justified right, or it might contain one or more leading spaces, and so on. To ensure that functions work properly, the combination of TRIM and LEFT is quite handy:

```
rc = index ( find_me, trim ( left ( now_ican))) ;
```

Similarly, you may wish to add the UPCASE or LOWCASE function to ensure that comparisons are made properly:

```
if upcase ( my_word ) = upcase ( yourword ) then
```

Handle Missing Values Consistently

Handling missing values properly is part of ERROR processing, and it requires careful thought. Do you want missing values to be handled without a warning, at a warning level, or at a complete error level? You must establish this convention prior to coding. It is easy to shrug off missing data as someone else's problem. After all, the data came in as missing, why should you worry about it? Unfortunately, missing data is often a symptom of a more serious situation.

You can easily ignore missing data by using forgiving constructs such as the SUM function:

```
fish_wt = sum ( fish_wt, fishstix ) ;
```

or you might prefer only to log such data with a warning:

```
if fish_wt = . or fishstix = . then
do ;
    file errorlog ;
    put 'missing values for variables' / _all_ ;
    file log ;
end ;
else
    fish_wt = sum ( fish_wt, fishstix ) ;
```

or you can treat missing data as serious errors and stop processing:

```
if fish_wt= . or fishstix = . then
do ;
    file errorlog ;
    put 'ERROR: missing values for variables' / _all_ ;
    stop ;
end ;
else
    fish_wt = sum ( fish_wt, fishstix ) ;
```

In most cases, you should log missing values at least once, and present this problem to the originator of the data for possible cleanup. It's considered good programming courtesy.

Speaking of missing data, you also need a graceful way of handling missing data on input. There are three ways to handle missing input using the INFILE statement. The FLOWOVER option is the default. It permits reading of data on the next line. However, this option is rarely satisfactory. If you allow input to wrap to subsequent records, then you are probably not familiar with the file format and not adjusting accordingly. Using the MISSOVER option is somewhat better because it prevents SAS from reading to the next line, but it still permits processing without error. Early on in the project, you might be content to use the FLOWOVER or MISSOVER option, but once you have a handle on the data and you have coded accordingly, you probably want to set the STOPOVER option when the code is in production.

Note: A fourth option, TRUNCOVER, is not really meant to handle missing data. Rather, it is a convenient way to handle input that might be shorter than expected. Its use should be application dependent. At times, a short field is acceptable; other times, it is not.

Take WARNINGS on the log seriously. In order to avoid the "crying wolf syndrome," try to suppress meaningless WARNINGS.

Centralize Coding Changes

As discussed in previous chapters, achieving modularity is essential for system building. Consider the following situation:

Marianne develops a brilliant program which, among its many functions, automatically formats SAS output into a WordPerfect document. Wind of this program spreads quickly, and others on the team are anxious to use her code. Marianne tells them the program name, and the programmers copy the appropriate sections of her code into their own programs (see Figure 8.1).

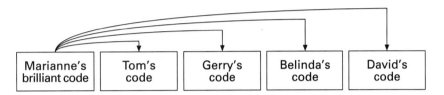

Figure 8.1   *The incorrect way to use common code.*

Marianne's work is so good that a competitor woos her to their organization for a substantial increase in pay. Two months later, Belinda discovers a bug in the "brilliant" code. However, there are now at least four copies of the code that exist in various and sundry forms in other programmers' programs. The team knows how to make the fix, but now the fix must be manually applied to everyone's program because the code was incorporated in different ways. Also, a couple of other programmers copied the code, unbeknownst to the programming team. Thus, their copies also contain this bug.

Here is an alternative means of using common code. Marianne should have copied her "brilliant" code into a centralized %INCLUDE library. Then any programmer can simply %INCLUDE that code into their program at the appropriate point. If the code has to be changed for any reason, then only one copy (the master in the %INCLUDE library) must be changed (see Figure 8.2).

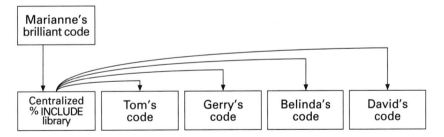

Figure 8.2   *The correct way to use common code.*

Remember, before copying someone else's code into your program, consider if the code may be reusable.

Allow for Field Expansion

Isn't it curious how highways are expanded? Suppose that an eight lane highway is increased by two lanes. Two years later, the highway needs further widening. Now, the total cost for two expansions is far greater than if the highway had been widened appropriately in the first place.

Programmers seem to fall into this same trap, protecting what they perceive as precious bytes of disk space. This leads to one of the subtlest forms of programming bugs. You can become so obsessed with efficiency (that is, saving a few bytes of storage) that you can easily introduce "overflow" errors that escape detection. Suppose that you define an employee key as containing two parts: marital status (MAR_STAT) and employee number (EMP_NUM).

```
mar_stat = "S" ;
emp_cnt = 100 ;

length emp_num $3 ;

emp_num= mar_stat || trim ( left ( emp_cnt )) ;
```

In this case, the value of EMP_NUM is truncated to "S10" rather than what was expected, "S100".

Think about Long Term Maintenance

In order for code to be robust, it should be able to handle any changes in the input data. For example, if an array has 17 elements, you can code:

```
do i = 1 to 17 ;
```

or you can make that code more dynamic:

```
do i = 1 to dim ( food_ary ) ;
```

or you can code the following equivalent, when the lower dimension does not start at 1:

```
do i = lbound ( food_ary ) to hbound ( food_ary ) ;
```

Incidentally, there is usually no need to hardcode values for the array dimensions because you can calculate them:

```
data _null_ ;
....
retain max_len ;
max_len = max ( max_len, length ( trim ( left ( the_var )))) ;
call symput ( 'fld_size', '$' || trim (left (max_len ))) ;
call symput ( 'ary_size', arraycnt ) ;
run ;

data _null_ ;
...
array my_ary { &ary_size } &fld_size _temporary_ ;
...
run ;
```

If You Are Going To Automate, Then Automate!

The entire purpose of using computers is to automate. Very often, it is tempting to automate part of the process and then finish the rest of the program manually. Here is an example where report output has a variable number of report columns. Sample report output might look like the following:

```
                ASPIRIN        ACETAMINOPHEN        PLACEBO
#Adverse          17               27                  7
Events
```

In contrast, a second report might look like this:

```
                VASODILATOR          PLACEBO
#Adverse            44                 26
Events
```

To automate the system, you can create a macro:

```
%macro ae_summ ( rpt_cnt = ,
                 severity = ,
                 druglist = ) ;
    ...
    data _null_ ;
    ...
    link header ;
    return ;
    ...
    header:
    ...
    return ;

    run ;
    ...
%mend ae_summ ;
```

and then invoke the macro as follows:

```
%ae_summ ( rpt_cnt = 1 ,
           severity = 4 ,
           druglist = %str(ASPIRIN, ACETAMINOPHEN, PLACEBO))

%ae_summ ( rpt_cnt = 2 ,
           severity = 4 ,
           druglist = %str (VASODILATOR, PLACEBO))
```

... and so on, for all 30 reports.

By now, you're pretty proud of yourself because your creation of a macro has eliminated a lot of repetitive coding. However, as a cheat, you code the HEADER routine in the above macro as:

```
header:
if &rpt_cnt = 1 then
      put @025 "ASPIRIN" @045 "ACETAMINOPHEN" @065 "PLACEBO" ;
else
if &rpt_cnt = 2 then
      put @040 "VASODILATOR" @070 "PLACEBO" ;
```

. . . and so on, for all 30 reports.

However, there is no need to manually calculate column locations for all of the variable headings. All of this can be automated. For example, start by setting up a few variables at the top of the program:

```
%let leftside = 20 ;   * Left side of columnar data begin here  ;
%let var_wid  =  20 ;  * Allocated space for one field           ;
%let rite_mar = 120 ;  * Right margin                            ;
%let page_wid = 70 ;   * Page width for variables                ;
```

Then, determine how many variables need to be printed:

```
length med_name $50 ;

if _n_ = 1 then
do ;
    drug_cnt = 1 ;
    do until ( med_name = " " ) ;
        med_name = scan ("&druglist", drug_cnt ) ;
        drug_cnt + 1 ;
    end ;
    drug_cnt = drug_cnt - 2 ;
end ;
```

Then, calculate the space between the variable fields:

```
blockgap =  int ( ( &page_wid - ( drug_cnt * &var_wid )) /
                ( drug_cnt - 1 )) ;
```

Now, the headings can be placed properly:

```
med_cnt = 1 ;

do until ( med_name = " " ) ;
    med_name = scan ("&druglist", med_cnt ) ;
    the_len = length ( trim ( left ( med_name))) ;
    spaces = int ((( &var_wid ) - the_len ) / 2 ) ;
    the_loc = &leftside + ((( med_cnt - 1 ) * blockgap )) +
            ((( med_cnt - 1 ) * &var_wid )) +
            + spaces + 1 ;
    if med_name ne " " then
        put @the_loc med_name  @ ;
    med_cnt + 1 ;
end ;

put ;
```

This method requires more work than does the original version. But it allows much more flexibility. It is immaterial whether you have to print two, three, or six variables. The program automatically calculates the appropriate header and its position. Also, if you need to change the left and right margins because of other layout changes, you can simply modify the macro variables at the top of the program.

Some Things Just Can't Be Coded

Fortunately, almost every kind of problem lends itself to a data processing solution. But some things are just better left alone. Here is an example of a programmer trying to be too clever. Assume that a comment field lists information about a patient's medical condition. You want to generate a listing of all those patients who have low blood sugar. Hence, you code the following:

```
comment = left ( upcase ( comment )) ;
find1 = index ( trim ( comment), "LOW BLOOD SUGAR" ) ;
find2 = index ( trim ( comment), "HYPOGLYCEMIA" ) ;
find3 = index ( trim ( comment), "LOW SUGAR" ) ;
...
find27 = ...
if find1 gt 0 or find2 gt 0 or.... then
     lowsugar = "Y" ;
```

However, this kind of code is fallible for a number of reasons:

- You cannot account for misspelled words.

- The word order is not determinable. You can't predict all the various and sundry representations.

- Negatives can wreak havoc with the logic.

Rather, it is better to manually examine the fields and set the low sugar field with a set of IF-THEN-ELSE statements. This code belongs in a %INCLUDE module (where you would put any code that contains literals and is not portable).

Pretend You Are the Customer

Before laying out a report or screen, think about how the customer is going to use your product. Apparently minor details in layout can mean the difference between a user-friendly product and a clunky one. For example, consider how you are going to format the date. If the dates are listed in chronological order, then using a format such as DATE7. will yield values such as:

```
12SEP89
02JAN90
22MAR90
```

This output does not provide good visual separation, and it requires considerable effort on the part of readers, who have to mentally calculate the difference between dates. On the other hand, using a format such as MMDDYY8. yields

```
09/12/89
01/10/90
03/22/90
```

This output more readily allows readers to scan for differences in dates.

Hide the Details from the Code

Coding involves many choices. In general, you want to select a method that is flexible, free from errors, and easy to understand. In the following example, age brackets are devised according to age. You can simply write code to select for age brackets using the SELECT statement:

```
select ;
    when ( age >= 1 and age  <=5  ) bracket = 1 ;
    when ( age >= 6 and age  <=10 ) bracket = 2 ;
    when ( age >= 11 and age <=15 ) bracket = 3 ;
    when ( age >= 16 and age <=20 ) bracket = 4 ;
    when ( age >= 21 and age <=25 ) bracket = 5 ;
    otherwise bracket = . ;
end ;
```

The biggest drawback of this method is that if age brackets are calculated in multiple places, then all these code fragments would have to be modified in case of an enhancement. A better method is to table the values. This ensures that all changes can be made in one place. PROC FORMAT would do just fine for this case:

```
proc format ;
    value bracket
    1-5   = 1
    6-10  = 2
    11-15 = 3
    16-20 = 4
    21-25 = 5
    other = .
    ;
run ;
```

The last (and arguably the best) method is to calculate the value whenever possible:

```
if age ge 1 or age lt 26 then
    bracket = ceil ( age / 5 ) ;
else
    bracket = . ;
```

Because "5" isn't very informative, you can also code this as:

```
if age ge 1 and age lt 26 then
    bracket = ceil ( age / &year_int) ;
else
    bracket = . ;
```

where the macro variable YEAR_INT is defined either (a) within the program if the value is used just once, or (b) in an initialization file if it is a variable likely to be used throughout a system:

```
%let year_int = 5 ; * Number of years in age bracket interval ;
```

Similar code can be set for the upper and lower bounds of the age.

What is the biggest advantage of using calculations? You avoid the risk of making a typographical error either in inline code or when creating tables.

Define Standards for Status Variables

At times, maintaining the status of certain system events is imperative. As a result, you can create status type variables. The status often requires more than two states. One common error is to create a variable that is simply an "on/off" switch. For example, suppose that you create a routine that returns the status of a record search. Your original status codes might be classified as "Good"/"Bad" or "Successful"/"Not Successful". This leads to maintenance problems later on when you need to differentiate between the messages "End-of-file" and "Record not found, but not End-of-file". One possible solution is to set up formats for input/output file handling. For example:

```
proc format ;
value file_io
    1 = "End of File"
    2 = "Record not found"
    3 = "Record found"
    4 = "Invalid input parameter"
    ... and so on.
    ;
run ;
```

Or, you can specify macro variables in an initialization file:

```
%let end_file = 1 ;
%let notfound = 2 ;
%let found    = 3 ;
%let bad_parm = 4 ;
... and so on.
```

This allows you to use mnemonic names throughout the program:

```
if last_rec then
    status = &end_file ;
...
if status = &end_file then ...
```

Keep Modules Small and Simple

Programmers tend to try to do everything with only a few DATA steps. To simplify the coding, try to minimize the number of functions for each DATA step. A good candidate for simplification is the DATA _NULL_ step used to generate reports. Instead of formatting all the output fields within the DATA NULL step, try to do that prior to the step. Most DATA _NULL_ steps tend to be busy. Let the DATA _NULL_ simply handle the code to output all the fields required for the report.

There is an additional advantage to this approach, and it relates to quality assurance. Suppose that you develop two versions of a program. If you perform all calculations and formatting prior to the DATA _NULL_ step, then you can simply run a PROC COMPARE of the final SAS data sets created. If, on the other hand, calculations and formatting occur in the final step, then additional manual checking needs to be done to determine the source of the differences. This may include the additional check of running a source file comparison.

Don't Hardcode, Don't Hardcode...but if you must...

Hardcoding data is strongly contraindicated when building structured systems. For example, deciding how to organize data as lookup tables has many faces. If the number of choices is small, you can use a series of IF-THEN-ELSE statements, such as:

```
if monitor = "Melton 2000" then
    resolute = "1024 X 768" ;
else
if monitor = "Norwalk 440" then
    resolute = "640 X 440" ;
else
if monitor = "Parlinto" then
    resolute = "1224 X 900" ;
else
if monitor = "Stanton-D" then
    resolute = "1024 X 768" ;
else
        put "Invalid Monitor type" ;
```

The biggest disadvantage of this kind of coding technique is that the details of the table are "buried" within the code. This can make maintenance difficult. To improve the modularity, you can recode this as a format lookup:

```
proc format ;
value $res
"Melton 2000"    = "1024 X 768"
"Norwalk 440"    = "640 X 440"
"Parlinto"       = "1224 X 900"
"Stanton-D"      = "1024 X 768"
other            = "Invalid type"
;

resolute = put ( monitor, $res. ) ;
```

Hopefully, you are convinced by now that hardcoding is a dangerous practice. However, the complete elimination of hardcoding is not always possible. For example, suppose that a database transfers data to a group of SAS data sets. Perhaps there is a problem with the data and the original database cannot, or will not, be fixed. Now you are on your own. In addition to the difficulty of maintaining hardcoded data, there is the danger of contaminating other source modules. You might find that you have to code something like:

```
if cust_num = '683824' and status = "Not available" then
    status = "Accepted" ;
```

You have two better (and safer) options:

1. As mentioned in Chapter 3, "Managing the Project," you can create two libraries of SAS data. The data originally transferred from the database is moved into a library called ORIGDATA. Then, data can be reformatted to your liking and moved into a library called DATA. This is a good time to handle hardcodes. To do so, create a module and call it NEWDATA. Enter the harcoded data in this module. Then, when you start a new project, you simply create another version of NEWDATA. In this way, hardcodes are not accidentally copied over into a new project.

2. The other option is to place all hardcoding into %INCLUDE modules (that have names such as HCODE_01, HCODE_02, HCODE_03, and so on) and to define the fileref in the initialization file. In this way, when the source code is copied to another destination, there is little chance that the hardcodes will be pulled in inadvertently. Because the initialization file is always in the driver module, the filerefs pointing to the hardcodes are immediately obvious.

Table-Driven Code

Modern programming emphasizes flexibility and customization. In order to achieve this goal, all literal references to data must be removed from the code and placed into sets of tables. These tables are typically set up in one module or, with larger systems, in several modules. Then, when a change is required, most revisions can be handled by modifying only the master tables. A concomitant feature of table-driven code is that literals are removed from the source code. Everything is calculated, no matter how trivial.

In the following example, an advertising agency is interested in determining the effects of various promotional pieces and then the effect of those pieces on sales. The agency is likely to be interested in generating descriptive statistics for its mailing pieces to determine which promotional pieces are more effective than others. You can drive this routine by setting up parameter lists in the driver or initialization module as follows:

```
%let weeklist = 1 2 4 8 12 16 ;
%let promo    = 1 2 17 19 23 ;
```

Then, within the reporting program, you can simply process these parameter lists to generate the necessary reports. The major advantage of this approach is that multiple programs can read this one parameter list. When you are ready for a change, you simply change the parameter list in one place, thus automatically updating all the programs.

You may be wondering why WEEKLIST and PROMO are not calculated by reading the input data. The reason is that data are rarely clean. By using the raw data to create the parameter list, the program expects values where they do not exist. Here is how you can use the WEEKLIST and PROMO parameters in a program:

```
%macro rpt_loop ;

    %local i j ;

    *********************************************************** ;
    *** The outer loop moves through the weeks of the mailing  *** ;
    *** promotion.  The inner loop moves through the list of   *** ;
    *** promotions                                             *** ;
    *********************************************************** ;

        %let i = 1 ;
        %do %until ( %scan ( &weeklist, &i ) = )   ;
            %let j = 1 ;
            %do %until ( %scan ( &promo, &j ) = )   ;
                data final ;
                    set promo
                    ( where = ( promo = %scan (&promo, &J ) and
                                week =  %scan (&weeklist, &i ))) ;
                run ;
                proc summary nway data = final ;
                    by promo ;
                    output out = finalrpt ( drop = _type_ _freq_ )
                                    min = minsale  max = maxsale
                                    std = stdsale  mean = meansale ;
                    var sales ;
                run ;
                proc print data = finalrpt ;
                run ;
                %let j = %eval ( &j + 1 ) ;
            %end ;
            %let i = %eval ( &i + 1 ) ;
        %end ;
%mend rpt_loop ;

    *********************************************************** ;
    *** Report the results of marketing promotions.           *** ;
    *********************************************************** ;

%rpt_loop
```

Error Handling

At least half of the code in a major system is devoted to error handling. Hence, it is imperative to have a consistent strategy for handling error situations. Two major strategies are:

- Abort the program and send the user a detailed description of the problem.

- Issue a warning and continue execution of the program.

In either case, you must develop conventions for error messages.

Where To Route the Error Messages

One issue you should consider as you develop your error handling strategy is the question of where to route error messages. If it is a critical error and the user is expecting output in the output queue, then you should route the message there. If you are running a batch run of the complete system, then route all warnings and errors to a special error file. You can use this format to define a master error log in the initialization file:

```
filename errorlog "filespec"  ;  * master error file ;
```

In addition, you may want to define error files for individual programs. You certainly can use the log file and then route it to disk. This involves creating a log directory and then routing to it all files with a .log extension. For example, if the source module is ELEMENT.SAS, then the log file is routed to the log subdirectory and is named ELEMENT.LOG. If you decide to use the log file for messages, then you want to ensure that your error messages don't get lost. You can mimic the SAS convention of prefixing all error messages with ERROR, or you can create your own. Just be consistent, and start with a keyword that you can search on, such as "ERROR FOUND".

Where to Perform Error Checking

When you design the system, you must also decide where you want to perform the error checking. One strategy is to run pre-filter programs that run through all the data sets and report potential errors. While this method does not obviate the need to include error trapping within individual modules, it can be beneficial for a variety of reasons:

- You can report your results back to the database administrator, who can clean up the data. The administrator certainly would appreciate an ordered list of error messages as opposed to being bothered randomly every time you find a potential error in the system.

- Running this kind of program early in the project helps you to become very familiar with the data.

- The act of creating this kind of program helps you focus on modular design considerations. Some systems require attention to data, and defining the module interfaces can be a critical issue.

In addition, individual modules must do their own error checking. But a critical decision is to determine if a given routine can expect data passed to it to be clean. Should data validation occur early and at a high level, or should you postpone validation to a more detailed level? Hopefully, you aren't waiting with bated breath for the answer. There is no simple solution. If you do error checking at every possible step, then a 100 line program becomes a

1000 line program. Furthermore, if you do all your checking at the detail level, the amount of checking mushrooms and may be redundant because it may have been performed by other modules. If you do all your error checking at a high level, then you can easily bypass detail-level concerns such as a "divide by 0" error. Perhaps a reasonable compromise is to concentrate on the most thorough checking at the module interface because problems there can mushroom throughout the system.

Dynamic Code

Another useful but underutilized coding technique is the use of dynamic code generation. This technique has several other names, such as flexcode or "coding on the fly." Regardless of the name, it involves a program that modifies itself while running. Specifically, this involves writing SAS code that is later %INCLUDEd into the program.

What is the advantage of dynamic code generation? You can easily and accurately code repetitive tasks without the inherent danger of making a typing error. Consider the following example. A SAS data set is created using survey data. However, someone realizes, after the survey responses are returned, that there is a flaw in the design of the questionnaire. Specifically, some of the questions are ambiguous, such that some of the answers could lead to confusion. For example, you may decide that, if any answer contains "bottom", "lowest" or "lower", then you want to recode all these values to "low". For a number of reasons, you might decide that formats are not the appropriate solution, so you might try something like this:

```
data permsas.clean ;
    set permsas.dirty ;

if quest_1 in ( "bottom", "lowest", "lower" ) then
    quest_1 = "low" ;

if quest_2 in ( "bottom", "lowest", "lower" ) then
    quest_2 = "low" ;
...
... and so on, for all 100 questions.

run ;
```

Undoubtedly, you can use the power of the editor and copy each segment of code 100 times and simply change the question number. Unfortunately, you can easily make a typing mistake, and then the appropriate field may never get changed. Or what if there are thousands of questions and a large number of variables that need to be recoded? Do you really want to make those changes manually? In these kinds of situations, writing dynamic code is a safer and much faster approach.

The key to developing dynamic code is to work backwards. Think about how you would write the code as if it were a normal DATA step. Most of the coding occurs in three phases:

1. What do you want to process before reading the first record? In other words, what do you want to do when _N_ = 1 ? This is the perfect time to set up the constants %INCLUDEd into the next step, such as the output data set, or the SET, FORMAT, RETAIN, LENGTH, or ATTRIB statements.

2. What do you want to accomplish upon reading each detail record?

3. What do you want to process after reading the last record?

Here is an example of how you can use dynamic code to accomplish the recoding in the example above:

```
libname permsas "libref" ;
filename instruct "fileref" ;


**************************************************************** ;
*** Get a list of variable names and their attributes.    *** ;
**************************************************************** ;

proc contents data = permsas.dirty
    out = contents ( keep = memname name type ) noprint ;
run ;

data _null_ ;
    set contents end = last_one ;

file instruct ;

retain char_var 2 ;              * Data is character ;

**************************************************************** ;
*** Write out just once:                              *** ;
*** (1) The data statement                            *** ;
*** (2) The set statement                             *** ;
**************************************************************** ;

if _n_ = 1 then
do ;
    put "data permsas.clean; " ;
    put "    set permsas.dirty ; " ;
end ;

**************************************************************** ;
*** Recode missing numeric data.                      *** ;
*** This is the code processed for EACH observation.   *** ;
**************************************************************** ;

if type = char_var then
do ;
    put " " ;
    put "if trim ( left ( " name ")) in "
      "('bottom','lowest','lower') then ";
    put "    " name "= 'low' ;" ;
end ;
```

```
******************************************************************* ;
*** After all detail records are processed, write out a      *** ;
*** run   statement.                                         *** ;
******************************************************************* ;

if last_one then
    put / " run ; " ;

run ;

******************************************************************* ;
*** Include the instructions that will now actually write    *** ;
*** out the new SAS data set.                                *** ;
******************************************************************* ;

%include instruct ;
```

Here is the code that is automatically generated. These statements appear in the log if options SOURCE2 is set:

```
+data permsas.clean;
+    set permsas.dirty ;
+
+if trim ( left ( QUEST_1 )) in ('bottom','lowest','lower') then
+    QUEST_1 = 'low' ;
+
+if trim ( left ( QUEST_2 )) in ('bottom','lowest','lower') then
+    QUEST_2 = 'low' ;
+
+if trim ( left ( QUEST_3 )) in ('bottom','lowest','lower') then
+    QUEST_3 = 'low' ;
+
...
... and so on for all 100 questions.
...
+ run ;
```

It is instructive now to look back at the code that generated the above %INCLUDE statement.

For more advanced use of dynamic code generation, refer to Coding Sample 6 in Appendix 1, "Coding Samples," which shows an enhancement to the parser routine introduced in Chapter 5, "Laying the Foundation with Good Design."

More Tips for Writing Dynamic Code

- Be sure to set the SAS system option SOURCE2 in order to view the dynamically created code. Alternatively, you can write to the log and debug one step at a time before changing the file to an external file.

- Once you have determined that your macro variables are working properly, set the macro option to NOSYMBOLGEN. Otherwise, the printing of the macro variables is completely embedded in the dynamic code. This makes reading difficult, and it obscures the logic.

- Be careful when you mix dynamic code with SAS data sets. When you create working variables, make sure they don't clash with those in the SAS data sets. You may choose to use a leading underscore or any established convention at your site.

- Try to use meaningful file names for your filerefs. After a while, TEMP1, TEMP2, TEMP3, and so on, start to all look alike.

- When you write the code, insert vertical and horizontal white spaces just as you would in normal coding. That way, when you retrieve the code, you can more easily detect logic flaws.

Seamless Coding

It was previously mentioned that it is of utmost importance to keep the literals out of the code. Here are some examples of how to do so. This first example uses traditional coding techniques. In this data set for a robotics factory, the variable names are the same as the part names:

```
model_id  plant  inspdate  head  neck  arm  leg  hip  knee  torso  foot  hand
   197     A-2     061297     1     1    2    3    1    8      1      3     2
   197     A-2     061397     .     1    .    .    1    .      .      .     2
   197     A-2     061397     1     .    2    3    1    8      .      3     2
... and so on.
```

You would like to rearrange the data so that it looks like this:

```
model_id  plant  inspdate  bodypart  part_val
   197     A-2     061297     head        1
   197     A-2     061297     neck        1
   197     A-2     061297     arm         2
... and so on, for all the body parts.
```

As a first attempt, you might try to solve the problem by using code such as this:

```
data new_data ( keep = model_id plant inspdate
                bodypart part_val );
    set old_data ;

length bodypart $8 ;

if head ne . then
do ;
    bodypart = "head" ;
    part_val = head ;
    output ;
end ;

if neck ne . then
do ;
    bodypart = "neck" ;
    part_val = neck ;
    output ;
end ;

... and so on, for all body parts.

run ;
```

Naturally, as the list of body parts becomes larger, the coding becomes more tedious. In addition, there is a greater chance for you to introduce buggy code. Most likely, you will use the editor and copy a block of code and modify the appropriate characters in each section. Still, you can easily make a typo and retrieve the wrong value for a body part.

Here is a second attempt at rearranging the data: much better, but still not perfect. First, define the following in your system initialization file:

```
%let partlist = neck head arm leg hip knee torso foot hand ;
```

Then, the core program reads as follows:

```
proc sort data = in_data out = _scratch ;
    by model_id inspdate plant ;
run ;

*****************************************************************  ;
*** Create a separate observation for each body part by      *** ;
*** model number, inspection date and plant code.            *** ;
*****************************************************************  ;

proc transpose data = _scratch out = _trans prefix = _value
    name = bodypart ;
    var &partlist ;
    by model_id inspdate plant ;
run ;

proc print data = _trans ;
run ;
```

At this point, it is easy to go astray. After studying the output from PROC PRINT, you determine that there are up to four columns of data per observation, listed as _VALUE1-_VALUE4. Because you want to eliminate all those records in which _VALUE1-_VALUE4 is missing, you write the following flawed code:

```
data out_data ;
    set _trans ;

if _value1 not = . then
    output ;
if _value2 not = . then
    output ;
if _value3 not = . then
    output ;
if _value4 not = . then
    output ;

run ;
```

Unfortunately, this code is not robust, and so changes in the input data can cause incorrect output. For example, changes in the input data might ultimately yield three or eight columns of data per observation instead of four. You can fix this problem permanently by automatically counting the columns and adjusting the code accordingly. For instance, you can replace the previous step with the following code:

```
data out_data ( drop = i _value: ) ;
    set _trans ;

array _value {*} _value: ;
do i = 1 to dim ( _value ) ;
    if _value {i} ne . then
    do ;
        part_val = _value {i} ;
        output ;
    end ;
end ;

run ;
```

Rather than hardcode values in a program, often it is easy to calculate a variable's value. For example, a report's footnote can be coded as a literal. This is a common practice, as is illustrated in the following footnote statements:

```
footnote1 "Superfund Site List: Cartera,Williams,Oxygen Transport" ;
```

or

```
footer = "Superfund Site List: Cartera,Williams,Oxygen Transport" ;
...
put @010 footer ;
```

Instead, you can calculate the footnotes, which is the robust solution:

```
data newsites ;
    set sites end = last_rec ;

length namelist $132 ;
retain namelist ;
...
...
if super = "Y" then
do ;
    if namelist = " " then
        namelist = trim (site) ;
    else
        namelist = trim (namelist) || "," || trim (site) ;
end ;
```

```
if last_rec then
do ;
    if namelist ne " " then
        call symput ( 'footer',"Supefund Site list: "
            || trim ( namelist )) ;
    else
        call symput
            ( 'footer',"No Superfund sites for this region" ) ;
end ;
...
...
run ;

data _null_ ;
    set newsites end = last_rec ;

...
... code to print report
...

if last_rec then
    put @010 "&footer" ;

run ;
```

The dreaded typographical error is always a concern, especially when you are typing in hundreds of values for a table. Whenever possible, try to automate the process. This is especially effective when you have a continuous table (that is, when there should be no gaps in the table). In the following example, assume that you want to calculate chemical toxicities based on a standard value. Here is a small piece of the input data for creating the formats. Imagine the complexity if hundreds of values were entered in the corresponding PROC FORMAT:

OBS	LOW	HIGH	TOXICITY
1	0	10	1
2	11	60	2
3	61	75	3
4	76	100	4
5	101	.	5

Assume that a missing value in the last field (HIGH) indicates no upper limit on the high value. The code can be set up as the following. (Note: for an alternative technique of using the CNTLIN option to create formats, refer to Coding Sample 3 in Appendix 1.)

```
filename makeform 'fileref' ;

data make_fmt ;
    set lab_vals end = last_one ;

file makeform ;
```

```
retain last_val . ; * Previous value ;
retain col_01 01 ;  * Position for print column ;
retain col_02 08 ;  * Position for print column ;
retain col_03 15 ;  * Position for print column ;
retain col_04 24 ;  * Position for print column ;

if _n_ = 1 then
do ;
    put @col_01 "proc format ;" ;
    put @col_02 "value labs" ;
    put @col_02 low @col_03 "- " high @col_04 "=" +2 toxicity;
end ;
else
do ;
    if last_one and high = . then
        put @col_02 last_val @col_03 "<-" "high"
            @col_04 "=" +2 toxicity ;
    else
        put @col_02 last_val @col_03 "<-" high
            @col_04 "=" +2 toxicity ;
end ;

last_val = high ;

if last_one then
do ;
    put @col_02 ";" ;
    put "run ;" ;
end ;

run ;

%include makeform ;
```

The dynamically created code produces:

```
proc format ;
value labs
0        - 10     =    1
10       <-60     =    2
60       <-75     =    3
75       <-100    =    4
100      <-high   =    5
;
run ;
```

System Coding Concerns

Many unique or particularly troublesome coding issues come into play when you build complete software systems.

Black Box Systems: Good or Bad?

In Chapter 9, "Program Verification and Testing Methodology," there is an extensive discussion about Black Box testing. However, the term Black Box has also been used to describe the components of a system. Before you read a definition, look at the diagram of a Black Box system in Figure 8.3.

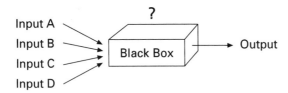

Figure 8.3   *A Black Box system looks a little like a magic show. Inputs are acted upon by some unknown process (Black Box) that produces output.*

Black Box systems are those in which the details of the process are hidden from the programmer. This is usually a good thing because many of the trivial details are handled behind the scenes, thus freeing up programmers to concentrate on other tasks. However, there is a catch. Black Box systems require more responsibility, namely documentation. It is imperative that you describe the system using both external documentation (that is, system specifications) and thorough internal documentation (that is, within the source code). Then, if someone later has to modify the code, the search shouldn't resemble a journey through an African jungle.

One familiar Black Box system is one that is written predominately with the macro language. Repeated calls to macros without concomitant documentation is irresponsible, but unfortunately, it is all too common.

Another type of Black Box can be created with SQL. SQL is very powerful. However, it can be complex, especially if there are a number of nested queries and complicated joins. When the output doesn't look right, debugging can become pretty nasty, especially when it's not your own code.

Black Box systems are not restricted to macros or SQL processing. Any system that exhibits a high degree of modularity is also a candidate. In summary, Black Box systems are very useful, but it's a good idea to document these systems carefully.

Data Duplication

One annoying problem is dealing with data duplication. If the record keys are identical, the fix is easy. In those situations, you simply use PROC SORT with the NODUPKEY option. A more pressing problem is the case of complete record duplication, where all variables in two or more records are identical. How do these records get created? Here are just a few of the ways:

- A database uses a transaction buffer that periodically updates the database. However, a system bug can cause the transaction buffer not to be flushed. Then, transaction records are once again added to the database.

- Flawed design logic can cause the incorrect updating of a database. For instance, some systems use transaction codes to update a database. This may entail a transaction flag whose values can be "A" for add, "C" for change, and "D" for delete. However, for this approach to work effectively, the transaction records must be passed in correct sequence. If the order of records is inadvertently changed, then you can accidentally delete valid records or add records that already exist in the database.

- System crashes combined with inadequate error recovery restart procedures can result in bizarre record sequences.

- When using an online interface for rapid data entry, it is often convenient to assign a function key as a screen duplicator. In that way, if one record is a near duplicate of another, the operator merely presses the duplication key and types over the changed fields. However, because of fatigue, or an unexpected interruption, a record can be inadvertently duplicated.

- Another typical online error is accidentally saving the data in the input buffer when the user requests to cancel the session.

- Normal SAS processing can also create duplicate records. This is quite common when using DROP and KEEP within the DATA step.

Regardless of the cause, it is usually necessary to remove these records at the outset. Otherwise, they can destroy most summaries and analysis. To remove exact duplicates, one method is to use the NODUPLICATES option with PROC SORT. However, you must remember that NODUPLICATES only removes duplicates records in consecutive order. To ensure the deletion of all duplicate records, you must sort by all variables:

```
proc sort data = painting out = no_dupes noduplicates ;
    by painter canvtype medium period  ;
run ;
```

When the number of variables in a data set becomes large, then writing this kind of code for every single data set becomes tedious. You can more easily eliminate duplicates by using the following:

```
%macro no_dupes ( lib = ) ;

    %local i ;        * Loop index ;
    %local member ;   * Library member name ;
    %local mem_cnt ;  * Number of members in library ;
```

```
proc sql noprint ;
    select distinct memname
    into :mem_list separated by " "
    from dictionary.columns
    where libname ="&lib"
    ;
    %let mem_cnt = &sqlobs ;
quit ;

%do i = 1 %to &mem_cnt ;
    %let member = %scan ( &mem_list, &i ) ;
    proc sort data = &lib..&member noduplicates ;
        by _all_ ;
    run ;
%end ;
%mend no_dupes ;

%no_dupes ( lib = WORK )
```

System Control Flags

Controlling an entire system with a control file (that is, an external file or SAS data set) is sometimes necessary because of coordination issues. For example, it may be required that file A should not be updated before file B is updated. One way to accomplish this is to use a SAS data set with control flags that are updated at the appropriate time. However, you need to be careful when you let flags exert such power, because even a subtle bug can be disastrous. Here is a classic way to install a little preventive medicine: Suppose that a master database transfers all the appropriate data directly into the SAS data sets. A simple addition to the process should be the transfer of a data set that contains a count of the expected records. For this example, assume that this count is stored in TRAN_CNT:

```
data _null_ ;
    set control nobs = contnobs  ;
    set trans ;

file errorlog ;

if tran_cnt ne contnobs then
do ;
    put "*** SERIOUS TRANSFER ERROR ***" ;
    put "Observations in Control Data Set is " contnobs ;
    put "Observations Reported in Transaction Data set is "
      tran_cnt ;
end ;
else
do ;
    put "Transfer successful" ;
    put "Observations in Transaction Data set is " tran_cnt ;
end ;

stop ;

run ;
```

As an exercise, you should consider testing for the presence of observations in both data sets.

Portrait and Landscape Printing

Another system coding concern is how to handle the thorny details of printing reports easily. For example, you may have a number of reports that may require printing in portrait mode and others that may require printing in landscape mode. There are several solutions to this problem:

- Create two batch files. First, manually set the print orientation to landscape. Then execute a program called BAT_LAN.SAS, which executes all programs printed in landscape mode. Then, set the print location to "Portrait" and execute a program called BAT_PORT.SAS, which runs all programs in portrait mode. This method has its drawbacks because it requires manual intervention and you have to maintain two files to accomplish one task.

- A similar method is to use only one file. You comment out one type of files and execute the job stream, and then reset the orientation to run the rest of the source files. Like the first option, this is a clumsy solution that requires user intervention between the job runs.

- One preferred option requires that each program set its page orientation within the program. This provides a very robust solution because once the orientation is set up, one batch file will automate the whole process. For example, a program would contain either:

```
%let orient = Landscape ;
```

or

```
%let orient = Portrait ;
```

Then, right before the DATA _NULL_ step, the program sends an escape sequence to the printer, specifying the codes for portrait or landscape orientation as needed. To determine these codes, you can consult the printer user guide for your specific printer. For example, for the Hewlett-Packard Laserjet 4Si, the following code does the trick:

```
data _null_ ;
....
file print_it ;
put "1B266C313F"x ;
run ;
```

After the program runs, do not forget to send the reset code, or you can surely make a lot of enemies!

```
data _null_ ;
....
file print_it ;
put "1B45"x ;
run ;
```

- What if a requirement is to route all the reports to a directory and then print later at a more appropriate time? How do you then know which reports are printed in landscape and which in portrait? One possibility is to use a part of the file name to designate the print mode. In DOS for example, you can use the file suffix as a tag. Here is a way to automate the whole process:

  - If the program determines that &ORIENT = portrait, then write the file out with a .txp ("text portrait") extension. If &ORIENT = landscape, then write out the file with a .txl ("text landscape") extension.
  - Run the batch program as before, first outputting the directory of landscape files to a file.
  - Send the escape sequence for landscape.
  - %INCLUDE and run the landscape programs.
  - Send the portrait escape sequence.
  - %INCLUDE and run the portrait programs.
  - Finally, send a reset escape sequence.

Good, you're paying attention. You may have noticed that the above method works best if you have your own printer. If you are running on a network, you should reset the escape sequences after each program in case somebody tries to slip their job in.

Initialization Options for Customized Software

When developing a complete software system, you will eventually have to deal with system initialization. Ideally, you want an environment that is clean and that does not contain any residual "garbage" from previously executed programs. Here are three major options for initializing the current environment:

- Utilize the SAS AUTOEXEC and CONFIG files

- %INCLUDE an initialization module at the start of each program

- Create a startup shell that runs an initialization program.

Utilize the SAS AUTOEXEC and CONFIG Files

SAS provides a convenient way of setting up your work environment. In fact, when you first load the SAS System, the SAS CONFIG file provides a default configuration. This can be modified so that at startup, you can customize the environment for your session. For the PC environment, you may enter options, such as the following, to increase your productivity:

```
-echo 'Are we feeling creative today?'
```

Similarly, you can set up SAS code to execute automatically at startup by including the code in the SAS AUTOEXEC file. For the PC environment, you can enter code as such:

```
libname mysongs   'c:\getting\closer\home' ;
filename bighits 'c:\beatles\early\lovemedo.dat' ;
```

Problems with Personal Startup Files

Using startup files this way is great for your personal environment, but it is less than ideal for systems building. There are many reasons why it falls short. For instance, you may be developing multiple systems at a site and you need a way to configure your environment for each system. You might think that a simple way around this is to invoke SAS using the configuration and AUTOEXEC options. However, this approach has several glaring weaknesses:

- You may forget to include the appropriate files when starting the system. Or, you could specify the incorrect configuration and AUTOEXEC files.

- Using an iconized version that includes the full specification is not practical. You would need a separate icon for each system or subsystem!

- It is not a very portable solution. When the system is moved to other platforms, the commands may not be interpreted properly. Code placed in these files is often specific to a particular operating system.

- It is not advisable if the software is being shipped to customer sites. You certainly don't want to force your clients to use your configuration and AUTOEXEC files. They probably have the environment configured the way they want and do not want you to override their default configuration.

Utilizing a %INCLUDE Startup File

Consider the alternative approaches to startup. One is to %INCLUDE a startup file in each of your source modules:

```
%include "c:\textiles\startup.sas" ;
```

At first, this may seem to contradict the earlier principle of hardwiring literals into the code. However, this is not as much of a problem as you might think. By placing this file at the beginning of each program, you can initialize and clean up the environment before running each program. A sample initialization file is given in Coding Sample 7 in Appendix 1.

But what if the directory changes, or you need to ship the program to a customer site? This is actually not a major problem because the %INCLUDE statement is quite unique. As a result, you can confidently run a utility to globally change this string for all the files in a directory. You would not have to worry about accidentally corrupting the source file with the "global find and replace" command.

Create a Startup Shell that Runs an Initialization Program

The third option is to create a startup shell that drives the whole system. A common way of doing this with the base SAS language is to create a display by using the WINDOW or %WINDOW command. Then, when the user makes a menu selection, the first item that runs is the appropriate initialization file for that program. A sample window to accomplish this is displayed in Figure 8.4.

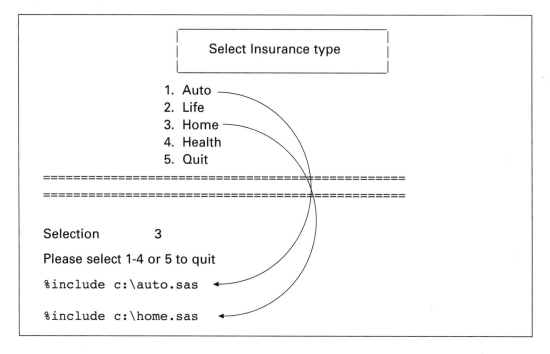

Figure 8.4 *Making a selection from the master menu causes the appropriate %INCLUDE file to be executed. This permits the loading of the requisite initialization options.*

The code to generate this window can be found in Coding Sample 8 in Appendix 1.

A Reporting System

This section examines a systems approach to reports development. The goal is to simplify the process so that you can handle repetitive tasks smoothly, expedite development time, and ensure high quality of output. Here is a step by step discussion of the tasks needed to develop such a system.

Segregate Titles and Footnotes

Placing titles and footnotes in their own file simplifies coding. Here are some reasons for doing so:

- In many systems, reports are assigned a sequence number, which is listed in either the header or footer of the report. If you have to change the sequence number (such as when you insert a new report in the middle of the chain), you can simply renumber the reports in one file. On the other hand, if you keep the report numbers in each source module, then you would have to modify each of these reports if you update the numeric sequence.

- A person without programming experience can learn to modify such a file with very little training. This allows the programmers to concentrate on the more difficult tasks.

- When this file is used in conjunction with other %INCLUDE modules, the exact positioning of titles and footnotes is automatically calculated.

- Global changes to titles, footnotes or groups of titles and footnotes can be changed easily in one place. You may, for example, decide that you want to globally capitalize a particular word.

- The titles can be read in from another program to be used for external documentation. This helps to keep the external documentation and report titles in synchronization.

Complete details of the titles file can be found in Coding Sample 9 in Appendix 1.

Eliminate Coding Steps

Often you are confronted with the task of ejecting a page before printing the next record in a group of records. You could write code to count the number of records in each group and store the count in a variable, NUM_RECS. Then you can write code in your program such as:

```
file print linesleft = remain ;

if remain - num_recs le 5 then
    put _page_ ;
```

However, you have to write this same code, over and over again, for each program with modifications. Instead, you can create a macro that can be called by all the programs to handle this repetitive chore. Then you can simply call one routine, regardless of the report. Here is the sample code to do so:

```
%macro getcount ( in_data = _last_ ,   /* Input data set */
                  var_name = ) ;       /* Var requiring count */

**************************************************************** ;
*** Produce a data set that contains a count of the records *** ;
*** for each grouping.                                      *** ;
**************************************************************** ;

    proc summary data = &in_data nway ;
        class &var_name ;
        output out = _count ( keep = &var_name _freq_ ) ;
    run ;

**************************************************************** ;
*** Prepare the data sets for merging.                      *** ;
**************************************************************** ;

    proc sort data = &in_data equals ;
        by &var_name ;

    run ;
```

```
*************************************************************** ;
*** Merge the data sets so that the input data set can get  *** ;
*** the record count.                                       *** ;
*************************************************************** ;

     data &in_data ;
         merge &in_data
                 _count ;
         by &var_name ;

     rename _freq_ = _rec_cnt ;

     run ;

%mend getcount ;
```

Then, call the macro as:

```
%getcount ( in_data = my_data ,
            var_name = finances )
```

Allow for Flexibility in Routing Output

Often, you will want the flexibility to print all your reports to the printer, terminal screen, or hard disk directory. With just a little preparation (as described in this section), this is a simple task. Establish a standard that each program will list its source file name as the first line in the program. The second line is to be the call to the master %INCLUDE module. For this section's example, call it C:\SCHOOL\INIT.SAS:

```
%let filename = grades.sas ;
%include "c:\school\init.sas" ;
```

Set Macro Variables for Routing

Examine more closely some of the statements in this example's master %INCLUDE module. These macro variables set up a destination for routing all your log and SAS output:

```
%let logout   = &drive:\machine\log ;
%let rptout   = &drive:\machine\reports ;
```

The REDIRECT macro variable can be set to TERMINAL, PRINTER, or STUDYDIR (hard disk). The following setting causes all reports to be routed to the user screen:

```
%let redirect = TERMINAL ;
```

The macro variable PRINT does not need to be reset by the programmer. If the output is redirected to the printer, the program automatically changes its value to redirect output to the local printer. This will become obvious to you after you see the PRINTLOC code, which is examined shortly:

```
%let print = print ;
```

Now, the process is ready to be automated. Simply call a macro routine PRINTLOC before the final DATA _NULL_ ;

```
%printloc

data _null_ ;
file &print ;
...
run ;
```

Now, the report output will be routed to the appropriate destination. Here is the code for the PRINTLOC module:

```
%macro printloc ;

**************************************************************** ;
*** Pick up the source code file name so that if the output *** ;
*** goes to disk, it can be routed to the appropriate dir-  *** ;
*** ectory.                                                 *** ;
**************************************************************** ;

    %let prefix = %scan ( &filename, 1, "." ) ;

**************************************************************** ;
*** The user can direct the output to any of the following: *** ;
***                                                         *** ;
*** (1) The study directories (save on disk)                *** ;
*** (2) The terminal                                        *** ;
*** (3) The printer                                         *** ;
**************************************************************** ;

    %if %upcase ( &redirect ) = STUDYDIR %then
    %do ;
        %let print = print ;
        proc printto print = "&rptout\&prefix..rpt"  new ;
        run ;
    %end ;

    %if %upcase ( &redirect ) = TERMINAL %then
    %do ;
        %let print = print ;
        proc printto ;
        run ;
    %end ;

    %if %upcase ( &redirect ) = PRINTER %then
    %do ;
        %let print = localprt ;
    %end ;

%mend printloc ;
```

Create a Skeleton Program

The final step is to create a shell program so you can automate as much of the process as possible. What are the reasons for using such a shell?

- to dramatically enhance the speed and accuracy of report development.

- to reinitialize the environment for each report, minimizing the chance of corrupting the current environment.

- to automatically parse data variables.

- to automatically calculate group counts for control breaks.

- to set the print destination to terminal, disk, or printer.

- to provide the option of printing in portrait or landscape mode, and setting system options accordingly.

- to standardize headers, footers, and titles.

Details of the shell components are discussed in Coding Sample 10 in Appendix 1.

Code Generators: Reporting at the Next Level

Writing a DATA _NULL_ step can be tedious. The next level of reporting involves using a layout program and having the program calculate the required statements for the DATA _NULL_. Full blown report generators can run thousands of lines of code to generate all the bells and whistles. Nevertheless, here is a simplified version that should be instructive.

The first step is to create a format so that the user can type in the report layout. First, note the bare bones layout:

:TITLES:

:HEADINGS:

:DETAIL:

:FOOTNOTES:

:BOTTOM OF PAGE:

Next, you simply fill in the layout as you envision the final report. The pound sign (#) has a dual purpose. One is to designate SAS variables. Thus "#broker" represents the position for the SAS variable BROKER. This enables the program to recognize that this is a variable position and that the variable should be written in that location. Otherwise, all other text prints as is. The second reason is to designate control characters. For example, in the TITLES section, two of the titles are preceded by "#L" and two are preceded by "#C". This tells the program to left justify and center justify the titles, respectively. Other options include "#R" (for Right Justification) and "#A" (for "As is"—the default). The "#" can be changed on the input parameter list because the report may require printing this character. Here is a completed version of the layout as you might fill it in:

:TITLES:

#L Student Study Assignment
#L Semester #2

#C   Top Stockbrokers in the U.S. Provide
#C   Their List of Top Picks for This Year

:HEADINGS:

Broker   Best Bets   Comments

:DETAIL:
#broker   #picks   #comments

:FOOTNOTES:

Internal Use Only
Dir: c:\broker\picks.sas - Miss Wanda Author - &sysdate

:BOTTOM OF PAGE:

Here is the input data set for this sample program:

OBS	COMMENTS
1	You can't go wrong with the standards, can you?
2	They are hot right now, but won't be next year.
3	I'm kinda conservative; stocks should be stable.
4	I never let you down with bad picks before, so why should I start now?
5	Cover all your bases. Buy low, sell high is the key to any success.
6	I got my brokerage degree by mail—you figure.
7	Good old American manufacturing is on the way back.

OBS	BROKER	PICKS
1	Stevens	Gold, Silver, Bronze
2	Rincon	Biotechnology, computer chips
3	Edwards	Utilities
4	Waller	Gold, Banking, Insurance
5	Ellis	High tech, Low tech and medium tech
6	Belxer	How should I know? I just got my license.
7	Alpine	Manufacturing, particularly textiles

Here is the report generated after executing RPT_GEN.SAS:

Student Study Assignment

Semester #2

```
                          Top Stockbrokers in the U.S. Provide
                          Their List of Top Picks for This Year


     _____

        Broker       Best Bets            Comments
     _____


        Alpine       Manufacturing,       Good old American manufacturing is on the
                       particularly         way back.
                       textiles
        Belxer       How should I         I got my brokerage degree by mail—you
                       know? I just         figure.
                       got my license.
        Edwards      Utilities            I'm kinda conservative; stocks should be
                                            stable.
        Ellis        High tech, low       Cover all your bases. Buy low, sell high is
                       tech, and medium     the key to any success.
                       tech
        Rincon       Biotechnology,       They are hot right now, but won't be next
                       computer chips       year.
        Stevens      Gold, Silver,        You can't go wrong with the standards, can
                       Bronze               you?
        Waller       Gold, Banking,       I never let you down with bad picks before,
                       Insurance            so why should I start now?
     _____


     Internal Use Only
     Dir: c:\broker\picks.sas - Miss Wanda Author - 10JUN96
```

The complete source code for RPT_GEN.SAS can be found in Coding Sample 11 in Appendix 1.

Summary

Coding comprehensive software systems requires an approach that allows rapid and accurate development of production–level software. Programming defensively is critical to trap for unexpected problems. If possible, keep the literals out of the code, and use table-driven techniques. Finally, develop a library of reusable tools that will enable you to simplify your coding process.

Exercises

1. The following DO loop processes record prices. However, record prices continuously change, and these values are hardcoded in many places throughout the source code. Thus, you would like to recode this fragment so that it will read from a table. Show how you can do this by setting up a %LET statement and a modification of the DO loop.

```
do recprice = 599, 799, 999, 1199 ;
    discount = int (recprice / 10) ;
    put 'Your total discount is ' discount ;
    sale = ( recprice - discount ) / 100 ;
    put 'And your cost for the record is ' sale dollar6.2 ;
end ;
```

2. How can you redirect your procedural output to a file that has the same prefix name as the source?

3. In your opinion, do you think duplicate records should be handled at a higher module level (early in a series of steps) or later, among lower level modules?

4. Why should you not ship your personal AUTOEXEC file as the startup file for a customer?

5. What are the main arguments for and against handling error processing at a high level?

6. Assume you want to set up LENGTH statements for a set of variables read in from input files. However, you do not want to set them too small, for fear of truncation. And you don't want the data sets to be too large because you don't want to waste space. How can you solve this problem?

7. Why is the NODUPLICATES option in PROC SORT usually inadequate to remove duplicate data?

8. What is the main reason for maintaining titles and reports in a separate file?

9. What kinds of maintenance changes benefit from defensive coding? Which of the four effects do you think defensive coding is most useful for?

10. What is the definition of "seamless coding"? Why is it important in building large software systems?

References

Jalote, P. (1997), *An Integrated Approach to Software Engineering*, New York: Springer.

Jensen, R.W. and Tonies, C.C. (1979), *Software Engineering*, Englewood Cliffs, NJ: Prentice-Hall.

Chapter 9

Program Verification and Testing Methodology

Introduction **190**

Black Box Testing **191**
   Types of Black Box Tests 191
   Equivalence Classes 191
   Boundary Values 194
   Maximize the Output Domain 195
   Miscellaneous Boundaries 195
   Error Guessing (Ad Hoc) Testing 197
   Random Testing 197

White Box Testing **198**
   Statement Coverage 199
   Branch Coverage 199
   Multiple Condition Coverage 200
   Implementing White Box Methodology: Path Testing 201
   Dynamic Data Flow Analysis 207

Black Box versus White Box Testing **211**
   Black Box Testing Conditions 211
   White Box Testing Conditions 211

Gray Box Testing **212**

Structured Testing Methodology **216**
   Module Testing 216
   Integration Testing 217
   System Testing 222

Bugging a Program **223**

Comparison Testing Techniques **223**

Summary **225**

Exercises **225**

References **228**

Introduction

A good definition of "testing" is critical to set proper goals for program and system verification. Here is an incorrect definition that has pervaded the software industry:

Testing is the process of proving a program is correct.

While an extremely popular notion, it is nonetheless wrong. You can never actually prove that a program is correct. No matter how many thousands of tests you execute, there is still an infinite number of checks that you can run. As an analogy, consider a scientific experiment comparing the effectiveness of two prescription drugs:

If drug "A" is effective in relieving the symptoms of headache in all 25 patients and drug "B" is ineffective for all 25 patients, what conclusions can be drawn? Namely, there is evidence that "A" is more effective than "B."

"What? You're putting me on! How much more evidence do you need than that?" Well, perhaps, there was a "bug" in the experimental design. For example, it is possible that the subjects in Group "B" were taking another medication that negated the effects of the treatment drug. Alternatively, the subjects in group "A" may have worked as suntan lotion testers, and the subjects in group "B" may have worked in the complaints department for lost baggage at a major airport.

The problems of incomplete testing are evident throughout every industry. From failed space missions to recalled automobiles, the manufacturers were "sure" that they inspected everything completely. Have you ever written a program that you swore was bug free? It was, until one day when brand new data caused your program to come crashing back to earth. Now we're ready for a better definition of testing:

Testing is the process of attempting to find errors in a program.

The difference between this definition and the previous one may seem subtle, but the importance is substantial. The latter is superior because it establishes a goal for the test plan. By attempting to find errors, you can plan to develop a battery of tests to examine a hypothesis (that there are bugs in the program). On the other hand, what kind of organized plan can you construct to prove a program is without fault?

Testing is probably the second most distasteful task for programmers (documentation wins the honors). Programmers must try to find fault with their programs, to trip them up, to bring them to their knees. Finding bugs in your own program seems to be an attack on your ego. It's no wonder that when a production problem arises, finger pointing is the initial reaction. You'll hear: "It couldn't be my program. You must have passed in lousy data!" or "I can't trap for everything!" Most programmers examine their programs at only a superficial level because it is easiest for them that way. Unfortunately, many programmers, from novice to advanced levels, lack a technical understanding of comprehensive software testing. That's why many latent bugs spring forward when real testing begins.

Black Box Testing

Testing strategies fall into two major categories. The first is Black Box testing, also known as functional, input/output or data-dependent testing. The term "Black Box" conjures an aura of mystery, but it really means nothing more than observed input and observed output. Think of a magician with an amazing hat that produces rabbits or handkerchiefs by the dozens. What you see is the hand reaching into the hat (input) and the seemingly miraculous extraction of rabbits (output). Because you cannot see the internal workings of the hat, the hat is a Black Box.

For nontechnical people, Black Box products are terrific because such products enable users to utilize very advanced technology with little or no knowledge about the internal mechanisms of the products themselves. These kinds of products are most prevalent in electronics, including such items as TVs, VCRs, CD players, computers, and automobiles. You don't need to know the internal mechanics of a CD player to listen to your favorite disk.

With Black Box testing, the tester is oblivious to the internal workings of the product. For instance, how do you test the braking system of a car? The tester may step on the accelerator, rev the car to breakneck speeds, and then slam on the brakes to determine the car's stopping distance before bowling over a row of test dummies. With this kind of testing, the tester doesn't consider the brake line, hydraulics, master cylinder, or any of the other mechanical parts in the braking system.

In Black Box testing of software, there is no concern about the internal workings of the program. Testers should not be peeking at the source code. They should concern themselves only with inputting various data and then noting the output.

Types of Black Box Tests

There are several types of Black Box tests, and they have varying degrees of effectiveness. The categories are: Equivalence Classes, Boundary Value, Error Guessing, and Random Testing.

Before investigating these strategies in more detail, it should be mentioned that testing is one of the most labor intensive factors on a large project. As previously stated, there are literally an infinite number of checks that can be performed on a software system, so you must develop an approach that maximizes the use of your time. It is imperative that you develop a plan such that the fewest number of cases determines the maximum number of bugs in a system. That is, performing 500 tests and discovering 20 bugs is a lot more efficient than performing 10,000 tests and finding only 10 bugs. You can improve each system's testing efficiency by implementing one or more of the following techniques.

Equivalence Classes

When you are developing test cases, it is important to maximize the effort by not repeating cases that are so similar that they are not likely to report new findings. Inputs that have a similar look and feel about them are likely to yield similar results. You can take advantage of this by using equivalence class testing. In equivalence class testing, the program's input space is divided into domains such that all inputs within a domain are equivalent in the sense that any input represents all inputs in that domain.

For example, assume a baker wants to ensure the quality of his doughnuts. The doughnuts are produced in lots of 100, and he wants to guarantee that the freshness and texture of each doughnut meets some expected standard. Observe the results of a sample inspection as given in Table 9.1.

# Doughnut	Quality
01–33	Pass
34–46	Not Tested
47–59	Pass
60–69	Not Tested
70–84	Pass
85–100	Pass

Table 9.1   *A sample inspection of a baker's doughnuts.*

Having observed the above results, it is likely that doughnuts 34-46 and 60-69 can also pass the quality test. All of this assumes independence of tests. If there is a glitch in the machine, then the doughnuts affected may not be random or may be calculable based on knowing the defect of the machine.

When setting up test cases for software, you want to adopt a similar approach. If one set of input data yields a given result, then a piece of similar data should yield similar results. Let's apply this to a very simple example. Assume that a program creates survey data for favorite television shows. Valid responses range from "1-10" with "1" meaning "Bomb" and "10" meaning "Addiction". As you set up equivalence classes, the following cases come to mind:

- a possible valid score
- a score less than the minimum valid score
- a score greater than the maximum score.

Then you can lay out the test data as follows:

```
data rating ;
input scores @@ ;
cards ;
-5 7 12
;
```

In this scenario, one value is chosen for each of the classes as a representative for that class. It is important to maintain a record of these cases as they are performed. For this example, the testing log is depicted in Table 9.2.

Test Case	Expected Output	Actual Output	Comments
–5	"Invalid Value"	"Invalid Value"	OK
7	"Entertaining"	"Entertaining"	OK
12	"Invalid Value"	"Bomb"	Bug

Table 9.2   *A log of test cases.*

Many testers recognize the importance of organizing their test cases and so they develop an outline to help facilitate their creation of test groupings. For the following example, assume that a part description is twenty bytes long and is composed solely of alphabetic characters, for example: NAIL, SCREW, HAMMER. (Note: an exhaustive list of invalid cases is not presented because these are examined more thoroughly in subsequent examples.) One possible set of equivalence classes can be identified by creating an outline:

A.   Input string is blank
B.   Input string is not blank
    1. String = Length of field
       a. Alphabetic characters found
         1. No matches found
         2. One or more matches found
       b. No alphabetic characters found

    2. String is smaller than length of field
       a. Alphabetic characters found
         1. No matches found
         2. One or more matches found
       b. No alphabetic characters found

For the next example, assume you have to develop equivalence classes for someone's weight in an all-male group. Because a person's weight can be represented by a range, the first step is to draw that range as shown in Figure 9.1.

```
   Invalid          Rock Star   Normal  Heavy    Obese    Talk Show   Time to
                                                          Interview    Diet
  <-----------|------|---------|------|-------|----------|------------>
   Negative    0      95        160    200     260        500         1000?
```

Figure 9.1   *It is easier to develop test cases by sketching the range of possible values.*

Diagrams can assist you when you develop test cases. Here, the range of equivalent tests quickly comes to mind:

Test Case	Rationale
-50	Invalid value to left of range
0	Absence of weight
167	Typical weight
+12	Possible leading positive sign
182.9	Typical weight with decimal places
123.745655	How is the program handling extra decimal places?
2356	Impossibly large value to the right of the range
.	Missing value

When you select a valid case, you must be aware of coincidental correctness. *Coincidental correctness* occurs when a value generates the correct answer even though the algorithm is wrong. This usually occurs with very small numbers or numbers that are on even boundaries, such as 10, 200, 1000, and so on. The following is an example of coincidental correctness. The Einstein prodigy should have developed the following formula:

$$Force = .5 * m * v ** 2 ;$$

but instead, his formula takes the form of:

Force = .5 * m * v * 2 ;

Inserting $m = 5$ and $v = 2$ yields identical results for both equations even though only the first equation is correct for this application. This is why many theorists advocate using a minimum of two valid test cases for each equivalence class.

Strings have their own equivalence classes. Consider a variable that is defined as:

```
attrib fav_city length = $20 label = "Favorite City in U.S." ;
```

Appropriate test cases would include:

Test Case	Rationale
" "	Empty string
"Pittsburgh"	Typical city in normal case
"pittsburgh"	Typical city in lower case
"PITTSBURGH"	Typical city in upper case
"PittsBUrgh"	Typical city in mixed case
"34t3943"	Garbage value
"New York"	Two or more words in the string
"New4York"	Misspelling
"Minneapolis/St.Paul"	How are special characters handled?
"Old Caster Waco City"	String equals length of field
"Shinnemahoning Yakima"	Variable overflow of length
" San Diego"	Leading spaces handled ok?
"Walla Walla"	Embedded extra spaces a problem?
"a b c d e f g h i j"	Maximum number of words in string

You can define additional equivalence cases by using the number of bytes in the string as its own separate case (such as "a", "be", "cee"). If time permits, this is as useful practice because it is difficult to predict which functions are being used to manipulate the data.

Boundary Values

Years of testing software demonstrates that a high percentage of errors occur at edges, or "domain boundaries." Hence, while Equivalence Partitioning can be very effective, you can also fine-tune your testing battery with Boundary Analysis to detect more errors.

Problems with boundary values are not a new phenomenon. Consider the following story:

> *One Roman turns to the other and says:"Can you believe it? Here it is 1 A.D. already and I'm <u>still</u> writing B.C. on my checks!"*

Returning to modern times for a second example, start with boundary considerations for this simple DO loop:

```
do i = 1 to 100 ;
    dollars + 1 ;
end ;
```

The values of i are incremented from 1 to 100. However, most errors can be detected at the extremes of the values of i. Specifically i should be examined at 0, 1, 100, and 101. These are the "edges" of the variable's dimension. Empirically, good cases are also established at just above the minimum and just below the maximum. In this case, 2 and 99 would also provide good input. There is another reason why 2 is considered useful for evaluating loops. Loops often work correctly for one iteration but improperly thereafter due to improper incrementing of the loop index.

Maximize the Output Domain

When you are examining boundary values, it is easy to think about minimizing and maximizing the input domain. That is, it is easy to consider very small and very large values as possible test cases. While these cases are certainly part of a good testing strategy, don't forget to minimize and maximize the output domain as well. Often, the input and output domains follow each other. For instance, if you enhance your personal gross income, the federal income tax also increases. If you increase the radius of a circle, the circumference shows a concomitant gain in size. But consider the following cases where the input and output domain do not follow each other:

- An investigator varies the amount of light from very dim to extremely bright. Subjects are asked to identify as many letters as possible on a vision chart.

- Subjects are exposed to various levels of arousal, from a soft whisper to a very loud bell. Then, their reaction time to a stimulus is measured.

This phenomenon of nonlinear (or curvilinear) variable relationships is actually quite common. Human physiological response, as demonstrated in the above examples, often exhibits this "bell-shaped" pattern. Thus, to ensure complete testing, watch for these boundaries as well. The programmer may not have allocated the appropriate data structure to handle these unexpectedly large or small output domains.

Miscellaneous Boundaries

Boundaries occur outside the program's code as well. Other boundaries that you should consider testing include:

- A program is expected to run on a PC with 8MB–16MB RAM. Try running the software on a computer with less and more RAM.

- Test a file with 0 and 1 observations.

- Test a missing file or missing SAS data set. This is useful for inspecting your error trapping routines.

- If a program is to wait 60 seconds for a user response, try a response at 59, 60, and 61 seconds.

The simplest boundary test is to keep all values within the normal range except for one value, which is inspected at its boundary. The most stringent boundary test involves inspecting the results when all values are tested at their boundaries. Combinations of values are most often useful at revealing program faults.

Testing at the edges is certainly a good strategy, but does not guarantee that other values in the input range cannot cause problems. Consider the following code. Instead of using a SAS procedure to calculate the median of some data, you decide to write your own procedure. Assume that your code calculates the median correctly for an odd number of observations, but incorrectly for an even number of observations. This is not so farfetched because, when you have an even number of observations, you have to split the difference between the two central values. Now, assume that the test data contain anywhere from 1 to 9 observations. If you examine only the edges (that is, 1 or 9), you would miss an obvious bug.

Another important "edge" is related to the FIRST. and LAST. variable processing that is provided by the SAS programming language. For example, as a tester, you might be provided with a list of plants that manufacture the parts for a jet airplane. The list is sorted by location, system, and supervisor. You should take extra care to test the boundary conditions of the sort, as indicated by the arrows in this report:

	OBS	LOCATION	SYSTEM	SUPERVISOR
==>	1	Greenville	Landing gear	2178
	2	Greenville	Landing gear	2249
	3	Greenville	Landing gear	3487
	4	Greenville	Landing gear	4340
==>	5	Greenville	Landing gear	4900
==>	6	Greenville	Cockpit Controls	1322
	7	Greenville	Cockpit Controls	3487
	8	Greenville	Cockpit Controls	6652
==>	9	Greenville	Cockpit Controls	6652
==>	10	Austin	Landing gear	8763
==>	11	Austin	Fueling system	1345
	12	Austin	Fueling system	1417
	13	Austin	Fueling system	1417
	14	Austin	Fueling system	1599
	15	Austin	Fueling system	2213
	16	Austin	Fueling system	6661
==>	17	Austin	Fueling system	8723

These boundaries are specific to the sort criteria and, as such, should be used to design the testing plan.

Error Guessing (Ad Hoc Testing)

While boundary value analysis and equivalence partitioning form the mainstay of comprehensive testing, Error Guessing is a useful adjunct. Error Guessing is based upon a tester's experience. Test masters have the wisdom to find the "soft spots." Here is a list of problematic items that might come to mind, based on their experience:

- expiration date (year 2000)
- noon or midnight
- date change at year boundaries
- leap year
- SAS variables at 200-character limit.

They might also try to test combinations such as the following:

- changing the order of expected input
- attempting to abort a program at unexpected places
- pressing various key combinations
- using function keys intended for other parts of the program
- testing zero because it can cause division by zero errors.

Random Testing

The last method of Black Box testing, and generally the least effective, is Random Testing. This is typically an automated approach that attempts to make up for lack of quality with sheer quantity. Normally when a massive number of inputs is created, each individual test case is not studied to verify its output. Often, testers simply visually scan the output for anomalies. Here is a quick and dirty sampling, to create integers between 1 and 1000, which can then be used as input for testing:

```
data testdata ( keep = testcase ) ;

seed1 = int ( time() ) ;

do i = 1 to 100 ;
    call ranuni ( seed1, new_num ) ;
    testcase = round ( new_num, .001) * 1000 ;
    output ;
end ;

run ;
```

White Box Testing

An alternate and complementary testing technique is called White Box testing, also called Glass Box, structural, or logic-driven testing. In White Box testing, the internal structure of the code is examined to determine test cases. Functional requirements are of secondary concern. Rather, the focus is to verify the consistency of logic to ensure that the program flow is correct. The goal of White Box testing is to be able to trace every possible path in the program. This can become a formidable task because the possible number of logic combinations can mushroom to gigantic proportions.

Consider the following diagram in which a curious child gets lost in downtown New York (see Figure 9.2). The parents start their search at each intersection (designated by a crosshair). Assuming their choices are completely random, the odds of finding their child after five decisions are: 1 / (4 * 4 * 4 * 4 * 4) = 1 in 1024.

Figure 9.2   *The number of decisions can mushroom very quickly, even when there are only a few decisions at each junction.*

For a programming logic example, assume that one simple program only contains 5 SELECT statements, each with 4 cases. That would yield the same number of decision points that the parents had. Thus, to ensure complete testing, 1024 test cases would have to be built for this modest program!

To determine all of the paths for a program, computer scientists have developed a number of different approaches. For simplicity, consider the three most widely used. In order from weakest to strongest coverage, the three traversal strategies are shown here:

- Statement Coverage

- Branch Coverage

- Multiple-Condition Coverage.

Statement Coverage

Statement Coverage is the most elemental type of White Box testing. To achieve Statement Coverage, you must traverse every statement in the program at least one time. Consider the following example:

```
if car = "Red" and power = "high" and model = "Corvette" then
do ;
    ticket = "Yes" ;
    fine  = 100.00 ;
end ;

if ticket = "Yes" or fine le 100 then      Ⓐ
    jail = "Yes" ;
```

Here, you can cause all statements in this code fragment to be executed by setting CAR to "Red", POWER to "High", and MODEL to "Corvette." However, the programmer may have intended to use AND instead of OR, or GE instead LE (marked Ⓐ in the example). In such cases, important logic paths would have been missed.

Statement Coverage is rarely considered adequate for serious applications development. However, due to time pressure, many organizations consider themselves fortunate to achieve coverage at this level.

Branch Coverage

Branch Coverage means that, at every decision point, test cases are arranged so that "True" and "False" conditions are both executed. Consider the following code fragment:

```
Branch #1:  if x = 1 and y = 2 then
                z = 3 ;

Branch #2:  if x = 2 and y = 3 then
                z = 4 ;
```

By setting the test cases as follows, both branch #1 and branch #2 are set to both "True and False":

1. (Sets Branch #1 to True, Branch #2 to False): `x = 1, y = 2`

2. (Sets Branch #1 to False, Branch #2 to False): `x = 0, y = 3`

3. (Sets Branch #1 to False, Branch #2 to True): `x = 2, y = 3`

By definition, Branch Coverage does not imply Statement Coverage, but for the sake of completeness, it should be part of Branch Coverage requirements. In SAS, for example, the SELECT construct also requires that each possible condition satisfied by the WHEN statement should be executed at least once.

Multiple Condition Coverage

A significant enhancement to Branch Coverage, Multiple Condition Coverage means that, at each branch point, each condition must take on all possible outcomes at least once. Consider the following code:

```
do until ( count gt maxcount or done = 'Y' or abort = 'Y' ) ;
    %get_more
end ;
```

For this example, eight test cases must be established:

1. `count gt maxcount, done = 'Y', abort = 'Y'`

2. `count le maxcount, done = 'Y', abort = 'Y'`

3. `count gt maxcount, done = 'N', abort = 'Y'`

4. `count le maxcount, done = 'N', abort = 'Y'`

5. `count gt maxcount, done = 'Y', abort = 'N'`

6. `count le maxcount, done = 'Y', abort = 'N'`

7. `count gt maxcount, done = 'N', abort = 'N'`

8. `count le maxcount, done = 'N', abort = 'N'`

Multiple Condition Coverage is considered the strongest type of coverage because virtually every combination of logic paths is examined.

Implementing White Box Methodology: Path Testing

Path Testing is a group of techniques based on the evaluation of program path execution. This section describes some terms and techniques associated with Path Testing.

Flowgraph

Flowgraph is a pictorial representation of program path execution. It is similar to old fashioned flowcharts, but with a few key differences:

- The flowgraph emphasizes decision making.
- All decision structures are included, no matter how trivial.
- Blocks of related code are condensed into one segment.

Process Block

A *process block* is a set of one or more program statements that are written so that if one of the statements executes, then all of the statements in the block execute. In other words, there are no statements that change the control flow. Here is an example of a process block:

```
x = y + 2 ;
a = scan ( counter, 1, "?" ) ;
b = index ( original, "bee" ) ;
```

Any SAS procedure is also a process block because all of the statements in the procedure step execute unconditionally.

Decision

A *decision* is any construct that can alter the flow of control. That is, at a decision point, the path that the program takes can be altered. The following constructs are decisions:

IF-THEN-ELSE	%IF-%THEN-%ELSE
SELECT	DO-WHILE
%DO-%WHILE	DO-UNTIL
%DO-%UNTIL	DO-END
%DO-%END	subsetting IF
WHERE	computed %GOTO

Don't forget that all DO-END constructs have an implicit level of decision because the loop index must be examined for each iteration of the DO loop.

The following constructs, while not decisions per se, can nevertheless alter the flow of control. This is particularly important when they are used in conjunction with a decision structure. Most often this would entail the use of an IF-THEN-ELSE construct. Hence, you must be aware of these constructs when determining program flow:

ABORT	DELETE
STOP	LINK
GOTO	%GOTO (not computed)
RETURN	

Junction

A *junction* is any point at which the flow of control comes to a common point. This can also be called a *merge point* for the control structure. The LABEL statement, which is the target of a GOTO instruction, is a junction.

Path Testing Example

Here is a simple example of how to convert some code into a flowgraph. This problem examines the flight of three amateur bank robbers. The starting and ending point of each process block is marked next to the source code. Any decision type structures, such as a DO loop or SELECT statement, are not marked because their logic flow is data dependent. Remember that the end of a DATA step is an implied loop, so leave the SET statement intact.

```
%let half_mil = 500000 ;              <<< start process block
%let ten_gees = 10000 ;               <<<
%let grand    = 1000 ;                <<<
%let one_mil  = 1000000 ;             <<<
                                      <<<
data _null_ ;                         <<< end process block
    set  robbers ;

length escape $30 ;                   <<< start process block
networth = diamonds  + saphires + cash ;   <<<
the_gang = "Dizzy" || " Earl" ||      <<<
 " Crazy Luke" ;                      <<<
                                      <<<
bank_rob = 0 ;                        <<< end process block

do until ( bank_rob = 5 or rob_cash gt &one_mil ) ;
    bank_rob + 1 ;
    rob_cash = sum ( rob_cash,  int ( ranuni (1414) * 1000 )) ;
end ;

split = int ( networth / 3 ) ;        <<< start process block
avg_haul = rob_cash / bank_rob ;      <<<
networth = networth + rob_cash ;      <<< end process block

select ;
    when (networth ge &half_mil)
        escape = "Private Jet" ;
    when (&ten_gees <= networth < &half_mil)
        escape = "Prop plane" ;
    when (&grand <= networth < &ten_gees)
        escape = "Automobile" ;
    otherwise
        escape = "Walk across border" ;
end ;

run ;                                 <<<  immaterial
```

The next step is to delete these marked portions of the process blocks so you can more easily follow the logic flow. If an element in a process block relates to ensuing decisions (for example, BANK_ROB = 0), leave it intact because it allows for easier test case generation.

```
set robbers ;

bank_rob = 0 ;

do until ( bank_rob = 5 or rob_cash gt &one_mil ) ;
    bank_rob + 1 ;
    rob_cash = sum ( rob_cash, int ( ranuni (1414) * 1000 )) ;
end ;

networth = networth + rob_cash ;

select ;
    when (networth ge &half_mil)
        escape = "Private jet" ;
    when (&ten_gees <= networth < &half_mil)
        escape = "Prop plane" ;
    when (&grand <= networth < &ten_gees)
        escape = "Automobile" ;
    otherwise
        escape = "Walk across border" ;
end ;
```

Converting to a Flowgraph

The first phase of converting to a flowgraph is to draw out the instructions similar to a flowchart (see Figure 9.3). The exact method of drawing (that is, left to right, up and down) is immaterial as long as you draw the flow correctly. Also, there is no requirement to write the exact SAS statement. You can write just enough so that you realize what the box represents. You can rewrite SELECT statements to look like multiple IF-THEN-ELSE constructs for readability. In addition, you can redraw a DO loop to emphasize its decision structure. This process helps you achieve the most comprehensive test coverage available—Multiple Condition Coverage.

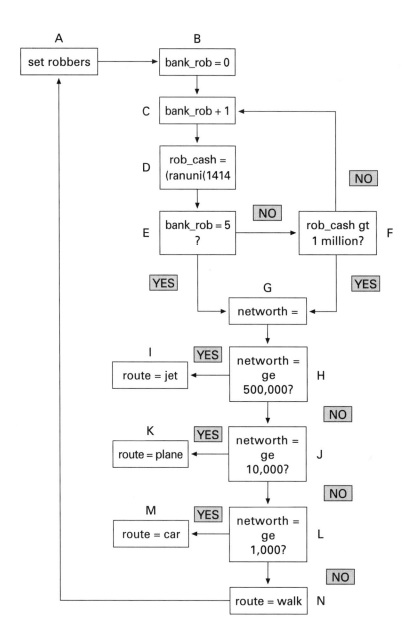

Figure 9.3   *The flowgraph looks a lot like a flowchart, except that the emphasis is on the decision points.*

After mapping out the logic flow, start at the top of the diagram and assign each statement a unique letter. Each statement is referred to as a "node." If a statement involves a decision, it is called a decision node. The next step involves creating a chart that reflects the possible test paths. Start with the simplest, most direct path. Then change each path by one node. From a testing perspective, if you detect a bug, this method makes it easier for you to determine the cause of the error. Save the more esoteric cases for when you have completed the basic cases:

Decision Nodes

Test Case	Path Trace	E	F	H	J	L
1	ABCDEGHJLNA	Yes	.	No	No	No
2	ABCDEGHJLMA	Yes	.	No	No	Yes
3	ABCDEGHJKA	Yes	.	No	Yes	.
4	ABCDEGHIA	Yes	.	Yes	.	.
5	ABCDEFCDEFGHJLNA	No	No*	No	No	No
6	ABCDEFGHJLNA	No	Yes	No	No	No

* For Test Case 5, the F node equals "No" for the first iteration, but equals "Yes" for the second iteration.

Test Case 4, by itself, achieves Statement Coverage because every statement in the source code executes at least once. To verify this, look at the source code, which shows that this path executes the DO loop one time and executes the first option in the SELECT statement. Would this be considered comprehensive testing? Intuitively, it is not.

Using the first five test cases meets Branch Coverage requirements. How do you know that? Look at the decision nodes. The E and F nodes form the DO loop combination. If one is set to "Yes" in any path trace and one is set to "No" in any path trace, then the requirements are met for this part of the program. Regarding the SELECT statement, all branches have to be selected at least once for Branch Coverage. Test Cases 1-4 execute each choice in the SELECT statement. Hence, for this program, complete Branch Coverage has been met by using just those five cases.

Test Case 6 is required for Multiple Condition Coverage, the most stringent path test. The reason is that the path segment E-F-G is not forced by Branch Coverage.

Reality Check

Real world programs are far more complex. Yet, one of the biggest obstacles to path testing is getting the code arranged so that logic paths are obvious to the tester. In other words, the tester wants to see the program trace as it executes. To ensure a complete source listing on the log, include the following at the beginning of the program:

```
options source source2 mprint ;
```

One disadvantage of using the log is that the code can look cluttered. Thus, whenever possible, use the original source code instead. This is possible under certain circumstances:

- if the level of nesting is not too deep with %INCLUDEd code. In this case, copy these %INCLUDE modules inline into the source code. After copying each module into the editor, continue to search for more %INCLUDE modules until all levels of nesting are accounted for inline.

- if the level of nesting is not too deep with the LINK statement. This is usually not overly difficult because the source code for the linked modules usually resides in the master source module.

- if the level of nesting is not too deep with macros. In this case, "demacro-ize" the macro, if possible, and bring these macros inline into the source code where the macro would have been invoked. Certainly, this does not work with all macro constructs because certain macros create and evaluate variables as they execute, such as the &&VAR&I macro.

- if no dynamic code is created. If there is code that is created with PUT statements that are later %INCLUDEd into the program, you must use the log because the source code is not predetermined.

Don't be discouraged by thinking that you have to draw out flowgraphs to achieve test cases. An alternate method for creating test cases is called "Linked-List" graphs. To use this methodology, list all the nodes in the program from top to bottom, compressing the process blocks into one node. Then, list next to it the node that executes. If a True/False condition exists, list the two possibilities.

```
A    start                => B
B                         => C
C    (loop)               => D
D                         => E
E    bank_rob = 5?        => G  (True)
                             F  (False)
F    rob_cash > mil?      => G  (True)
                          => C  (False)
G                         => H
H    networth >= .5 mil?  => I  (True)
                             J  (False)
I                         => A
J    networth >= 10,000?  => K  (True)
                          => L  (False)
K                         => A
L    networth >= 1000?    => M  (True)
                          => N  (False)
M                         => A
N                         => A
```

If this still seems tedious and beyond the realm of anyone outside of professional testers, you might consider using path testing on only the most complex modules. These are where errors tend to congregate. Nevertheless, the exercise of creating flowgraphs or linked-list graphs can be very revealing about the source code, and it provides valuable information for future development. Mapping program flow can provide information about:

- software complexity
- programs that are under- or over-modularized
- whether SELECT and IF-THEN-ELSE constructs are seamless
- failure to trap for logic or boundary errors

Dynamic Data Flow Analysis

Another aspect of White Box testing involves watching the data transitions from one state to the next. Many programming bugs are related to the improper declaration, initialization, and utilization of variables. A variable can exist in one of four states: declared, defined, used, or killed.

Declared

For this discussion, the "declared" state is only considered for DATA step variables (without a concomitant RETAIN). Their declaration allocates a fixed storage size and is therefore related to potential bugs. Declaration can result from any of the following statements:

1. LENGTH
2. ATTRIB
3. ARRAY

Defined

A "defined" DATA step variable appears on the left side of the equal (=) operator. A "defined" macro variable is created a number of ways, including:

1. %DO-END constructs
2. %GLOBAL
3. %INPUT
4. %LET
5. %LOCAL
6. %MACRO
7. %SYMPUT
8. %WINDOW
9. INTO statement from PROC SQL

Used

A "used" variable appears on the right side of the equal sign or is used as an object of a command:

```
if the_var gt 7 ;
put new_var 6.2 ;
```

Killed

A "killed" variable is no longer available for program processing. For example, if you omit a variable by using the DROP statement, it is "killed," in that it is not available in the next step.

There are 16 possible pairs of variable states. Some of these are part of normal processing while others are potentially problematic. As some of the more interesting combinations are examined in this section, remember that these combinations refer to consecutive references to a variable. Also, keep in mind that these 16 states can take on many more permutations, depending on the application. Use the following as a general guideline only:

Declared, Defined – normal, but there is no warning if the variable assignment is greater than the allocated length:

```
length new_var $25 ;
new_var = "This new variable is a bit too long" ;
```

Declared, Declared – this pathological state creates a warning in the log if the variable type is character:

```
length new_var $8 ;
...
length new_var $12 ;
```

Declared, Used – this pathological state creates a note in the SAS log:

```
length new_var 8 ;
old_var = new_var * 7 ;
```

Declared, Killed – usually harmless, but should be cleaned up:

```
data out_data ;
    set old_data ;

length new_var 8;
drop new_var ;
```

Defined, Declared – potential bug due to character truncation:

```
new_var = calc_var ;
length new_var $12 ;
```

Defined, Defined – Case I. This state is usually harmless and is most likely used to override default:

```
%let rpt_type = payroll ;
...
%let rpt_type = acct_pay ;
```

Defined, Defined – Case II. This is a potential bug because a variable being reinitialized without intervening use is cause for concern:

```
data re_use ;
...
my_var = 25 ;
...
...
my_var = 18 ;
```

Used, Declared – normal state that is used to change the length of a variable:

```
data out_data ;

length old_var $12 ;
set new ;
```

Killed, Used – a potential bug that is a common error with macro variables:

```
%macro pot_bug ;
    %local new_var ;
    %let new_var = 20 ;
%mend pot_bug ;

data _null_ ;
..
calc_var = 17 + &new_var ;
```

Killed, Defined – potential bug. Be careful mixing global macro variables and local macro variables:

```
%macro pot_bug ;
    %local new_var ;
    %let new_var = 20 ;
%mend pot_bug ;

%let new_var = 30 ;
```

Killed, Killed – probably harmless. It produces a warning on the log:

```
data new_data ;
    set old_data ;
drop a ;
....
run ;

data out_data ;
    set new_data ;
drop a ;
run ;
```

Here is a table that summarizes the state combinations and their potential for problems. Note that the actual result may differ according to the application as there are literally hundreds of permutations that can be generated from these 16 variable combinations. Remember, Table 9.3 is only a guideline for potential problems:

State 1	State 2	Typical Result
Declared	Declared	Warning on log
Declared	Defined	OK, watch truncation
Declared	Used	Note on log
Declared	Killed	Probably Harmless
Defined	Declared	Potential Bug
Defined	Defined	Possible bug/Normal
Defined	Used	OK
Defined	Killed	OK
Used	Declared	OK
Used	Defined	OK
Used	Used	OK
Used	Killed	OK
Killed	Declared	OK
Killed	Defined	Caution
Killed	Used	Potential Bug
Killed	Killed	Warning on log

Table 9.3 *Variable state combinations and their potential for problems.*

For the tester, there are a few points to remember about data dynamics:

- Don't ignore warnings from the SAS supervisor!

- A clean log does not mean that there are no anomalies.

- Modern programming is becoming more and more table driven. This means that data become a much larger segment of the code, so there is a concomitant increase in data-related errors.

- Variable state anomalies are application dependent.

- Be acutely aware of referencing environments. Be suspicious of same name macro variables used both for local and global environments. Or, in the same vein, be wary of same name variables used in two different local environments. If the programmer utilizes the %LOCAL statement, then there shouldn't be a problem. However, in the absence of the %LOCAL statement, there is certainly a chance of variables clashing.

Black Box Testing versus White Box Testing

In a typical software environment, complete testing involves a combination of White Box and Black Box testing. The two complement each other, and both are required to maximize testing success. However, each method has its strengths and weaknesses, and each is more appropriate for certain applications.

Black Box Testing Conditions

Black Box testing is appropriate when:

- you have built customized systems. Customization is, by definition, the development of software according to modified functional specifications. The emphasis of testing such systems is on ensuring that modifications adhere to the new functional requirements.

- if for security reasons, the source code is not to be accessed by testers.

- the SAS code is shipped to the customer using the Compiled Stored Facility, thus making the DATA step inaccessible.

- you need user acceptance testing, but the customer lacks the technical expertise to implement White Box techniques.

- the code is too massive, at the system level, to implement White Box techniques.

- testing time is limited. Black box testing does not require you to have any comprehension of the source code. While the time to develop test cases for White Box testing may not be considerable for small programs, this changes rapidly as the complexity of the program grows. This is most evident in programs laced with many macros, %INCLUDE modules, and a lot of decision making. Hence, in general, Black Box testing is generally more efficient to quickly create test cases.

Two other points to consider are:

- Nontechnical project managers generally believe that Black Box testing is the only testing necessary.

- Programs generated primarily by PROCS are generally not amenable to White Box testing.

White Box Testing Conditions

White Box testing is more appropriate when:

- you are testing utility software. These tests emphasize Glass Box techniques because you want to formulate educated guesses about the most frequently traversed logic paths.

- you are testing at the module level. Good design implies relative independence of modules.

- the testers have a strong theoretical training. Then, a whole new set of tools is available to them.

Two other points to consider are:

- Complex algorithms should be examined internally.

- Programs that have a significant amount of DATA _NULL_ and/or macro processing are good candidates for logic flow analysis. Complex querying with PROC SQL may also lend itself to logic-based testing.

Gray Box Testing

Up to this point, this chapter has examined two major branches of testing. However, there is a shady area, between the two extremes, which has been coined "Gray Box testing." This type of inspection can take on two forms. In one case, programmers do not actually look at the code, but their knowledge of programming techniques allows them to make hunches about the kinds of processing. Then they create equivalence classes from these hunches. Examples of constructs that fall into this category include:

_N_	the first observation
FIRST.	the first observation in a group
LAST.	the last observation in a group
END=	last observation
BY	by-group processing

The other kind of Gray Box testing occurs when you look at the source code and create equivalence cases based on your perusal of the logic. For example, if a programmer used a lot of hexadecimal processing, you should examine the domain edges using hexadecimal boundaries. For instance, if a variable has a valid range of $30x$ to $39x$ (a decimal equivalent of 0–9) then it would be prudent to inspect $29x$ and $40x$ as boundary conditions. The latter are called "hidden boundaries" because they would not be evident without first looking at the source code.

The MERGE statement creates its own set of input domains. Each input data set and its intersection (or lack of intersection) creates its own partition space. For instance, examine the following MERGE statement:

```
data applepie ;
     merge apples ( in = in_apple )
           crust  ( in = in_crust )
           sugar  ( in = in_sugar ) ;
```

This domain space can be depicted as in Figure 9.4:

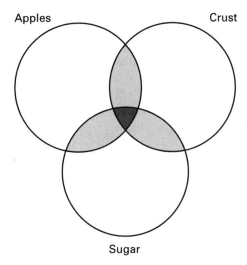

Figure 9.4 *The input boundaries can overlap, leading to interesting scenarios.*

The following partition spaces are identified based on the presence of the following ingredients and their corresponding IN operator.

sugar only	(in_sugar)
crust only	(in_crust)
apples only	(in_apple)
apples and crust	(in_apple and in_crust)
crust and sugar	(in_crust and in_sugar)
apples and sugar	(in_apple and in_sugar)
apples, crust and sugar	(in_apple and in_crust and in_sugar)
no ingredients	(all data sets empty)

In general, the number of test cases is determined as 2^n where n is the number of data sets that are merged. It is very handy to have the list of test cases laid out on paper, especially when the number of merged data sets becomes large. Here is a sample program that quickly lays this out:

```
%macro set_var ( list = ) ;

    %local word ;        * One word in the input list ;
    %local new_list ;    * Creates list for proc freq ;
    %local pointer ;     * Points to next word in the input list ;

    data domain ;

    %let pointer = 1 ;
```

```
%do %until ( &word = %str ( ) ) ;
    %let word = %scan ( &list, &pointer ) ;
    %if &word ne %then
    %do ;
        %if &pointer = 1 %then
            %let new_list = &word ;
        %else
            %let new_list = &new_list * &word ;
        &word = "Yes" ;
    %end ;
    %let pointer = %eval ( &pointer + 1 ) ;
%end ;

output ;

%let pointer = 1 ;
%do %until ( &word = %str() ) ;
    %let word = %scan ( &list, &pointer ) ;
    %if &word ne %then
    %do ;
        &word = "No" ;
    %end ;
    %let pointer = %eval ( &pointer + 1 ) ;
%end ;

output ;
run ;

proc freq data = domain noprint ;
    tables &new_list/ sparse out = dom_list
    ( drop = count percent ) ;
run ;

proc print data = dom_list ;
    title 'Input domain based on MERGE statement' ;
run ;

%mend set_var ;
```

Invoking this macro with five data sets produces the following output:

```
%set_var ( list = peaches crust sugar filling cinnamon )
```

```
                 Input domain based on MERGE statement

     OBS      PEACHES      CRUST      SUGAR      FILLING      CINNAMON

      1        No          No         No         No           No
      2        No          No         No         No           Yes
      3        No          No         No         Yes          No
      4        No          No         No         Yes          Yes
      5        No          No         Yes        No           No
      6        No          No         Yes        No           Yes
      7        No          No         Yes        Yes          No
      8        No          No         Yes        Yes          Yes
      9        No          Yes        No         No           No
     10        No          Yes        No         No           Yes
     11        No          Yes        No         Yes          No
     12        No          Yes        No         Yes          Yes
     13        No          Yes        Yes        No           No
     14        No          Yes        Yes        No           Yes
     15        No          Yes        Yes        Yes          No
     16        No          Yes        Yes        Yes          Yes
     17        Yes         No         No         No           No
     18        Yes         No         No         No           Yes
     19        Yes         No         No         Yes          No
     20        Yes         No         No         Yes          Yes
     21        Yes         No         Yes        No           No
     22        Yes         No         Yes        No           Yes
     23        Yes         No         Yes        Yes          No
     24        Yes         No         Yes        Yes          Yes
     25        Yes         Yes        No         No           No
     26        Yes         Yes        No         No           Yes
     27        Yes         Yes        No         Yes          No
     28        Yes         Yes        No         Yes          Yes
     29        Yes         Yes        Yes        No           No
     30        Yes         Yes        Yes        No           Yes
     31        Yes         Yes        Yes        Yes          No
     32        Yes         Yes        Yes        Yes          Yes
```

This table can guide the test plan toward completeness with an otherwise complicated testing scheme.

Remember that examining equivalence classes is not a complete testing battery, but merely a part of a complete test package.

Structured Testing Methodology

Up to this point, the focus of this chapter has been on the mechanics of testing. In this section, the focus is on the aspects of testing that relate to the entire software system. To get a handle on organizing large systems testing, you need a plan for organizing the process. Normal protocol requires software systems to be inspected at the module level, followed by integration and, lastly, system testing.

Module Testing

Testing each module separately has a number of advantages. Most notably, you can more easily isolate and correct errors in elemental structures. This is in contrast to trying to find bugs in large systems and then laboriously tracing the cause of the error. Another advantage is that you can simultaneously test multiple modules before assembling the system. It is important to note that that the ability to perform effective unit testing depends on a module having clearly specified inputs and outputs.

Module testing tends to be largely White Box testing, with enough Black Box testing to ensure functionality. This is partly due to the fact that White Box testing is often not feasible at integration or system levels.

Considerations for Testing a Module

You want to ensure that all variables in the parameter list are handled appropriately. For this example, consider a macro module. If a variable has no default, then it is critical to test for its existence. Here is an example:

```
%macro dance ( lesson  = ,
               teacher = ,
               type = ) ;

    data bad_recs ( keep = err_msg ) ;

    length err_msg $100 ;

    %if %length (&lesson) = 0 %then
    %do ;
        err_msg = 'parameter &lesson is missing' ;
        output ;
    %end ;

    %if %length (&teacher) = 0 %then
    %do ;
        err_msg = 'parameter &teacher is missing' ;
        output ;
    %end ;

    %if %length (&type) = 0 %then
    %do ;
        err_msg = 'parameter &type is missing' ;
        output ;
    %end ;

    stop ;
    run ;

%mend dance ;
```

At this point, you can test invoking the macro with missing parameters:

```
%dance ( lesson = 3 ,
         type = Salsa )
```

The following is then written to the error data set:

```
parameter &teacher is missing
```

Another problem to watch for is inconsistencies or redundancy in the parameter list. For example, you may create a macro that requests the output device and a minimal acceptable resolution:

```
%macro out_dev ( device = ,
                 min_res = ) ;
```

How do you handle the problem of specifying a device as a printer, but a resolution for a monitor? It is useful, after creating a macro, to list all the variable dependencies and verify that there is appropriate error trapping for each of these inconsistencies.

Integration Testing

At the unit testing level, modules are tested as discrete entities. When performing integration testing, you must demonstrate that the modules function together as a group. Integration testing is effective at demonstrating faults in three major areas: interfaces, module combinations, and global data structures.

Interfaces

An interface is the means of passing data from one module to the next. The goal of this phase of testing is to ensure "integration integrity," which means that data passed from one module to the next should not be lost or corrupted. What kinds of interface errors are possible?

1. The calling and called routines are not in synchronization on the number of arguments that they use.

2. The called routine receives the wrong type of argument.

3. The data somehow disappears (for example, macro variables.)

4. There are conflicts in global variables.

Module Combinations

The second kind of possible error is when modules act in combination. For example, perhaps modules are not called in correct sequence.

Global Data Structures

The third type of integration testing involves global data structures. This testing may involve external files, SAS data sets, database access and update, and %GLOBAL macro variables.

Integration Strategies

There are two general strategies for integration testing: "Big Bang" (or non-incremental testing) and the incremental approach. With Big Bang testing, you do thorough testing only after the completion of individual modules testing. Some might argue that overall testing time is less because unit testing is bypassed to concentrate on the "real system." However, "Big Bang" testing is rather shortsighted. Upon discovering a bug, how do you isolate the source of the error?

The second (and more sound) approach is "Incremental Testing," which consolidates software components after testing individual modules. This can involve consolidation through Bottom-Up or Top-Down strategies.

Top-Down Testing

Top-down testing involves testing individual components only when all of an element's parents have already been tested. Thus, by definition, you would test the topmost module before examining any other modules. In the following example, the programmer creates a macro-based system to teach Spanish to students. Assume that any shaded module in Figure 9.5 has been coded.

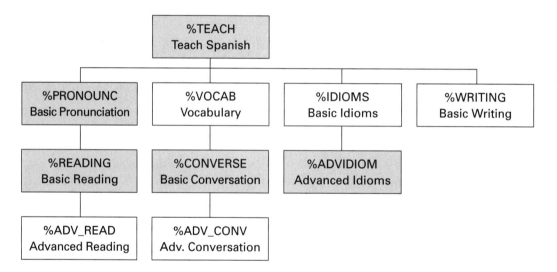

Figure 9.5   *An example of Top-Down Testing.*

In this example, test the %TEACH macro first. Then, test %PRONOUNC and %READING respectively. Note that you cannot test any modules before coding and testing the parent modules. You can test %READING, but it is the parent to %ADV_READ, which has not been coded. In this case, you must create a "programming stub."

Stubs

These programming stubs (or dummy modules) may range from being trivial in nature to being very complex. At the simplest level, the stub just may be a subroutine (LINK, %INCLUDE, or macro) that returns a message that lets the calling routine know that it was called. This is allowable when the calling routine requires no data transferred from the called routine. For example, here is sample code that is based on the example in the previous section:

```
%macro adv_read ;
     %put Yes you entered the adv_read subroutine! ;
%mend adv_read ;
```

At the next level of complexity, the calling routine may expect one or more parameters to be passed back to the master routine. The parameters passed back must not only return the expected number of arguments, but must also have the attributes of the parameters:

```
data _null_ ;

link grades ;
return ;

grades:
name = "My friends call me Pokey"  ;
ssn = "118-55-3935" ;
major = "Pre-med Why not?" ;
gpa = 1.815 ;
return ;
```

At the most complex level, the calling routine may pass, to the stub, data that involves calculations before returning to the caller. In addition, the called routine may expect a range of responses, such as 1-10. The master program should be able to test for each of these responses. One way is to create a test data set that reflects all these combinations. For the following example, assume that your children want to open up a drink stand for making big summer money. To help them appreciate the importance of marketing, you require them to market their product by using different drinks, prices, and locations. To ensure complete coverage, you would need to code something similar to the following:

```
data level_01 ;

infile cards ;
length drink $40. ;
input drink  @@ ;

cards ;
Lemonade Juice Milk Soda
;
```

```
data level_02 ;

infile cards ;
length location $20. ;
input location @@ ;

cards ;
Mall Home Street
;

data level_03 ;

infile cards ;

input price @@ ;
cards ;
.25 .50 .75 1.00 1.25 1.50 1.75 2.00 2.50
;

data testdata ;
    set level_01 level_02 level_03  ;
run ;

proc freq data = testdata noprint  ;
    tables drink * location * price  /
        sparse out = test_out
          ( keep = drink location price ) ;
run ;

proc print data = test_out ;
    where drink ne " " and location ne " " and price ne . ;
run ;
```

I guess you're a pretty strict parent because such a the marketing approach requires 108 tests!

Bottom-Up Testing

Bottom-up testing is similar to top-down testing except that you start at the bottom of the programming hierarchy and move upwards in the testing of modules. Consider again the example of the macro-based system to teach Spanish to students. As in Figure 9.5, shaded areas in Figure 9.6 indicate modules that have been coded.

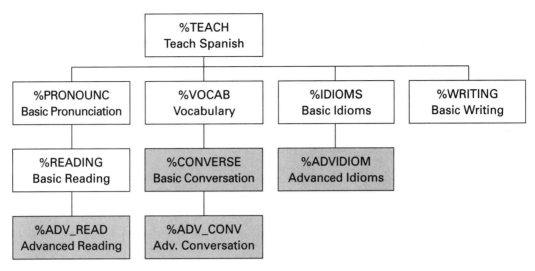

Figure 9.6   *An example of Bottom-Up Testing.*

Drivers

In bottom-up testing, it is necessary to create driver modules. These drivers are temporary blocks of code that define data and the control interface that the block needs for execution. In the example above, %ADV_READ has been coded. In order to test it, you must create a driver because %READING has not yet been coded. On the other hand, %ADV_CONV needs no driver because its parent module %CONVERSE has already been coded. Note, however, that %CONVERSE needs a driver because %VOCAB has not been coded yet. Creating code for drivers is similar to programming stubs. You must create enough code to ensure minimum functionality for the driver. At the simplest level, this may just involve allowing the module to be called from the parent module:

```
%macro reading ;
    %put I am calling the converse module now ;
    %converse
%mend reading ;
```

At the more complex level, the driver may require such functions as accessing a database, performing a calculation, massaging data, or passing a list of parameters to the called routine.

Comparison of Top-Down Testing versus Bottom-Up Testing

Theorists debate about whether bottom-up or top-down testing is easier and more practical to implement. However, the majority prefer top-down for two major reasons:

- Drivers are generally more difficult to write than stubs.

- Testing the high-level modules first can expose critical design-related problems early in the software development process.

System Testing

System testing is the final step in the testing continuum. At times, the term "Validation Testing" is used because the goal is to determine if the final product works according to specifications. Included in system testing are the following subsets:

- Volume testing
- Stress testing
- Conversion/parallel testing
- Acceptance testing.

Volume Testing

Volume testing stresses the program with massive input. For example, you can do any of the following:

- Create SAS data sets of incredible size. This should be tested in two dimensions. One is to create a data set with a large number of observations. Secondly, if the program produces data sets of variable width, create a data set as wide as possible.
- Create input and output files of huge proportions.
- If linked lists are involved, construct as many links as possible.
- Attempt to break the program by taxing memory to the limit.
- Send large amounts of data to any peripheral device.
- Run the program for hours or days.

Stress Testing

Stress testing tests a program's response to peak bursts of activity. For example, you can:

- Key information into an input field as fast as possible.
- Simultaneously update a database using multiple users.
- Submit multiple jobs to a network printer at the same time.
- Attempt multiple access to too few communication lines.

Conversion/Parallel Testing

Conversion/parallel testing can verify that a product runs on different platforms, or it can compare the manual version against the automated version.

Acceptance Testing

Acceptance testing is the last of the testing phases. If there are few customers, then the customers evaluate the product. If there is a large customer population, then some of the customers may perform an alpha test at the developer's site. This is then followed by a beta test, which is a preliminary shipment to a select group of customers. Beta tests are of enormous benefit because many "real world" bugs are discovered and fixed before the finished product is shipped to the entire customer base.

Bugging a Program

How do you measure the effectiveness of testing? One technique is to plant bugs in a program. By counting how many of these bugs the tester uncovers, you can extrapolate the number of bugs remaining in the rest of the program. The formula to predict latent bugs is:

$$\text{Bugs remaining} = ((\text{ PB / PBF }) * \text{ OBF }) - \text{OBF} + (\text{ PB} - \text{PBF }) ;$$

where PB = # of Planted Bugs
    PBF = # of Planted Bugs found
    OBF = # of Other (non-planted) bugs found

For example, if the programmer planted 50 bugs in a program and the tester finds 10 of these bugs and 70 others, then the number of bugs in the program is:

$$\begin{aligned}\text{Bugs remaining} &= ((\text{ 50 / 10 }) * 70) - 70 + (\text{ 50} - 10) \\ &= 350 - 70 + 40 \\ &= 320\end{aligned}$$

Bugging a program has two major criticisms:

1. The planted bugs must have the same chance of being detected as other bugs. Otherwise, the program can seriously underestimate or overestimate the bug rate and, thus, waste of a lot of project time.

2. The political consequences of bugging a program can irk both the tester and the programmer. This is especially true when neither have been notified about the bugging process.

Comparison Testing Techniques

One of the most powerful ways to ensure the quality of the output is to compare the program output from different sources. Some of the options include the following:

- computer software versus manual calculations: Most programmers probably do this type of testing to a certain degree. Sometimes this involves just pulling out a hand calculator and computing statistics against the SAS output.

- computer software versus multiple manual calculations: SAS output is generated and at least two other individuals calculate the expected output manually. This technique is especially useful when the functional specifications are complex. Walking through the data "by hand" to generate statistics can be quite revealing. On numerous occasions, functional specifications have been modified after the fact. This type of comparison is imperative for critical applications, such as clinical trials that test the effectiveness of a medication. In this case, it is typical for several members of the medical team to calculate the numbers manually and compare their output against the SAS programmer's output.

- SAS System versus other languages: SAS output is verified against the results of another language. This is imperative when converting from another language to SAS or vice versa. The most direct way to compare results is to write SAS data to an ASCII file, have the target language do the same, and then compare output. Alternatively, the ASCII file can be converted to a SAS data sets, and you could then run PROC COMPARE on the two data sets.

- SAS versus SAS (same algorithm): You calculate output using two different SAS techniques. For instance, you might calculate results with DATA step MERGE processing and then compare it with the output generated by PROC SQL processing. Or, you may calculate statistics with PROCS such as PROC UNIVARIATE or PROC MEANS, and then compare against the same calculations produced by a DATA _NULL_. This technique is also useful to test a program that is rewritten for efficiency reasons. For example, you can run PROC COMPARE on the final data sets to compare the original and rewritten versions.

- SAS versus SAS (different algorithm): This may be one of the most powerful techniques because it helps to minimize programming bias. For example, to determine if a routine has a circular link, you can calculate this indirectly or directly. The indirect method would entail the following. The key elements for determining circular links are marked in bold :

```
do until (list_ary {arrow} = '  ') ;
    do a = 1 to ary_cnt ;
        if trim ( left ( list_ary {arrow} )) =
            trim ( left ( from_ary {a} )) then
        do ;
            list_cnt + 1 ;
            if list_cnt gt &max_poss then
            do ;
                put 'Circular link detected' ;
                bad_rec = 'yes' ;
                return ;
            end ;
            list_ary {list_cnt} = to_ary {a} ;
        end ;
    end ;
    arrow + 1 ;
end ;
```

The above algorithm is indirect. If the link list attempts to go into an infinite loop, then you can infer that a circular loop has been created. An alternative algorithm (direct approach) is to trace the links. If at any time a link is repeated within the list, then a circular link has been identified. Recoding this routine demonstrates the difference. Once again, the key elements for determining circular links are marked in bold:

```
do until (list_ary {arrow} = '  ') ;
    do a = 1 to ary_cnt ;
        if trim ( left ( list_ary {arrow} )) =
            trim ( left ( from_ary {a} )) then
        do ;
            do b = 1 to list_cnt ;
                if to_ary {a} = list_ary {b} then
                do ;
                    put "circular link begins at " to_ary {a} ;
                    return ;
                end ;
            end ;
            list_cnt + 1 ;
            list_ary {list_cnt} = to_ary {a} ;
        end ;
    end ;
    arrow + 1 ;
end ;
```

Summary

Testing methodology is more of a science than most people realize. While most programmers test their programs at a superficial level, rarely do they examine their code at comprehensive White Box and Black Box levels. You can discover many errors by doing a systematic analysis of logic paths and functional specifications, and by isolating input vector domains. Functional requirements lend themselves to Black Box techniques, while program logic can be analyzed by White Box techniques. Supplementing these methodologies with Gray Box Testing can form a complete testing battery.

To incorporate Integration Testing, test modules using top-down testing or bottom-up testing. Usually, this involves writing test harnesses or dummy modules to simulate the completion of a module.

System Testing is the final phase in the test process. This is the ultimate test because you have the opportunity to prove that the system can stand up to the pressures of real world situations.

Exercises

1. Without informing the team, the not-so-popular project leader decides to plant 100 bugs in a system. The tester discovers 5 of these bugs and 25 other bugs. Assuming that the planted bugs have the same likelihood of discovery as all other bugs, how many bugs remain in the system?

2. Identify each of the following as White Box, Gray Box or Black Box Testing:

   a. You want to develop a sweeter kind of corn. You create hybrids using ten different types of corn. You note the sweetness of each hybrid.

   b. After peeking at the source code, you notice that equivalence classes are set up using PROC FORMAT. You then develop your own equivalent classes and note the output.

   c. A macro redirects logic flow according to the value of its input parameters. You trace this logic after inputting various parameters.

   d. A tire's durability is tested by puncturing it, using a large nail, with incrementally greater force. You watch to determine the force required to puncture the tire.

   e. You test an airline reservation system by entering 1, 10, and 99 reservations for one passenger.

   f. You notice that BY group processing is used to calculate totals on a report. You look at the report and manually calculate totals for each BY group.

   g. You slam your fists on the keyboard and observe the computer's response.

   h. You test each case in a SELECT statement and watch which subroutine is called for each case.

3. A new cable television system has the following channels available:

03-12

17-45

49

55-66

Set up an INPUT statement and a CARDS statement to test for boundary values.

4. After entering your login ID, you must enter a two character code (your password) and then press the ENTER key. What would be the major equivalence classes?

5. How many equivalence classes should be created for the following DATA step?

```
data commute ;
    set auto
        train
        bus
        trolley
        ;
    by fare ;
```

6. Explain why Statement Coverage is inadequate to test the following code fragment:

```
if animal = in ("Carnivore", "Herbivore") then
    if foodtype = "Beef" then
        meal = "Y" ;

if animal = "Herbivore and meal = "Y" then
    satisfied = "Y" ;
```

7. What is a good set of test cases for the following DO loop index?

```
do i = 1 to &max_cnt ;
    val = old_val + new_val ;
end ;
```

8. In the following diagram, assume that the shaded boxes represent modules that have been coded. If you are doing top-down testing, which modules must be programmed as dummy stubs if you want to commence testing?

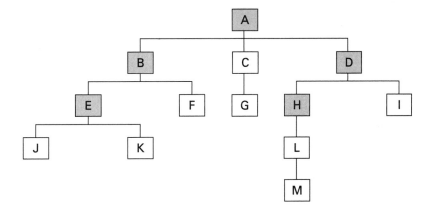

9. In the following diagram, assume that the shaded boxes represent modules that have been coded. If you are doing bottom-up testing, which modules must be programmed as driver modules if you want to commence testing?

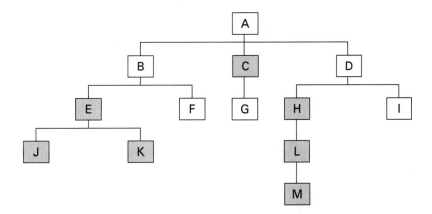

10. What is the principal reason for performing a data flow analysis on a SAS program?

References

Andriole, S.J. (1986), *Software Validation Verification Testing and Documentation*, Princeton, NJ: Petrocelli Books.

Beizer, B. (1990), *Software Testing Techniques*, New York: Van Nostrand Reinhold.

Cave, W.C. and Maymon, G.W. (1984), *Software Lifecycle Management: The Incremental Method*, New York: Macmillan Publishing.

Jack, O. (1996), *Software Testing for Conventional and Logic Programming*, Berlin: Walter de Gruyter.

Hausen H. (1983), *Software Validation*, Amersterdam: North-Holland.

Kaner, C. (1988), *Testing Computer Software*, Blue Ridge Summit, PA: Tab Professional and Reference Books.

Marick, B. (1995), *The Craft of Software Testing*, Englewood Cliffs, NJ: Prentice Hall PTR.

Miller, E. and Howden, E. (1981), *Tutorial: Software Testing & Validation Techniques*, New York: IEEE Computer Society Press.

Myers, G.J. (1979), *The Art of Software Testing*, New York: John Wiley & Sons.

Parikh, G. (1986), *Handbook of Software Maintenance*, New York: John Wiley & Sons.

Perry, W. (1988), *A Structured Approach to Systems Testing*, Wellesley, MA: GED Information Systems.

Chapter 10   # Digging Out with Debugging Techniques

Introduction **230**

The Anatomy of Bugs **230**

General Debugging Strategies **231**
    Brute Force 231
    Induction 232
    Deduction 232

Debugging Tactics **234**

Preventive Maintenance **242**
    Designing In/Instrumenting 242
    "Bug Catcher" Routines 243

Regressive Bugs **244**

Debugging Dynamic Code **245**

Macro Debugging Tips **246**

The SAS DATA Step Debugger **249**
    Running the Debugger without Interruption 250
    Running the Debugger One Step at a Time 251
    Additional Debugger Features 255

Summary **255**

Exercises **256**

References **256**

Introduction

Steve was having a really lousy day. Seventeen prisoners escaped from maximum security after the electronic surveillance system failed for the first time ever. The software he installed and tested for that system had been infallible for the last seven years. Until today. Where did he go wrong? Was the problem related to hardware, software, or in the controller itself? Could this be a freak accident, or is there a serious problem? What methods could he use to avert future disasters like this one?

The situation that Steve encountered happens every day in the programming community, but for most programmers, their story is not as dramatic as Steve's. Programming bugs can be trivial, or they can be incredibly elusive. This chapter examines the methods of debugging that must be in every programmer's arsenal. Specifically, it focuses on bugs that are related to faulty logic. It is assumed that you already understand how to eliminate syntactical errors. Consequently, this class of errors is not discussed in this chapter.

The Anatomy of Bugs

If you were to survey programmers and ask them what a bug is, most would reply, "A coding error." However, bugs can appear at any time during a project. Here is a brief description of bugs based on their relative location in the software lifecycle:

Analysis/Design: This is the worst kind of bug because its effects can ripple throughout the system.

Coding: These bugs are created by faulty programming logic or technique. Such bugs are the focus of this chapter.

External Documentation: The programmer may be coding according to external specifications, and the original specifications may be correct. However, when the code is reformatted for use in, for instance, a WordPerfect document, an error occurs in the translation.

Internal documentation: The comments within the program are not updated or, for whatever reason, they do not match the code.

Testing: The tester creates a test case, notes an error (incorrectly), and reports the error to the programmer.

Maintenance: A programmer makes a fix to a known bug, but creates another bug in its wake. This is incredibly common.

General Debugging Strategies

Effective debugging should not be a random act. Rather, there are a number of techniques that you can utilize to systematically uncover program faults. See Figure 10.1 for a summary of the major debugging strategies.

Brute Force

The daughter of King Ferdinand is abducted in the middle of the night. The despondent king orders his soldiers to sweep the countryside. He tells his men to search every home, every field, behind every tree, and into the mountains, looking anywhere and everywhere.

The king is relying on "brute force" in an attempt to find his daughter. Does this brute force method have its counterpart in SAS software? It certainly does. One variation is to use the PUT _ALL_ construct. This statement requests that every single variable in the Program Data Vector be displayed in the SAS log. What are the pros and cons of such a method?

The PUT_ALL_ Construct

The advantages of using the PUT_ALL_ construct are:

- You can easily display variables of interest.
- Because it does not disrupt the source code to a great degree, it is a simple matter to remove the PUT statement when debugging is completed.

The disadvantages are:

- Because it is a "snapshot," it does not effectively show the dynamics of program processing.
- Unless you place an incredibly large number of PUT statements in the DATA step, many key variables may not be exposed at the exact moment that the error occurs. For example, it is easy to overlook the re-initialization of variables and the updating of array elements.
- Most likely, the programmer is not thinking about the problem. Odds are that he isn't studying his code for logic flaws.
- The Program Data Vector can be massive, especially if large arrays are defined in the DATA step. This can dramatically increase the programmer's search time.

Note: Save your vision (and your sanity) by requesting a line return or two between observations for easier debugging:

```
put // _all_ ;
```

The PRINT Procedure

A second variation of brute force in SAS software is the use of PROC PRINT after each and every DATA step and PROC step. The pros and cons of using PROC PRINT are basically the same as using PUT _ALL_, but with the following additional advantages:

- It provides a snapshot at a good logical boundary, which is at a data interface. Thus, it is effective in helping you to isolate a problem to a given DATA step. It is interesting to note that creating smaller DATA steps can, thus, be advantageous from a debugging standpoint.

- Isolating a bug in a large system is more methodical, thus saving considerable debugging time.

However, the additional disadvantage is that it does not show logic errors within a module.

Induction

Our miserable king finds that his methods of brute force are futile, so he decides to use his gray matter, hoping to find clues. He remembers that not a soul has seen his beautiful princess since last night. The bedroom window, usually shut, is now ajar. The flowers next to her bed are crushed. There is also the gentlest scent of cologne permeating the air.

In the same way as the king, you can use induction to find errors in your programs. For instance, suppose that program totals are not being calculated properly. The clues might include: (1) the error only occurs after the first observation, (2) the bug only surfaces in the first record in a BY group, (3) if there is only one record in the BY group, the problem does not appear. From these clues, you develop a hypothesis. In this case, you theorize that the variable TOTAL is reset at the inappropriate place in the DATA step. Also, the first record is immune because a RETAIN statement initialized that variable. Hence, you make a program fix, and then test the hypothesis. If the output is still incorrect, you continue the iteration of finding clues, making a hypothesis, and testing the hypothesis until the program is fixed.

Deduction

The king is getting desperate. The clues do not give him a single idea. Now he is ready to work the other way around. He remembers that outside, in the courtyard (before the gates were locked), Sir Wallace, Sir Raleigh, Sir Scott, and William, the peasant, were milling around. It must be one of them!

In like manner, you come up with a list of possible suspects. For the previous example, you develop the following theories:

- A lookup table calculates totals. However, there have been updates to the PROC FORMAT that creates this table.

- The variables used to calculate the total are not initialized in the correct location.

- The SQL query in the previous step is not constructed properly.

- The algorithm for calculating the total is flawed.

Each hypothesis is tested in turn until the problem is uncovered. Just as in the case of induction, the hypothesis is tested until it is verified.

P.S. *As it turns out, the princess actually ran away from home. So here is a good lesson—if there is an error in the problem definition, the project is set up for failure.*

(A) Brute Force

(B) Induction

(C) Deduction

Figure 10.1   *The three major strategies for program debugging:*
a. Brute Force implies a sweep of the application space without regard to any theories.
b. Induction involves looking at the clues and forming a hypothesis.
c. Deduction involves creating a list of suspects and testing each of these candidates in turn.

Debugging Tactics

Here is a list of suggestions for assisting you in debugging code.

Never assume anything!

It is common for programmers to think in the following manner: "Well, I know that variable x has to be 7 here, and variable y has to be 12 there, and variable z is definitely 24 there." Step back and verify that these values are really what you think they are. Many bugs are silly oversights, such as forgetting a RETAIN or a LENGTH statement.

Print out all raw data for the program.

Running a PROC PRINT for all data used in the program is invaluable. Whenever you are testing and debugging, it is imperative to go back to the raw data. As in the previous point, NEVER assume that output from any intermediate procedure step or DATA step is correct.

Simplify by isolating the problem.

The execution of a program requires the successful operation of many factors including software, hardware, interfaces to peripheral devices, data sharing, database access, and network operations, just to name a few. For example, suppose that you have developed a program in an operating environment that converts SAS output into Microsoft Word format and sends the output directly to the printer. What if the program bombs while executing in a new environment?

Isolate the problem: Does the output look okay if directed to the terminal? What happens if you run the program stand-alone (as opposed to executing on the network)? What version of SAS is executing? What version of Word is loaded? What version of the database is resident?

Change only one thing at a time.

When debugging, you often form a hypothesis about the problem. If you change only three things, then the odds of determining the change that affects the output is 2 * 2 * 2, or 8 possibilities.

If the SAS environment is acting peculiar, start again.

Sometimes, strange things can happen after you create even simple syntax errors such as unbalanced quotes. Simply do a complete reboot, cancel your session, or run an Initial Program Load, as appropriate for your operating system.

Don't ignore messages in the SAS log. Don't ignore messages in the SAS log! DON'T IGNORE MESSAGES IN THE SAS LOG!!

Do you avoid the doctor like the plague? After all, your symptoms are certainly benign—just like those warnings on the SAS log. If you value your computer's health more than your own, you need to take corrective action to suppress these warning messages.

Be consistent about marking the code that you create for debugging.

Removing debugging code should not be a major task. Accidentally leaving this code in the source can introduce new bugs! The debugging code should stand out (and not resemble your comment blocks). Several suggestions include:

- Create a keyboard definition such as:

```
%keydef F9 'include c:\find_bug.sas' ;
```

Then, pressing F9 includes the following text at the point of the cursor:

```
*>>>>>>>>>>>>>>>>>>>>>>>>>>>>>>>>>>>>>>>>>>>>>>>>>>>>>>>>>>>>> ;
*>>>>>>>>>>>>>>>>>>>>>>>>>>>>>>>>>>>>>>>>>>>>>>>>>>>>>>>>>>>>> ;
*>>>                                                    >>> ;
*>>>            D E B U G G I N G   S T A R T           >>> ;
*>>>                                                    >>> ;
*>>>>>>>>>>>>>>>>>>>>>>>>>>>>>>>>>>>>>>>>>>>>>>>>>>>>>>>>>>>>> ;
*>>>>>>>>>>>>>>>>>>>>>>>>>>>>>>>>>>>>>>>>>>>>>>>>>>>>>>>>>>>>> ;


*>>>>>>>>>>>>>>>>>>>>>>>>>>>>>>>>>>>>>>>>>>>>>>>>>>>>>>>>>>>>> ;
*>>>>>>>>>>>>>>>>>>>>>>>>>>>>>>>>>>>>>>>>>>>>>>>>>>>>>>>>>>>>> ;
*>>>                                                    >>> ;
*>>>             D E B U G G I N G   E N D              >>> ;
*>>>                                                    >>> ;
*>>>>>>>>>>>>>>>>>>>>>>>>>>>>>>>>>>>>>>>>>>>>>>>>>>>>>>>>>>>>> ;
*>>>>>>>>>>>>>>>>>>>>>>>>>>>>>>>>>>>>>>>>>>>>>>>>>>>>>>>>>>>>> ;
```

- Some programmers like to flag debugging code with pet symbols such as:

```
*zzzzzzzz ;
```

- Other programmers prefer to write all code in lowercase, but use uppercase for debugging code.

- Require that all code be tested in a debug directory. Then the programmer does not have to insert "prettyprint" to designate debugged code.

Regardless of the method that you use, it is always advisable to run a source code comparison of the old and current production versions. This can help catch debugging aids left lingering in the code.

Watch out for variables clashing into each other.

It has been mentioned throughout this book that you have to watch for variables overlaying one another. But sometimes this kind of bug can be really elusive. Here is one situation that is baffling if you don't prepare for it:

```
data float ;
    merge rootbeer ( in = in_root )
          icecream ( in = in_ice )
          ;
    by taster ;
...
run ;
```

And as you go along, whistling your merry way, you are ready to calculate the calories consumed:

```
data calories ;
    set float ;

tot_cals = in_root + icecream ;

run ;
```

which displays:

```
TOT_CALS=.
NOTE: Variable IN_ROOT is uninitialized.
```

Because the variable IN_ROOT is also the name of the IN operand in the previous step, the variable IN_ROOT is dropped from the data set.

If the program creates temporary files, erase them before the job has completed.

Nothing can be more frustrating than assuming that everything is just fine until you find that a temporary file is not updated properly. Within the source code, delete these files either at the beginning or the end of the program. Otherwise, the temporary file that you may be debugging may not have been modified at all. To avoid nasty warning or error messages, you can check of the existence of the file before you try to delete it:

```
filename testing  "c:\find_bug.sas" ;

data _null_ ;

if fexist ('testing') then
    call system  ("del c:\find_bug.sas") ;

run ;
```

Patience, patience, patience . . .

With the advent of modern computers and their high processing speeds, there is a growing tendency towards the vicious cycle of code, compile, test .... code, compile, test. Such a scattershot debugging process most likely indicates that you aren't thinking about the problem carefully. A more careful debugging process not only makes you think about logic, but may uncover other errors as well.

Start with a small number of observations.

It is easiest to start with a small number of records. You can subset on a common variable, such as all of the observations in one BY group. For example, if you are looking at aviary data, instead of using this code:

```
set birds (obs = 100) ;
```

use this code instead:

```
set birds ;
    where birdtype in ("Woodpecker") ;
```

Then, to increase the number of observations, add more birds with:

```
set birds ;
    where birdtype in ("Woodpecker", "Cardinal", "Bluejay") ;
```

Fragmented data sets can cause their own processing problems, particularly in BY-group processing.

Flowchart the program and carefully trace through the logic.

Flowcharts are very useful to help you find both design and system flow errors. As mentioned in Chapter 9, "Program Verification and Testing Methodology," you should test your program thoroughly by using multicondition coverage.

Watch your boundaries.

As mentioned in Chapter 9, many bugs congregate in the corners. Look carefully at boundary conditions for sources of errors.

Check the module interfaces.

Intraprogram and interprogram communications are a large source of errors. Verify that parameters are being passed properly. If the program uses macro functions, ensure that all parameters are correct when the macro begins to execute. If the program uses DATA steps, use PROC PRINT liberally to catch interface errors.

Completely lost? Use the binary search technique.

If you haven't got a clue as to where the program has gone astray, use the binary search technique. Suppose that you have a program with 10,000 lines of code. Start searching at a DATA or PROC step boundary near line 5000. Does the error surface here? If not, restart your search near line 2500. Does the error surface here? If so, cut this partition in two and look at a place near line 3750. Continue this iterative process until you locate where the code has gone astray.

Be careful with efficiency rewrites.

It is easy to change the basic algorithm. A classic example is rewriting a MERGE statement using PROC SQL.

Be wary of patches.

Naturally, you wouldn't consider placing a patch in a program to handle exception conditions. But they may exist in someone else's code and may not always be obvious. The obvious case is when literals are embedded in code that otherwise looks quite normal. Usually the IF statement combined with literals is a dead giveaway:

```
if codename = "jamesbond" then
    ammo = "gone" ;
```

However, patches may be less easy to detect by some "clever" programmers who try to disguise the patch. In this instance, a programmer has a bug in which single digit numbers work fine but two and three digit numbers halve the value, hence the patch:

```
proc format ;
    value value
    10-high = 2
    other = 1 ;
run ;
```

The devious programmer doesn't worry because the formats are buried in a far off library. Surely, no one would notice this innocent construct:

```
final = base_val * num *  (put ( num, value.)) ;
```

Use a closing RUN statement for DATA and procedure steps.

If you ignore this rule, then be alert for (a) disappearing titles, and (b) unresolved variables created by CALL SYMPUT.

Change the names of the data sets instead of rewriting to the same data set.

For example, to save work space, you probably have written code like this:

```
data banking ;
    set banking ;
... code for first DATA step
run ;

data banking ;
    set banking ;
... code for second DATA step
run ;

... more DATA steps that continually write over the BANKING data
set.
```

Now, if you insert a PROC PRINT statement after each DATA step, you may not remember what each step does, and the PROC PRINT output becomes confusing. Instead, to help jog your memory, use a descriptive name for each data set created. Then, debugging with PROC PRINT statements becomes manageable:

```
data teller ;
    set banking ;
... code for first DATA step
run ;

proc print data = teller ;
    title 'teller transactions' ;
run ;

data balance ;
    set teller ;
... code for second DATA step
run ;

proc print data = balance ;
    title 'statement balance' ;
run ;
```

Yes, optical illusions do occur in programming.

Sometimes the silliest errors occur because "1" looks like "l" or "0" looks like "O". Usually, the error message "uninitialized variables" in the log can help to detect these bugs.

Walk away. Start another day.

If you're tired, you are better off walking away from the program and getting a fresh start tomorrow. Debugging requires a clear mind. Amazingly, solutions often come to mind while you are driving home from work.

Observe flags for potential errors.

Make a list of program flags and watch their behavior. Some programmers like to use a lot of flags to control logic flow, but this is not a great idea. Flags are often the source of program bugs for the following reasons:

1. They often lack adequate documentation. FLAG1 can mean just about anything.

2. In general, they tend to make the code more convoluted. Because SAS has all the structural constructs for developing modular programs, it is often possible to rewrite sections of code to eliminate some or all of these flags.

3. Flags are often ignored because the programmer who is maintaining the code may not believe that their value affects any code modification.

Rubbish In, rubbish out . . .

Be careful how you process the INPUT statement. In production systems, new forms of input can cause problems, and it is difficult to predict every permutation with defensive programming. One simple way to check the input data is by using the PUT _INFILE_ statement, which displays, in the SAS log, the format of the input data.

Rewrite spaghetti code.

If you don't understand the code because it is convoluted and you can't find anyone to explain it to you, then try rewriting the module. You may discover a more straightforward way of writing the code.

Use the PAGE compiler option for each new module.

You may want to do this for %INCLUDE modules, macros, linked subroutines, and even DATA steps. Then you can lay out the pages on the desk or floor in front of you. You may even want to draw up a rough chart, on paper or on a chalkboard, that shows the flow of modules. Now, you're ready for serious debugging!

Change the WORK library.

Debugging can be tedious, in fact, downright exhausting. When running a stream of programs or long executing jobs, you may find it useful to save the contents of the WORK library for further examination at a later time. The simplest way is to reroute the WORK library by using the SAS keyword USER. By creating a libref with a two-level name, you can save the SAS data in a permanent library. The syntax for two variations is:

> libname user '*SAS-data-library*' ;

or

> libname worklib '*SAS-data-library*' ;
> options user = worklib ;

Thereafter, one-level libnames are written to the USER library.

Debug en masse.

When you are creating a stream of programs, it is tedious to verify the SAS log every single time you execute a program. However, warnings and errors have to be dealt with. To circumvent this problem, route all your program output into a log subdirectory. Then, you can execute a program that spins through all the entries that report errors, warnings, and notes of interest.

Each program will have to redirect its output by using the PRINTTO procedure. In this example, &SAS_NAME is the name of the source file and &LOGOUT is the directory where you wish to redirect the log files. For a complete description of this technique, refer to the section that is entitled "Allow for Flexibility in Routing Output" in Chapter 8, "System Coding Principles."

```
proc printto log = "&logout\&sas_name..log" new ;
run ;
```

The complete source code that you can use to route your program logs is contained in Coding Sample 12 in Appendix 1, "Coding Samples." Here is a small piece of the output created by ERRORLOG.SAS:

```
AEDRUG.LOG
NOTE: Variable FIRST.BODY_SYS is uninitialized.

AESEVREL.LOG
NOTE: Variable CONT_06 is uninitialized.
NOTE: Variable CONT_07 is uninitialized.
NOTE: Variable CONT_08 is uninitialized.
NOTE: Variable CONT_09 is uninitialized.
NOTE: Variable CONT_10 is uninitialized.

DEMOG.LOG
NOTE: Variable PRIMRISK is uninitialized.
ERROR: Variable PRIMRISK not found.
ERROR: Variable PRIMRISK not found.
NOTE: Variable PRIMRISK is uninitialized.

LABNORMS.LOG
ERROR: Variable LAB_TEST not found.
ERROR: Variable LAB_ID not found.
ERROR: Variable SEX not found.
NOTE: Variable REC_CNT is uninitialized.
NOTE: Variable LAB_LOC is uninitialized.
NOTE: Variable SEX is uninitialized.
NOTE: Variable MIN_VAL is uninitialized.
NOTE: Variable MAX_VAL is uninitialized.
NOTE: Variable UNITS is uninitialized.
ERROR: BY variable LAB_TEST is not on input data set WORK.NORM.
ERROR: BY variable LAB_ID is not on input data set WORK.NORM.
ERROR: BY variable SEX is not on input data set WORK.NORM.
```

Preventive Maintenance

A little preparation can pay big dividends if you want to write code that is immune to subtle programming bugs. Undoubtedly, writing structured, documented code goes a long way to this end. In addition, it helps to have a few of the following tools at your side.

Designing In/Instrumenting

While a program may be working perfectly well, there may be nasty little bugs lurking around, ready to spring forward at the slightest crack. It is useful for a program to keep tabs on certain processes to warn you of potential problems. For instance, your program may be utilizing a number of arrays on a PC where memory is at a premium. The program can track the status of these arrays and provide a summary at the end of the program:

```
data project ;
...
... SAS code
...
max_cnt  = max ( max_cnt , cnt ) ;
max_copy = max ( max_copy , copy_cnt ) ;
max_dupe = max ( max_dupe , dupe_cnt ) ;
max_subs = max ( max_subs , subs_cnt ) ;
max_str  = max ( max_str , str_cnt ) ;
max_len  = max ( max_len , link_len ) ;
...
if last_rec then
do ;
    call symput ( 'max_len'  , put ( max_len , 4. )) ;
    call symput ( 'max_cnt'  , put ( max_cnt  , 4. )) ;
    call symput ( 'max_copy' , put ( max_copy , 4. )) ;
    call symput ( 'max_dupe' , put ( max_dupe , 4. )) ;
    call symput ( 'max_subs' , put ( max_subs, 4. )) ;
    call symput ( 'max_str'  , put ( max_str , 4. )) ;
end ;


data final ;
    set project end = last_rec ;
...
... SAS code
...
if last_rec then
do ;
    title 'Summary Statistics' ;
    file print ;
    put // ;
    put @001 'Max elements in count array.... ' "&max_cnt" ;
    put @001 'Max elements in copy array..... ' "&max_copy" ;
    put @001 'Max elements in dupe array..... ' "&max_dupe" ;
    put @001 'Max elements in subs array..... ' "&max_subs" ;
    put @001 'Max elements in string array... ' "&max_str" ;
    put @001 'Max string length............. ' "&max_len" ;
end ;
```

As the last PUT statement demonstrates, you also need to know about the "Great Divide," that is, any variable that threatens to cross the 200 byte boundary. If variables can potentially be larger than 200 bytes, a critical redesign of the program may be required to handle the parsing and linking chores.

"Bug Catcher" Routines

Certain kinds of logic errors are not flagged by SAS either during compilation or execution. However, you must be aware of their existence because these errors are easily overlooked. To combat these logic errors, you can develop a library of "bug catcher" programs and run them as a batch against the source code. For example, have you ever been bitten by an ELSE statement followed by an inadvertent semicolon? This is not a syntax error, but is an insidious bug. Here is some code that will warn you of the problem:

```
filename the_file 'fileref' ;

data _null_ ;

infile the_file length = the_len ;
input sas_line $varying150. the_len ;

findelse = index ( trim ( left ( upcase ( compress
          ( sas_line )))), "ELSE;" ) ;

if findelse then
do ;
    file log ;
    put "At line " _n_ " Warning: An ELSE with a semicolon??!!" ;
end ;

run ;
```

Here's another killer. A MERGE statement used with no BY statement will not report a syntax error. Usually, the coder had intended to include the BY statement:

```
proc sort data = first ;
    by type ;
run ;

proc sort data = last ;
    by type ;
run ;

data mixture ;
    merge first ( in = in_first )
          last  ( in = in_last )
          ;
       <=== (Whoops! forgot the BY statement)
    run ;
```

The code to detect this problem can be found in Coding Sample 13 in Appendix 1.

Here is a bug that can make you feel silly. While editing, you may accidentally push source code wide right out of view of the screen. This is the kind of bug where you can stare at the screen all day long and yet the bug remains well concealed. For example, the source code may read as follows:

```
<========== Width of screen display =========><==Beyond display==>

my_song = "Shoobie-doobie-do, wa do-be-woosy" ;        a = 25 ;
```

Fortunately, you can catch this one pretty easily by using the following code:

```
************************************************************** ;
*** Name of SAS source file.                             *** ;
************************************************************** ;

filename the_file 'fileref' ;

************************************************************** ;
*** Set maximum length of allowable fields               *** ;
************************************************************** ;

%let max_rite = 72 ;   * Defined in init file ;

data _null_ ;

************************************************************** ;
*** Read the SAS source file.                            *** ;
************************************************************** ;

infile the_file length = the_len ;
input sas_line $varying200. the_len ;

************************************************************** ;
*** Flag any fields beyond expected right side of source. *** ;
************************************************************** ;

leftover = substr ( sas_line, ( &max_rite + 1 )) ;
if leftover ne " " then
     put "Extra characters beyond source boundary at line " _n_ ;

run ;
```

Regressive Bugs

The customer complains to the auto mechanic: "There is a terrible rumbling noise in the trunk. I'll leave the car with you and I'll come back tomorrow." The next day the customer returns and test drives the "repaired car." Now the radio is locked onto one station which continuously blasts Rock and Roll. The customer complains, to which the mechanic retorts: "What are you complaining about? I'll bet you can't hear the rumbling in the trunk anymore."

So goes the nature of programming bugs. You fix one bug and another appears mysteriously, perhaps not on this execution, but next month during critical end-of-year processing.

How do you know if a bug is fixed once and for all? One method is to retest the program against standardized test data. The new version of the program should produce output that is identical to the previous version. This test data can be created and maintained in a test/debug library. Whenever changes are made to the software, the program uses the test data sets and compares the old output to the new output. This technique is known as "regression testing" and is often overlooked in systems development.

Regressive bugs are a special class of programming bugs. By definition, these are bugs created while attempting to fix another bug. What are some good techniques to avoid regressive bugs?

- Use as few system flags as possible.

- Whenever possible, do not use one flag to set another flag:

```
if status = "Y" then rec_flag = "N" ;
```

- Be careful of introducing new variables into the Program Data Vector without first checking if that variable already exists. It is usually a simple task to list all the variables in the libraries:

```
proc contents data = 'libref'._all_ ;
```

A good rule of thumb is—if you aren't sure the fix is correct, then you have probably created another bug.

Debugging Dynamic Code

Because dynamic code is %INCLUDEd code, you must set the option SOURCE2 to view this code. (Refer to Chapter 8, "System Coding Principles," for a discussion of code generation.) Possibly the biggest problem that you may encounter is the confusion of literals and variables. As a journeyman SAS programmer, you will eventually stumble upon code like this:

```
put 'length '"_v&i._var "'$'_v&i._len";";
```

Who is responsible for this mess? No matter. To unscramble this clutter, break the line into literals and nonliterals. You can do this simply by moving the cursor along the line and pressing the ENTER key (causing a line feed) every time you discover the first occurrence of a single or double quote. Don't press ENTER again until you find the matched quote on the other side. In this way, each line will contain a literal or variable.

Actually, an extra line feed provides even better visual separation, as shown in the following code. Now the code should be crystal clear. Incidentally, it's also a good idea to insert extra spaces around the quotes because two single quotes can easily be mistaken for double quotes.

```
put

'length '

" _v&i._var "

'$'

_v&i._len

";"

;
```

This code looks a lot better. The programmer was trying to write dynamic code that would produce:

```
length _v1_var $7 ;
```

Macro Debugging Tips

Here is a list of tips specifically for debugging macro code.

If you are really stuck, then "de-macroize."

The macro language adds another layer of complexity to the SAS code. In many cases (not all unfortunately), you can rewrite the code by converting macro parameters to equivalent %LET statements. Then, you can step through the code as you would a regular SAS DATA step. For instance:

```
%macro nasty ( shape = ,
               radius = ,
               shade = ,
               border = ,
               font = ) ;

     ... macro code

%mend nasty ;
```

is normally invoked as:

```
%nasty ( shape = circle ,
         radius = 1.25 ,
         shade = .25 ,
         border = Yes ,
         font = Times )
```

which should be replaced by killing the macro definition and coding:

```
%let shape  = circle ;
%let radius = 1.25 ;
%let shade  = .25 ;
%let border = Yes ;
%let font   = Times ;
```

Note that you are replacing local macro variables with global macro variables. Hence, it is prudent to first use %PUT _GLOBAL_ to ensure that there are no conflicts with previously defined globals. If so, you can temporarily rename any of the new globals to avoid this conflict.

Temporarily remove the macro quoting functions.

Debugging macros can be a difficult task, especially when someone else wrote the macro code. One tip to use when you pick up someone else's code is to temporarily strip out the quoting functions by globally replacing them with blanks. The quoting functions are used to help resolve "problem" characters. However, they dramatically decrease the readability of the code. When you have a handle on the code, you can restore the original source code and pay attention to the details provided by the quoting functions.

Delimit the macro variable.

When you use the %PUT statement with macro variables, it is helpful to use a leading and trailing character such as the pound sign (#). This helps you to view the number of leading and trailing spaces (as specified by a quoting function), which can be critical for logical comparison or string manipulation operations. For example, this code:

```
%put *&look_mom* ;
```

would then display the following:

```
*    No hands!    *
```

Use the key macro options SYMBOLGEN, MPRINT, and MTRACE.

However, including them all at once can really fill up the log. Start with SYMBOLGEN. Many errors can be caught by simply displaying the values of the macro variables. Then, you can add MPRINT and MTRACE incrementally.

Debug from the inside out.

Debug macros from the inside out rather than from the outside in. That is, start with the innermost macro and test the code carefully. Then, when you are comfortable that the innermost macro is functioning properly, move to the next outermost level, until you reach the outermost layer. In this way, you can gain confidence in the foundation layers, which are most likely to be used in other applications.

```
%macro inner ;
    ... SAS code       <===== Start debugging here.
%mend inner ;

%macro middle ;
    ...
    %inner
    ...
%mend middle ;

%macro outer ;
    ...
    %middle
    ...
%mend outer ;

%macro loop ;
    ...
    %outer
    ...
%mend loop  ;

%loop
```

Display macro tables.

The %PUT statement is useful for listing the contents of various macro variables. The most useful options for the %PUT statement include:

USER	are variables created by the programmer, including both LOCAL and GLOBAL macro variables. This may be the most useful option because you can see possible interactions between GLOBAL and LOCAL macro variables.
ALL	lists every type of macro variable defined for all referencing environments. Sometimes this just creates too much clutter because every single macro variable is listed.
LOCAL	displays all macro variables in the current referencing environment.
GLOBAL	displays all user created variables that are global in scope. This does not include SAS generated globals.
AUTOMATIC	displays all SAS generated variables. These are all GLOBAL with the exception of SYSPBUFF. The _AUTOMATIC_ variables are usually not the source of bugs, but SYSPBUFF may be useful.

As an example, the %PUT statement can be placed strategically in the macro. Consider the following code fragment:

```
%let title1 = "Aspirin vs. Placebo" ;
%let title2 = "Sports Related Injuries" ;

%macro ae_summ ( rpt_cnt  = ,
                 severity = ,
                 druglist = ,
                 studyarm = ) ;
    ...
    ... SAS code
    ...
    %put _user_ ;

%mend ae_summ ;
```

Then, invoking the macro as:

```
%ae_summ ( rpt_cnt = 3 ,
           druglist = %str ('ASPIRIN', 'PLACEBO') ,
           studyarm = ORTHOPEDIC )
```

produces the following in the log:

```
AE_SUMM RPT_CNT 3
AE_SUMM SEVERITY
AE_SUMM DRUGLIST _'ASPIRIN'_ 'PLACEBO'_
AE_SUMM STUDYARM ORTHOPEDIC
GLOBAL TITLE1 "Aspirin vs. Placebo"
GLOBAL TITLE2 "Sports Related Injuries"
```

Immediately, it is obvious that the local macro variable SEVERITY was never assigned a value.

On the flip side, you can use this technique to your advantage while coding. Using %PUT _ALL_, or merely %PUT _LOCAL_, prior to the MEND statement lists all local macro variables. This is a good reminder to define, as appropriate, any local macro variable as LOCAL in scope.

The SAS DATA Step Debugger

SAS offers a source-level debugger that provides an online interactive environment for debugging programs. For a complete discussion of the DATA step debugger and all of its options, refer to *SAS Software: Changes and Enhancements, Release 6.11*. Here are some coding situations for which you should consider using the DATA step debugger:

- when you have isolated the error to a given DATA step. Because the debugger can only be applied to a DATA step, you have to at least know where the error occurred.

- when you think you have made a silly error. Simple errors can be discovered quite easily with the debugger. For example, forgetting to initialize, or to re-initialize, a variable is usually discovered pretty quickly.

- to debug arrays.

- to debug a DATA step generated by macro code.

- to debug DO loops, including the infamous endless loop.

When is the DATA step debugger not so useful?

- with PROCS or stand-alone macros (debugging only works with the DATA step).

- if you would only end up trying to use Brute Force on a very complex problem. If the DATA step is very large or complex or both, you should develop a hypothesis about the source of the problem. Otherwise, you could spend a lot of time tracing with the debugger and becoming frustrated. There is also a tendency to create a quick bug fix after spending a lot of mechanical time trying to isolate a bug.

- if you don't know where the bug is located in the program.

Running the Debugger without Interruption

To run the debugger, you must first associate a DATA step with the DEBUG option:

```
data help_me / debug ;
...
run ;
```

After you submit this program with the DEBUG option, the DATA step debugger is loaded and then displays two windows:

1. The *Source Window*: contains a listing of the program statements. The highlighted line indicates the statement that is about to execute.

2. The *Dialog Window*: allows you to enter debugging commands.

The default for the debugger is that the program runs to completion unless it is interrupted. These intentional interrupts include the following:

STEP   causes the program to walk through the source code one (or more) statements at a time. While the programmer may list multiple source statements on one line, it is easier to follow the code with separate statements on each line.

BREAK   causes the program to suspend execution at a prespecified breakpoint.

WATCH   suspends the program when a prespecified variable changes its value.

After you invoke the debugger, the GO command starts executing the program; or if the program has already started, GO resumes execution. Normally, you wouldn't start off with the GO command unless you suspect that your program has a logic flow problem. In that case, as soon as the debugger is invoked, set

```
> Trace On
```

The TRACE command ensures that a listing of DATA step execution is recorded while the programming is running. Then enter

```
> Go
```

The program executes without interruption and then displays all the lines in the source window that were executed:

```
Stepped to line 180 column 1
Stepped to line 181 column 5
Stepped to line 182 column 5
Stepped to line 183 column 9
Stepped to line 184 column 5
Stepped to line 183 column 9
Stepped to line 184 column 5
Stepped to line 185 column 1
Stepped to line 187 column 1
Stepped to line 189 column 1
The DATA step program has terminated, there is no active program
environment
```

In this way, you can quickly discern logic path errors without having to step through the program or set breakpoints.

Note: If you happened to enter the commands above, then you have to restart the debugger. So type QUIT at the debugger command prompt, and then resubmit your program.

Running the Debugger One Step at a Time

Consider a program in which you need to move more slowly to track down a bug. You know that the variable TOT_COST for this program should yield 516, not '.' ($5.16 for the price of a meal and meal tax, which is 10 cents per item). However, you suspect the problem is with the variable MEALCOST. As before, append the DEBUG option to the first line in the DATA step. Don't forget to leave PROC FORMAT alone. You can't use the debugger to step through procedure steps.

Now submit the following code:

```
proc format ;
    value $foodval
    "Burrito"        =    150
    "Chimichanga"    =    179
    "Cola"           =     89
    "Refried Beans"  =    119
    "Rice"           =     59
    "Taco"           =     79
    "Tortilla"       =     49
    ;
run ;

data goodmeal /debug ;

retain order "Rice,Burrito,Tortilla,Refried Beans,Cola" ;

students =   "Danny Richey Susana Kerry Martin" ;
teachers =   "Womack Penderton Stafford Kilgore" ;
schools  =   "Whitman Bradley Pasqual Escondido" ;
county   =   "Alameda Diegito Northern" ;
```

```
fooddate = today() + 7 ;
mealcost = 0 ;

length food $50 ;

food_cnt = 1 ;
do until ( food = " " ) ;
    food = left ( scan ( order, food_cnt, "," )) ;
    food_cnt + 1 ;
    mealcost = mealcost + put ( food, $foodval. ) ;
end ;

food_cnt = food_cnt - 2 ;
tot_cost  = mealcost + ( food_cnt * 10 ) ;

stop ;
run ;
```

Start debugging by walking through the code one step at a time. To do so, you can type the STEP command and then press the ENTER key.

```
> STEP
```

The program executes the current statement and moves the highlight bar to the next statement in the program.

Note: You may wish to select the TILE window option to view all the windows simultaneously.

The program now displays with the current line highlighted (shown in bold, below):

```
13 data help_me  /debug ;
14
15 retain order "Rice,Burrito,Tortilla,Refried Beans,Cola" ;
16
17 students =  "Danny Richey Susana Kerry Martin" ;
18 teachers =   "Womack Penderton Stafford Kilgore" ;
19 schools  =  "Whitman Bradley Pasqual Escondido" ;
20 county   =  "Alameda Diegito Northern" ;
21
22 fooddate = today() + 7 ;
23 mealcost = 0 ;
24
25 length food $50 ;
26
27 food_cnt = 1 ;
28 do until ( food = " " ) ;
29     food = left ( scan ( order, food_cnt, "," )) ;
30     food_cnt + 1 ;
31     mealcost = mealcost + put ( food, $foodval. ) ;
32 end ;
33
34 food_cnt = food_cnt - 2 ;
35 tot_cost = mealcost + ( food_cnt * 10 ) ;
36
37 run ;
```

Because the ENTER key is assigned the STEP command, you can simply press the ENTER key to walk through the program. It is also possible to step a specified number of times. (But don't do the following instruction now—we're in the middle of a tutorial!)

```
> STEP 10
```

EXAMINE is a powerful statement that allows you to view any and all variables at the time of execution. The syntax is simply:

EXAMINE *variable*

So, for this example, look at MEALCOST:

```
> EXAMINE mealcost
```

As expected, the program displays:

```
MEALCOST = .
```

Most of the debugger commands have an alias that allows you to enter fewer characters. In this case, the alias for EXAMINE is simply "E".

Rather than display one variable at a time, which can be quite tedious, it is a simple matter to display all of the variables:

```
> E _ALL_
```

In this case, the following data lines display:

```
ORDER = Rice,Burrito,Tortilla,Refried Beans,Cola
STUDENTS = Danny Richey Susana Kerry Martin
TEACHERS =
SCHOOLS =
COUNTY =
FOODDATE = .
MEALCOST = .
FOOD =
FOOD_CNT = 0
TOT_COST = .
_ERROR_ = 0
_N_ = 1
```

After a while, you may grow weary of constantly typing the EXAMINE _ALL_ command. Fortunately, you can assign function keys to the debugger commands. Simply open the KEYS window and, for the key you choose, type in the DSD command followed by the debugger command. If you wish to enter multiple commands, then enclose the commands in quotes (separated by semicolons). Here are examples of commands you can enter in the KEYS window:

```
DSD E _ALL_
DSD 'Examine i; set j = 5;'
```

Usually, you have a good idea where you want to inspect the program. Therefore, instead of stepping through every single statement, you can set break points, such as the start or end of a DO loop. Now, the program continues to execute and only stops at the break point. In this example, you know that MEALCOST is not calculating correctly, so you can set a break at the end of the DO loop by specifying the line number. The line number in your session will most likely be different from the one in this example:

```
> Break 32
> Go
```

The SOURCE window displays with the break point line highlighted with an exclamation mark in the margin:

```
  27 food_cnt = 1 ;
  28 do until ( food = " " ) ;
  29     food = left ( scan ( order, food_cnt, "," )) ;
  30     food_cnt + 1 ;
  31     mealcost = mealcost + put ( food, $foodval. ) ;
! 32 end ;
  33
  34 food_cnt = food_cnt - 2 ;
  35 tot_cost  = mealcost + ( food_cnt * 10 ) ;
  36
  37 run ;
```

Then, look at MEALCOST:

```
> E mealcost
```

which displays

```
MEALCOST = 59
```

You can continue to visit this break point by continually typing the GO command to examine MEALCOST. Notice that MEALCOST increases until the last iteration. MEALCOST suddenly drops to missing! Fortunately, the fix is simple. MEALCOST should not be recalculated when the SCAN function fails to find a food.

Incidentally, you can kill these break points easily by using the DELETE command:

```
> delete 32
```

To delete all of the break points, type:

```
> delete _ALL_
```

You can also aid your debugging efforts by changing the value of any variable at any time:

```
> set mealcost = 466
```

The problem is that MEALCOST was set incorrectly to missing. Now you can execute the rest of the program and determine if TOT_COST was calculated properly:

```
> go
```

When the program has finished executing, the following message is displayed:

```
The DATA step program has terminated, there is no active
program environment.
```

You cannot restart the program at this point, but you may wish to examine variables:

```
> E tot_cost

TOTCOST = 516
```

To return to the SAS editor, simply type

```
> Quit
```

Additional Debugger Features

Let's quickly mention two more features of the debugger. One of the most valuable features is the WATCH command. Often, you know that the value of a variable is being corrupted somewhere, but you don't know where this is happening. WATCH suspends execution when the value of the watched variable changes:

```
> WATCH mealcost
```

A second useful debugger feature is the JUMP command. By using the JUMP command, you can jump directly to another part of the program without executing the intervening statements:

```
> JUMP 33
> GO
```

However, you should use this feature with caution. It is easy to assume that the intervening statements have no effect, but this may not be true. Unless the execution of intervening statements requires a coffee break, it is usually preferable to advance to that routine with a BREAK statement instead.

Summary

Debugging code should be done systematically. The major strategies that emerge are brute force, induction, and deduction. You can save much time by using good preventive maintenance practices. Also, you should design code to trap for potential errors. However, for certain kinds of errors, especially when you isolate an error to a particular DATA step, the DATA step debugger can be an invaluable tool.

Exercises

1. When are deduction and induction more likely to be successful than brute force?

2. When do you think the PUT _ALL_ statement is most useful?

3. When do you think PROC PRINT is particularly useful?

4. When you are testing, it can be troublesome to use a small number of observations instead of selecting all records in a BY group. Explain why.

5. Some of the nastiest bugs are ones that are difficult to repeat. Give a couple of examples of bugs that you think are difficult to repeat.

6. How can overmodularizing a program make debugging difficult?

7. Why do you think that, sometimes, you might suddenly realize the source of a bug while you are discussing a problem with a co-worker?

8. Why do you think the INPUT statement is the source of many bugs?

9. Why do many programming bugs occur at boundaries?

10. The following bug is caused by a common optical illusion. What do you think the programmer intended? Hint: the entire construct was supposed to execute 500 times. What kind of logic could you use to find these kinds of errors?

```
do i = 1 to 10 ;
    do j = i to 10 ;
        do k = 1 to 5 ;
            count + 1 ;
            tot_val = count * net_val ;
        end ;
    end ;
end ;
```

References

Brooks F.P. (1995), *The Mythical Man-Month*, Reading, MA: Addison-Wesley.

Bruce, R.C. (1980), *Software Debugging for Microcomputers*, Reston, VA: Prentice-Hall.

Johnson, W.L. (1986), *Intention-Based Diagnosis of Novice Programming Errors,* London: Pittman Publishing.

Lazzerini, B. and Lapriore L. (1992), *Program Debugging Environments*, New York: Ellis Harwood.

Peterson, I. (1995), *Fatal Defect*, New York: Random House.

Rosenberg, J.B. (1996), *How Debuggers Work*, New York: John Wiley & Sons, Inc.

Rustin, R. (1970), *Debugging Techniques in Large System*s, Englewood Cliffs, NJ: Prentice-Hall.

Chapter 11

Putting It All Together with a Demonstration: The Site Map System

Introduction **258**

Background **258**

Important Terms **258**

Problem Definition **259**

Analysis **260**
   Functional Requirements 260
   Feasibility Study 260
   Selecting a Language/Prototyping 260

Design **261**
   1. Determine the general physical layout 261
   2. Determine the order of navigating elements 261
   3. Calculate logical grid coordinates 262
   4. Adjust logical coordinates, if needed 262
   5. Calculate physical grid coordinates 262
   6. Draw the boxes and codes 264
   7. Draw the arrows connecting the boxes 264

Coding **266**

Testing **267**
   Unit Testing/Debugging for ERRORRTN 267
   Unit Testing/Debugging for Single String Processing (SSP) 267
   Unit Testing/Debugging for Logical Grid Coordinates 269
   Unit Testing/Debugging for DRAWMAP 269
   Unit Testing/Debugging for POWER 269
   Integration Testing/Debugging 270
   System Testing/Debugging 270

User Acceptance **270**

Maintenance **271**

Introduction

This chapter presents a complete system, a sample walk through of all phases of the software life cycle. This project (hereafter referred to as the Site Map System) was selected for several reasons:

- This system is medium sized (about 15,000 lines of SAS code for the SAS prototype and roughly twice that for the executable C/C++ version).

- This project demonstrates the use of linked-list methodology, which is not frequently used by SAS programmers.

- Nearly 95% of the project was written using the base SAS product, which is the core of this book. Only the final portion of the module DRAWMAP uses the Annotate facility of SAS/GRAPH software.

If certain terms used here are new to you, please reference Appendix 2, "Definitions for the Site Map System."

This was a real project in which the author participated. It is presented here as if you are making the decisions yourself, based on the project parameters given you by the Environmental Protection Agency (EPA).

Background

The EPA has classified over 1300 sites as being extremely toxic as a result of contamination of soil, water, or work areas, or because of chemical spills. This group of sites, known as the Superfund National Priority List (NPL), is targeted for immediate cleanup.

The cleanup process will be incredibly expensive, ranging from hundreds of thousands of dollars at smaller sites, to multimillion dollar cleanups at some of the highly contaminated areas. Thus, it is imperative that EPA decision makers have access to current and accurate information relating to the cleanup events at each site. This leads to the creation of a whole subsystem referred to as the Site Map System.

Important Terms

To understand the description of this project, you will need these definitions:

Activity   any type of legal activity at the site. This may include negotiations, settlements, court orders, and bankruptcies.

Event   any action related to the cleanup of a site. This may include preliminary assessments, feasibility studies, community reaction, execution of the cleanup, and short and long term maintenance.

Node   the symbolic representation of the events and activities, usually in the form of a code. For instance, the code 01FS1 represents a feasibility study, and the code 00PA1 is a preliminary assessment. These codes are what will actually appear on the Site Map.

Link   a relationship between two nodes. A link implies causality. Thus, if 00PA1 links to 01FS1, then it also causes 01FS1.

Problem Definition

The EPA requires a graphics-based system that will allow users to easily visualize the ongoing cleanup events and litigation activities at a Superfund site.

Expanded Problem Definition

Each site has a unique and constantly changing configuration that needs to be mapped both online and on hardcopy. Prior to this time, the only hardcopy available has been hand-drawn maps. The problems inherent in hand drawing site maps are the following:

- Map drawing is extremely tedious, involving hours (or even days!) of research, in addition to the time required to draw the maps.

- Maps are static. To add, delete, or change elements, you have to redraw the entire map.

- There is no uniform expertise regarding the technical aspects of the Site Map System. As a result, many maps are being drawn incorrectly.

- There is no online version of the map available.

- Maps that overflow one page are a nightmare to follow. Visions of old fashioned flow-charts begin to resurface.

Figure 11.1 shows part of a computer-generated site map.

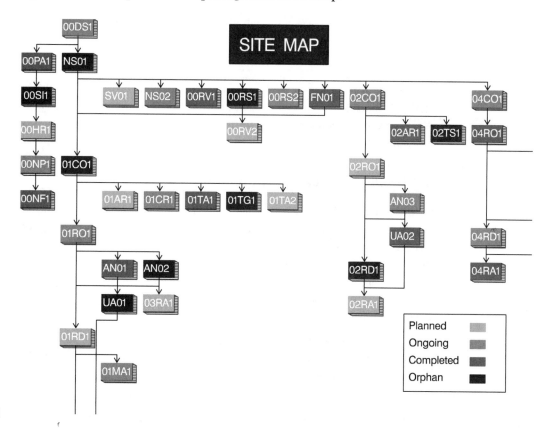

Figure 11.1

Analysis

For this project, becoming familiar with the task requires studying hundreds of hand-drawn maps. The other source of information is the EPA site map "bible" entitled "The Links Programmatic Coding Guidance," which contains literally hundreds of rules for drawing Site Maps by hand. It is disconcerting when you discover that many of the hand-drawn maps were not drawn following the established guidelines.

Functional Requirements

- The maps should conform to the rules set down in "The Links Programmatic Coding Guidance."
- The maps must be dynamic. Insertion or deletion of elements should not present a problem.
- The program should be functional on a PC-386 or higher.
- The program should be functional with Version 5 of DOS or higher.
- The program should produce hardcopy on any laser printer.
- Online updating should be available.
- The program should actually calculate the links (that is, it should be an expert system).
- The maps should have minimal line crossings.

Feasibility Study

Before investing a tremendous amount of resources, you have to develop an algorithm that can withstand the complexity of sites with over 200 nodes. Fortunately, an algorithm and demonstration become available within a short period of time. Hence, you are ready to forge ahead!

Selecting a Language/Prototyping

Determining the implementation language is fairly complex. Here is the scenario: the EPA has very strict guidelines about developing software on their LAN. For example, user-written software cannot modify the EPA database directly. Data must first be moved from the database to a user work area. This is not a major concern because the database is updated only once a day and it occurs in the wee hours of the morning. Because FOXBASE is the only language approved by the EPA for interfacing with the database, you have no choice about data retrieval.

Likewise, only FOXBASE can update the database. However, FOXBASE is limited for developing visually pleasing screens. As a result, you decide to use FOXPRO for developing the front-end selection screens.

SAS is chosen for the prototype. The word "prototype" is used here loosely because, in essence, the entire system is to be coded in SAS, and then your team will translate it to another target language for the "real-time" execution. Why take such an unusual approach? Primarily because programming development in SAS requires a fraction of the development time required for low level languages. The entire system can be coded, tested, debugged, and demonstrated in a short time frame. However, the final program requires lightning execution speed. Hence, the core language to be used for drawing the Site Map System maps is a combination of C and C++. Figure 11.2 shows the sequence of the project's proposed real-time execution.

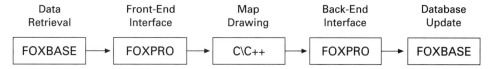

Figure 11.2 *In general, you want to strive for simplicity by writing an entire system in one language. However, as in this project, creating projects with multiple vendors can force certain constraints.*

Design

This section presents the seven major design components.

1. Determine the general physical layout

Site Maps should adhere to the rules set forth in the "Links Programmatic Coding Guidance." In other words, their layout should look as if someone drew the map by hand—correctly. The general considerations include:

- Allow for as many possible elements as you need on one screen/page without causing a cramped look.

- When you draw lines from parent to child nodes, strive for simplicity and minimize the line crossings.

- Use bridges or connectors to minimize ambiguity at line crossings.

- A child node must always reside below all of its parents nodes (note that a child may have more than one parent).

2. Determine the order of navigating elements

It is decided to navigate elements using an ordered binary search algorithm. Here is the general navigation strategy:

- Start at the tree head.

- Trace through elements that apply to the entire site before tracing specific cleanup and litigation nodes.

- Navigate cleanup and litigation elements relative to their chronological occurrence.

- Trace litigation before cleanup when both occur at about the same chronological time.

That was a simplified explanation of the complete algorithm. For a comprehensive discussion, refer to Appendix 4, "Tutorial of Navigation Rules," and the more comprehensive version in Appendix 5, "Summary of Navigation Rules."

Output from this module produces Table 11.1.

Position	Node	Code on Map
1	Discovery	00DS1
2	Assessment	00PA1
3	Hazard Ranking	00HR1
4	Investigation	01RI1
5	Feasibility Study	01FS1
6	Record of Decision	02RO1
⋮	⋮	⋮

Table 11.1   *A typical linked list after navigating all the activities and events at a site.*

3. Calculate logical grid coordinates

The next step is to calculate the relative position of the nodes. At this stage, the exact physical position of the nodes is immaterial. Rather, how they relate to each other is important. For example, to state that "Litigation" appears directly above "Negotiations" is a reference to the nodes' logical, or relative, position.

Using the data from the previous example, the nodes are placed into a two dimensional array, as depicted in Table 11.2.

Y coord.	X coord. =======>		
	1	2	3
1		00DS1	
2	00PA1	01RI1	
3	00HR1	01FS1	02RO1

Table 11.2   *The X and Y coordinates are calculated for each node.*

4. Adjust logical coordinates, if needed

At this point, all the elements are laid out on the page in their respective positions. However, there may be cases in which a child appears at the same level or above its parent record. This is relatively rare, but it happens because of the appearance of "late blooming" parents. That is, one of a child's parents may be positioned long after the child's position is determined. For the simple cases, you drop the child node down as far as necessary. For more involved cases, entire blocks of nodes need to be repositioned.

5. Calculate physical grid coordinates

The next step is to calculate the exact physical location of the elements on the page. For instance, the tree head should be mapped at X coordinate = 1 and Y coordinate = 1, but where exactly do you draw this? Should it be 1 inch from the top of page, or .5 inches, or .567 inches? The answer depends on a number of factors and is related to the users' preferences. For instance, users may want to see the site in a compressed form with as many nodes as possible on one screen. Or, they may prefer a zoomed-in version with the larger-sized boxes on the printout.

You can calculate the exact location of a node on the physical page/screen by using these parameters:

- page size/screen size

- size of the margins

- width and height of the boxes

- space separating the boxes

After determining these parameters, you can calculate the number of elements that will fit on one screen or page:

> # Horizontal elements =
> Horizontal page size – Left margin – Right margin
> / (box width + horizontal space between boxes)

> # Vertical elements =
> Vertical page size – Top margin – Bottom margin
> / (box height + vertical space between boxes)

After you determine the number of boxes that can be drawn on a page, you will have to readjust the logical coordinates. When you first create these logical grid coordinates, imagine that you are working on one very large page of infinite dimensions. Now, you can readjust the coordinates according to the page number. For example, suppose that you can fit 10 boxes on a page both in the vertical and horizontal dimension. If the logical coordinates of a node are X = 23 and Y = 34, then you can calculate the page number of the node. The formula is simply:

> X page = round up (X coordinate / # boxes on page in X dimension)
> Y page = round up (Y coordinate / # boxes on page in Y dimension)
> new X coordinate = remainder of X page division
> new Y coordinate = remainder of Y page division

Based on user options, Figure 11.3 displays sample measurements.

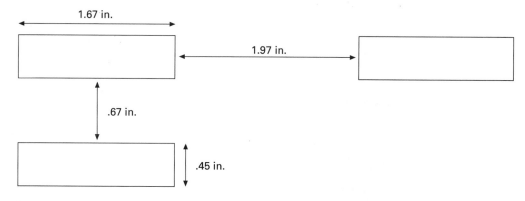

Figure 11.3   *User preferences dictate the dimensions of the site map elements.*

6. Draw the boxes and codes

The actual drawing of the nodes requires the Annotate facility of SAS/GRAPH software (see Figure 11.4). It is important that the code be portable to C, so the boxes are drawn using the POLY function to move from one segment to the next. This is preferable to using the BOX function, which does not have the concomitant function in C. The logic is simply:

1. Position point at upper left hand corner of box as determined by the equations discussed earlier in the section "5. Calculate physical grid coordinates."

2. Draw a line from the upper left corner to the lower left corner.

3. Draw a line from the lower left corner to the lower right corner.

4. Draw a line from the lower right corner to the upper right corner.

5. Draw a line from the upper right corner to the upper left corner.

6. Center the code name in the box. To do so, determine the width of the box and the width of the lettering used in the code name.

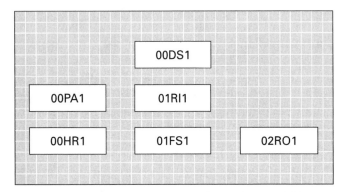

Figure 11.4   *In the first phase of map drawing, the nodes are laid out on the master grid.*

7. Draw the arrows connecting the boxes

The next step is to connect all the parents to their children. While at times this procedure is simple, at other times this presents a challenge because of nodes blocking the direct path from parent to child. Here are three major strategies for connecting nodes:

The "B-52 Bomber" Approach

If there are no blocking elements, draw a line directly from the parent to the child if the two nodes have the same X coordinates. If the two nodes reside in different X coordinates, then drop a line halfway down between the parent and child box. Then move laterally until you are directly above the child. Finally, draw a line from this point down to the top of the child. The term "Bomber" comes from the fact that you can drop straight down from the top as if a bomb were being dropped.

If there are blocking elements between the parent and child, then one of the following two methods is used.

The "Tomahawk Cruise Missile" Approach

This approach means that you drop down as far as possible from the parent's node and then move laterally until just above the child's node. The term "Tomahawk Cruise Missile" was derived from the fact that the line that is drawn is often a long line that lies close to the child's node.

The "Stealth" Approach

This approach is employed as a last resort. It means that you have to find an alleyway to connect the boxes. This involves dropping down half a box size, moving laterally into the alley between the boxes, dropping straight down again until just above the child, and then moving laterally again until just above the child. This "Stealth" method derives its name form the fact that a convoluted path is followed in order to meet up with the target, despite all the obstacles in the way.

After you draw the arrows connecting the nodes, the map should appear as in Figure 11.5.

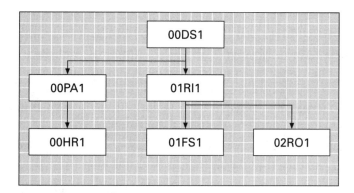

Figure 11.5   *The final site map.*

Coding

Figure 11.6 depicts the core programs in the system.

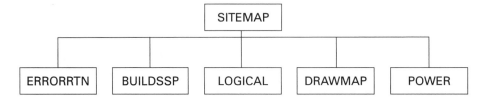

Figure 11.6   *The core modules required to draw a site map.*

Following is a brief description of the modules, starting with the two essential %INCLUDE modules:

CODES provides a convenient way to refer to groups of elements such as project support elements.

RPT_HEAD allows uniformity of reports and is used not only for this project but for all report output given to the EPA.

Here are the main modules:

ERRORRTN examines all the linked relationships in the database and reports any serious errors. These take on three forms: circular links, multiple tree heads, and multiple trees. (Refer to Appendix 3, "A Links Primer," for the complete description of these errors.) If a site exhibits any of these critical errors, the site map is not drawn for that site. Instead, an error log is issued and distributed to the appropriate project leader at EPA.

BUILDSSP creates the navigation order and places the nodes into a single list in a SAS data set called SASDATA.SSP_LIST.

LOGICAL calculates the logical grid coordinates for the drawing of the site map.

DRAWMAP has several functions. Based on the coordinates created from the LOGICAL module, as well as the type of output (terminal, printer, plotter), the exact positioning of the nodes are calculated. After the nodes are drawn, the lines connecting the nodes are drawn. Finally, the text associated with each node is added, along with the appropriate shading and coloring.

POWER is a miniature expert system. Normally, the site maps are created by reading the links that reside in the database. However, the user has the option of recreating the links from scratch. The POWER module assists the user by suggesting a list of links that is then confirmed by the user.

Testing

The layout of the modules in the previous section is based on two factors. First, the modules, as described, provide good logical units. Secondly, it is important to ensure that the output from the SAS prototype corresponds to the output produced by the executable C and C++ programs. This is accomplished by producing intermediate ASCII files after each module is executed. The final module, DRAWMAP, can be broken down into more than one module, but nothing is gained in comparative testing. The reason is that C has access to every picture element on the screen and, thus, extreme precision is attainable, while SAS depends on the Black Box output of SAS/GRAPH. After the execution of each of these modules, SAS can generate a flat file from its SAS data set and can be compared, record for record, with the C output, noting any mismatches.

The raw data from the master database provides an excellent test file for input to the first module—BUILDSSP. Approximately 30,000 links records are available for testing. However, additional links combinations have to be created, both valid and invalid.

Unit Testing/Debugging for ERRORRTN

The ERRORRTN module traps serious errors including circular links, multiple tree heads, and multiple trees. (See Appendix 3, "A Links Primer," for a description of these errors.) To verify that the routine is working properly, you identify the list of links that is creating this circular route. You then provide this list to the EPA so that they can fix the data.

Unit Testing/Debugging for Single String Processing (SSP)

A valid link contains two nodes, both a "from" link and a "to" link. As noted in Figure 11.7, each node contains three parts: (a) the operable unit, (b) the op code, and (c) the sequence number:

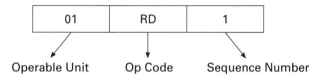

Figure 11.7   *The core components of a node.*

The rules are the following for each component part:

1. The operable unit refers to a major cleanup operation. This part of the node is only valid for an event and must range from 00-99. For activities, this part of the field should be blank.

2. The Op Code is a two letter combination, which is an abbreviated form of the full name that describes an event or activity for the EPA. For example, "RD" represents "Remedial Design", "RA" is "Remedial Action," and "RI" is "Remedial Investigation." The Op Codes are unique, so that you can determine if a node is an activity or event merely by looking at the Op Code.

3. The sequence number must be 01-99 for an activity and 1-9 for an event.

Now you can set up equivalence classes for testing, including boundary value analysis. Descriptions of each type of test appear next to the input field:

```
input node $char06. ;
cards4 ;
00RD1        Valid event at boundary (zero causes problems?)
01RD1        Valid event just inside boundary
-1RD1        Invalid operable unit at boundary
99RD1        Valid event at boundary
100RD1       Invalid op unit at boundary
03RZ1        Invalid op code
03AN1        Op unit with activity
03RD9        Sequence number at boundary
03RD10       Invalid sequence at boundary
RD1          Missing operable unit
03RD         Missing sequence number
031          Missing op code
03           Operable unit only
1            Sequence number only
RD           Op code only
AN00         Invalid activity at boundary (zero cause problems?)
AN01         Valid activity at boundary
AN-1         Invalid operable unit at boundary
AN99         Valid activity at boundary
AN100        Invalid sequence # at boundary
RQ03         Invalid op code
RD99         Has sequence number for an event
AN           Missing sequence number
Blank node
;;;;
```

The next level of testing involves link combinations. It is *theoretically* possible to test all combinations because there are approximately 40 types of events and 40 types of activities. There are four basic possibilities of linking:

```
Event    ==> Event
Event    ==> Activity
Activity ==> Activity
Activity ==> Event
```

Thus, there are (40 * 40) * 4 = 6400 combinations. However, operable codes are processed as groups; hence, equivalence classes can be set up. You want to set up at least enough equivalence classes to form all legitimate combinations. For example:

> Litigation   ==> Negotiations
> Negotiations ==> Remedy
> Remedy   ==> Negotiations
> Search   ==> Removal

For White Box testing, you want to trace through the program and verify that all these combinations are accounted for.

Now, assume that the simplest test cases are completed. The difficult part remaining is to test the BUILDSSP logic. There is no standard for comparing the string output. Rather, you find that you have to create your own rules to determine if the BUILDSSP output is "sensible." For example:

> NS01 ==> 01RD1 ==> 03RD1 ==> 01RA1 ==> 01RA2

is potentially flawed because operable units should be processed in order, "01" before "02" before "03" and so on. However, there are exceptions, and these can only be discerned by viewing the raw links to determine if the BUILDSSP logic is wrong. So, you write routines that provide "Warnings" for potentially troublesome linked lists. Another confounding factor is that the raw data can contain invalid links because the customer inadvertently created them incorrectly. Though time consuming, you find that the best approach is to scan the raw list of "from" and "to" links, and then draw an appropriate linked list. Then, you can compare this against the computer generated output.

You design two tests to assist you in testing/debugging. One test verifies that the number of links in the final SSP string is the same as the number of nodes. The second test verifies that each node is represented once and only once in the final string (a correspondence error).

Unit Testing/Debugging for Logical Grid Coordinates

You emphasize White Box testing to ensure that all logic paths are tested for every conceivable parent-child links relationship. You defer serious testing of modules for integration testing, as is explained shortly.

Unit Testing/Debugging for DRAWMAP

Fortunately, hand-drawn site maps are available for hundreds of site maps. The computer generated version is then compared against these manual drawings. Logic errors can be discerned very rapidly this way.

Unit Testing/Debugging for POWER

Testing the automated generation is tedious. It involves viewing the DRAWMAP output created from this module, and comparing it against the list of raw "from" and "to" links. In general, the hand-drawn maps are less useful than they are for the SITEMAP routine because POWER does not attempt to link every single node. Rather, only major events and corresponding activity settlements are linked. Difficult link relationships, such as litigation, can only be determined with serious research. Hence, these are manually linked online.

Integration Testing/Debugging

Fortunately, when the final output is online, "What-You-See-is-What-You-Get" greatly simplifies testing. Sites can be batched such that the system can generate maps for an entire region (approximately 125 sites per region). In processing order, the system reads the database links, generates the SSP, creates logical grid coordinates, calculates physical position, and finally draws the map online. Optionally, the program can generate hardcopy output. If there is a discrepancy between the hand-drawn maps and the computer-generated version, it is immediately obvious. Debugging entails checking the module interfaces. This involves dumping permanent data sets at each phase of the process. This allows you to isolate program bugs to one of the major modules.

System Testing/Debugging

The program is tested on different configurations from 286 to 486 machines with varying amounts of memory and disk space. The system is first tested stand-alone, and then on a Novell network. Output is directed to all types of VGA monitors as well as a variety of laser printers. The most pressing problem that you encounter is running short on memory with the C version. This is particularly evident with the larger sites, which contain 150–200 links. Because many arrays are used (including one two-dimensional array), it is easy to run short on memory. To combat the problem, you use the following approach.

- All arrays are dynamically allocated.
- The C programs are divided into smaller modules than their SAS counterparts.
- Programs are swapped out of memory utilizing a memory manager.
- When possible, output files are created in intermediate steps.
- The program checks for other memory resident programs and asks the user to logoff and re-logon without these programs installed.

User Acceptance

The customer tests the software at their site. Unit testing is performed for the BUILDSSP module, the final Site Map System module (DRAWMAP), and the POWER module, because these are the three components that the customer uses in their day to day functions.

Maintenance

The customer is pleased with the rapid display of the maps online. However, hardcopy output remains painfully slow. The list of enhancements generated by the customer includes adding the abilities to do the following:

- output to a plotter

- view legal and financial data online by clicking on a node

- provide an iconized version of the site map to enable nontechnical people to understand links relationships

- restore the original site map quickly if current edits have to be canceled

- move alternatively between sites without returning to the master menu.

Chapter 12   **Answers to Exercises**

Chapter 2

1. Quick Analysis ==> Coding ==> Very Quick Testing ==> Debugging

2. • Prototyping has become much more important. Hence, the need for fast, flexible tools.

   • Testing is performed throughout the software life cycle.

   • Test Plans are written before the project starts.

   • With the advent of fast programming and design tools, maintenance on dinosaur systems is dying. Companies are throwing out old code and starting over with new and better methodologies. This can cause a shift in the relative amount of time spent in each phase of the life cycle.

3. • People don't think it is cost effective.

   • Deadline pressures force teams to skip or skimp on certain phases.

   • People just don't understand the process.

   • Managers don't believe in it, thinking that programmers should be coding, not planning.

   • People mistakenly believe that the development of modern software tools (such as CASE, Object Oriented Programming, GUI tools, and so on) replace many of the requirements for planning.

4. The later they are discovered in the life cycle, the more expensive they are to correct. For example, design bugs discovered near the end of the project may be 100 times as expensive to fix than when they are discovered early in the process. In the worst case scenario, a project team may not really understand the customer's problem and, so, may develop a system to faulty specifications. In such a case, all or much of the work may have to be scrapped.

5. • The requirements for communication increase dramatically as the number of programmers increase.

   • Documentation has to be continually updated and distributed.

   • More meetings and memos are required to allow for interprogrammer communication.

   • Library management has to be installed so programmers don't trash each other's work.

   • And of course, it is difficult to move through the software life cycle properly when the total timeline is very short. People have different strengths and weaknesses and move at a different pace. You can't just move these 12 people all into the analysis phase and all 12 people into the design phase, then into the coding phase, and so on.

Chapter 3

1. **a. SAS macro autocall facility advantages:**

   - Macros are stored in a common area.
   - The name of the file and macro have the same name for quick reference.

   SAS macro autocall facility disadvantages:

   - Multiple macros can be placed in this file, thus causing organizational problems.
   - Placing nonmacro code in a file can result in bizarre bugs because the code is only executed the first time.

   b. SAS compiled stored facility advantages:

   - Macros are stored in a common area.
   - There are CPU savings because of one-time compilation.

   SAS compiled stored facility disadvantages:

   - Source code can be lost or might not match up with the executing macro.

   c. General %INCLUDE library advantages:

   - You can keep, in one area, various types of constructs that have a common function.

   General %INCLUDE library disadvantages

   - Programmers are not accustomed to this kind of organization. It's hard to break habits.

2. The programming team may code for the visible range of values. When the database is updated with a new range of values, the current code becomes obsolete and can lead to unexpected results.

3. The automatic macro variable &SYSSCP can be tested to conditionally execute code (such as library and file name definitions).

4. The treatment is effective if oral temperature is reduced by at least 1.50 degrees Fahrenheit as compared to baseline using a W-7 oral thermometer. Only one such reduction is required to provide evidence of efficacy. Baseline temperature is measured at 6 a.m. (Note: the exact methodology of utilizing an oral thermometer should also be made explicitly clear).

5. **a. Advantages of centralized libraries:**

   - Their use allows all macros to be stored in one place, thus everyone knows where macros are stored.
   - Duplication of names is not possible. With proper documentation, users can be made aware of the various and sundry macros available for their use.

   b. Disadvantages of centralized libraries:

   - The number of macros can be imposing and frustrating to the user who is overwhelmed by hundreds (or thousands!) of macros, many of those being of no interest to the user.

c. Advantage of decentralized libraries:

- Being smaller, they are more manageable. They allow users to be exposed primarily to just the macros they need to be using.

d. Disadvantages of decentralized libraries:

- Two different libraries may have the same name for a macro, thus creating confusion.

- Time may be wasted because two or more people in the organization are developing a macro with the same function.

- A user may not be aware that a certain valuable macro exists in some far-off library.

Chapter 4

1. They must assess:

   - cost

   - technical barriers

   - external agents

   - timeline constraints

2. If the system needs to be rewritten for machine efficiency, you want to be careful that you don't destroy the old logic. Therefore, you must comprehend the system fully.

3. Earlier versions of SAS software lacked the full functionality to make it practical for central data storage. Most notably, SAS lacked the indexing capabilities for rapid retrieval. In addition, the user interfaces were not as developed as they are today. As customers become enlightened to many of the new features of the SAS System, they will gradually be swayed into using SAS for most, if not all, of their information needs.

4. Data set organization must provide maximum efficiency and ease of use for the programming team, and it should eliminate data redundancy. Only after modeling a comprehensive system can you get a good feel for these considerations.

5. Analysis means to study something by breaking it down into its constituent parts. The analyst can start at the gross level and continue to break down the task into its atomic elements.

Chapter 5

1. Top-Down design is based on the principle of abstraction, which is a thought process that categorizes objects by focusing on their similarities. In Top-Down design, you begin at a high, general level of abstraction, and then formulate down to more specific, detailed levels.

2. Bottom-Up design is based on the principle of concatenation. You think of small objects as tiny entities in their own right. Bottom-Up development involves stringing together specific details in order to formulate higher levels of abstraction.

3. It is easy to forget the variable's attributes, which can lead to programming bugs. This is particularly a problem with character variables. There is an additional concern when a variable is alive for a long time. There is a good chance for the variable to corrupt the values of other variables, or for itself to be corrupted.

4. a. Possibly (2)

b. Probably (1)

c. Probably (1)

d. Probably not (3)

e. Probably not (3)

f. Probably (1)

g. Possibly (2)

h. Probably not (3)

i. Probably not (3)

5. The module should have one function, a small parameter list of common functions, and a high degree of portability.

6. This would be advantageous to process variables as a list, such as this set of exams: &EXAM1–&EXAM9

7. When multiple languages are involved in a system, an ASCII file is a good medium for everyone to read.

8. Companies are realizing that the cost of constructing software is becoming prohibitive when the user is not satisfied. A "throwaway" prototype is code that is trashed at the end of the modeling phase. An "evolutionary" prototype is code that is used for both the model and the final implementation.

9. Move it into a DATA step variable and then manipulate the DATA step variable as you wish. In that way, you don't trash the macro variable for other's use.

10. Developing these lists allows you to think more deeply about the design and, thus, build in flexibility. Nothing can be more frustrating to users than telling them that what they perceive as a small modification is actually a nightmare for the programming team.

Chapter 6

1. a. Other team members may have to do a lot of horizontal scrolling when they have to view your files.

b. There is a tendency to build expressions that are too complex, such as stacking multiple functions.

c. Wide screens encourage deep nesting of DO loops and IF-THEN-ELSE constructs.

2. Everyone has been exposed to different languages and operating systems. +1 may mean "success" to you, but it may signify "failure" to another programmer.

3. a. Use a verb and object to describe the module's function, such as FIX_TIME.

b. Use a name that describes what the function returns, such as TIMESPAN.

4. Calculate the number of categories with, say, a PROC FREQ and then:

```
    do k = 1 to &num_cats ;
```
or
```
    do k = 1 to num_cats ;
```

5. a. Some people abhor typing.

   b. Programming is, by nature, terse.

   c. Some people actually believe that typing time is the rate limiting factor in coding development.

   d. Programs become too long.

   e. Long names make the code unreadable.

6. a. Use standard computer abbreviations such as EOF or IO.

   b. Separate logical parts of words with an underscore.

   c. Use standard industry abbreviations.

   d. Avoid meaningless suffixes.

7. They provide landmarks that enable you to quickly skim source code to find the section that requires maintenance.

8. The source code and comments may not match, thus confusing the maintenance programmer.

9. a. Alignment is a continual maintenance problem.

   b. The comments must be very short.

   c. The comments may not elucidate the overall function of the code.

10. The biggest advantage is that it provides good visual separation. The biggest disadvantage is that everyone on the team may have their own conventions, thus leading to confusion. This becomes particularly annoying when modules are merged into one routine.

11. "Documentation density" is the percentage of the source code devoted to comments. Documentation density is affected by the programming language. Very low languages tend to be cryptic and to require a higher level of documentation.

Chapter 7

1. a. to avoid the excessive use of flag setting

   b. to avoid the use of GOTOs

   c. to abort a routine

2. a. Use PROC FORMAT.

   b. LINK to a subroutine.

   c. Use the SELECT statement.

3. a. Use the KEEP and DROP data set option or statement.

   b. Move global variables into a DATA step variable.

   c. Consider using CALL SYMPUT to bring forward a smaller number of variables in the program.

   d. Define module macro variables as LOCAL in scope.

   e. Be judicious in the selection of GLOBAL macro variables.

4. a. It forces you to think about the design process. Otherwise, you might dash straight to the terminal and commence coding.

   b. You can discover design and logic flaws during the translation process.

   c. It's a good way to ensure that the code is documented.

5. a. A variable is declared with a LENGTH or ATTRIB statement and is then used (without assignment).

b. A variable is extracted improperly from another variable.

c The programmer forgot to use a RETAIN statement.

d. Names are duplicated for the initialized variable and another variable in the Program Data Vector.

6. Measuring software complexity is useful because

a. it is useful for predicting problematic modules.

b. it can be used to suggest when a module should be subdivided.

c. it can predict modules that are difficult to test.

d. it can predict the error rate for a module.

While there are proponents for both sides, metric complexity is probably more useful as a prospective tool. Changing a number of modules just to improve the metric complexity is potentially dangerous. There is a significant chance of creating bugs in the program because the logic may be inadvertently changed. Most proponents feel that it is useful as a learning tool for future projects.

7. a. It is easier to ensure that cases aren't missed.

b. There is a tendency to use literals in IF-THEN-ELSE statements, which is difficult to maintain.

c. It centralizes code for easier maintenance.

8.
```
if prelim in ( &fever, &rash ) then
    if nitetime in ( &chills, &sweats ) then
        if signs in ( &pale, &flushed ) then
            call = urgent ;
```

9. If a variable has a long span, there is a greater opportunity for the variable to corrupt other variables or for itself to be altered inadvertently.

10. a. to avoid messy flag setting

b. to go to the end of a macro routine.

Chapter 8

1.
```
%let recprice = 599 799 999 1199 ;

rec_cnt = 1 ;
do until ( recprice = " " ) ;
    recprice = scan ( "&recprice", rec_cnt ) ;
    if recprice ne " " then
    do ;
        discount = int (recprice / 10) ;
        put 'Your total discount is ' discount ;
        sale = ( recprice - discount ) / 100 ;
        put 'And your cost for the record is ' sale dollar6.2 ;
    end ;
    rec_cnt + 1 ;
end ;
```

2. In the source file, specify a macro variable such as:

```
%let filename = movefile.sas ;
```

In the master driver file, specify the output location:

```
%let outloc = &drive\data\reports ;
```

Then, in the calling module, code:

```
%let prefix = %scan ( &filename, 1, "." ) ;

proc printto print = "&outloc\&prefix..rpt" new ;
run ;
```

3. Both times are important. Encountering duplicate records early in the process may be indicative of problems in the database. On the other hand, duplicate records can also be caused by flawed logic or system problems later in the process.

4. It is unrealistic to expect a customer to use your commands because they probably have their own file they like to use for setting up their environment. Also, a customer could easily forget that the AUTOEXEC file contained special commands when they recreate their own version.

5. **Advantage:** Error processing at higher levels avoids redundancy of coding.

Disadvantage: Low level errors, particularly execution-time errors, would be missed. A good example is the "divide by zero" condition.

6. Each time you read the input file, dynamically calculate the longest length of each variable. Then, in the following DATA step, you can create LENGTH statements based on these calculated lengths. For an example of the technique, refer to Coding Sample 6 in Appendix 1, "Coding Samples."

7. This option removes duplicates only if the records are consecutive and identical. You have to sort by all of the variables to effectively remove all of the exact duplicates.

8. to assure proper sequencing of report numbers and to allow global changes to titles and footnotes.

9. a. changes to data passed in to the program
b. changes in program specifications
c. changes in the module interfaces
d. changes in the coding algorithm

The first effect is the best candidate because changes in the data can almost always be handled by good coding practices.

10. "Seamless coding" means making the code airtight so that changes in the data do not result in unexpected errors. It is important in large systems because the programmer should not be concerned about constantly trying to maintain every module whenever there are changes to the system. Ideally, changes to a system should be managed by a handful of modules.

Chapter 9

1. Bugs remaining = $((100 / 5) * 25) - 25 + (100 - 5)$
   $$= 500 - 25 + 95$$
   $$= 570$$

2. a. Black Box
   b. Gray Box
   c. White Box
   d. Black Box
   e. Black Box
   f. Gray Box
   g. Black Box
   h. White Box

3. ```
   input channel @@ ;
   cards ;
   02 03 12 13 16 17 45 46 48 49 50 54 55 66 67
   ;
   ```

4. a. Valid two-character entry
   b. Invalid two-character entry
   c. Valid first-character entry, invalid second-character entry
   d. Invalid first-character entry, valid second-character entry
   e. Both characters missing

   Note: Extra classes can be developed to test case sensitivity.

5. 16

6. The programmer probably did not intend to include "Herbivore" in the first statement. This logic error would be caught by more comprehensive White Box tests.

7. 0, 1 , 2, &max_cnt – 1, &max_cnt, &max_cnt + 1

8. J,K,F,C,L,I

9. B,D (be careful—not A, because module G is not coded yet)

10. Many programming errors are related to the invalid sequences of data declaration and usage. These kinds of errors are becoming even more prevalent as modern day programming emphasizes table-driven programming.
   ```

Chapter 10

1. Nontrivial errors are difficult to track down by brute force. Without forming a hypothesis first, you may have to run countless executions. Also, it is tempting to make a fix as soon as you find the location of the error without realizing the bug may be more involved than you first thought.

2. It can effectively catch simple logic errors such as forgetting to use a LENGTH or RETAIN statement.

3. PROC PRINT is especially useful at locating gross logic flaws because they become immediately obvious when you print the results before and after a DATA step or PROC step. Particular constructs causing these errors may be misuse of MERGE, PROC SQL, SET and UPDATE, and improper handling of missing values for procedures.

4. Data lookups and MERGE processing can easily get out of synchronization.

5. a. bugs related to date and time.
   b. bugs related to timing issues. For example, programs requiring user input may react differently depending on when the user responds.
   c. bugs created when a random number generator is involved.

6. Trying to trace logic through many layers is difficult. It is easy to get lost. In addition, if data are passed continuously through all these channels, there are numerous opportunities for the data to be corrupted.

7. Because it is probably the first time that you seriously walked through the logic.

8. Most programmers are probably not as familiar with the input data as they ought to be. Also, too often, the data is assumed to be clean when it really is not.

9. Programmers do not take the care to think carefully about these boundaries. It is very easy to code "LT" when you meant "LE". Also, you may have set a counter or total that is initialized according to a loop index. It is easy to let these get out of synchronization by changing one of them without thinking how the other is affected.

10. The programmer intended to code the following in the second line:

    ```
    do j = 1 to 10;
    ```

    You could write a program to find a DO statement and then the first nonblank character after the equal sign. You may want to provide a warning if it is not numeric or only if "i" , "l" or "o" is encountered.

Coding Samples

Summary of Coding Samples

The following programs are introduced throughout this book. Here is a brief description of each program:

Coding Sample   **Description**

1   creates formats automatically using the CNTLIN feature of PROC FORMAT.

2   validates the transmission of data from a database into permanent SAS data sets.

3   provides a frequency distribution of data.

4   runs a batch job for submitting multiple SAS source modules.

5   a parser routine that allows one or more words to be wrapped properly for report output.

6   an enhancement to the parser routine in Coding Sample 5. The program calculates the maximum formatted value for all variables in a data set.

7   a sample initialization file. This program can be a sample master driver module that is included at the beginning of each source file.

8   demonstrates a sample selection screen using the WINDOW statement.

9   a sample titles and footnotes file. This file works in conjunction with other programs to automatically place titles and footnotes in the appropriate program.

10   a sample report shell.

11   code for a report generator.

12   scans a log directory and reports all ERROR and WARNING messages, and NOTES of interest.

13   finds a MERGE without a concomitant BY statement.

Coding Sample 1

```
****************************************************************** ;
***                                                          *** ;
*** Source:    MAKEFORM                                      *** ;
***                                                          *** ;
*** Type:      Utility                                       *** ;
***                                                          *** ;
*** Function:  Automatically creates PROC FORMATS            *** ;
***                                                          *** ;
*** Usage:     You must pass in the following parameters:    *** ;
***                                                          *** ;
***            DATASET   which contains the name of the SAS  *** ;
***                      data set containing the table data. *** ;
***                                                          *** ;
***            FORMNAME  is the format name that you wish to *** ;
***                      create in the PROC FORMAT statement.*** ;
***                                                          *** ;
***            VALUE     is the variable name in the SAS data*** ;
***                      set that contains the lookup values.*** ;
***                                                          *** ;
***            DESCRIPT  is the description that each value   *** ;
***                      maps to.                            *** ;
***                                                          *** ;
*** Example:   You have a data set named LOOKUP.ETHNIC       *** ;
***            that contains a mapping of race codes and     *** ;
***            their respective races. The value of ETHNICID *** ;
***            maps to ETHNICGR:                             *** ;
***                                                          *** ;
***            obs  ethnicid ethnicgr                        *** ;
***             1      4      Asian                          *** ;
***             2      7      White                          *** ;
***             3      9      Black                          *** ;
***                                                          *** ;
*** Assume that you want to create a format called "race".   *** ;
*** You would then call the macro as follows:                *** ;
***                                                          *** ;
*** %makeform ( dataset = lookup.ethnic ,                    *** ;
***             formname = race ,                            *** ;
***             value = ethnicid ,                           *** ;
***             descript = ethnicgr )                        *** ;
***                                                          *** ;
****************************************************************** ;

%macro makeform ( dataset = ,
                  formname =,
                  value = ,
                  descript = ) ;
```

```
******************************************************************* ;
*** Set up variables required by the CNTLIN option of PROC   *** ;
*** FORMAT. START contains the value, LABEL is the des-      *** ;
*** cription and FMTNAME is the format name you wish to       *** ;
*** assign.                                                    *** ;
******************************************************************* ;

     data control ( rename =
        ( &value = start &descript = label )) ;
           set &dataset ;

     fmtname = "&formname" ;
     run ;
%mend makeform ;


******************************************************************* ;
*** Create the formats automatically                          *** ;
******************************************************************* ;

%makeform ( dataset = lookup.ethnic ,
            formname = race ,
            value = ethnicid ,
            descript = ethnicgr )

proc format cntlin = control ;
run ;
```

Coding Sample 2

```
******************************************************************* ;
***                                                           *** ;
*** Source:     QADATA.SAS                                    *** ;
***                                                           *** ;
*** Type:       Utility                                       *** ;
***                                                           *** ;
*** Function:   To ensure that data are transferred correctly *** ;
***             from the in-house data base to the production *** ;
***             SAS data sets.                                *** ;
***                                                           *** ;
*** Logic:      Data from the data base are written out to a  *** ;
***             set of text files.  The name of the file      *** ;
***             should correspond to the name of the SAS      *** ;
***             data set. i.e. CONCOM.SSD and CONCOM.TXT.     *** ;
***             Then, the SAS data sets are read to gather     *** ;
***             information about their format. This allows    *** ;
***             you to write code that generates the proper    *** ;
***             input and length statements for reading the    *** ;
***             text file into a SAS data set. Then, the two   *** ;
***             sets of SAS data are compared with PROC        *** ;
***             COMPARE.  If the two data sets are equal,      *** ;
***             we can feel pretty confident that the trans-   *** ;
***             fer process is occurring correctly.            *** ;
***                                                           *** ;
```

```
*** Usage:      The two key variables are the pointers to the *** ;
***             SAS data sets and the text file directory.    *** ;
***             These are set up in the macro %LIBCHEK.        *** ;
***                                                            *** ;
***             %libchek ( lib = permsas ,                     *** ;
***                        text_dir = c:\ascii ,               *** ;
***                        maxlrecl = 256 ,                    *** ;
***                        titlecnt = 3 )                      *** ;
***                                                            *** ;
**************************************************************** ;


**************************************************************** ;
*** This format will be used to differentiate between char-  *** ;
*** acter and numeric variables.                             *** ;
**************************************************************** ;

proc format ;

value _vartype
    1 = ' '
    2 = '$'
    ;
run ;


%macro libchek ( lib = work ,        /* Input SAS data library */
                 text_dir = ,        /* Input text file library */
                 maxlrecl = 256 ,    /* Max length of text files */
                 titlecnt = 3 ) ;    /* Where to place title */

**************************************************************** ;
***                                                          *** ;
***                  V A R I A B L E S                       *** ;
***                                                          *** ;
**************************************************************** ;
%local i ;            * Loop counter ;
%local mem_list ;     * List of library members ;
%local mem_cnt ;      * Number of members in library ;
%local memname ;      * Library member name ;

%let lib = %upcase ( &lib ) ;

**************************************************************** ;
*** Get a list of all the library members and place it into  *** ;
*** a macro variable.  Also, get a count of the number of    *** ;
*** members in the library.                                  *** ;
**************************************************************** ;

proc sql noprint ;
    select memname into : mem_list separated by " "
    from dictionary.columns
    where libname = "&lib"
    ;
    %let mem_cnt = &sqlobs ;
quit ;
```

```
******************************************************** ;
*** Pick off the current member name.  This allows us to   *** ;
*** find both the SAS data set and ASCII text file with that *** ;
*** name.                                                  *** ;
*** Continually call MEMCHEK which does the actual creating *** ;
*** of the secondary SAS data set as well as  the file     *** ;
*** comparison.                                            *** ;
******************************************************** ;

%do i = 1 %to &mem_cnt ;
    %let memname = %qscan ( &mem_list, &i ) ;
    %memchek ( sasdata = &lib..&memname,
               textfile = &text_dir\&memname..txt,
               lrecl = &maxlrecl
             )
%end ;

%mend libchek ;


******************************************************** ;
*** MEMCHEK will read the first record of the text file to *** ;
*** retrieve the SAS variable names.  Then a PROC CONTENTS *** ;
*** will enable us to retrieve the variable attributes of  *** ;
*** the SAS variables.  This will provide the requisite    *** ;
*** information to create the appropriate length and input *** ;
*** statements for the text file.                          *** ;
******************************************************** ;

%macro memchek ( sasdata = _last_ , /* SAS input data set    */
                 textfile = ,       /* Comma separated direct. */
                 lrecl= ,           /* logical record length  */
                 titlecnt = 3 ) ;   /* Title loc for report   */


******************************************************** ;
***                                                    *** ;
***                 V A R I A B L E S                  *** ;
***                                                    *** ;
******************************************************** ;
%local i ;           * Loop counter ;
%local len_list ;    * Holds lengths of all variables ;
%local inp_list ;    * Holds list of input variables ;
%local fixlist  ;    * List of variables that must be fixed ;

%if %upcase ( &sasdata) = _LAST_ %then
    %let sasdata = &syslast ;

filename _in "&textfile" ;

******************************************************** ;
*** Read just the first record of the text file. This con- *** ;
*** tains the list of SAS variable names.                  *** ;
******************************************************** ;

data _textvar ( keep = var seq ) ;

length var $ 8 ;
infile "&textfile" dsd missover obs = 1 ;
input var $ @ ;
```

```
            do while ( var ^= " " ) ;
                seq + 1 ;
                output _textvar ;
                input var $ @ ;
            end ;
            run ;

            proc contents data = &sasdata noprint
                out = _sas_var ( keep = name length type format ) ;
            run ;

            proc sql noprint ;

            create table _specs as
                select name, length, type, format, seq
                from _textvar as csv, _sas_var as sas
                where upcase ( var ) = name
                order by seq
                ;

            select name || put ( type, _vartype.) || put ( length, 4. )
                into : len_list separated by " "
                from _specs
                ;

            select case
                when ( type = 1 and format = "DATETIME" ) then
                    name || " :" || "MMDDYY8. "
                when ( type = 2 ) then
                    name || ' $'
                else name
                end
                into : inp_list separated by ' '
                from _specs
                ;

            %let fixlist = ;
            select name || '=86400 * ' || name
                into : fixlist separated by ";"
                from _specs
                where format = "DATETIME"
                ;

            quit ;

            ******************************************************************* ;
            *** We now know how to input the fields from the ASCII file. *** ;
            *** The LENGTH and INPUT statements were established from   *** ;
            *** previous steps.                                         *** ;
            ******************************************************************* ;

            data _text ;
                infile "&textfile" dsd firstobs = 2 ;
                length &len_list ;
                input &inp_list ;
                &fixlist ;
            run ;
```

```
********************************************************************** ;
*** Compare the original SAS data set with the one that was   *** ;
*** created from the text file.  If the transfer was ok,      *** ;
*** then the procedure should report no differences.          *** ;
********************************************************************** ;

title&titlecnt "Summary comparison for &sasdata and &textfile" ;

proc compare base = &sasdata compare = _text
    criterion = .00001 brief;
run ;


********************************************************************** ;
*** Clean up the environment.                                 *** ;
********************************************************************** ;

proc datasets lib = work ;
    delete _textvar _sas_var _specs _text ;
quit ;

filename _in clear ;

%mend memchek ;
```

Coding Sample 3

Note: In the following code, you might want to substitute PROC FREQ with PROC UNIVARIATE and the ROUND option if you want to reduce the number of unique values generated. This is particularly useful for continuous data.

```
********************************************************************** ;
***                                                           *** ;
*** Source:     DATAFREQ.SAS                                  *** ;
***                                                           *** ;
*** Type:       Utility                                       *** ;
***                                                           *** ;
*** Function:   Creates a listing of all values for all       *** ;
***             data sets in this library.                    *** ;
***                                                           *** ;
*** Data sets: Uses all data sets in library.                 *** ;
***                                                           *** ;
*** Usage:      Set the macro variable &DROPVARS to those     *** ;
***             variables that you want to drop from the      *** ;
***             PROC FREQ.  This list globally drops these    *** ;
***             variables from all the work data sets. If the *** ;
***             variable is not found in a data set, a Warn-  *** ;
***             ing is issued by SAS, but the step continues  *** ;
***             to execute.                                   *** ;
***                                                           *** ;
***             %let dropvars = date_cre date_end ;           *** ;
***                                                           *** ;
***             If you prefer not to drop any variables,      *** ;
***             set the macro variable to null:               *** ;
***                                                           *** ;
***             %let dropvars = ;                             *** ;
```

```
***                                                       ***  ;
***             Also, set the library with &LIB.          ***  ;
***                                                       ***  ;
***************************************************************  ;

%let lib = MAPS ;

***************************************************************  ;
*** DROPVARS is a macro variable that lists all the vari-  ***  ;
*** ables you do not want to run a PROC FREQ on.  These    ***  ;
*** variables are dropped from their respective data sets. ***  ;
***************************************************************  ;

%let dropvars = ;

***************************************************************  ;
*** Set up a scratch file.                                 ***  ;
***************************************************************  ;

filename instruct "c:\instruct.dat" ;

***************************************************************  ;
*** Get a list of all the library members in this directory. ***  ;
***************************************************************  ;

proc contents data = &lib.._all_
     short noprint out = contents ;
run ;

***************************************************************  ;
*** We do not need the variables in each SAS data set.  We ***  ;
*** just want a list of the library members.               ***  ;
***************************************************************  ;

proc sort data = contents nodupkey
     out = final ( keep = memname )   ;
     by memname ;
run ;

***************************************************************  ;
*** This step loops through the list of library members,   ***  ;
*** creates a temporary SAS data set, drops any variables   ***  ;
*** specified by &DROPVARS, and runs a PROC FREQ for all    ***  ;
*** remaining variables in that data set.                   ***  ;
***************************************************************  ;

data _null_ ;
     set final ;

***************************************************************  ;
*** Write instructions out to a file that are %INCLUDED     ***  ;
*** later.                                                  ***  ;
***************************************************************  ;

file instruct ;

put "proc freq data = &lib.." memname "(drop = &dropvars) ;" ;
put "title1 " "Raw data dump for &lib.." memname " ;" ;
```

```
                put "tables _all_  ;" ;
                put "run ;" ;

                run ;


                *************************************************************** ;
                *** Now execute the SAS instructions set up in the previous *** ;
                *** step.                                                   *** ;
                *************************************************************** ;


                %include instruct ;
```

Coding Sample 4

```
                *************************************************************** ;
                ***                                                        *** ;
                *** Source:     STUDYRUN.SAS                               *** ;
                ***                                                        *** ;
                *** Type:       Utility                                    *** ;
                ***                                                        *** ;
                *** Function:   Runs all source modules in a given directory. *** ;
                ***                                                        *** ;
                *** Usage:      Set the following macro variables:         *** ;
                ***                                                        *** ;
                ***             DIR_LIST is the filename of directory list *** ;
                ***             SAS_CODE is scratch area for instructions  *** ;
                ***             SAS_DIR is directory that contains source.  *** ;
                ***                                                        *** ;
                *************************************************************** ;


                *************************************************************** ;
                *** Scratch files                                          *** ;
                *************************************************************** ;

                %let dir_list = c:\mysas\dir_list.dat ;
                %let sas_code = c:\mysas\sas_code.sas ;
                %let sas_dir  = c:\mysas ;

                *************************************************************** ;
                *** Filename references for scratch files.                 *** ;
                *************************************************************** ;

                filename dir_list  "&dir_list" ;
                filename sas_code  "&sas_code" ;

                *************************************************************** ;
                *** We do not want user to have to interact with DOS.      *** ;
                *************************************************************** ;

                options noxwait ;

                *************************************************************** ;
                *** Erase old copies of output file, easier for debugging!  *** ;
                *************************************************************** ;

                x  "erase &dir_list" ;
                x  "erase &sas_code" ;
```

```
******************************************************************* ;
*** Get a listing of all the SAS source code files.       *** ;
******************************************************************* ;

x "dir/b &sas_dir\*.sas | sort > &dir_list" ;

x "type &dir_list" ;

data _null_ ;
    infile "&dir_list" truncover ;

length the_file $12 ;   * Scratch file ;
input the_file $ ;      * Work area for file entries ;

******************************************************************* ;
*** Write entries back out to temp file.                  *** ;
******************************************************************* ;

file "&sas_code" ;

put "%include "  "'" "&sas_dir\" the_file "'"   " ; " ;

run ;

******************************************************************* ;
***  Code to execute the source files one at a time.      *** ;
******************************************************************* ;

%include sas_code ;
```

Coding Sample 5

```
******************************************************************* ;
***                                                       *** ;
*** Source:    PARSER.SAS                                  *** ;
***                                                       *** ;
*** Type:      %INCLUDE Module                             *** ;
***                                                       *** ;
*** Function: Parsing routine.  Sometimes because of space *** ;
***           limitations, it is necessary to split a var- *** ;
***           iable (parse it) over two or more observations.*** ;
***           This routine will only update a SAS data set *** ;
***           by adding an observation whenever needed to  *** ;
***           accommodate the parsed variable.             *** ;
***                                                       *** ;
*** Usage:     Set up the following:                       *** ;
***                                                       *** ;
***            &VARS is the variable(s) to be parsed.      *** ;
***                                                       *** ;
***            &IN_DATA is data set that contains the parsed *** ;
***            variable(s).                                *** ;
***                                                       *** ;
***            &LEN_MAX is the maximum number of characters *** ;
***            that you wish to allow for the variable per *** ;
***            output line on the report.  For example, if *** ;
***            you set &LEN_MAX to 20 and your variable    *** ;
```

```
***              contains 63 characters, your output will       *** ;
***              probably be parsed to 4 lines.  I say          *** ;
***              probably because the parser will never allow a *** ;
***              variable to be split in the middle of a word,  *** ;
***              so it is possible that the parsed word may     *** ;
***              occupy more lines than anticipated.            *** ;
***                                                             *** ;
***              &KEEPVARS are any variables that you wish to   *** ;
***              keep on continuation lines besides the parsed  *** ;
***              variables.  If you only want the parsed var-   *** ;
***              iables, then set &KEEPVARS to null.            *** ;
***                                                             *** ;
***              &SPACES is the number of spaces you want to    *** ;
***              indent for each line after the first one.      *** ;
***              This is usually preferred since cosmetically   *** ;
***              it is easier to read the output.  You can      *** ;
***              specify 0 if you do not want any indention.    *** ;
***              My personal preference is 2. Remember, that if *** ;
***              you decide you want indention for subsequent   *** ;
***              lines, you must specify the $CHAR format for   *** ;
***              the parsed variable in the output report.      *** ;
***                                                             *** ;
***              Example: (for parsing one variable)            *** ;
***                                                             *** ;
***              %let vars = crf_term ;                         *** ;
***              %let in_data = adverse ;                       *** ;
***              %let len_max = 45 ;                            *** ;
***              %let spaces = 2 ;                              *** ;
***              %let keepvars = body_sys organ ;               *** ;
***              %include parser ;                              *** ;
***                                                             *** ;
***              Example: (for parsing several variables)       *** ;
***                                                             *** ;
***              Make sure that for multiple variables that you *** ;
***              specify a length (&LEN_MAX) and indention       *** ;
***              (&SPACES) for EACH variable that you parse:     *** ;
***                                                             *** ;
***              %let vars = histolog cause_of body_sys         *** ;
***              %let in_data = pat_info ;                       *** ;
***              %let len_max = 30 45 25 ;                       *** ;
***              %let spaces =   2  0  2 ;                       *** ;
***              %let keepvars = pat_num ;                       *** ;
***              %include parser ;                               *** ;
***                                                             *** ;
***              Note:                                          *** ;
***              Two variables will be added to your data set.  *** ;
***              One is _LINEPOS which stands for "line          *** ;
***              position".  This may be useful to allow a more *** ;
***              cosmetic formatting of the output.  For         *** ;
***              example, you may want to only print the        *** ;
***              continued parsed out variable on the contin-   *** ;
***              uation lines, not the rest of the detail       *** ;
***              record.  Let us say, you have a report in      *** ;
***              which you want to print the patient number     *** ;
***              (PAT_NUM), the body system (BODY_SYS) and      *** ;
***              costart term (COSTART).  The body system       *** ;
***              term (BODY_SYS) is the variable that is to be  *** ;
```

```
***            parsed. After calling the parser routine as    *** ;
***            specified above, you would include the follow-  *** ;
***            ing code in your DATA _NULL_. This code would   *** ;
***            cause all report variables to print on the      *** ;
***        .   first line, but only the parsed out variable    *** ;
***            on subsequent lines.                            *** ;
***            The other variable is _SEQ_NUM.  This identi-    *** ;
***            fies the observation number from the original   *** ;
***            data set. Thus, if the first record is parsed   *** ;
***            into three records, the _SEQ_NUM will be "1"     *** ;
***            for all three records and the _LINEPOS will be   *** ;
***            "1", "2" and "3" respectively for the three      *** ;
***            records.                                         *** ;
***                                                             *** ;
***            if _linepos = 1 then                             *** ;
***                put @010 pat_num                             *** ;
***                    @030 body_sys $char.                     *** ;
***                    @50  costart                             *** ;
***                    ;                                        *** ;
***            else                                             *** ;
***                put @030 body_sys $char. ;                   *** ;
***                                                             *** ;
****************************************************************** ;


****************************************************************** ;
*** Add a variable to the original data set which is the    *** ;
*** sequence number for each record.  This will ensure that *** ;
*** the data is merged back properly.                       *** ;
****************************************************************** ;

data  &in_data _final ;
    set &in_data ;

retain _seq_num 0 ;

_linepos = 1 ;

_seq_num + 1 ;

output ;

run ;


****************************************************************** ;
*** Point to the first variable in the &VARS list. Also,    *** ;
*** pick up the length and indention specified by the user. *** ;
****************************************************************** ;

%let count = 1 ;

%let var_name = %scan ( &vars, &count ) ;
%let max_len =  %scan ( &len_max, &count ) ;
%let indent =   %scan ( &spaces, &count ) ;
```

```
*******************************************************************  ;
***            B E G I N N I N G   O F   M A C R O       ***  ;
*******************************************************************  ;

%macro parse ;

%do %until ( &_abort = "YES" or &var_name = ) ;

*******************************************************************  ;
*** Create a scratch data set which keeps just the parsed   ***  ;
*** variable, the total lines occupied by the parsed var-   ***  ;
*** iable, and the variables used to sort the data set.     ***  ;
*******************************************************************  ;

data _scratch ( keep = &var_name _linepos _seq_num &keepvars ) ;
    set &in_data ;

*******************************************************************  ;
***                                                         ***  ;
***                    V A R I A B L E S                    ***  ;
***                                                         ***  ;
*******************************************************************  ;
length _avail     8     ;  * Available space on line.          ;
length _indent    8     ;  * Indention for lines 2 and greater ;
length _linenum   8     ;  * Line number(record)               ;
length _linepos   8     ;  * Line position (record)            ;
length _old_len   8     ;  * Length of old word                ;
length _new_len   8     ;  * Length of new word                ;
length _textout   $200  ;  * Text to be written out to file    ;
length _word      $200  ;  * Field to be parsed into words     ;
length _wordcnt   8     ;  * Which word am I parsing in variable? ;

*******************************************************************  ;

*******************************************************************  ;
*** The repeat function always gives one more space than the***  ;
*** user specified, so we want to correct this.            ***  ;
*******************************************************************  ;

_indent = &indent - 1 ;

*******************************************************************  ;
*** Start at first line and first word.                    ***  ;
*******************************************************************  ;

_linenum = 1 ;
_wordcnt = 1 ;

*******************************************************************  ;
*** Save parsed variable in hold area.                     ***  ;
*******************************************************************  ;

_string = &var_name ;
```

```
*******************************************************************  ;
*** Continually parse out one word at a time from the string.***  ;
*** If a word is greater than the available space on the     ***  ;
*** line, and can not be parsed then set up abort variables.***  ;
*******************************************************************  ;

_linepos = 0 ;

do until ( _word = " " ) ;
    _word = scan ( _string, _wordcnt, " " ) ;
    _len = length ( trim ( _word )) ;
    if _linepos = 0 then
        _avail = &max_len - 1 ;
    else
        _avail = &max_len - &indent - 1 ;
    if length ( trim ( _word )) gt _avail then
    do ;
        call symput ( '_abort', 'YES' ) ;
        call symput ( '_reason', 'PARSER' ) ;
        call symput ( '_string', _string ) ;
        call symput ( '_word', _word ) ;
        call symput ( '_len', _len ) ;
        call symput ( '_max_len', &max_len ) ;
        call symput ( '_indent', &indent ) ;
        call symput ( '_varname', "&var_name" ) ;
        stop ;
    end ;

*******************************************************************  ;
*** If this is the last word and more than one word is pro- ***  ;
*** cessed and this is not first line for this parsed text, ***  ;
*** then blank out all variables on the next line except the ***  ;
*** parsed word, which is kept and indented the amount      ***  ;
*** requested by the user.                                  ***  ;
*******************************************************************  ;

    if _word = " " and _wordcnt gt 1 then
    do ;
        if _linenum gt 1 then
        do ;
            if _indent ge 0 then
                _textout = repeat ( " ", _indent ) || trim
                   (_textout) ;
            else
                _textout = trim ( _textout ) ;
        end ;
        &var_name = trim ( _textout ) ;
        _linepos + 1 ;
        output ;
        _linenum + 1 ;
        file log ;
        put _linepos= _linenum= ;
    end ;
    if _wordcnt = 1 then
        _textout = _word ;
```

```
****************************************************************** ;
*** Here we add up the length of the current string so far  *** ;
*** and the current word.  If the total of these two is     *** ;
*** greater than the maximum length allowed for the line    *** ;
*** (specified by &MAX_LEN), then we need to output the      *** ;
*** record and start building a string on the next line.    *** ;
****************************************************************** ;

        if _word ne " " and _wordcnt gt 1 then
        do ;
            _old_len = length ( trim ( left ( _textout ))) ;
            _new_len = length ( trim ( left ( _word ))) ;
            if _old_len + _new_len gt ( &max_len - &INDENT -1 ) then
            do ;
                if _linenum gt 1 then
                do ;
                    if _indent ge 0 then
                        _textout = repeat ( " ", _indent ) ||
                            trim ( _textout ) ;
                    else
                        _textout = trim ( _textout ) ;
                end ;

****************************************************************** ;
*** Here we output the record and start building the string *** ;
*** for the next line.                                       *** ;
****************************************************************** ;

                &var_name = trim ( _textout ) ;
                _linepos + 1 ;
                output ;
                _linenum + 1 ;
                _textout = _word ;
                put _linepos= _linenum= ;
            end ;

            if _old_len + _new_len le ( &max_len - &indent - 1 ) then
                _textout = trim ( _textout) || " " || trim ( _word ) ;
        end ;

****************************************************************** ;
*** Increase word count, so we can parse out the next word. *** ;
****************************************************************** ;

    _wordcnt + 1 ;

end ;

return ;
```

```
******************************************************************* ;
***   This step will continually add the parsed variables to *** ;
***   the master SAS data set.                              *** ;
******************************************************************* ;

data _final ;
    update _final
           _scratch
           ;
    by _seq_num _linepos ;
run ;

******************************************************************* ;
*** Update the count so that we can pick off the next var-  *** ;
*** iable to be parsed and its maximum length and indention.*** ;
******************************************************************* ;

%let count    =    %eval ( &count + 1 ) ;
%let var_name =    %scan ( &vars, &count ) ;
%let max_len  =    %scan ( &len_max, &count ) ;
%let indent   =    %scan ( &spaces, &count ) ;

%end ;

******************************************************************* ;
*** Replace the original data set with the final data set.  *** ;
******************************************************************* ;

data &in_data ;
    set _final ;
run ;

******************************************************************* ;
*** Clean up.                                               *** ;
******************************************************************* ;

proc datasets ;
    delete _scratch _final ;
run ;

%mend parse ;

******************************************************************* ;
***                E N D   O F   M A C R O (parse)          *** ;
******************************************************************* ;


******************************************************************* ;
*** This macro is the main driver routine for parsing the   *** ;
*** variables in the SAS data set.                          *** ;
******************************************************************* ;

%parse
```

Coding Sample 6

Consider the following data set:

```
    The search for the perfect city

OBS    CITY                    SIZE

 1     Gainesville    Small enough to be country
 2     Seattle        Fairly large and growing
 3     New York       Can you spell intimidating


OBS    HUMIDITY

 1     Better have a good pair of flip-flops
 2     Moderate
 3     With all this crime, who notices?


OBS    RAINFALL

 1     Tremendous downpours in summer
 2     A constant drizzle
 3     Intermittent
```

There are two reasons why it would be great to know in advance the maximum length of each field and each word to assist the programmer in formatting reports.

The LENGTH assigned to a SAS variable can easily overestimate the amount of space required on the report. For instance, if a variable has a LENGTH of 50 for a list of cities and the longest city has 15 characters, then you only want to allocate 15 spaces on the report.

Many variables have formats associated with them which belie their true length. For example, suppose that a field is represented by numeric codes 1–5. Their formatted lengths may range from 10–50 characters. Hence, you want to allocate 50 spaces for this field, not 2 spaces. It would be useful for a program to calculate the maximum formatted length for a variable. The following program will accomplishes this task.

Here is sample output of this program using the above data:

```
          Maximum word/variable lengths for CITYDATA

                                              Maximum
           Variable    Maximum Length           Word
OBS          Name      of Entire Field        Length

 1         CITY               11                 11
 2         SIZE               26                 12
 3         HUMIDITY           37                 10
 4         RAINFALL           30                 12
```

The values in the Maximum Word Length column indicate the absolute minimum length that must be allocated for a variable on a report because parsing occurs on word boundaries. The values in the Maximum Length of the Entire Field column indicate the maximum length required for any field if you choose not to word wrap that field. This information can then be utilized by a parser routine to calculate the amount of space to allocate for each field. (See Coding Sample 5 earlier in this appendix.)

Before looking at PREVIEW.SAS, which actually creates this dynamic code, look at the dynamic code that is created and %INCLUDEd into the program. This first section is created by the %INCLUDE module named FIND_MAX:

```
11459 +data _str_len ;
11460 +set testdata end = last_one ;
11461 +
11462 +length _workvar $200 ;
11463 +length _origvar $8 ;
11464 +length _chunk $200 ;
11465 +length _delim $50 ;
11466 +retain ;
11467 + _delim = "&delim" ;
11468 +
11469 +
11470 + _len = length ( trim  ( left (  CITY  ))) ;
11471 +_workvar = trim  ( left ( CITY  )) ;
11472 +_v1_len  = max ( _len , _v1_len  ) ;
11473 +
11474 + _partcnt = 1 ;
11475 + _maxpart = 0 ;
11476 +do until ( _chunk = ' ' ) ;
11477 +    _chunk = scan ( _workvar  , _partcnt, _delim ) ;
11478 +    _partlen = length ( trim ( left ( _chunk ))) ;
11479 +    _maxpart = max ( _maxpart, _partlen ) ;
11480 +    _partcnt + 1 ;
11481 +end ;
11482 + _v1_max  = max ( _v1_max , _maxpart ) ;
11483 +
11484 +
11485 + _len = length ( trim  ( left (  HUMIDITY  ))) ;
11486 + _workvar = trim  ( left ( HUMIDITY  )) ;
11487 + _v2_len  = max ( _len , _v2_len  ) ;
11488 +
11489 + _partcnt = 1 ;
11490 + _maxpart = 0 ;
11491 +do until ( _chunk = ' ' ) ;
11492 +    _chunk = scan ( _workvar  , _partcnt, _delim ) ;
11493 +    _partlen = length ( trim ( left ( _chunk ))) ;
11494 +    _maxpart = max ( _maxpart, _partlen ) ;
11495 +    _partcnt + 1 ;
11496 +end ;
11497 + _v2_max  = max ( _v2_max , _maxpart ) ;
11498 +
11499 +
11500 + _len = length ( trim  ( left (  RAINFALL  ))) ;
11501 + _workvar = trim  ( left ( RAINFALL  )) ;
11502 + _v3_len  = max ( _len , _v3_len  ) ;
11503 +
11504 + _partcnt = 1 ;
```

```
11505 +_maxpart = 0 ;
11506 +do until ( _chunk = ' ' ) ;
11507 +    _chunk = scan (    _workvar   , _partcnt, _delim ) ;
11508 +    _partlen = length ( trim ( left ( _chunk ))) ;
11509 +    _maxpart = max ( _maxpart, _partlen ) ;
11510 +    _partcnt + 1 ;
11511 +end ;
11512 +_v3_max  = max ( _v3_max , _maxpart ) ;
11513 +
11514 +
11515 +_len = length ( trim  ( left (  SIZE  ))) ;
11516 +_workvar = trim  ( left (  SIZE  )) ;
11517 +_v4_len  = max (  _len , _v4_len  ) ;
11518 +
11519 +_partcnt = 1 ;
11520 +_maxpart = 0 ;
11521 +do until ( _chunk = ' ' ) ;
11522 +    _chunk = scan (    _workvar   , _partcnt, _delim ) ;
11523 +    _partlen = length ( trim ( left ( _chunk ))) ;
11524 +    _maxpart = max ( _maxpart, _partlen ) ;
11525 +    _partcnt + 1 ;
11526 +end ;
11527 +_v4_max  = max ( _v4_max , _maxpart ) ;
11528 +
11529 +if last_one then
11530 +do ;
11531 +    file set_attr ;
11532 +    %put_len ;
11533 +    title1 Maximum word/variable lengths for TESTDATA  ;
11534 +end ;
11535 +
11536 +run ;
```

This section of code is created by the %INCLUDE module named SET_ATTR:

```
11537 +
11538 +length    _v1_var $ 11  ;
11539 +label     _v1_var = CITY  ;
11540 +format    _v1_var 11. ;
11541 +
11542 +length    _v2_var $ 37  ;
11543 +label     _v2_var = HUMIDITY  ;
11544 +format    _v2_var 10. ;
11545 +
11546 +length    _v3_var $ 31  ;
11547 +label     _v3_var = RAINFALL  ;
11548 +format    _v3_var 12. ;
11549 +
11550 +length    _v4_var $ 26  ;
11551 +label     _v4_var = SIZE  ;
11552 +format    _v4_var 12. ;
```

Here is the source code for PREVIEW.SAS, which dynamically generates the code listed above:

```
****************************************************************** ;
***                                                          *** ;
*** Source:    PREVIEW.SAS                                   *** ;
***                                                          *** ;
*** Type:      Source module                                 *** ;
***                                                          *** ;
*** Function:  To allow the user the opportunity to first    *** ;
***            preview the maximum lengths of formatted var-*** ;
***            iables and maximum word sizes before using    *** ;
***            the parser routine.                           *** ;
***                                                          *** ;
*** Usage:     Specify &IN_DATA, which is your input data set*** ;
***            DELIM which is the delimiters other than      *** ;
***            blank that are acceptable for causing a word  *** ;
***            break to the next line.  For example:         *** ;
***                                                          *** ;
***            %let in_data = sasdata.concom ;               *** ;
***            %let delim = / ;                              *** ;
***            %include preview ;                            *** ;
***                                                          *** ;
****************************************************************** ;


****************************************************************** ;
***          F I L E N A M E   D E F I N I T I O N S         *** ;
****************************************************************** ;

filename find_max "find_max.sas" ;  * Find max var lengths    ;
filename set_attr "set_attr.sas" ;  * Set variable attributes ;

%let lib = WORK ;
%let member = SUNNY ;
%let delim = / ;


****************************************************************** ;
*** List out the member names of the data set.  Place the   *** ;
*** list of names into a macro variable and also into a data*** ;
*** set.                                                     *** ;
****************************************************************** ;

proc sql noprint ;
    create table contents as
        select name, type, format
        from dictionary.columns
        where libname = "&lib" and memname = "&member" ;
    select name into : _thelist separated by " "
    from dictionary.columns
    where libname = "&lib" and memname = "&member" ;
    %let mem_cnt = &sqlobs ;
quit ;
```

```
*****************************************************************  ;
*** Source:     PUT_LEN                                   ***  ;
*** Type:       macro                                     ***  ;
*** Function:   Will write out variable lengths.         ***  ;
*****************************************************************  ;

%macro put_len ;
    %do  i = 1 %to &varcount ;
        _origvar = "%scan ( &_thelist, &i )" ;
        put  ;
        put "length  "  "_v&i._var" " $ " _v&i._len " ; " ;
        put "label    "  "_v&i._var" " = " _origvar  " ; " ;
        put "format   "  "_v&i._var "  _v&i._max +(-1) "." " ; " ;
    %end ;
%mend put_len ;


*****************************************************************  ;
*** Source:     MAX_SIZE.SAS                              ***  ;
*** Type:       macro                                     ***  ;
*** Function:   Will spin through all the SAS data sets and ***  ;
***             find the largest formatted value for each   ***  ;
***             variable.                                 ***  ;
*****************************************************************  ;

%macro max_size ;

*****************************************************************  ;
*** Write out code on the fly to determine the maximum size ***  ;
*** formatted size of each variable.                     ***  ;
*****************************************************************  ;

    data _null_ ;
        set contents end = last_one  ;

    file find_max ;

*****************************************************************  ;
*** You only want to write out one time the important infor- ***  ;
*** mation for doing the calculations in the included file. ***  ;
*****************************************************************  ;

    if _n_ = 1 then
    do ;
        put "data _str_len ; " ;
        put "set &lib..&member end = last_one ; " ;
        put / "length _workvar $200 ; " ;
        put   "length _origvar $8 ; " ;
        put   "length _chunk $200 ; " ;
        put   "length _delim $50 ; " ;
        put   "retain ; " ;
        put   '_delim = "&delim" ; ' ;
    end ;

    retain _count 0 ;
    length _var $8 ;
    length char_cnt $8 ;
```

```
if format = '$' then
    format = " " ;

_count + 1 ;
char_cnt = _count ;
_var = "_v" || trim ( left ( char_cnt )) || "_len" ;

put / ;

if format ne " " then
do ;
    put "_len = length ( trim ( left  ( put
      ( "  name " , " format " )))) ; " ;
    put "_workvar = trim ( left  ( put
      ( "  name " , " format " ))) ; " ;
end ;
else
do ;
    put "_len = length ( trim  ( left (  "  name " ))) ; " ;
    put "_workvar = trim  ( left (  "  name " )) ; " ;
end ;

put _var " = max (  _len , " _var " ) ; " ;

str = "_v" ||  trim ( left ( char_cnt )) || "_max" ;

put " " ;
put "_partcnt = 1 ; " ;
put "_maxpart = 0 ; " ;
put "do until ( _chunk = ' ' ) ; " ;
put "    _chunk = scan ( _workvar  , _partcnt, _delim ) ; " ;
put "    _partlen = length ( trim ( left ( _chunk ))) ; " ;
put "    _maxpart = max ( _maxpart, _partlen ) ; " ;
put "    _partcnt + 1 ; " ;
put "end ; " ;
put str " = max ( " str ", _maxpart ) ; " ;

call symput ('varcount', _count ) ;

if last_one then
do ;
    put / "if last_one then " ;
    put "do ; " ;
    put "    file set_attr ; " ;
    put "    %" "put_len ;" ;
    put "    title1 Maximum word/variable lengths for
      &lib..&member ;" ;
    put "end ; " ;
    put / "run ; " ;
end ;

run ;
```

```
**************************************************************** ;
*** Include code that finds the maximum length of each var- *** ;
*** iable.                                                   *** ;
**************************************************************** ;

     %include find_max ;

     data _str_len ;

**************************************************************** ;
*** Set the variables attributes here.                      *** ;
**************************************************************** ;

     %include set_attr ;

     run ;

**************************************************************** ;
*** Get a list of variables in the final data set that con- *** ;
*** tains the maximum lengths for all variables.            *** ;
**************************************************************** ;

     proc contents data = _str_len noprint out = _str_len ;
     run ;

**************************************************************** ;
*** Print the variables and their maximum lengths.          *** ;
**************************************************************** ;

     proc print label data = _str_len split = "*" ;
         var label length formatl ;
         where upcase ( substr ( left (  name ) , 1, 2 )) = "_V" ;
         label label   = "Variable*Name"
               length  = "Maximum Length*of Entire Field"
               formatl = "Maximum*Word*Length" ;
     run ;

%mend max_size ;

**************************************************************** ;
***                   E n d   o f   m a c r o (MAX_SIZE)    *** ;
**************************************************************** ;


**************************************************************** ;
*** This is the main driver routine that will determine the *** ;
*** maximum formatted length of the variables.              *** ;
**************************************************************** ;

%max_size
```

Coding Sample 7

```
***************************************************************** ;
***                                                         *** ;
*** Source:    INIT.SAS                                     *** ;
***                                                         *** ;
*** Type:      %INCLUDE MODULE                              *** ;
***                                                         *** ;
*** Function: This module sets up the study environment.    *** ;
***           All global definitions for each study should  *** ;
***           be placed in this module.  In addition, any   *** ;
***           initialization programs should also be run    *** ;
***           here.  This module should be included at the  *** ;
***           beginning of each program.                    *** ;
***                                                         *** ;
*** Usage:     Please read the documentation carefully and  *** ;
***            you should be able to modify this INIT file  *** ;
***            for any study.  Note:  Whenever setting up a *** ;
***            list using a macro variable, use a space as  *** ;
***            a delimiter.                                  *** ;
***                                                         *** ;
***            %let conc = 100 300 600 900 ;                *** ;
***                                                         *** ;
***************************************************************** ;
```

First, set up variables that are global in scope for the remainder of the SAS session. You can start by defining system-wide options. Here is a list of suggested options and the comment providing the rationale. This set is particularly useful if you rarely utilize PROC step output for production.

```
options nocenter ;        * Maximizes display, avoids scrolling ;
options ls = 90 ;         * Your terminal width, avoids scrolling ;
options missing = "." ;   * To change SAS default in one place ;
options source2 ;         * %INCLUDE used often, aids in debugging ;
options nocaps ;          * Can always UPCASE if need to ;
options nodate ;          * Prefer own data formatting ;
options fmterr ;          * Must be alerted to format error ;
options nonumber ;        * Use your own page numbering schemes ;
options noreplace ;       * Don't accidentally overwrite data ;
options obs = max ;       * Often changed when debugging ;
options pagesize = 86 ;   * Perfect for portrait mode ;
options source ;          * Useful for debugging ;
options symbolgen ;       * Best macro debugger known on earth ;
title1 ;                  * Write your own title positioning rtn. ;
footnote ;                * Write your own footnote pos. rtn. ;
```

Reset the system-wide global variables:

```
%let _abort = NO ;        * If need to abort, set this to YES ;
%let _reason =   ;        * Reason for aborting program.      ;
%let misschar = '.' ;     * What to print for missing char values;
```

Including the drive specification is handy. This allows a simple transition for work at home. All you have to do is set up a directory structure that mimics the structure at work, and change the drive variable to the hard drive (usually "c:") on your home computer.

```
%let drive = g ;
```

Next, define variables that are appropriate for each subsystem. For example, if you are running a clinical trials study and there are different phases of the system, each of these subsystems would have variables defined to set up the study.

```
%let code_loc = &drive:\medstudy\source ;
%let study = Diabetes ;
%let phase = Phase IV ;
%let all_conc = 10 20 40 60 80 120 220 ;
```

The following allows maximum flexibility in routing the log and output data. The following code sets up global parameters used by all files in the system:

```
****************************************************************** ;
***                                                          *** ;
*** These variables control the routing of output.          *** ;
***                                                          *** ;
*** &REDIRECT determines where you want to direct the output*** ;
*** of your log files and report output.  The options are:  *** ;
***                                                          *** ;
*** TERMINAL   which is the default and routes your output   *** ;
***            to the terminal.                              *** ;
***                                                          *** ;
*** PRINTER    sends your output to a local printer as       *** ;
***            specified in the filename LOCALPRT.           *** ;
***                                                          *** ;
*** STUDYDIR   routes your output to the files specified     *** ;
***            in the RPTOUT and LOGOUT variables.           *** ;
***                                                          *** ;
*** &RPTOUT    specifies the directory where you want to     *** ;
***            route your report output. (You must specify   *** ;
***            REDIRECT = STUDYDIR)                           *** ;
***                                                          *** ;
** &LOGOUT     specifies the directory where you want to     *** ;
***            route your log output. (You must specify      *** ;
***            REDIRECT = STUDYDIR)                           *** ;
***                                                          *** ;
*** &PRINT     Is an option on the file statement.  You do   *** ;
***            not need to set this.  The program auto-      *** ;
***            matically changes this on the fly to redirect *** ;
***            your output.                                  *** ;
***                                                          *** ;
*** &STUDYRUN is a flag to determine if this is a batch      *** ;
***            study run.  You do not need to change this.   *** ;
***            If you are running the utility program        *** ;
***            STUDYRUN.SAS, this variable is automatically  *** ;
***            changed to YES at the appropriate time.       *** ;
***                                                          *** ;
*** &RESET     resets the printer to normal mode for the HP  *** ;
***            LASER JET 4SI. This should not be changed     *** ;
***            unless you change printers.                   *** ;
***                                                          *** ;
```

```
*** &LANDCODE Sets escape sequence characters to force the  ***  ;
***           printer to print in landscape mode.  You      ***  ;
***           should not change this unless you change       ***  ;
***           printers.                                      ***  ;
***                                                          ***  ;
*************************************************************** ;

%let datadump = &drive:\medstudy\datadump ;
%let landcode = '1B266C314F'x ;
%let logout   = &drive:\medstudy\log ;
%let orient = portrait ;
%let print = print ;
%let redirect = TERMINAL ;
%let rptout   = &drive:\medstudy\reports ;
%let reset    = '1B45'x ;
%let studyrun = NO ;
%let sysfoot = 0 ;
```

Set up library definitions:

```
libname sasdata   "&drive:\medstudy\&study\data" ;
libname origdata  "&drive:\medstudy\&study\origdata\sasdata" ;
libname lookup    "&drive:\medstudy\&study\origdata\lookup" ;
... and so on.
```

Set up filename definitions:

```
%let inc_loc = includes ;  * Location of include files ;
filename abortit    "&drive:\medstudy\&inc_loc\abortit.sas" ;
filename cleanup    "&drive:\medstudy\&inc_loc\cleanup.sas" ;
... and so on.
```

Set up default print margins for printing in portrait mode for the current printer's pitch and font. These values allow for 1 inch margins for font LINEPRINTER of pitch size = 8:

```
%let bot_mar =   82 ;          * Bottom Print margin          ;
%let left_mar =  16 ;          * Left Print Margin            ;
%let linesize = 133 ;          * linesize for page width      ;
%let rite_mar = 121 ;          * Right Print margin           ;
%let page_wid = 133 ;          * Page width for printed output;
%let top_mar =   05 ;          * Top print margin             ;
```

Execute programs to rename variable and set up formats:

```
%include rename ;
%include formats ;
```

```
****************************************************************** ;
*** This macro is useful to change the print destination    *** ;
*** without having to change the REDIRECT variable in this   *** ;
*** module. Thus, the OVERRIDE macro variable can be set to  *** ;
*** YES in another program to temporarily change the value   *** ;
*** the REDIRECT variable.  REDIRECT will be reset to its    *** ;
*** default value after the other program finishes executing.*** ;
*** Note: OVERRIDE is initially set outside of INIT.SAS      *** ;
****************************************************************** ;

%macro override ;
    %if &override = YES %then
        %let redirect = STUDYDIR ;
%mend override ;


****************************************************************** ;
*** Change the print destination if the user changed the     *** ;
*** override macro variable = "YES".                         *** ;
****************************************************************** ;

%override
```

Coding Sample 8

```
****************************************************************** ;
*** Project:    Insurance                                    *** ;
*** Source:     FINDINIT.SAS (Find proper init file)         *** ;
*** Type:       Source module                                *** ;
*** Function:   To load the appropriate initialization file  *** ;
***             based on the user selection.                 *** ;
****************************************************************** ;

data _null_ ;

retain ;

****************************************************************** ;
***                 V A R I A B L E S                        *** ;
****************************************************************** ;

length choice   $  1 ;    * User selection ;
length err_msg  $ 60 ;    * Error message ;
length prom_msg $ 60 ;    * Prompt message ;

retain col_01    20 ;    * Field location ;
retain col_02    30 ;    * Field location ;
retain left_mar   3 ;    * Left margin ;
retain prom_msg "Please select 1-4 or 5 to quit" ;

%let tit_col  = red ;     * Title color ;
%let text_col = blue ;    * Text color ;
%let err_col  = pink ;    * Error color ;
%let inp_col  = green ;   * Input field color ;
%let bot_col  = red ;     * Bottom of screen color ;
%let prom_col = blue ;    * Prompt message color ;
```

```
bot_line = repeat ( "=", 60 ) ;
choice = " " ;

********************************************************** ;
*** Create the selection window.                    *** ;
********************************************************** ;

window start_up

#1   @col_01    "_____" color = &tit_col
#2   @col_01    "|                                       |" color = &tit_col
#3   @col_01    "|        Select  Insurance type         |" color = &tit_col
#4   @col_01    "|_____|" color = &tit_col

#6   @col_02    " 1.   Auto"    color = &text_col
#7   @col_02    " 2.   Life"    color = &text_col
#8   @col_02    " 3.   Home"    color = &text_col
#9   @col_02    " 4.   Health"  color = &text_col
#10  @col_02    " 5.   Quit"    color = &text_col

#12  @left_mar bot_line color = &bot_col protect = yes
#13  @left_mar bot_line color = &bot_col protect = yes

#16  @left_mar "Selection" @col_01 choice $1. color = &inp_col
#18  @left_mar prom_msg protect= yes   persist= yes
   color = &prom_col
#19  err_msg  protect= yes   persist= yes
   color = &err_col ;

display start_up ;

************************************************************ ;
*** Include the appropriate startup file based on selection. *** ;
************************************************************ ;

if choice ge 1 and choice le 5 then
do ;
    if choice = 1 then
        call execute ( "%include 'c:\insure\auto.sas' ; " ) ;
    if choice = 2 then
        call execute ( "%include 'c:\insure\life.sas' ; " ) ;
    if choice = 3 then
        call execute ( "%include 'c:\insure\home.sas' ; " ) ;
    if choice = 4 then
        call execute ( "%include 'c:\insure\health.sas' ; " ) ;
    stop ;
end ;
else
    err_msg = choice || " is an invalid selection. Try again." ;

run ;
```

Coding Sample 9

```
******************************************************************* ;
***                                                            *** ;
*** Source:      TITLES.SAS                                    *** ;
***                                                            *** ;
*** Type:        External flat file                            *** ;
***                                                            *** ;
*** Function:    Contains titles and footnotes for all medical *** ;
***              summary programs                              *** ;
***                                                            *** ;
*** Usage:       You create this file by writing titles and    *** ;
***              footnotes for an entire study in this file.    *** ;
***              There are 3 types of titles and footnotes and *** ;
***              they must appear in this order:                *** ;
***              (1) Study wide titles                         *** ;
***              (2) Report specific titles and footnotes       *** ;
***              (3) Study wide footnotes                       *** ;
***                                                            *** ;
***              The first entry in this file is the studywide *** ;
***              titles.  Directly under this entry, enter      *** ;
***              zero, one or as many titles that you wish.     *** ;
***              These titles will appear at the top of your    *** ;
***              report before any report specific titles.      *** ;
***              Next enter a line that contains the            *** ;
***              "stopsign" for processing this code.  The      *** ;
***              stopsign symbol is set up in the include       *** ;
***              module HEADFOOT.SAS if you wish to change it. *** ;
***              This symbol tells the SAS program to end       *** ;
***              processing of this component and start         *** ;
***              processing the next one.                       *** ;
***              The next set of entries (and the bulk of this *** ;
***              file) contains report specific titles and      *** ;
***              footnotes. First enter the SAS program name    *** ;
***              followed by the word titles and the report     *** ;
***              number.  The report number should start at     *** ;
***              one and be incremented by 1 for each add-      *** ;
***              itional report.  In the SAS program itself     *** ;
***              (that generates the medical summary), you      *** ;
***              must set a macro variable RPT_CNT = 1 ; to     *** ;
***              to process the first report, RPT_CNT = 2 ; to *** ;
***              process the second report etc. Finally, enter*** ;
***              the stopsign symbol as noted above. The logic*** ;
***              for footnotes is the same as for the titles.  *** ;
***                                                            *** ;
***              The last entry at the bottom of the file is   *** ;
***              the study wide footnotes. These will appear    *** ;
***              at the bottom of the report page, following    *** ;
***              the report specific footnotes.  You do not     *** ;
***              have to worry about their location, page       *** ;
***              breaks etc. This is all taken care of in the  *** ;
***              SAS include modules headfoot, header, footer  *** ;
***              and in the beginning of the DATA NULL step     *** ;
***              that makes reference to the LINE_CNT.          *** ;
***                                                            *** ;
```

```
***              NOTE: You should include a titles and foot-  *** ;
***              notes entry for every program, even if it is *** ;
***              blank. You will note that many of the pro-   *** ;
***              grams in this file have no footnotes. The    *** ;
***              blank spaces between entries is not required,*** ;
***              they are there for readability.              *** ;
***                                                           *** ;
***              Footnotes are by default centered.  However, *** ;
***              if you wish footnotes to be centered, but    *** ;
***              all left justified underneath one another,   *** ;
***              enclose the footnotes in double quotes. This *** ;
***              may be useful if you are listing items such  *** ;
***              as Lab locations.                            *** ;
***              If you want to left justify your footnotes to *** ;
***              the left margin, then precede the footnote   *** ;
***              with #L and begin the actual footnote in     *** ;
***              column 4.                                    *** ;
***                                                           *** ;
*************************************************************** ;


- - - - - - - - - Study Wide Titles - - - - - - - - - - - - -
STUDYWIDE TITLES
#L Diabetes Trial 3CM
++++


- - - - - - - - Report Specific Titles/Footnotes - - - - - - - -


AE_DATA.SAS TITLES 1
#L Data Listing 8
Patients Adverse Events
(All Patients)
PAGE HOLDER
++++
AE_DATA.SAS FOOTNOTES 1
#L 1 All terms mapped to preferred terms of Costart version 4.
++++


AE_ARA.SAS TITLES 1
#L Safety Summary Table 31
Number of Adverse Events by Relationship to Study Drug
(All Patients in Lymphoma and Leukemia Arms)
PAGE HOLDER
++++
AE_ARA.SAS FOOTNOTES 1
#L "Note:  All data are listed in data listing 8."
#L "        Includes only new events or changes in severity"
++++


AE_ARA.SAS TITLES 2
#L Safety Summary Table 31
Number of Adverse Events by Relationship to Study Drug
(All Patients in Lymphoma and Leukemia Arms)
PAGE HOLDER
++++
AE_ARA.SAS FOOTNOTES 2
```

```
#L "Note:  All data are listed in data listing 8.
++++


AE_DRUG.SAS TITLES 1
#L Safety Summary Table 29
Number of Adverse Events by Relationship to Study Drug
(All Patients Receiving Study Drug)
PAGE HOLDER
++++
AE_DRUG.SAS FOOTNOTES 1
#L "Note:  All data are listed in data listing 11"
++++


- - - - - - - - - - Study Wide Footnotes - - - - - - - - - - - -
STUDYWIDE FOOTNOTES

#L Company Confidential
++++
```

Coding Sample 10

In this program sample, everything in bold is part of the shell. Anything not in bold is provided by the programmer. The letters next to the text are described below the shell in case you are interested in further details for any of these components.

```
****************************************************************** ;
***                                                          *** ;
*** Project:    Home Based Business                          *** ;
***                                                          *** ;
*** Source:     MONEY.SAS                                    *** ;
***                                                          *** ;
*** Type:       Source module                                *** ;
***                                                          *** ;
*** Function:   To create a report that shows how much money *** ;
***             is made by selling magazine subscriptions    *** ;
***             over the telephone.                          *** ;
***                                                          *** ;
*** Data sets: sasdata.mags                                  *** ;
***                                                          *** ;
****************************************************************** ;


****************************************************************** ;
*** Call routine that initializes project environment.    *** ;
****************************************************************** ;

%let filename = money.sas ;
%include "c:\home\includes\init.sas" ;
```

Ⓐ

```
******************************************************************* ;
*** Sort the data for report ordering.                        *** ;
******************************************************************* ;

proc sort data = sasdata.mags out = mags ;
    by cust_num ;
run ;

******************************************************************* ;
*** Several variables are too wide for the report and need    *** ;
*** to be parsed.                                             *** ;
******************************************************************* ;

%let len_max = 20 30 ;
%let vars = custname address ;
%let spaces = 0 0 ;                        Ⓑ
%let in_data = mags ;
%let keepvars = cust_num ;
%include parser ;

******************************************************************* ;
*** Add variable _REC_CNT to data set so that you have a      *** ;
*** count of records per group.                               *** ;
******************************************************************* ;

%getcount ( in_data = mags ,                        Ⓒ
            var_name = cust_num )

proc sort data = mags ;
    by _seq_num _linepos cust_num ;
run ;

******************************************************************* ;
*** Set the report counter.                                   *** ;
******************************************************************* ;

%let rpt_cnt = 1 ;

******************************************************************* ;
*** Set the print destination.                                *** ;
******************************************************************* ;

%include printloc ;        Ⓓ

******************************************************************* ;
*** Include this module whenever you print in landscape.      *** ;
******************************************************************* ;

%include landscap ;        Ⓔ

******************************************************************* ;
*** Print the report.                                         *** ;
******************************************************************* ;

data _null_ ;
```

```
******************************************************************** ;
*** Abort the program if a previous step requests this.    *** ;
******************************************************************** ;

%include abortit ;        ❻

    set mags end = last_one ;
    by _seq_num _linepos cust_num ;

file &print ;

******************************************************************** ;
*** Retrieve module that gets titles and footnotes.        *** ;
******************************************************************** ;

%include headfoot ;       ❼

******************************************************************** ;
*** Print the header before reading first record.          *** ;
******************************************************************** ;

if _n_ = 1 then
    link header ;

%let dash_cnt = %eval (&rite_mar - &left_mar + 1 ) ;

******************************************************************** ;
*** If near the bottom of the page and cannot print all of  *** ;
*** the records for one group, then eject a new page.        *** ;
******************************************************************** ;

if first._seq_num and line_cnt gt ( bot_mar - _rec_cnt + 1 ) then
do ;
    put @&left_mar &dash_cnt*'_' ;
    put @&left_mar "'.' Indicates Data are Missing"
        @ ( &left_mar + &dash_cnt -11 ) "(Continued)" ;
    link footer ;
    link header ;
end ;

if first._seq_num then
do ;
    line_cnt + 1 ;
    put ;
end ;

******************************************************************** ;
*** Print the detail records.                               *** ;
******************************************************************** ;

retain col_01  21 ;
retain col_02  35 ;
retain col_03  57 ;
retain col_04  72 ;

if _linepos = 1 then
put @ ( col_01 + 0 ) cust_num
    @ ( col_02 + 0 ) custname
```

```
        @ ( col_03 + 4 ) money $2.
        @ ( col_04 + 0 ) address
        ;
else
put
        @ ( col_02 + 0 ) custname
        @ ( col_04 + 0 ) address
        ;

line_cnt + 1 ;

*************************************************************** ;
*** Processing after all records have been read           *** ;
*************************************************************** ;

if last_one then
do ;
    put @&left_mar &dash_cnt*'_' ;
    put @&left_mar " '.' Indicates Data are Missing" ;
    link footer ;
end ;

return ;

*************************************************************** ;
*** Print the titles.                                     *** ;
*************************************************************** ;

%include header ;      🅗

*************************************************************** ;
*** Print underlines around column headings.              *** ;
*************************************************************** ;

put @&left_mar &dash_cnt*'_' ;
put ;
line_cnt + 2 ;

*************************************************************** ;
*** Print the column headers.                             *** ;
*************************************************************** ;

put  @ ( col_01 + 0 ) "Customer"
     @ ( col_02 + 0 ) "Customer"
     @ ( col_03 + 1 ) "Cash from"
     @ ( col_04 + 0 ) "Address"
     ;

line_cnt + 1 ;

put  @ ( col_01 + 1 ) "Number"
     @ ( col_02 + 2 ) "Name"
     @ ( col_03 + 0 ) "Transaction"
     ;

line_cnt + 1 ;
```

```
*******************************************************************  ;
*** Print underlines around column headings.                ***  ;
*******************************************************************  ;

put @&left_mar &dash_cnt*'_' / ;
line_cnt + 2 ;

return ;

*******************************************************************  ;
*** Print the footnotes.                                     ***  ;
*******************************************************************  ;

%include footer ;      ❶

run ;

*******************************************************************  ;
*** Cleanup the environment.                                 ***  ;
*******************************************************************  ;

%include cleanup ;     ❿

*******************************************************************  ;
***            E N D   O F   M O D U L E  (money)           ***  ;
*******************************************************************  ;
```

Ⓐ See Coding Sample 7.

Ⓑ See Coding Sample 5 and the enhancement to the parser (PREVIEW.SAS) in Coding Sample 6.

Ⓒ See the section "Eliminate Coding Steps" in Chapter 8, "System Coding Principles."

Ⓓ See the section "Allow for Flexibility in Routing Output" in Chapter 8.

Ⓔ

```
*******************************************************************  ;
*** Source:   LANDSCAP.SAS                                   ***  ;
*** Type:     %INCLUDE Module                                ***  ;
*** Function: Sets parameters properly for printing in       ***  ;
***           landscape mode.                                ***  ;
*** Use:      Include this module anywhere before your       ***  ;
***           DATA _NULL_                                    ***  ;
** Example :  %include landscap ;                            ***  ;
*******************************************************************  ;

*******************************************************************  ;
***         G L O B A L   S Y S T E M   O P T I O N S        ***  ;
*******************************************************************  ;

options ls = 175 ;       * Set default linesize              ;
options pagesize = 66 ;  * Set page size                     ;
```

```
**************************************************************** ;
***                  G L O B A L   V A R I A B L E S       *** ;
**************************************************************** ;

%let bot_mar  =  67 ;          * Bottom print margin          ;
%let left_mar =  16 ;          * Left print margin            ;
%let linesize = 175 ;          * Sets the linesize for centering ;
%let orient   = landscape ;    * Print in landscape mode      ;
%let page_wid = 175 ;          * Page width                   ;
%let rite_mar = 159 ;          * Right print margin           ;
%let top_mar =   05 ;          * Top print margin             ;
```

F

```
**************************************************************** ;
***                                                        *** ;
*** Source:     ABORTIT.SAS                                *** ;
***                                                        *** ;
*** Type:       %INCLUDE Module                            *** ;
***                                                        *** ;
*** Function:   The function of this routine is to abort a *** ;
***             program.  This may happen for example, when *** ;
***             the user tries to parse a variable and sets *** ;
***             the maximum length of the parsed variable less *** ;
***             than the length of one of the words to be  *** ;
***             parsed.                                    *** ;
***                                                        *** ;
*** Usage:      Include this module at the very beginning of *** ;
***             your DATA _NULL_.                          *** ;
***                                                        *** ;
***             Example:                                   *** ;
***                                                        *** ;
***             DATA _NULL_ ;                              *** ;
***             %include abortit ;                         *** ;
***                                                        *** ;
***             To turn on ABORT in your routine, set _ABORT *** ;
***             and &_REASON                               *** ;
***                                                        *** ;
***             Example:                                   *** ;
***                                                        *** ;
***             %let _abort = YES ;                        *** ;
***             %let _reason = Laboratory file is Missing!  *** ;
***                                                        *** ;
**************************************************************** ;

retain _colinit 20 ;   * Where to print ERROR messages.        ;
...
... code to handle other abort situations
...
if "&_abort" = "YES" and "&_reason" = "PARSER" then
do ;
    _xname   = "&_varname" ;
    _xword   = "&_word" ;
    _xlen    = "&_len" ;
    _xmaxlen = "&_max_len" ;
    _xindent = "&_indent" ;
    _xstring = "&_string" ;
    file log  ;
```

```
      %include parsemsg ;
      file print   ;
      %include parsemsg ;
      stop ;
end ;
```

where PARSEMSG contains the error messages for a parser type
error:

```
**************************************************************** ;
***                                                        *** ;
*** Source:    PARSEMSG.SAS                                 *** ;
***                                                        *** ;
*** Type:      %INCLUDE Module                              *** ;
***                                                        *** ;
*** Function: The function of this routine contains the    *** ;
***           message returned from the PARSER.SAS %INCLUDE *** ;
***           module.                                       *** ;
*** Usage:     Is automatically included when a program    *** ;
***            aborts because of a parsing problem.         *** ;
***                                                        *** ;
**************************************************************** ;

put @_colinit'**********************************************' ;
put @_colinit '***                                        ***' ;
put @_colinit '***                 E R R O R              ***' ;
put @_colinit '***                                        ***' ;
put @_colinit '***                 E R R O R              ***' ;
put @_colinit '***                                        ***' ;
put @_colinit '***                 E R R O R              ***' ;
put @_colinit '***                                        ***' ;
put @_colinit '*** Your program has aborted.  This is a   ***' ;
put @_colinit '*** programmer created abort situation.    ***' ;
put @_colinit '*** When using the parser routine, a word  ***' ;
put @colinit  '*** was longer than allowed based on para- ***' ;
put @_colinit '*** meters passed into the parser.  The    ***' ;
put @_colinit '*** following parameters are causing the   ***' ;
put @_colinit '*** problem:                               ***' ;
put @_colinit '***                                        ***' ;
put @_colinit '    The variable name:              ' _xname ;
put @_colinit '    The parsed word:                ' _xword ;
put @_colinit '    The word length:               ' _xlen ;
put @_colinit '    The maximum length specified   ' _xmaxlen ;
put @_colinit '    The indention  specified:      ' _xindent ;
put @_colinit '    The string containing the word is:      ***' ;
put @_colinit ' ' ;
put @_colinit '    ' _xstring ;
put @_colinit '***                                        ***' ;
put @_colinit '***                                        ***' ;
put @_colinit '*** In order to correct this problem,      ***' ;
put @_colinit '*** resubmit your program, but either      ***' ;
put @_colinit '*** increase the maximum length allowed for ***' ;
put @_colinit '*** a variable to be parsed (&len_max)      ***' ;
put @_colinit '*** and/or decrease the amount of indention ***' ;
put @_colinit '*** for the continuation lines (&spaces).   ***' ;
put @_colinit '***                                        ***' ;
put @_colinit '***                 E R R O R              ***' ;
put @_colinit '***                                        ***' ;
```

```
put @_colinit '***                  E R R O R               ***' ;
put @_colinit '***                                           ***' ;
put @_colinit '***                  E R R O R               ***' ;
put @_colinit '***                                           ***' ;
put @_colinit '*********************************************' ;
```

Ⓖ

```
************************************************************ ;
***                                                     *** ;
*** Source:    HEADFOOT.SAS                             *** ;
***                                                     *** ;
*** Type:      %INCLUDE Module                          *** ;
***                                                     *** ;
*** Function: Used by all reports to generate header titles *** ;
***           and footnotes.                            *** ;
***                                                     *** ;
*** Use:       Include this module at the beginning of your *** ;
***            DATA _NULL_                               *** ;
***                                                     *** ;
************************************************************ ;


************************************************************ ;
***                                                     *** ;
***                                                     *** ;
***                    IMPORTANT NOTE                   *** ;
***                                                     *** ;
*** Variables have been defined so that the following spec- *** ;
*** ifications are met for the reports:                 *** ;
***                                                     *** ;
*** (1) Header margins should be approximately 1 inch.  *** ;
*** (2) Footer margins should be approximately 1 inch.  *** ;
*** (3) The left margin should be at least 1.5 inches.  *** ;
*** (4) The right margin should be at least 1 inch.     *** ;
***                                                     *** ;
*** Reports are currently printed with the following font: *** ;
***                                                     *** ;
*** Lineprinter pitch 8                                 *** ;
***                                                     *** ;
*** If either the font changes or the margin requirements *** ;
*** change it will be  necessary to adjust the numbers in *** ;
*** the following variable table to account for these   *** ;
*** changes.                                            *** ;
***                                                     *** ;
************************************************************ ;


************************************************************ ;
***                                                     *** ;
***                  V A R I A B L E S                  *** ;
***                                                     *** ;
************************************************************ ;
%let cont_cnt = 2 ; * Count of lines needed for continuation  ;
%let stopsign = ++++ ;       * End of record in titles file  ;
%let sysfoot1 = Company Confidential ;
%let sysfoot = 2 ;    * Count of system footnotes            ;
************************************************************ ;
array tit_ary  {*} $200 title_01-title_10 ; * Report titles  ;
array foot_ary {*} $200 foot_01-foot_10 ; * Report footnotes  ;
************************************************************ ;
```

```
length fetch_it    $3 ;  * Whether or not to grab next record    ;
length _type       $9 ;  * Type of record ( title or footnote )  ;
length _word_      $12 ; * Scratch area for word                 ;
****************************************************************** ;
retain bot_mar        0 ;     * Bottom margin , is calculated        ;
retain foot_cnt   0 ;         * Number of footnotes for this report;
retain foot_01-foot_10 ;      * Holds report footnotes              ;
retain fetchit 'no' ;         * Whether or not to grab next record ;
retain in_len 133 ;           * Input record length for input file ;
retain titlecnt 0 ;           * Number of titles for this report   ;
retain title_01-title_10 ;    * Holds report titles                ;
retain _type " " ;            * Type of record (footnote or header);
****************************************************************** ;

****************************************************************** ;
*** Read in the TITLES file to get a list of study specific *** ;
*** titles and footnotes.                                   *** ;
****************************************************************** ;

infile titles length = in_len end = last_rec ;

****************************************************************** ;
*** If this is first record read, then process this routine. *** ;
*** The title file will be read in its entirety.  First      *** ;
*** search on studywide titles and add these to the title    *** ;
*** array. Then using the filename as the search key         *** ;
*** (i.e. DEMODATA.SAS ), scan for this filename and grab    *** ;
*** all the titles associated with this report.  Then grab   *** ;
*** the footnotes that are used in this report and put them  *** ;
*** in the footnote array.                                   *** ;
****************************************************************** ;

if _n_ = 1 then
do until ( last_rec ) ;
    input in_line $varying133. in_len ;
    check = index ( in_line, "&stopsign" ) ;
    if check gt 0 then
        fetch_it = 'no' ;
    if fetch_it = 'yes' and _type = 'TITLES' then
    do ;
        titlecnt + 1 ;
        tit_ary ( titlecnt ) = in_line ;
    end ;
    if fetch_it = 'yes' and _type = 'FOOTNOTES' then
    do ;
        foot_cnt + 1 ;
        foot_ary ( foot_cnt ) = put ( in_line, $char133. ) ;
    end ;

    check = index ( in_line, "STUDYWIDE FOOTNOTES" ) ;
    if check gt 0 then
    do ;
        _type = 'FOOTNOTES' ;
        fetch_it = 'yes' ;
    end ;

    check = index ( in_line, "STUDYWIDE TITLES" ) ;
    if check gt 0 then
```

```
                    do ;
                         _type = 'TITLES' ;
                         fetch_it = 'yes' ;
                    end ;
                    _word_ = scan ( in_line, 1, " " ) ;
                    check = index ( _word_, ".SAS" ) ;
                    if check gt 0 then
                    do ;
                         _type = scan ( in_line, 2, " " ) ;
                         rpt_cnt = scan ( in_line, 3, " " ) ;
                    end ;
                    if upcase ( _word_ ) = upcase ( "&filename" )
                         and rpt_cnt = &rpt_cnt then
                    do ;
                         fetch_it = 'yes' ;
                    end ;
              end ;

        **************************************************************** ;
        *** Here you calculate the logical bottom of the page. It is *** ;
        *** determined by starting at the system determined bottom   *** ;
        *** margin and subtracting the system footer count, the      *** ;
        *** report specific footer count (one additional line if     *** ;
        *** there is at least one footnote, so that you can have a    *** ;
        *** separation between the bottom of the report, the report  *** ;
        *** footer and the studywide footer), the lines needed for   *** ;
        *** the continuation text and continuation and one more      *** ;
        *** space between the continuation text and the bottom of    *** ;
        *** the report.                                              *** ;
        **************************************************************** ;

        if foot_cnt = 0 then
             bot_mar = &bot_mar - &sysfoot - &cont_cnt - 1 ;
        else
             bot_mar = &bot_mar - &sysfoot -foot_cnt -1 - &cont_cnt - 1 ;
```

H

```
        **************************************************************** ;
        ***                                                          *** ;
        *** Source:    HEADER.SAS                                    *** ;
        ***                                                          *** ;
        *** Type:      %INCLUDE Module                               *** ;
        ***                                                          *** ;
        *** Function: Prints report headers.                         *** ;
        ***                                                          *** ;
        **************************************************************** ;


        **************************************************************** ;
        *** This routine simply centers the titles and prints them. *** ;
        **************************************************************** ;

        header: ;

        **************************************************************** ;
        *** Eject a new page.                                       *** ;
        **************************************************************** ;

        put _page_ ;
```

```
****************************************************************** ;
*** Set the line count = top margin.                        *** ;
****************************************************************** ;

line_cnt = &top_mar ;

****************************************************************** ;
*** Center and print each title. The titles are stored in   *** ;
*** the title array.  They were originally placed there by   *** ;
*** the %INCLUDE module HEADFOOT.SAS.                        *** ;
****************************************************************** ;

length _scratch $200  ;

do i = 1 to titlecnt ;
    the_len = trim ( length ( tit_ary {i} )) ;
    check = index ( tit_ary {i}, "#L" ) ;
    if check gt 0 then
    do ;
        _scratch = substr ( tit_ary {i}, 4 ) ;
        put #line_cnt @&left_mar _scratch ;
    end ;
    else
    do ;
        the_loc = ( &page_wid - the_len + 2 ) / 2 ;
        put #line_cnt @the_loc tit_ary {i} ;
    end ;
    line_cnt + 1 ;
end ;
```

❶

```
****************************************************************** ;
***                                                         *** ;
*** Source:    FOOTER.SAS                                   *** ;
***                                                         *** ;
*** Type:      %INCLUDE Module                              *** ;
***                                                         *** ;
*** Function: Prints the footnotes at bottom of the page.   *** ;
***                                                         *** ;
****************************************************************** ;

footer: ;

****************************************************************** ;
*** If the code #L is found in the footnote array, then the *** ;
*** foot note is left justified, otherwise it is center     *** ;
*** justified.                                              *** ;
****************************************************************** ;

length scratch $175 ;     * scratch work area ;

do i = 1 to foot_cnt ;
    the_len = trim ( length ( foot_ary {i} )) ;
    foot_out = translate ( foot_ary {i},' ','"') ;
    check = index ( foot_out, "#L" ) ;
    if check gt 0 then
    do ;
```

```
                              scratch = substr ( foot_out, 4 ) ;
                              put # ( bot_mar + i + 3 ) @&left_mar
                                scratch $varying175. the_len ;
                    end ;
                    else
                    do ;
                        the_loc = (( &page_wid - the_len + 2 ) / 2 ) ;
                        put # ( bot_mar + i + 3 ) @the_loc
                          foot_out $varying175. the_len ;
                    end ;
            end ;

            put # ( bot_mar + i + 3 ) @ ( &left_mar + 1 )
                  "Dir: &code_loc\&filename - &coder - &sysdate &systime" ;

            return ;
```

J

```
    *************************************************************** ;
    ***                                                       *** ;
    *** Source:    CLEANUP.SAS                                *** ;
    ***                                                       *** ;
    *** Type:      %INCLUDE Module                            *** ;
    ***                                                       *** ;
    *** Function: Does general report cleanup.                *** ;
    ***                                                       *** ;
    *************************************************************** ;

    *************************************************************** ;
    *** Redirecting report output closes the print file and   *** ;
    *** allows you to view any recently created file in the    *** ;
    *** program editor. In addition, resetting procedure output *** ;
    *** is useful for debugging.                              *** ;
    *************************************************************** ;

    proc printto ;
    run ;

    *************************************************************** ;
    *** If this is a study run, then put the page number on each *** ;
    *** SAS program output.                                   *** ;
    *************************************************************** ;

    %macro putpage ;
        %if &redirect = STUDYDIR %then
            %include putpage ;
    %mend putpage ;

    %putpage

    *************************************************************** ;
    *** Deleting the work library is useful if you are running *** ;
    *** multiple jobs in a batch.                             *** ;
    *************************************************************** ;

    proc datasets library = work kill memtype = ( data ) ;
    run ;
    quit ;
```

Coding Sample 11

```
*****************************************************************  ;
***                                                         ***  ;
*** Source:    RPT_GEN.SAS (Report Generator)               ***  ;
***                                                         ***  ;
*** Type:      Utility                                      ***  ;
***                                                         ***  ;
*** Function: To automatically generate a DATA _NULL without ***  ;
***            coding any PUT statements by using a pre-     ***  ;
***            formatted layout program.                    ***  ;
***                                                         ***  ;
*** Inputs:    RPTGEN fileref points to the proposed report ***  ;
***            layout.                                       ***  ;
***            DATASET is the name of the SAS data set that  ***  ;
***            is input to the report generator.            ***  ;
***                                                         ***  ;
*** Vars:      See below                                    ***  ;
***                                                         ***  ;
*****************************************************************  ;


*****************************************************************  ;
*** Input data set and report layout                        ***  ;
*****************************************************************  ;

libname sasdata "c:\mysas" ;         * Name of SAS library ;

%let dataset = sasdata.stocks ;      * Name of input data set ;

filename rptgen    "c:\rptgen.dat" ;

*****************************************************************  ;
*** Input variables to this routine                         ***  ;
*****************************************************************  ;
%let control = # ;            * Character to designate control   ;
%let delim = / ;              * Delims besides space for parser? ;
%let page_wid = 78 ;          * Screen or report width           ;
%let preview = N ;            * Do not want preview of variables ;
%let sort_by = broker   ;     * Sort data set by this variable   ;
%let spaces = 2 ;             * # spaces to indent contin. lines ;
%let varstart = "#" ;         * Character that starts var position;
*****************************************************************  ;
***                     G L O B A L S                       ***  ;
*****************************************************************  ;

%let need_cut = N ;           * Assume no variables need parsed  ;


*****************************************************************  ;
***          F I L E N A M E   D E F I N I T I O N S        ***  ;
*****************************************************************  ;

filename parsemsg   "c:\parsemsg.sas" ;
filename layout     "c:\layout.sas" ;
filename setparse   "c:\setparse.sas" ;
filename head       "c:\head.inc" ;
filename layout     "c:\layout.sas" ;
```

```
filename foot      "c:\foot.inc" ;
filename parser    "c:\parser.sas" ;
filename abortit   "c:\abortit.sas" ;

***************************************************************** ;
*** Clear out title and footnote definitions.          *** ;
***************************************************************** ;

footnote1 ;                    * Clear out footnotes          ;
title1 ;                       * Clear out titles             ;


***************************************************************** ;
*** Get a list of variables for the SAS data set.      *** ;
***************************************************************** ;

proc sort data = &dataset out = sas_data nodupkey ;
    by &sort_by ;
run ;

proc contents data = sas_data noprint out = sas_cont ;
run ;


***************************************************************** ;
*** Make a first pass through the file to determine the  *** ;
*** amount of space required for each variable.          *** ;
***************************************************************** ;

data max ( keep = the_word word_loc ) ;

infile rptgen length = in_len ;

***************************************************************** ;
*** Find the start of the detail lines.                 *** ;
***************************************************************** ;

maxcount = 1 ;
do until ( det_chk gt 0 or maxcount gt 50 ) ;
    input @001 in_line $varying200. in_len ;
    det_chk = index ( in_line, ":DETAIL:" ) ;
    maxcount + 1 ;
end ;


***************************************************************** ;
*** Now input the next line which contains the list of vars.*** ;
***************************************************************** ;

input @001 in_line $varying200. in_len ;

***************************************************************** ;
*** Now find the maximum allocated space for each variable. *** ;
*** In this step, just find each word and its starting      *** ;
*** location.                                               *** ;
***************************************************************** ;

length the_word $9 ;

var_num = 0 ;
col_pos = 1 ;
do until ( col_pos gt in_len ) ;
```

```
          byte = substr ( in_line, col_pos, 1 ) ;
          if byte = &varstart then
          do ;
               var_num + 1 ;
               word_loc = col_pos ;
               on_word = 'Y' ;
               the_word = " " ;
          end ;
          if byte not in ( " ", &varstart ) then
          do ;
               on_word = 'Y' ;
               the_word = trim ( left ( the_word )) || byte ;
          end ;
          if ( byte = " " or col_pos = in_len )  and on_word = 'Y' then
          do ;
               on_word = 'N' ;
               output ;
               the_word = " " ;
          end ;
          col_pos + 1 ;
     end ;

     stop ;
     run ;

     ****************************************************************** ;
     *** Now find the maximum allocated space for each variable. *** ;
     ****************************************************************** ;

     data max ( keep = maxparse label ) ;
          set max end = last_01 ;

     length lastword $8 ;   * The previous word                       ;
     retain last_loc 0 ;    * Location of last word                   ;
     retain lastword " " ;  * The previous word                       ;

     ****************************************************************** ;
     *** Compare the current word location with the start loc-   *** ;
     *** ation of the next word.                                 *** ;
     ****************************************************************** ;

     if _n_ gt 1 then
     do ;
          maxparse = word_loc - last_loc - 1 ;
          label = upcase ( lastword ) ;
          output ;
     end ;

     ****************************************************************** ;
     *** The last word cannot use the next word as a boundary, so *** ;
     *** use the right margin.                                    *** ;
     ****************************************************************** ;

     if last_01 then
     do ;
          label = upcase ( the_word  ) ;
          maxparse = &page_wid - word_loc ;
          output ;
     end ;
```

```
*****************************************************************  ;
*** Keep track of the last word and its location.         ***  ;
*****************************************************************  ;

lastword = the_word ;
last_loc = word_loc ;

run ;


*****************************************************************  ;
*** The true length allocated for the variable is meaning-  ***  ;
*** less. We want to determine the maximum formatted length ***  ;
*** of each variable in the data set.  This module will     ***  ;
*** return the maximum actual formatted length of each var- ***  ;
*** iable and will be used to calculate how much space is    ***  ;
*** allocated for each variable on the report.             ***  ;
*****************************************************************  ;

%include "c:\preview.sas" ;   * See Coding Sample #6 ;


*****************************************************************  ;
*** We want to merge the results of the preview module with ***  ;
*** maximum number of spaces allocated for each variable by ***  ;
*** reading the physical layout.                           ***  ;
*****************************************************************  ;

proc sort data = _str_len ;
    by label ;
run ;

proc sort data = max ;
    by label ;
run ;


*****************************************************************  ;
*** Determine if we have to do a wordwrap on any variables. ***  ;
*** Pass the number of wrapped variables and the variable   ***  ;
*** names through global macro variables.                  ***  ;
*****************************************************************  ;

data final ( keep = label maxparse length need_cut type ) ;
    merge  max      ( in = in_max )
          _str_len ( in = In_var ) ;
    by label ;

length parsvars $200 ;   * Name of all parsed variables        ;
length max_size   $200 ; * Maximum size list of parsed vars    ;
retain parsvars ;         * Name of all parsed variables        ;
retain max_size ;         * Maximum size list of parsed vars    ;
retain cut_cnt 0 ;        * Increment if variable needs parsing ;

if in_max and not in_var then
do ;
    put '*** Warning ***' ;
    put 'There are variables in layout but not in SAS data set' ;
    put '*** Warning ***' ;
end ;
```

```
if in_max and in_var ;

if length gt maxparse then
    do ;
        need_cut = "Y" ;
        cut_cnt + 1 ;
        parsvars = trim ( left ( parsvars )) || " " || label ;
        put parsvars= label= ;
        max_size   = trim ( left ( max_size )) || " "
          || maxparse ;
        call symput ('parsvars', parsvars ) ;
        call symput ('max_size', max_size ) ;
    end ;
else
    need_cut = "N" ;

call symput ( 'cut_cnt', cut_cnt ) ;

run ;

**************************************************************** ;
*** Dynamically create the input parameters to the parser.  *** ;
**************************************************************** ;

data _null_ ;

length curr_var $8 ;     * the current variable                ;
length max_size $200 ;   * maximum size of parsed variables    ;
length parsvars $200 ;   * parsed variables                    ;

parsvars = "&parsvars" ;
max_size  = "&max_size" ;

if &cut_cnt gt 0 then
do ;
    file setparse ;
    put "%"  "let in_data = sas_data ; " ;
    put "%"  "let sort_by = ; " ;
    do i = 1 to &cut_cnt ;
        if i = 1 then
            put "%" "let vars = " ;
        curr_var = scan ( parsvars, i ) ;
        put curr_var ;
    end ;
    put " ; " ;
    do i = 1 to &cut_cnt ;
        if i = 1 then
            put "%" "let len_max = " ;
        max_var = scan ( max_size, i ) ;
        put max_var ;
    end ;
    put " ; " ;
    do i = 1 to &cut_cnt ;
        if i = 1 then
            put "%" "let spaces = "   ;
        put "&spaces"   ;
    end ;
```

```
         put  "  ;  "  ;
         put  "%include parser ; "  ;
     end  ;

     stop  ;

     run  ;

     *************************************************************** ;
     *** The last step dynamically created the input parameters  *** ;
     *** to the parser routine.  Now run the parser.             *** ;
     *************************************************************** ;

     %include setparse ;

     title1 ;

     *************************************************************** ;
     *** Dynamically create the final DATA_NULL_ step that will  *** ;
     *** actually write out the report.                          *** ;
     *************************************************************** ;

     data _null_ ;

     parsvars = "&parsvars" ;
     max_size = "&max_size" ;

     file layout ;
     put    @001 "data _null_ ; " ;
     put /  @001 "%include abortit ; " ;
     put    @001 "set sas_data end = last_01  ; " ;
     put    @005 "by  &sort_by  ; " ;
     put /  @001 "file print linesleft = numlines ; ";
     put    @001 " " ;

     infile rptgen length = in_len ;

     maxcount = 1 ;

     do until ( titcheck gt 0 or maxcount gt 50 ) ;
         input @001 in_line $varying200. in_len ;
         titcheck = index ( in_line, ":TITLES:" ) ;
         maxcount + 1 ;
     end ;

     head_chk = 'N' ;

     put "if _n_ = 1 then " ;
     put "    link header ; " ;
     put " " ;

     file head ;

     put "header: ; " ;
```

```
**************************************************************** ;
*** Print titles.                                          *** ;
**************************************************************** ;
titcount = 0 ;
do until ( head_chk gt 0 ) ;
    input @001 in_line $varying200. in_len ;
    head_chk = index ( in_line, ":HEADINGS:" ) ;
    if head_chk = 0 then
    do ;
        titcount + 1 ;
        length new_word $2 ;
        new_word = "&control" || "A" ;
        a_check = index ( in_line, new_word ) ;
        if a_check gt 0 then
        do ;
            in_line = substr ( in_line, ( a_check + 2 )) ;
            put 'put @001' '"' in_line $char. '"'   ' ; ' ;
        end ;
        new_word = "&control" || "L" ;
        l_check = index ( in_line, new_word ) ;
        if l_check gt 0 then
        do ;
            in_line = "   " ||
              trim ( left ( substr ( in_line,( l_check + 2 )))) ;
            put 'put @001' '"' in_line '"'   ' ; ' ;
        end ;
        new_word = "&control" || "R" ;
        r_check = index ( in_line, new_word ) ;
        if r_check gt 0 then
        do ;
            in_line = trim ( left ( substr
              ( in_line, r_check + 2 ))) ;
            the_len = length ( trim ( left ( in_line ))) ;
            rite_pos = ( &page_wid - the_len ) ;
            put 'put @' rite_pos  '"' in_line '"'   ' ; ' ;
        end ;
        new_word = "&control" || "C" ;
        c_check = index ( in_line, new_word ) ;
        if c_check gt 0 then
        do ;
            in_line = trim ( left ( substr
              ( in_line, c_check + 2 ))) ;
            the_len = length ( trim ( left ( in_line ))) ;
            cent_pos = int (( &page_wid - the_len ) / 2 )  + 1 ;
            put 'put @' cent_pos  '"' in_line '"'   ' ; ' ;
        end ;
        if a_check = 0 and l_check = 0 and r_check = 0
           and c_check = 0 then
        do ;
            the_len = length ( trim ( left ( in_line ))) ;
            cent_pos = int (( &page_wid - the_len ) / 2 ) + 1  ;
            put 'put @' cent_pos  '"' in_line '"'   ' ; ' ;
        end ;

    end ;
end ;

put " " ;
```

```
****************************************************************** ;
*** Print headings.                                           *** ;
****************************************************************** ;

head_cnt = 0 ;
maxcount = 1 ;
do until ( det_chk gt 0 or maxcount gt 50 ) ;
    input @001 in_line $varying200. in_len ;
    det_chk = index ( in_line, ":DETAIL:" ) ;
    if det_chk = 0 then
    do ;
    head_cnt + 1 ;
    the_len = length ( trim ( in_line )) ;
    put 'put @001 ' '"' in_line $varying200. the_len '"'  ' ;' ;
    end ;
    maxcount + 1 ;
end ;

put " " ;

put "return ; " ;

****************************************************************** ;
*** Print detail lines.                                       *** ;
****************************************************************** ;

file layout ;

length testword $8 ;
length the_word $9 ;

input @001 in_line $varying200. in_len ;

var_num = 0 ;
col_pos = 1 ;
do until ( col_pos gt in_len ) ;
    byte = substr ( in_line, col_pos, 1 ) ;
    if byte = &varstart then
    do ;
        var_num + 1 ;
        word_loc = col_pos ;
        on_word = 'Y' ;
        the_word = " " ;
    end ;
    if byte not in ( " ", &varstart ) then
    do ;
        on_word = 'Y' ;
        the_word = trim ( left ( the_word )) || byte ;
    end ;
    if ( byte = " " or col_pos = in_len ) and on_word = 'Y' then
    do ;
        on_word = 'N' ;
        char_var = "N" ;
        pointer = 1 ;
```

```
            do until ( pointer gt num_obs ) ;
                set sas_cont nobs = num_obs point = pointer ;
                if trim ( left ( upcase ( name ))) =
                    trim ( left ( upcase (the_word )))
                       and type = 2 then
                       char_var = "Y" ;
                pointer + 1 ;
            end ;
            the_len = 0 ;
            do i = 1 to &cut_cnt ;
                testword = scan ( parsvars, i ) ;
                if upcase ( trim ( left ( testword ))) =
                    upcase ( trim ( left ( the_word ))) then
                       the_len = scan ( max_size, i ) ;
            end ;
            if var_num = 1 then
                put "put " ;
            put "      " "@" word_loc the_word @ ;
            if char_var = "Y" and the_len gt 0 then
                put " $char" the_len +(-1) "." ;
            else
                put ;
            the_word = " " ;
        end ;
        col_pos + 1 ;
    end ;

put "      ; " ;

put /  @001  "if last_01 then" ;
put     @005  "link footer ; " ;
put /  @001  "return ; " ;

**************************************************************** ;
*** Print footnotes.                                       *** ;
**************************************************************** ;

file foot ;

put "footer: ; " ;

max_cnt = 1 ;

do until ( foot_chk gt 0 or max_cnt = 50 ) ;
    input @001 in_line $varying200. in_len ;
    foot_chk = index ( in_line, ":FOOTNOTES:" ) ;
    if foot_chk gt 0 then
    do until ( bot_chk gt 0 ) ;
        input @001 in_line $varying200. in_len ;
        bot_chk = index ( in_line, ":BOTTOM OF PAGE:" ) ;
        if bot_chk = 0 then
            put 'put @001' '"' in_line $char. '"'  ' ; ' ;
    end ;
    max_cnt + 1 ;
end ;
```

```
         put "return ; " ;

         stop ;
         run ;

         %include layout ;
         %include head ;
         %include foot ;

         run ;
```

Coding Sample 12

```
         *************************************************************** ;
         ***                                                       *** ;
         *** Source:    ERRORLOG.SAS                               *** ;
         ***                                                       *** ;
         *** Type:      Utility                                    *** ;
         ***                                                       *** ;
         *** Function: Searches the log directory and reports all  *** ;
         ***           references to warnings and errors.          *** ;
         ***                                                       *** ;
         *** Note:     You can actually use certain utilities like *** ;
         ***           Norton's Filefind or other micro based utili-*** ;
         ***           ties to perform a similar function. I use this*** ;
         ***           program to fine tune or customize my searches *** ;
         ***           exactly the way I want them, and format the  *** ;
         ***           output the way I prefer.                     *** ;
         ***                                                       *** ;
         *** Usage:    Set the macro variable &path to the location *** ;
         ***           of the SAS logs.                            *** ;
         ***                                                       *** ;
         ***           In the macro FIND_ERR, you can customize this*** ;
         ***           program to print off the messages that are of*** ;
         ***           interest to you.                            *** ;
         ***                                                       *** ;
         ***           A file is created in the log directory      *** ;
         ***           called ERROR.LST.  You can print it off and *** ;
         ***           note all references to ERRORS and WARNINGS. *** ;
         ***                                                       *** ;
         *************************************************************** ;

         %let path = c:\protocol\pls2g\log ;

         *************************************************************** ;
         *  Dont force user to press enter key for DOS commands.      ;
         *************************************************************** ;

         options noxwait ;

         *************************************************************** ;
         *** This is the file that will create the output listing. *** ;
         *************************************************************** ;

         filename errorout  "&path\error.lst" ;
```

```
***************************************************************** ;
*  Delete old listing, because we are using mod file option    ;
***************************************************************** ;

data _null_ ;

if fexist ('errorout') then
    call system  ("del &path\error.lst") ;

run ;

***************************************************************** ;
*** These are intermediate work files that will be used by  *** ;
*** DOS to create a file with the listing of all *.log files.*** ;
***************************************************************** ;

%let rawlist = rawdata.dir ;

***************************************************************** ;
*** Get a list of all files in the log subdirectory.        *** ;
***************************************************************** ;

x "dir &path/b > &path\&rawlist" ;

***************************************************************** ;
***   Macro        Logscan                                  *** ;
***   Function:  Scans the file that contains the complete   *** ;
***              list of log entries and pulls out 1 log file *** ;
***              at a time.                                  *** ;
***************************************************************** ;

%macro log_scan ;

data _null_ ;

length in_line $80 ;          * Each input record ;

infile "&path\&rawlist" length = in_len eof = no_more ;

***************************************************************** ;
*** Input the record at the present record pointer.         *** ;
***************************************************************** ;

input #&rec_pos in_line $ varying. in_len ;

***************************************************************** ;
*** Retrieve the name of the log file.                      *** ;
***************************************************************** ;

new_log = scan ( in_line, 1, ' ' ) ;
call symput ( 'logentry', put ( new_log,$12.) ) ;

stop ;

no_more:
call symput ( 'all_done','Y' ) ;

run ;
```

```
data _null_ ;

length in_line $120 ;              * input record ;
retain entrycnt 0 ;                * # times this entry written  ;

infile "&path\&logentry" length = in_len ;

input in_line $ varying. in_len ;

*************************************************************** ;
*** Search for the words "ERROR:" AND "WARNING".  If found, *** ;
*** write out to the error file. Also search for "NOTES" of *** ;
*** interest.                                            *** ;
*************************************************************** ;

find_err = index ( upcase ( in_line ) , 'ERROR:' ) ;
findwarn = index ( upcase ( in_line ) , 'WARNING:' ) ;
findnote = index ( upcase ( in_line ) , 'NOTE:' ) ;

*************************************************************** ;
*** Here you can ignore any WARNINGS that you choose.     *** ;
*************************************************************** ;

if findwarn gt 0 then
do ;
    findlib = index ( upcase ( in_line ) ,
     'IS ALREADY ON THE LIBRARY' ) ;
    if findlib gt 0 then
        findwarn = 0 ;
    find_exp = index ( upcase ( in_line ) , 'THE BASE PRODUCT' ) ;
    if find_exp gt 0 then
        findwarn = 0 ;
end ;

*************************************************************** ;
*** Select any NOTES that you wish to print.             *** ;
*************************************************************** ;

if findnote gt 0 then
do ;
    findzero = index ( upcase ( in_line ) , 'DIVISION BY ZERO' ) ;
    findunin = index ( upcase ( in_line ) , 'IS UNINITIALIZED.' ) ;
    find_wd  = index ( upcase ( in_line ) , 'W.D. FORMAT' ) ;
end ;

if find_err gt 0 or findwarn gt 0 or findunin gt 0 or
  find_wd gt 0 or findzero gt 0 then
do ;
    entrycnt + 1 ;
    file errorout mod ;
    if entrycnt = 1 then
        put / "&logentry" ;
    put in_line ;
    file log ;
end ;

run ;

%mend log_scan ;
```

```
********************************************************************** ;
*** Macro        MASTER                                      *** ;
*** Function:   This is the master routine that will drive   *** ;
***             the whole application.                       *** ;
********************************************************************** ;

%macro master ;
    %local all_done rec_pos ;
    %let all_done = N ;
    %let rec_pos = 1 ;
    %do %until ( &all_done = Y ) ;
        %log_scan
        %let rec_pos = %eval ( &rec_pos + 1 ) ;
    %end ;
%mend master ;


%master


********************************************************************** ;
*** This will help to determine if program runs OK.          *** ;
********************************************************************** ;

x "type &path\error.lst | more" ;


********************************************************************** ;
*** Clean up.                                                 *** ;
********************************************************************** ;

x "del &path\&rawlist" ;
```

Coding Sample 13

```
********************************************************************** ;
***                                                          *** ;
*** Source:    MERGE_BY (Find MERGE and no BY)               *** ;
***                                                          *** ;
*** Type:      Utility                                       *** ;
***                                                          *** ;
*** Function: To find a MERGE without an associated BY       *** ;
***           statement.                                     *** ;
***                                                          *** ;
*** Inputs:    Specify the name of the SAS program to be     *** ;
***            scanned.                                      *** ;
***                                                          *** ;
*** Limits:    For the sake of brevity, we will assume the   *** ;
***            following limitations of this routine:        *** ;
***                                                          *** ;
*** (1) There are no comments imbedded within the code       *** ;
*** (2) There are no quoted fields within the code           *** ;
*** (3) We will only scan one file. For an example of pro-   *** ;
***     cessing multiple files, refer to Coding Sample 12.   *** ;
***                                                          *** ;
********************************************************************** ;

data _null_ ;

infile 'fileref' truncover ;
```

```
input in_line $120. ;
in_line = upcase ( in_line ) ;

retain in_merge 0 ;    * Are you in a merge area ;
retain semi_one 0 ;    * Find first semicolon after merge? ;
retain semi_two 0 ;    * Find second semicolon after merge? ;
retain curr_loc 1 ;    * Where is the current file pointer? ;

*************************************************************** ;
*** In not in a MERGE, then check if in a MERGE statement. *** ;
*** If in a MERGE then mark the location.                  *** ;
*************************************************************** ;

curr_loc = 1 ;

if in_merge = 0 then
do ;
    in_merge = index ( in_line, 'MERGE' ) ;
    if in_merge gt 0 then
        curr_loc = in_merge + 5 ;
end ;

*************************************************************** ;
*** If in a MERGE statement and you have not found the     *** ;
*** first semicolon, look for it and mark its location.    *** ;
*************************************************************** ;

if in_merge gt 0 and semi_one = 0 then
do ;
    semi_one = index ( substr ( in_line, curr_loc ) , ";" ) ;
    if semi_one gt 0 then
        curr_loc = semi_one + 1 ;
end ;

*************************************************************** ;
*** In found semicolon, then look for a BY statement and   *** ;
*** another semicolon.  Compare their relative locations to *** ;
*** see if there is an error.                              *** ;
*************************************************************** ;

if semi_one gt 0 then
do ;
    find_by = index ( substr ( in_line, curr_loc ), "BY" ) ;
    semi_two= index ( substr ( in_line, curr_loc ), ";" ) ;
    if semi_two gt 0 then
    do ;
        if ( find_by gt 0 and find_by gt semi_two ) or
           ( find_by = 0 ) then
            put "BY statement expected on or before line #" _n_ ;
        in_merge = 0 ;
        semi_one = 0 ;
        semi_two = 0 ;
        curr_loc = 1 ;
    end ;
end ;

run ;
```

Appendix 2   # Definitions for the Site Map System

Array:

an area in computer memory used to hold a table or list of fields. Because these fields are contained in adjacent areas, data can be processed at very high speeds.

Artificial Intelligence:

a sophisticated branch of software engineering that attempts to simulate human thought processes in order to solve complex problems.

Bubble Sort:

a software technique allowing efficient sorting on tables that have a small number of elements. Essentially, in an alphabetic sort, each field in a table is compared with the element below it. The two fields are swapped if the second element is lower in alphabetic sequence.

Cascade:

a computer technique that helps you to examine a linked list. For example, assume that you want to know all the events and activities that would be affected by changing the status of one particular field. The technique of cascading (like a waterfall) determines those fields that are affected by changing another field. For example, consider a site that contains 01CO1, which links directly or indirectly to all of the following fields: 01RO1, 01RD1, and 01RA1. If the completion date of the 01CO1 field is delayed, then potentially, 01RO1, 01RD1, and 01RA1 can be affected.

Choice Table:

a table that is set up in computer memory to assist in navigating a tree. The Choice Table is simply a list of choices that a particular field can link to.

Circular Link:

a field that links back to itself either directly or indirectly. For example, if A links to B and B links to A, then an endless loop has been created.

Code Table:

a table that is set up in computer memory, it contains a list of all unique events and activities at a site. This list is useful in error testing because it can be compared with the Final Table. If the BUILDSSP module navigated a site properly, then the Code Table and Final Table should be identical.

Depth First Search:

a type of tree searching routine in which all the elements at one branch are scanned for the requisite data before every other branch is searched.

Direct Link:

a field that links to another field as defined by the "From" and "To" links in the master database. For example, an 01RD1 field often links to an 01RA1 field. This is a direct link because there is no intervening activity or event between the two fields.

Field:

an activity or event, this term is used interchangeably with "node".

Final Table:

a table that is set up in computer memory, it contains the final programmatically ordered list of events and activities at a site.

Indirect Link:

two fields that are causally related but not directly linked. For example, at a site, negotiations may lead to a consent decree which in turn leads to a remedial design. The negotiations and remedial design are not directly linked. However, they are related through an intervening field. Hence, negotiations and the remedial design are said to be indirectly linked.

Navigation Factor:

a component of the Navigation Priority. It is the most significant factor for determining the trace path in the BUILDSSP algorithm. For example, preremedial events have a lower Navigation Factor (and hence a higher Navigation Priority) than events have at other operable units.

Navigation Priority:

a term that refers to a numeric value that is assigned to each event and activity. The BUILDSSP program uses a mathematical formula to determine these values, which describe the linked ordering of data.

Node:

an activity or event, this term is used interchangeably with "field."

Parallel Routes:

a term that describes tree navigation situations where activities separate from the main pipeline and re-link back into the pipeline further down the tree. These activities are said to parallel the events in that they provide parallel routes of navigation.

Programmatic Ordering:

describes a list of events and activities where ordering is based on the rules set down in "The Links Programmatic Coding Guidance."

Table:

a list of fields. The list is usually maintained in computer memory, but can also be contained in a file.

Tree Head:

the field that resides at the top of the link pointer chain. Normally this would be the Discovery, because all other fields are linked from this point, either directly or indirectly.

Tree Searching:

describes moving through a tree-shaped database to access data. Powerful tree searching logic is required to scan quickly through large databases that have extensive branching.

Walking the chain:

expression that refers to tracing a list of linked fields.

Appendix 3   # A Links Primer

Definition of a Link. **341**
   "1 to 1" Relationship 341
   "1 to Many" Relationship 342
   "Many to 1" Relationship 342

Invalid Link Relationships **343**
   Circular Link 343
   Multiheaded Tree 343
   Multitree. 344

Here is a quick refresher course on hierarchical data relationships. This may be useful if you are interested in gaining a deeper understanding of the concepts presented in Chapter 11, "Putting It All Together with a Demonstration: The Site Map System."

Definition of a Link

Two records are said to be *linked* if they relate to each other. For example, when the Environmental Protection Agency (EPA) receives an initial phone call describing a potential toxic site, an element, called a Discovery record, is added to the database. The first and immediate event thereafter is to investigate the situation. This is called a Preliminary Assessment record. These records are said to be linked.

"1 to 1" Relationship

Think of the box on top as being the causative agent and the box on the bottom as being the result. Stated another way, the Discovery "caused" the Preliminary Assessment. Thus, the two elements are related or "linked." The record on top is called the "parent" record. The record on bottom is called the "child" record. As depicted in Figure A3.1, there is one parent and one child, or a "1 to 1" links relationship.

Figure A3.1   *A simple "1 to 1" link relationship.*

"1 to Many" Relationship

Consider the scenario in Figure A3.2.

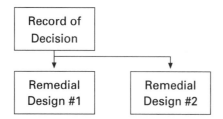

Figure A3.2   *A parent record can have multiple children.*

In this example, the EPA has formalized its decision and created a Record of Decision. This parent record caused two remedies: Remedial Design #1 and Remedial Design #2. Hence, the Record of Decision links to its child records, Remedial Design #1 and Remedial Design #2. In this diagram, there is one parent and two children. This is called a "1 to Many" links relationship.

"Many to 1" Relationship

The final type of linked relationship is displayed in Figure A3.3.

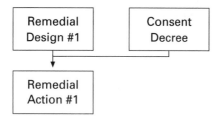

Figure A3.3   *A child can have more than one parent.*

Here, both the Remedial Design #1 and the Consent Decree caused the actual cleanup, also known as the Remedial Action #1. There are two parent records and one child record. This is known as a "Many to 1" links relationship.

Invalid Links Relationships

Here are three types of invalid links constructs in the Site Map System.

Circular Link

A circular link (Figure A3.4) occurs when either an element links to itself or a series of links causes a return to the original element:

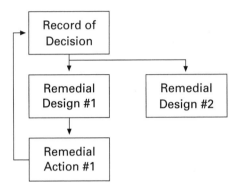

Figure A3.4   *A circular link.*

Multiheaded Tree

A multiheaded tree (Figure A3.5) is a construct that has more than one node at the top of a tree. It is invalid because there can be only one node at the very top of a tree.

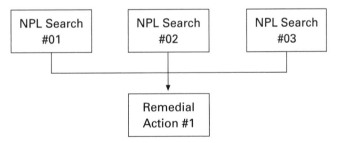

Figure A3.5   *A multiheaded tree.*

Multitree

A third invalid construct is called a multitree (Figure A3.6). A multitree is really a subset of multiheaded trees except that complete separate link trees are formed for one site.

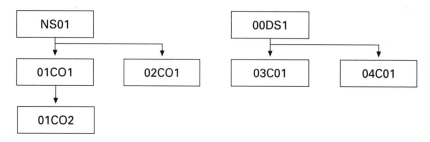

Figure A3.6   *A multitree.*

Appendix 4   # Tutorial of Navigation Rules

Introduction **345**

Pointer Approach **345**

Sample Site **346**

Logic for Navigation **346**

Gather All of the Links Relationships at a Site 346
Set Up a Table that Contains all Unique Codes 347
Determine the Tree Head 347
Walk the Chain 347
Assign the Priorities 348

Introduction

To create a site map, you need a strategy for navigating elements in proper sequence. That is, which element should be drawn first, second, third, and so on? This is a critical design challenge because utilizing the wrong order can complicate coding to an extreme level. The following discussion refers to the Single String Processor module (BUILDSSP).

Pointer Approach

One way to create a linked list is by tracing a site from the head of the tree all the way to the bottom. Obviously, you cannot traverse a tree from top to bottom in one pass (unless there is no branching). However, it is possible to trace all branches at a site by selecting a path from the head of the tree to the bottom of one path, and then backing up to pick up those fields that you missed on the first pass. This process may require only one pass or as many as a hundred passes, depending on the branching (complexity) of the site.

This process of "Tree Searching" is a common and accepted technique used in Artificial Intelligence (AI). In some applications, tree searching can be very expensive in terms of computing power. Hence, in applications such as games, code is usually written in very low languages to maximize execution speed. On the other hand, medical diagnostic programs may be written with higher level languages. However, to offset this disadvantage, the programs are usually run on very large powerful mainframes.

In the Site Map System, search paths are relatively small, thus allowing great flexibility in the various kinds of programs that can be developed.

Sample Site

The sample site was selected because it is of intermediate complexity. Also, navigating this site typifies the types of problems that you will encounter when negotiating the search path at most sites.

Logic for Navigation

Here is the algorithm for navigating a site in detail.

Gather All of the Links Relationships at a Site

Specifically, read the database and gather all the "From" and "To" links. Place these fields into two tables in memory. Linked data may be accessed on the mainframe by reading four fields in the hierarchical database:

C2432 Linked events
C2433 Linked activity
C2452 Linked events
C2453 Linked activities

Here is a list of all of the linked fields for this site:

From	To	From	To
AN01	CD01	01C01	01MA1
CD01	01RA1	01CO1	01RO1
CD01	01RD1	01CO1	01TA1
CD01	02RA1	01CO1	01TG1
CD01	02RD1	01CO1	01WP1
CD01	03RA1	01OM1	00ND1
CD01	03RD1	01RA1	01OM1
FN01	01CO1	01RD1	01RA1
NS01	FN01	01RO1	AN01
NS01	NS02	01RO1	01RD1
NS01	SV01	01RO1	02RD1
NS01	00RS1	01RO1	03RD1
NS01	00RS2	02RA1	02OM1
NS01	01CO1	02RD1	02RA1
01CO1	01RA1	03RA1	03OM1
01CO1	01CR1	03RD1	03RA1

The two tables are called the From Table (that is, an event or activity that links to another field) and the To Table (that is, the field to which the "From" event or activity is linked).

Set Up a Table that Contains all Unique Codes

Later on, you will need to ensure that every field is counted only once. To accomplish this, create a list of all activities and events at each site. This list of linked fields can be compared with fields attained by navigating a site. To set up these codes:

1. Create a blank table in memory. Call it the Codes Table.

2. Step through each field in the From Table. If that field is not already found in the Codes Table, add it to the table.

3. Step through each field in the To Table. If that field is not already in the Codes Table, add it to the table.

4. Finally, alphabetize the Codes Table by using a bubble sort.

Determine the Tree Head

A tree head is, logically, any field that does not have a record linking to it. Therefore, candidates for a tree head must be found in the From Table. Remember that if a field is found in the To Table, then something is linking to it and, therefore, it cannot be a tree head.

As an aside, the Discovery should be the tree head, but many regions have not linked their preremedial data. As a temporary solution, two other fields can be designated the tree head. The NPL Search (NS01) or Responsible Party Search (RP01) are acceptable tree heads if Discovery (DS01) is not present. To locate the tree head:

1. Examine each field in the From Table.

2. Determine if that field is found in the To Table. If it is, then it is not a tree head.

3. If it is not found in the To Table, it is a tree head.

4. Count up all the tree heads. If there is more than one (that is, you have a multiheaded tree), the site is rejected; so you proceed with the next site.

Walk the Chain

Set up two more tables. One is called the Final Table because it contains the programmatic ordering of links. The other is called the Choice Table. Its purpose is clarified shortly.

The first step is to initialize the Final Table, which contains the final list of programmatic strings:

Codes
NS01

Note: The shaded cell always indicates the current pointer in the Final Table. At this site, NS01 is the tree head, so place NS01 into the first slot in the Final Table. It is also important to determine the current location in this table. This is accomplished by setting the Final Table pointer to 1. From NS01, you can navigate in six different directions!

From here, there are six possibilities:

- Combined RI/FS (01CO1)
- RI/FS Negotiations (FN01)
- Second NPL Search (NS02)
- Section 107 Litigation (SV01)
- First Removal Investigation (00RS1)
- Second Removal Investigation (00RS2)

To make the proper navigation decision, place these six choices in a table, (that is, the Choice Table that was alluded to earlier). Then assign each choice a priority based on mathematical formulas which are presented in the next section.

Assign the Priorities

Before you examine the mathematical formulas, review this abbreviated, nontechnical summary of the rules. For a comprehensive discussion of the rules, refer to Appendix 5, "Summary of Navigation Rules."

Nontechnical Summary of the Rules

- There should be only one tree head and it is the first element. A multiple headed tree should be rejected.

- A circular link must be rejected.

- All events and activities that do not feed into a pipeline are considered higher priority than those fields that do link back into a pipeline.

- Any PRP searches beyond the sitewide point should be listed immediately after the site wide point.

- Activities are generally listed before events.

- With all else equal, lower numbered sequence numbers are listed before higher numbered sequence numbers.

- Lower numbered operable units should be negotiated before higher numbered operable units.

Formulas for Assigning Priority

From a logical standpoint, the ordering of events and activities is as follows:

NS01	(because it is the tree head)
NS02	(secondary search)
SV01	(activity that does not link back into the pipeline)
00RS1	(event that does not link back into the pipeline)
00RS2	(event that does not link back into the pipeline)
FN01	(an activity that links back into the pipeline)
01CO1	(an event that is part of a pipeline)

Here is the basic formula coming off the sitewide point:

Activity Navigation Priority =
    Navigation Factor + lowest op unit that an activity links to +
    (sequence number / 100)

where Navigation Factor =
    05, if activity = NS or RP
    20, if activity does not link back to a pipeline
    40, if activity does link back to a pipeline

Event Navigation Priority =
    40 + operable unit number + .5 + (sequence number /100) +
    (Event Sort Priority/10,000)

if the Event has an operable unit of 00, then

    Event Navigation Priority =
    10 + (sequence number /100)

Now assign each field in the Choice Table a priority based on the aforementioned formulas.

Code	Navigation Priority
NS01	0
01CO1	40 + 01 + .5 + 01/100 + 96/10000
FN01	40 + 01 + 01/100
NS02	05 + 0 + 02/100
00RS1	10 + 01/100
00RS2	10 + 02/100
SV01	20 + 0 + 01/100

The previous table resolves to this:

Code	Priority
NS01	0
01CO1	41.606
FN01	41.01
NS02	5.02
00RS1	10.01
00RS2	10.02
SV01	20.01

Now sort the fields so that the higher priority items (that is, the smaller numbered items) float to the top. Like before, use a bubble sort to move these fields within the table.

Code	Priority
NS01	0
NS02	5.02
00RS1	10.01
00RS2	10.02
SV01	20.01
FN01	41.01
01CO1	41.606

Because the correct sort order has been realized, transfer these six fields into the Final Table right after the current pointer:

Codes
NS01
NS02
00RS1
00RS2
SV01
FN01
01CO1

Whenever choices have been added to the Final Table, certain housekeeping functions are required:

- Add 1 to the pointer (which is now at the second field).

- Count the total number of fields (in this case, seven).

With the pointer now at 2 (that is, pointing to NS02), examine the To Table and note that there are no fields that link from NS02. This is the easiest scenario. You simply increment the pointer by 1 and look for fields that link from the third field.

00RS1	no links, add 1 to the pointer.
00RS2	no links, add 1 to the pointer.
SV01	no links, add 1 to the pointer.

The pointer now is a 6 and is pointing to FN01. Examine the To Table and note that FN01 links to 01CO1. This field has one choice in the Choice Table. Under normal circumstance, 01CO1 would be added to the Final Table. However, because 01CO1 is already represented in the Final Table, it is not added.

Once again, increment the pointer by 1. The pointer is now at 01CO1. This time there are seven choices in the Choice Table:

Codes
01WP1
01AR1
01CR1
01RO1
01MA1
01TA1
01TG1

There are six project support events. Their Navigation Priority is:

30 + operable unit number + (sequence number /100) +
(Place in Alphabetical Ordering Table/10,000)

where the Alphabetical Ordering Table is simply a list of all project support events in alphabetical order. Here is the Choice Table with Navigation Priorities included:

Code	Navigation Priority
01WP1	30 + 01 + 01/100 + 106/10000
01AR1	30 + 01 + 01/100 + 001/10000
01CR1	30 + 01 + 01/100 + 013/10000
01RO1	40 + 01 + .5 + 01/100 + 102/10000
01MA1	30 + 01 + 01/100 + 058/10000
01TA1	30 + 01 + 01/100 + 081/10000
01TG1	30 + 01 + 01/100 + 094/10000

The previous table resolves to this:

Codes	Priority
01WP1	31.01106
01AR1	31.01001
01CR1	31.01013
01RO1	41.51102
01MA1	31.01058
01TA1	31.01081
01TG1	31.01094

Now, sort in priority order:

Codes	Priority
01AR1	31.01001
01CR1	31.01013
01MA1	31.01058
01TA1	31.01081
01TG1	31.01094
01WP1	31.01106
01RO1	41.51101

As before, put these seven fields from the Choice Table into the Final Table:

Codes
NS01
NS02
00RS1
00RS2
SV01
FN01
01CO1
01AR1
01CR1
01MA1
01TA1
01TG1
01WP1
01RO1

At this stage, the pointer is at 8 and is looking at 01AR1. It points to nothing, as do all the project support fields, so increment the pointer by 1 until you reach the last field 01RO1. There are four choices for 01RO1: AN01, 01RD1, 02RD1, 03RD1. Proceeding according to the rules, here are the results:

Code	Navigation Priority
01RD1	40 + 01 + .5 + 01/100 + 111/10000
02RD1	40 + 02 + .5 + 01/100 + 111/10000
03RD1	40 + 03 + .5 + 01/100 + 111/10000
AN01	40 + 01 + 0 + 01/100

The previous table resolves to this:

Codes	Priority
01RD1	41.51111
02RD1	42.51111
03RD1	43.51111
AN01	41.01081

Sorting these fields in the Choice Table yields:

Codes	Priority
AN01	41.01
01RD1	41.51111
02RD1	42.51111
03RD1	43.51111

It is now clear why events get an additional .5 compared to the activities. This maintains the programmatic rule that if both events and activities link to the same pipeline, the activity has a higher priority.

Transferring these fields to the Final Table gives the following:

Codes
NS01
NS02
00RS1
00RS2
SV01
FN01
01CO1
01AR1
01CR1
01MA1
01TA1
01TG1
01WP1
01RO1
AN01
01RD1
02RD1
03RD1

The pointer is now on AN01, and there is one choice: CD01. In this case, CD01 must be inserted after AN01 but before 01RD1. Because the choice count is 1, it is necessary to slide the present table down 1 starting at 01RD1:

Codes
NS01
NS02
00RS1
00RS2
SV01
FN01
01CO1
01AR1
01CR1
01MA1
01TA1
01TG1
01WP1
01RO1
AN01
01RD1
02RD1
03RD1

Inserting CD01 into the Final Table gives the following:

Codes
NS01
NS02
00RS1
00RS2
SV01
FN01
01CO1
01AR1
01CR1
01MA1
01TA1
01TG1
01WP1
01RO1
AN01
CD01
01RD1
02RD1
03RD1

The pointer is at CD01. This case causes fine tuning of the original rule set. CD01 applies to six fields: 01RD1, 01RA1, 02RD1, 02RA1, 03RD1, and 03RA1. Because three of the fields (all the RD fields) already exist in the Final Table, these fields should not be added. As far as the RA fields are concerned, they are ultimately included because each of these fields is linked by another event. In this case, there are no fields to be transferred to the Final Table, so simply move the pointer to 01RD1.

01RD1 links to RA1. As before, you insert it and move the pointer up one to 01RA1. Again there is only one choice, 01OM1; so you insert it and move the pointer to 01OM1. This field, in turn links to 00ND1; so you insert it and move the pointer to 00ND1, which points to nothing. Now the table looks like this:

Codes
NS01
NS02
00RS1
00RS2
SV01
FN01
01CO1
01AR1
01CR1
01MA1
01TA1
01TG1
01WP1
01RO1
AN01
CD01
01RD1
01RA1
01OM1
00ND1
02RD1
03RD1

Move the pointer to 02RD1. The logic here is straightforward and similar to the first operable unit, resulting in this Final Table:

Codes
NS01
NS02
00RS1
00RS2
SV01
FN01
01CO1
01AR1
01CR1
01MA1
01TA1
01TG1
01WP1
01RO1
AN01
CD01
01RD1
01RA1
01OM1
00ND1
02RD1
02RA1
02OM1
03RD1
03RA1
03OM1

All Done!!

Appendix 5   # Summary of Navigation Rules

Introduction **357**

Navigation Strategy **357**

Find the Tree Head 357

Walk the Chain 358

Transfer Choices to the Final Table 360

Insert Fields 360

Handle Exceptions 360

Continue Navigation 361

Error Checks **361**

Introduction

Here are two general rules to follow:

- No attempts are made to correct bad links data. Further, no efforts are made to compensate for data that may be linked differently due to regional preferences. All sites are linked by the same rules, and all sites must link the same way every time.

- Circular links are rejected. If one is detected, then this message is sent to the error log: "Circular link detected."

Navigation Strategy

Here is a list of the navigation rules in detail.

Find the Tree Head

1. To find the tree head, search the list of linked fields. If a "From" link is found that does not have a listing in the "To" links, then you have located the tree head.

2. Count the total number of tree heads. If the tree head count is greater than one, then this message is sent to the error log, "Too many head records." Processing for this site is then stopped.

3. If the tree head count equals zero, then this message is sent to the error log: "No head record." Processing for this site is then aborted.

4. If the tree head count equals 1, then the tree head must be 00DS1, NS01, or RP01.

Ultimately, when all regions link their preremedial data, 00DS1 becomes the only acceptable tree head. If the tree head does not meet this criteria, then a message is sent to the error log: "... is not a valid tree head." Then processing is halted for this site.

Walk the Chain

Create a linked list using the following basic algorithm.

Start by placing the tree head into a table (call it the Final Table). Also, maintain a pointer that indicates the current position in the Final Table. Next, search the list of links and determine all fields that link from the tree head. There are two basic scenarios at this stage:

(1)   There is one link from the tree head. In this case, simply append the "To" field to the Final Table. In addition, increment the Final Table pointer by 1 so that the table pointer is at the second field.

(2)   There is more than one field that links from the head record. All these choices are placed into the Choice Table. In this case, you must determine a priority of the various choices in the table. This priority is determined by establishing a mathematical formula that provides a method of weighing each field so that activities and events with higher priority are navigated first and those with lower priority are navigated later.

Important note: Fields that are of higher priority are actually assigned a lower number than fields of lower priority. Conceptually, this may seem backwards; however, this is necessary because the choices are eventually sorted with the lower numbers floating to the top of the table.

The general formula for deciding on navigation priority is as follows:

Navigation Priority = Navigation Factor + operable unit number + Event Factor + (sequence number/100) + (Event Sort Priority/10,000)

Now examine the formula in more detail. Navigation Factor is the major determinant of link ordering:

Navigation Factor =

00 for preremedial events
05 for NS or RP
10 for operable unit 00 events
20 for activities that do not link back into a pipeline
30 for project support events
40 for all other events and activities that link back into a pipeline

Please note several important points:

- This ordering causes the NPL searches to appear before all other activities and events (except preremedials). Also, project support events appear immediately after the event they support because the next event in the pipeline has a navigation priority of at least 40.

- The second determinant is the operable unit number. It is imperative to traverse lower numbered operable units first, so the operable unit number is added to the basic navigation priority. Thus, an event at operable unit 01, at this point, has a total score of 40 + 01 (or 41), and an event at operable unit 05 has a total navigation score of 40 + 05 (or 45).

- Of course, an activity does not have an operable unit, but it must be determined if an activity is associated with an operable unit (that is, if the activity links to a pipeline either directly or indirectly). This is accomplished by using a computer technique called "cascading." Cascading allows you to search from the current field to the bottom of the tree by examining all possible branches. If cascading demonstrates that an activity links into a pipeline, then the Navigation Priority must be adjusted. The Navigation Factor must be reset from 20 to 40 (that is, similar to an event) and is added to the lowest operable unit that it links to. For example, if AN02 links to operable units 02 and 03, then the priority of AN02 at this point becomes 40 + 02 (or 42). If AN02 did not link back into a pipeline, then its priority at this stage would be 20 + 0 (or 20).

- At this point, you might note that an activity that links into a pipeline may have the same total navigation score as the operable unit to which it links. However, it is preferable that activities be navigated before events at the same level in the pipeline. Hence, you must change the priority of either the activity or the event. It is decided to add .5 to all events. In that way, an activity has a lower navigation total and, hence, is traversed first. This .5 constant is termed the "Event Factor," as noted in the above formula.

The next element is the sequence number. A lower numbered sequence number is navigated before a higher numbered one. This is a relatively minor determinant compared to some of the other parameters. As a result, the sequence number is divided by 100 and then added to the total navigation total. Thus, 01CO1 yields, at this point, the following navigation formula:

$$40 + 01 + .5 + 01/100 = 41.51$$

This compares with 01CO3, which yields:

$$40 + 1 + .5 + 03/100 = 41.53$$

Hence, 01CO1, with a lower overall score, is navigated first.

The final component to consider is "Event Priority." Each event in the pipeline has a "normal linking order." For instance, a ROD should appear before an RD in the same operable unit. Likewise, a RI/FS should appear before a ROD in the same operable unit. Thus, there is a default ordering of events from discovery to deletion. By assigning a low score to fields that should appear earlier in the pipeline, you ensure that these events are navigated first. The reason that this parameter is required is due to the following possible scenario:

CD01 applies to operable unit one because it links to both 01RD1 and 01RA1 at the first operable unit. According to the previous rule, CD01 is navigated prior to the pipeline events with which it is associated. However, when pointing to CD01, there are two choices: 01RD1 or 01RA1. Based on the other calculations, their scores would be identical, that is:

01RD1 = 40 + 01 + .5 + 01/100 = 41.51
01RA1 = 40 + 01 + .5 + 01/100 = 41.51

This explains why an Event Priority must distinguish between these two fields. The method of determining the Event Priority is as follows:

(1)   Set up a table that contains the list of events in programmatic order:
DS,PA,SI,ES,HR,NP,NR,NF,SE,AA,RS,RC,PR,IR,RV,UR,AS,HA,
AR,TO,TR,EV,OS,IM,WP,RM,CR,FP,RI,ED,FS,CO,TS,RO,NA,EO,
MA,RD,RA,FA,OF,OM,LR,OH,DA,TA,ER,TG,ER,TG,ND,PD

(2)   Count from the left of the table and determine the position for that event. Then divide that number by 10,000. For example,

PA is at position 4, so PA event priority = 4/10,000
SI is at position 7, so SI event priority = 7/10,000

Referring to the previous example:

$$01RD1 =   40 + 01 + .5 + 01/100 + 112/10,000 = 41.5212$$
$$01RA1 =   40 + 01 + .5 + 01/100 + 115/10,000 = 41.5215$$

Thus, 01RD1 would be navigated first.

Transfer Choices to the Final Table

At this point, all the choices have been assigned a numeric priority. The list of choices (the Choice Table) is sorted so that the fields associated with the higher priority (a lower number) float to the top, while those with a lower priority (a higher number) move to the bottom of the table.

These choices are then appended to the final field in the Final Table. As before, the Final Table pointer must be increased by one.

Insert Fields

Normally, all the choices in the Choice Table are appended to the end of the Final Table. However, if there are presently fields in the Final Table that are below the pointer, then these fields must be inserted after the present pointer but before the rest of the fields in the Final Table.

Handle Exceptions

Here are situations in which one of the choices is not placed into the Final Table:

1. if the choice already exists in the Final Table.

2. if an activity links to more than one operable unit. Then, only the event at the lowest operable unit is placed in the Final Table. However, if an event in one of the other operable units does not get linked by any other fields, it must also be added to the FINAL TABLE.

3. If an activity links to more than one event within an operable unit, then place only the event that cannot be linked from any other point into the Final Table. For instance, CD01 may link to 01RD1 and 01RA1. 01RA1 is linked later on by 01RD1 and therefore should be omitted from the Final Table. On the other hand, note that the link to 01RD1 (01RO1) is already in the Final Table. Thus, 01RD1 has no more opportunities to be linked and must be included at the present time.

Continue Navigation

The pointer is set at two (that is, pointing at the second field) in the Final Table. As before, determine all the elements that link from this field. There are three possibilities:

1. There is no link from the present field. If so, increase the Final Table pointer by one and process the next field.

2. There is one link from this field. In this case, simply append the "To" field to the Final Table. In addition, increment the Final Table pointer by one so that the third field becomes the current one.

3. There is more than one field that links from the head record. Like before, all these choices are placed into a Choice Table. Use the same formula used in the Tree Head routine above for determining Final Priority. Transfer the fields from the Choice Table into the Final Table.

Repeat the above process until the pointer reaches a blank field in the FINAL TABLE. At this point, no more fields need to be processed.

Error Checks

In addition to the test for an invalid tree head and circular links, the following validation is conducted at each site:

- Create a list of unique fields at each site and place them into a Code Table. This is accomplished by scanning the "From" link list for unique codes and placing them into the Code Table. The same is done for the "To" list of links. Sort the Code Table and Final Table alphabetically. Both the Code Table and Final Table should have the identical number of elements. If not, a message is sent to the error log: "Navigated count does not match the code count." In addition, step through each table one field at a time and compare their contents. If they are not identical at each location, a message is sent to the error log: "Correspondence error: Fields do not match."

- If an invalid code is encountered during any phase of program execution, a message is sent to the error log: "Invalid activity or event."

- The Final Table should be in operable unit order. This test is accomplished by creating a list of events. If the operable unit of an event is less than the previous event, there is an error. The exception is PD and ND because these operable units are 00 and they link below the first operable unit.

- Events should be in correct priority order within one operable unit. If the sequence CO ==> RO ==> RD ==> RA ==> OM is not observed, then this message is sent to the error log: "Events out of sequence." This test can be expanded in future releases to handle all events.

Index

A

ABORT statement, organizing DATA step
    statements 121
abstraction, definition 50
acceptance testing 222
activities, definition 258
ad hoc testing 197
analysis phase
    backtracking trees 41-42
    choosing a language 46-47
    data modeling 45-46
    decision tables 39-40
    definition 8
    digraph-directed graphs 42-43
    example 260-261
    feasibility studies 44
    functional requirements 43
    preliminary assessment 43
    pruning trees 41-42
    structured analysis 43-44
    traditional methods 44
    tree searching 40-42
arrays, definition 339
artificial intelligence, definition 339
attributes, definition 45
AUTOEXEC file 178-180
automation 157-159

B

backing up files 20-21
backslash (\), in pathnames 16
backtracking trees 41-42
binary searches 237
Black Box systems 174
Black Box testing
    boundary values 194-196
    coincidental correctness 193-194
    domain boundaries 194-196
    equivalence classes 191-194
    random testing 197
    test cases, developing 193-194
    types of 191
    versus White Box testing 211
Bohm 117
bottom-up design 52-53
bottom-up testing
    definition 220-221
    versus top-down testing 221

boundaries, debugging 237
boundary values 194-196
branch coverage 199-200
breakout mechanisms, organizing DATA step
    statements 120-121
bubble sorts, definition 339
bugs
    planting 223
    regressive 244-245
    types of 230-231
BUILDSSP module 266
BY statements, missing
    code sample 337-338
    debugging 243

C

cardinality, definition 45
cascade, definition 339
case sensitivity
    and system coding 153
    in internal documentation 97
    LOWCASE function 153
    UPCASE function 153
case statements, structured coding 118-120
checklist, project progress 24-25
choice tables, definition 339
circular links, definition 339
classical cohesion 61-62
code, maintenance 156
code changes, centralizing 155
code details, hiding 160-161
code generators 184-186
code tables, definition 339
CODES module 266
coding on the fly
    See dynamic code
coding phase
    definition 9
    example 266
coding samples
    See examples
coincidental cohesion 59-60
coincidental correctness 193-194
comment density 111
comments
    See also internal documentation
    counting 111
    delimited style 107-108

disadvantages 104
end-line style 105-106
flowerbox style 104
macro style 108
mixed case 106-107
on data declarations 112-113
statement style 107-108
top-line style 106
variable length boxes 107
common code 155
common coupling 68-69
communicational cohesion 63
compiled stored macro facility 22-23
concatenation, definition 52
CONFIG file 178-180
content coupling 66-67
continuation lines 96
CONTINUE statement, organizing DATA step
    statements 128-130
control coupling 67-68
conversion/parallel testing 222

D

data coupling 71-73
data dependent testing
  See Black Box testing
data duplication, avoiding 175-176
data modeling 45-46
DATA _NULL_ step 184-186
DATA step statements, organizing
  See also structured coding
  ABORT statement 121
  breakout mechanisms 120-121
  CONTINUE statement 128-130
  DELETE statement 121
  IF-THEN-ELSE constructs 122-126
  LEAVE statement 128-130
  loops 126-128
  loops, breaking out of 128-130
  readability 125
  STOP statement 121
  straight-line code 121-122
  subsetting IF statement 121
  WHERE clause 121
DATA steps, and modules 57-58
data transformation 29-31
data transmission
  validating 29
  validating, code sample 285-289
database management
  data transfer, verifying 29
  data transformation 29-31
  formats 26-27

multipurpose variables 28
preformatted values 26-27
quality assurance 29
user formats 27
debugging
  See also SAS DATA step debugger
  See also testing
  binary searches 237
  boundaries 237
  bugs, types of 230-231
  code off screen 244
  deduction 232
  displaying variables 231
  dynamic code 245-246
  ELSE statements 243
  extraneous semicolons 243
  flags 239
  flowcharting 237
  induction 232
  input data 240
  isolating problems 234
  limiting number of observations 236-237
  macros 246-249
  MERGE statements 243
  missing BY statements 243
  module interfaces 237
  MPRINT macro option 247
  MTRACE macro option 247
  optical illusions 239
  PAGE compiler 240
  patches 238
  preventive maintenance 242-244
  PRINT procedure 231-232, 234
  PUT_ALL_ construct 231
  regressive bugs 244-245
  removing debugging code 235
  SAS log 234
  SYMBOLGEN macro option 247
  systems approach to 6-7
  tactics for 234-241
  temporary files 236
  variables, overlaying 235
  WORK library 240-241
debugging phase, definition 9
decision tables 39-40
decisions, definition 201
deduction 232
defensive coding 153
DELETE statement, organizing DATA step
    statements 121
delimited comment style 107-108
depth first searches, definition 339
design phase

bottom-up design 52-53
definition 8
example 261-265
Future Enhancements list 83
modular design 50
Must Have lists 83
stepwise refinement 54-55, 83-84
tools, choosing 82
top-down design 50-52
Would Be Nice lists 83
detail level documentation 110
digraph-directed graphs 42-43
Dijkstra, E. W. 116
direct links, definition 339
DO loops, and modules 58
documentation, external
  See external documentation
documentation, internal
  See internal documentation
documentation density 111
domain boundaries 194-196
DRAWMAP module 266
drivers, testing 221
dummy modules 51-52
dynamic code
  debugging 245-246
  generating 166-169
dynamic data flow analysis 207-210

E

eight-character name limitation 98, 101
ELSE statements, debugging 243
end-line comment style 105-106
entities, definition 45
Entity Relationship Diagram (ERD) 45
equivalence classes 191-194
ERD (Entity Relationship Diagram) 45
error guessing 197
error handling
  error checking, early versus late 165-166
  error files, defining 165
  routing error messages 165
  typographical errors 172-173
ERRORRTN module 266
events 258
evolutionary prototyping 82
examples
  analysis phase 260-261
  BY statements, missing 337-338
  coding phase 266
  design phase 261-265
  designing a module 85-86
  feasibility study 260

flowgraphs 203-205
footnotes 311-313
formats, creating 284-285
frequency distributions 289-291
initialization file 306-309
internal documentation 79-81
internal documentation, aligning 94
log directories, scanning 334-337
MERGE statements, missing BY statements 337-338
path testing 202-207
problem definition phase 259
prototyping 260-261
report generators 325-334
report shell 313-324
reports, word wrapping 292-298
selection screen 309-310
software life cycle 10-14
source code 94
source code, aligning 94
submitting SAS source modules 291-292
testing 267-270
titles 311-313
user acceptance phase 270
validating data transmission 285-289
variables, calculating values for 299-305
external documentation 32-33, 90
external documentation phase, definition 9

F

feasibility studies 44
  example 260
field expansion 156
fields, definition 340
files
  backing up 20-21
  organizing by function 19
final tables, definition 340
flags, debugging 239
flexcode
  See dynamic code generation
flowcharting, as debugging tool 237
flowerbox comment style 104
flowgraphs
  definition 201
  example 203-205
FLOWOVER option, INFILE statement 154
footnotes
  code sample 311-313
  reports 180-181
formats
  creating, code sample 284-285
  database 26-27

frequency distributions, code sample 289-291
functional cohesion 64-65
functional requirements 43
functional testing
    See Black Box testing
Future Enhancements list 83

G

Glass Box testing
    See White Box testing
global data structures, testing 217
global macro variables
    and common coupling 68-69
    passing parameters 76-77
GOTO constructs, structured coding
    alternatives to 129
    definition 116
    using 130-131
Gray Box testing 212-216

H

Halstead Software Science Metrics 137-138
hardcoding data 162-163
history, structured coding 116

I

IF-THEN-ELSE constructs, organizing DATA step
        statements 122-126
%INCLUDE construct, and modules 58
%INCLUDE libraries
    creating 23
    for common code 155
%INCLUDEd code, and modules 75
incremental testing 218
independence, module 58
indirect links, definition 340
induction 232
INFILE statement 154
informational cohesion 63
initialization file, code sample 306-309
inline code, and modules 74
input data, debugging 240
input/output testing
    See Black Box testing
integration strategies 218
integration testing 217-221
interfaces, testing 217
internal documentation
    See also comments
    alignment 92-94
    alignment, examples 94
    and monitor width 95
    continuation lines 96

    definition 90
    detail level 110
    documentation density 111
    eight-character name limitation 98, 101
    example 79-81
    layout 90
    literals, avoiding 96-97, 102
    logging code changes 113-114
    missing semicolons 95
    mixed case 97
    module level 110
    naming conventions 98
    naming modules 98
    naming variables 99-101
    numeric flags 102-103
    one statement per line 91
    parentheses 94
    program level 109-110
    separating code blocks 91-92
    white space 92, 95
internal documentation phase, definition 9
internal subroutines, and modules 75
iteration, structured coding 117-118

J

Jacopini 117
job stream, creating a 32
JUMP command 255
junctions, definition 202

K

KEEP data set option, structured coding of
        variables 132
keyword parameters 75
Knot count 137

L

large projects, characteristics of 7-8
LEAVE statement, organizing DATA step
        statements 128-130
LENGTH statement 153
%LET statement, table-driven code generation
        163-164
library organization 16-19
lifetime of variables 131
LINK statement, and modules 58
links
    circular 339, 343
    definition 258, 341
    direct 339
    indirect 340
    "Many to 1" 342
    multiheaded trees 343

multitree 344
"1 to Many" 342
"1 to 1" 341
literals, avoiding 96-97, 102, 169-174
local macro variables 76
log directories, scanning
    code sample 334-337
logging
    code changes 113-114
    SAS log, and debugging 234
    test results 206-207
logical cohesion 60-61
LOGICAL module 266
logic-driven testing
    See White Box testing
loops
    breaking out of 128-130
    breaking out of, organizing DATA step
        statements 128-130
    DATA step statements, organizing 126-130
    DO loops, and modules 58
    organizing DATA step statements 126-128
LOWCASE function 153

M

macro comment style 108
macro variables
    global 76-77
    listing 248-249
    local 76
macros
    and modules 74-75
    compiled stored macro facility 22-23
    debugging 246-249
    multiple per file 22
    nonmacro code 22
    organizing 21-23
    SAS macro autocall facility 21-22
McCabe's Cyclomatic Complexity 134-136
McCabe's Essential Complexity 136
MERGE statements
    debugging 243
    missing BY statements, code sample 337-338
missing values 154
MISSOVER option, INFILE statement 154
modular design 50
modular programs, definition 7
module cohesion
    classical 61-62
    coincidental 59-60
    communicational 63
    definition 59
    functional 64-65

informational 63
    logical 60-61
    procedural 62
    temporal 61-62
module combinations, testing 217
module coupling
    common 68-69
    content 66-67
    control 67-68
    data 71-73
    definition 65-66
    stamp 69-71
    tramp 67
module interfaces, debugging 237
module level documentation 110
module testing 216-217
modules
    converting to SAS code 73-75
    DATA step 57-58
    definition 50
    design tips 83-84
    DO loops 58
    dummy 51-52
    %INCLUDE construct 58
    %INCLUDEd code 75
    independence 58
    inline code 74
    internal subroutines 75
    LINK statement 58
    macros 74-75
    naming 98
    passing parameters 59, 71-73
    SAS functions 58
    SAS library macros 58
    SAS procedures 57
    SAS programs 57
    SAS programs versus traditional programs 56
    simplicity 58
    size 55, 161-162
    stubs 51-52
    user-defined macros 58
monitor width, and internal documentation 95
MPRINT macro option, as debugging tool 247
MTRACE macro option, as debugging tool 247
multiple condition coverage 200
Must Have lists 83

N

naming conventions
    filerefs 169
    internal documentation 98
    source modules 22
navigation factors, definition 340

Navigation Priority, definition 340
nested IFs, structured coding 118
nodes 258, 340
NODUPLICATES option, SORT procedure 175-176
numeric flags 102-103

O

observations, limiting during debugging 236-237
operating system, determining 34
operating system version, determining 34
optical illusions 239
ordinality, definition 45

P

PAGE compiler, as debugging tool 240
page ejection 181-182
parallel routes, definition 340
parameters, passing
  data coupling 71-73
  keyword parameters 75
  LINK statement 77-78
  minimizing 59
  number of arguments 79
  positional parameters 75
  to macros 75-77
  using external files 77
  using global macro variables 79
  using open code 77-78
  using SAS data sets 77
parentheses (( )), in internal documentation 94
patches, debugging 238
path testing
  definition 201-202
  example 202-207
PDL (Program Design Language), structured coding 139-147
persistence of variables 131-133
portability 34
  and external files 74
positional parameters 75
POWER module 266
preformatted database values 26-27
preliminary assessment 43
PRINT procedure, as debugging tool 231-232, 234
printing
  See also reports
  page orientation 177-178
  raw data 31
problem definition phase
  definition 8
  example 259

risk/reward evaluation 38-39
procedural cohesion 62
procedure output, routing to external files 73-74
process blocks 201
Program Design Language (PDL), structured coding 139-147
program level documentation 109-110
programmatic ordering, definition 340
programming language, choosing for a project 46-47, 260-261
programs, portability 34
project management
  assigning programming tasks 25-26
  choosing a language 46-47
  creating a job stream 32
  external documentation, 32-33
  portability 34
  printing raw data 31
  progress checklist 24-25
  setting standards 23-24
  test plans 26
  version control 25-26
prototyping 81-82
  example 260-261
pruning trees 41-42
Pseudocode, structured coding 139-147
PUT_ALL_ construct, as debugging tool 231

R

random testing 197
readability, DATA step statements 125
readability, source code
  See internal documentation
regressive bugs 244-245
report generators 184-186
  code sample 325-334
report shell, code sample 313-324
reports
  See also printing
  footnotes 180-181
  page ejection 181-182
  routing to output device 182-184
  titles 180-181
  word wrapping, code sample 292-298
RETAIN statement 153
risk/reward evaluation 38-39
RPT_HEAD module 266

S

sample code
  See examples
SAS complexity, scoring 138
SAS DATA step debugger

definition 249-250
JUMP command 255
jumping routines 255
running step by step 251-255
running uninterrupted 250-251
WATCH command 255
watching variables 255
SAS functions, and modules 58
SAS library macros, and modules 58
SAS log, as debugging tool 234
SAS macro autocall facility 21-22
SAS procedures, and modules 57
SAS programs, and modules 57
SAS source modules
submitting, code sample 291-292
seamless coding 169-174
SELECT clause, ordering elements 119
selection, structured coding 117
selection screen, code sample 309-310
semicolon (;)
extraneous 243
missing 95
separating code blocks 91-92
sequence, structured coding 117
Site Map System
analysis 260-261
BUILDSSP module 266
CODES module 266
coding 266
connecting nodes 264-265
design 261-265
drawing nodes 264
DRAWMAP module 266
ERRORRTN module 266
feasibility study 260
functional requirements 260
logical grid coordinates 262
LOGICAL module 266
maintenance 271
module descriptions 266
navigation order 261-262
physical grid coordinates 262-263
physical layout 261
POWER module 266
problem definition 259
programming language, choosing 260-261
prototyping 260-261
RPT_HEAD module 266
testing 267-270
user acceptance 270
site maps, navigating
assigning priorities 348-356
creating linked lists 345

error checking 361
exception handling 360
finding the tree head 347, 357
inserting fields 360
listing linked fields 346
navigation algorithm 346-356
pointer approach 345
transferring choices to final table 360
tree searching 345
walking the chain 347-348, 358-360
software life cycle
See also analysis phase
See also design phase
See also problem definition phase
See also Site Map System
coding phase 9, 266
debugging phase 9
definition 8
example 10-14
external documentation phase 9
internal documentation phase 9
large projects, characteristics of 7-8
systems approach to programming 6-7
testing phase 9
user acceptance phase 9, 270
software metrics
definition 134
Halstead Software Science Metrics 137-138
knot count 137
McCabe's Cyclomatic Complexity 134-136
McCabe's Essential Complexity 136
scoring SAS complexity 138
software quality, measuring
See software metrics
software systems
large, characteristics of 7-8
software testing
See structured testing methods
See testing
source code
See also internal documentation
aligning 92-94
aligning, examples 94
organizing 21-23
source modules, naming conventions 22
span of variables 131
stamp coupling 69-71
startup options 178-180
startup shells 180
statement comment style 107-108
statement coverage 199
status variables 161
stepwise refinement 54-55, 83-84

STOP statement, organizing DATA step statements 121

STOPOVER option, INFILE statement 154

straight-line code, organizing DATA step statements 121-122

stress testing 222

structural testing
See White Box testing

structured analysis 43-44

structured coding
See also DATA step statements, organizing
See also system coding
See also variables
case statements 118-120
definition 116
GOTO constructs, alternatives to 129
GOTO constructs, definition 116
GOTO constructs, using 130-131
history 116
iteration 117-118
nested IFs 118
Program Design Language (PDL) 139-147
Pseudocode 139-147
selection 117
sequence 117

structured programming
See also structured coding
definition 7

structured testing methods
acceptance testing 222
bottom-up testing, definition 220-221
bottom-up testing versus top-down testing 221
conversion/parallel testing 222
drivers 221
global data structures 217
incremental testing 218
integration strategies 218
integration testing 217-221
interfaces 217
module combinations 217
module testing 216-217
stress testing 222
stubs 219-220
system testing 222
top-down testing 218
top-down testing, versus bottom-up testing 221
volume testing 222

stubs 51-52
and testing 219-220

subsetting IF statement, organizing DATA step statements 121

SYMBOLGEN macro option, as debugging tool 247

&SYSSCP macro variable 34

system coding
See also structured coding
automation 157-159
Black Box systems 174
case sensitivity 153
centralizing code changes 155
common code 155
data duplication 175-176
defensive coding 153
field expansion 156
hardcoding data 162-163
hiding code details 160-161
%INCLUDE libraries 155
maintenance 156
missing values 154
module size 161-162
printing, page orientation 177-178
simplicity 152
status variables 161
system control flags 176-177
truncation 153
user perspective 159
variables, retaining values 153
variables, specifying length 153

system control flags 176-177

system definitions, definition 32-33

system testing 222

systems approach to programming
advantages of 6-7
definition 7

&SYSVER macro variable 34

T

table-driven code generation 163-164

tables, definition 340

temporal cohesion 61-62

test cases, developing 193-194

test plans 26

testing
See also Black Box testing
See also debugging
See also structured testing methods
See also White Box testing
ad hoc 197
bugs, planting 223
comparing results 223-224
definition 190
error guessing 197
example 267-270
Gray Box 212-216
random 197

testing phase, definition 9

throwaway prototyping   81-82
titles
   code sample   311-313
   reports   180-181
top-down design   50-52
top-down testing   218
   versus bottom-up testing   221
top-line comment style   106
tracing programs   205-207
tramp coupling   67
tree heads, definition   340
tree searching   40-42
   definition   340
truncation   153
TRUNCOVER option, INFILE statement   154

U

UPCASE function   153
user acceptance phase
   definition   9
   example   270
user formats, databases   27
user-defined macros, and modules   58

V

variables
   See also structured coding
   calculating values for, code sample   299-305
   database, multipurpose   28
   declared   207
   defined   207
   displaying   231
   killed   208
   naming   99-101
   overlaying   235
   retaining values   153
   specifying length   153
   state combinations   208-210
   structured coding, initializing   133-134
   structured coding, KEEP data set option   132
   structured coding, lifetime   131
   structured coding, persistence   131-133
   structured coding, referencing   131
   structured coding, span   131
   used   208
   watching   255

version control   25-26
volume testing   222

W

walking the chain
   definition   340
   navigating site maps   347-348, 358-360
WATCH command   255
WHERE clause, organizing DATA step statements
   121
White Box testing
   branch coverage   199-200
   decisions   201
   definition   198-199
   dynamic data flow analysis   207-210
   flowgraphs, definition   201
   flowgraphs, example   203-205
   junctions   202
   logging results   206-207
   multiple condition coverage   200
   path testing   201-202
   path testing, example   202-207
   process blocks   201
   statement coverage   199
   tracing programs   205-207
   variables, declared   207
   variables, defined   207
   variables, killed   208
   variables, state combinations   208-210
   variables, used   208
   versus Black Box testing   211-212
white space
   dynamic code generation   169
   internal documentation   92, 95
WORK library, and debugging   240-241
Would Be Nice lists   83

Special Characters
\ (backslash), in pathnames   16
( ) (parentheses), in internal documentation   94
; (semicolon)
   See semicolon (;)

Call your local SAS® office to order these other books and tapes available through the Books by Users℠ program:

An Array of Challenges — Test Your SAS® Skills
by **Robert Virgile** . . . . Order No. A55625

Applied Multivariate Statistics with SAS® Software
by **Ravindra Khattree**
and **Dayanand N. Naik** . . . . Order No. A55234

Applied Statistics and the SAS® Programming Language, Fourth Edition
by **Ronald P. Cody**
and **Jeffrey K. Smith** . . . . Order No. A55984

Beyond the Obvious with SAS® Screen Control Language
by **Don Stanley** . . . . Order No. A55073

The Cartoon Guide to Statistics
by **Larry Gonick**
and **Woollcott Smith** . . . . Order No. A55153

Categorical Data Analysis Using the SAS® System
by **Maura E. Stokes, Charles E. Davis,**
and **Gary G. Koch** . . . . Order No. A55320

Common Statistical Methods for Clinical Research with SAS® Examples
by **Glenn A. Walker** . . . . Order No. A55991

Concepts and Case Studies in Data Management
by **William S. Calvert**
and **J. Meimei Ma** . . . . Order No. A55220

Essential Client/Server Survival Guide, Second Edition
by **Robert Orfali, Dan Harkey,**
and **Jeri Edwards** . . . . Order No. A56285

Extending SAS® Survival Analysis Techniques for Medical Research
by **Alan Cantor** . . . . Order No. A55504

A Handbook of Statistical Analyses using SAS®
by **B.S. Everitt**
and **G. Der** . . . . Order No. A56378

The How-To Book for SAS/GRAPH® Software
by **Thomas Miron** . . . . Order No. A55203

In the Know ... SAS® Tips and Techniques From Around the Globe
by **Phil Mason** . . . . Order No. A55513

Learning SAS® in the Computer Lab
by **Rebecca J. Elliott** . . . . Order No. A55273

The Little SAS® Book: A Primer
by **Lora D. Delwiche**
and **Susan J. Slaughter** . . . . Order No. A55200

Mastering the SAS® System, Second Edition
by **Jay A. Jaffe** . . . . Order No. A55123

Painless Windows: A Handbook for SAS® Users (for Windows 95 and Windows NT)
by **Jodie Gilmore** . . . . Order No. A55769

Painless Windows 3.1: A Beginner's Handbook for SAS® Users
by **Jodie Gilmore** . . . . Order No. A55505

Professional SAS® Programming Secrets, Second Edition
by **Rick Aster**
and **Rhena Seidman** . . . . Order No. A56279

Professional SAS® User Interfaces
by **Rick Aster** . . . . Order No. A56197

Quick Results with SAS/GRAPH® Software
by **Arthur L. Carpenter**
and **Charles E. Shipp** . . . . Order No. A55127

Quick Start to Data Analysis with SAS®
by **Frank C. Dilorio**
and **Kenneth A. Hardy** . . . . Order No. A55550

Reporting from the Field: SAS® Software Experts Present Real-World Report-Writing Applications . . . . Order No. A55135

SAS® Applications Programming: A Gentle Introduction
by **Frank C. Dilorio** . . . . Order No. A55193

SAS® Foundations: From Installation to Operation
by **Rick Aster** . . . . Order No. A55093

SAS® Programming by Example
by **Ron Cody**
and **Ray Pass** . . . . Order No. A55126

SAS® Programming for Researchers and Social Scientists
by **Paul E. Spector** . . . . Order No. A56199